Lifestyle Changes

A Clinician's Guide to Common Events, Challenges, and Options

Vera Sonja Maass

Routledge
Taylor & Francis Group
New York London

Routledge
Taylor & Francis Group
270 Madison Avenue
New York, NY 10016

Routledge
Taylor & Francis Group
2 Park Square
Milton Park, Abingdon
Oxon OX14 4RN

International Standard Book Number-13: 978-0-415-96057-1 (Hardcover)

Library of Congress Cataloging-in-Publication Data

Maass, Vera Sonja.
  Lifestyle changes : a clinician's guide to common events, challenges, and options / Vera Sonja Maass.
    p. ; cm.
  Includes bibliographical references and indexes.
  ISBN 978-0-415-96057-1 (hardcover : alk. paper)
    1. Life change events--Psychological aspects. 2. Lifestyles--Psychological aspects. 3. Adjustment (Psychology) 4. Change (Psychology) I. Title.
  [DNLM: 1. Life Change Events. 2. Stress, Psychological--therapy. 3. Adaptation, Psychological. 4. Family--psychology. 5. Mental Disorders--therapy. 6. Psychotherapy--methods. WM 172 M111L 2008]

  RC455.4.L53M37 2008
  616.9'8--dc22   2007046337

Visit the Taylor & Francis Web site at
http://www.taylorandfrancis.com

and the Routledge Web site at
http://www.routledge.com

Contents

Preface

Changes, great and small, are frequent topics of discussion in the world at large and in psychotherapy in particular. Many changes are of such a magnitude that they initiate significant modifications in a person's overall lifestyle. How to respond to such changes, what outcomes to expect, how to prepare for them, and how to cope with them are just a few of the many questions that arise. Changes bring conditions of uncertainty with them and many people experience discomfort in the face of uncertainty because of their negative expectations.

But uncertainty does not necessarily mean that the outcome of the changing situation will be dark or threatening. There may be promising opportunities to choose from as well as less desirable options; there will be losses of the familiar as well as gains of the unknown. In the pages of this book there are accounts of those who forged new directions and adventures out of the situations they were in and of those who may have missed opportunities by blinding their vision with their preoccupation on what they had to give up. Their concentration on the losses seemed to have prevented them from recognizing the opportunities for gain or profit.

The topics for the chapters of this book were determined by clients and the particular situations they sought help for. Similar experiences from people in the community at large and figures in the public domain were added for a balanced presentation of the topics. The material discussed in this book is not part of any structured research. The individuals and couples encountered in the pages of this book have not been selected on a random basis. Some have been clients; some are volunteers from the general population and some are college students. Although they are from various ethnic and cultural backgrounds, the majority of them come from White middle-class and African-American backgrounds. Their names have been changed and their circumstances disguised for reasons of confidentiality. There is no claim that the individuals whose stories have been related are representative of all individuals in the general population.

Acknowledgments

The individuals and couples who agreed to share their stories have become a significant part of this book. Their generosity with time and information is greatly appreciated. Their enthusiasm about participating was contagious. For reasons of confidentiality their names have been changed and in some cases their circumstances have been disguised. They know who they are and my gratitude is extended to each of them.

Special thanks go to Mr. Dana Bliss, editor, behavioral sciences, for his willingness to make himself available when needed, and to the members of the "Word by Word" writers' group for their patience in reading many parts of the manuscript and offering feedback and helpful personal discussions. Carole Carlson, Nancee Harrison, Mary McCorkle, Linda Thornton, Richard Stott, Jim Gamble, and Bob Hall—thank you all.

CHAPTER 1

Yesterday's Guarantees— Today's Uncertainties

There is nothing more certain than change. No matter what aspect of life we are looking at, not much remains the same. A hundred years ago people could imagine their lives to be similar to that of their parents. Where once lifestyles were passed on from one generation to another, today many individuals' lifestyles change drastically and more than once within their lifetime.

Whether it is one's family lifestyle, professional and occupational lifestyle, the adjustments that individuals in recovery from an addictive lifestyle face, or retirement lifestyle, change is the common thread through all of them. The security of marriage—once only threatened by widowhood— has given way to the insecurities of divorce, repeated singleness, single parenthood, and cohabitation. Careers that were once chosen for a lifetime of employment today encounter confrontation with early retirement or even obsoleteness of skills for many employees. The loyalty of generations of workers, who were employed by the same companies throughout their working lives, is disintegrating as their sons and daughters are confronted with reduced health care benefits and smaller retirement packages than their parents and grandparents had earned. In some cases, the employers have closed their doors and ceased to exist.

Pessimists might point to the end of a way of life, seeing nothing but chaos and decay; optimists might enthusiastically greet changes, waiting for a new utopia to unfold; and realists would view such dramatic changes as presenting challenges that call for adaptation to those changes as well as offering options for exploration of new paths and new adventures.

Reasons for Change

There are those who for various reasons emigrate from one country to another or just move from one region of the country to another. In some cases, people are confronted with the necessity to learn a different language; in many cases they are faced with the requirement to adapt to different cultures and customs. Overall, they often trade some parts of their previous daily life for new ways of existing.

People's decisions in significant areas of their lives are often lifestyle decisions—decisions that are dictated or at least influenced by the lifestyle they found themselves in at the moment. For instance, a young, independent person would be able to choose a career for his or her interest in the particular field and also look for future opportunities to engage more deeply in those interests. On the other hand, a young man who has already made commitments to a wife and children may consider other variables in his career choices, such as the amount of the beginning salary and whether it is sufficient to consider buying a house for his developing family.

A divorced or widowed mother, living in the suburbs for the sake of her children's safety, may have to trade her career-oriented job in the city for a less exciting employment opportunity closer to home because, as a single mother, she cannot afford the commuting time or the money it would cost to hire a nanny for the time she is away from her children. She may have to put her career plans on hold for the next several years or find other ways to make her new job meaningful.

Job and relationship choices made earlier in life make an impact on the financial and psychological well-being of individuals later in life, as Susan Krauss Whitbourne, a psychology professor tracking three generations of college students, observed. As reported in the *APA Monitor on Psychology* (Clay, 2003), people who changed jobs early in adulthood scored higher on measures of having a sense of productivity in work and a desire to generate a legacy for future generations than did individuals who settled down and stayed within an occupation for 20 or more years. The job changes that people made in their 20s and 30s seemed to have beneficial influences in midlife; they saved them from feeling stuck. On the other hand, Whitbourne found that changes in personal relationships (such as divorce) early in life tended to have a detrimental effect on people's psychological well-being in midlife.

Thinking about retirement, individuals may volunteer their services in an area of high personal interest, something they always wanted to be active in but could not afford to gamble at when faced with family responsibilities. Following retirement from their jobs and with their children grown, they may consider a whole new career—one that includes increased personal satisfaction. They may even want to start a whole new business. In the end, it is the individual's decision on how to approach the significant changes in his or her style of life.

The situation is somewhat different in the case of forced early retirement, especially when no big severance packet is in the offing; instead of the "golden parachute," the person may receive nothing more than a "pink slip." This person's decision on the basis of his or her lifestyle change may amount to taking any available job, regardless of chances for future advancement, hopes for significant increases in salary, or even promises for meaningful or exciting activities.

Reactions to Change

Confronted with the circumstances of forced lifestyle changes, people initially tend to focus on the losses they experience with the change. "I was looking forward in my retirement to have a house and a boat along the coast of Florida, just fishing and taking it easy in the warm weather," the hard-working man who is now forced into early retirement may complain. Similarly, health problems can wreck the best-laid plans and force individuals to cope with significant changes in their lifestyles. It is natural that the thought of losses becomes the first consideration in many of these situations.

Other changes may present themselves in the form of opportunities that are too tempting to resist. The young woman who has waited for years for a certain career opportunity exclaims:

> I just found this exciting job that entails a lot of travel and meeting interesting people, but my husband resents having to be responsible for our children while I am gone. Now I have to decide between my career and my family; it's not fair!"

Her husband may respond:

> My father never had to do the dishes, cook, and take care of us children when he came home from work. Now I am supposed to do all that while my wife travels around the country. I have a career to think about, too; it's not fair!

As people are contemplating the losses they are incurring as consequences of these changes, they often engage in a one-directional way of thinking and may blind themselves to the existence of possible options inherent in the new situation. In fact, often they are not even aware of this type of thinking; they may see themselves as faced with a decision where they have to choose one scenario to the exclusion of the other—much like the young woman who saw her choices as between her family and her career. Both choices were extremely important to her, yet she had to give up one of them. As she was weighing the desirability of either one, she could not help but feel a loss in whichever choice she made. If accused of one-directional thinking, she would defend herself, insisting that she was considering *both* sides, not just one.

But there is more than just deciding between two choices. Much of our thinking is dichotomous, occurring along the lines of good and bad, bright and dark, right and wrong, and so on. When we apply this type of thinking, what we perceive as losses in those lifestyle changes automatically take on the meaning of bad, dark, and wrong. And developments that grow out of these changes seem superimposed on the losses and automatically become experienced with the negative flavor associated with losses. Yet as the actual scenario of most lifestyle changes unfolds, there is another dichotomy at work: Those situations present both challenges and options. Confronting the challenges of change may be extremely painful, but in most situations it is unlikely that there is only one way to approach the challenge.

The Case of Bad Being Stronger Than Good

The case has been made for the greater power of bad events over good ones in everyday situations, major life events, interpersonal interactions, and learning processes (Baumeister, Bratlavsky, Finkenauer, & Vohs, 2001). The reasoning is that bad impressions form faster in people's minds and are more resistant to modification or extinction than are good ones. Bad pieces of information and bad feedback appear to have greater impact than good ones. We spend more attention on processing bad information than on considering good information and we are more motivated to avoid bad self-definitions than to follow up on good ones. "To say that bad is stronger than good is thus to say that bad things will produce larger, more consistent, more multifaceted, or more lasting effects than good things" (Baumeister et al., 2001, p. 325).

This reasoning could be applied in some cases of individuals suffering from a particular phobia. For instance, a small child having difficulty getting out of a swimming pool may develop a strong fear that will last to adulthood and keep him from ever entering a swimming pool or any other body of water again. The boy's fear will overshadow the fun he had at times when he played in the water prior to the frightening incident.

From an evolutionary point of view it might appear adaptive to focus more intently on bad than on good things. Organisms that were better in tune with bad events would have been more likely to survive threats and therefore would have had an increased probability of passing on their genes to future generations. Thus, when considering changes and options, focusing on the possible negative outcomes might appear to be an adaptive movement because ignoring the possibility of a positive outcome may induce regret later for having missed an opportunity for pleasure or advancement, but it does not become a matter of life or death.

Applying these findings to the relationship domain, Gottman (1994) developed a diagnostic index for the evaluation of relationships. For a successful relationship, positive interactions must outnumber negative ones by at least five to one, he proposed. This would indicate that bad events or interactions are about five times as powerful as good ones in close relationships.

Although people may reject the notion of keeping track of their own positive and negative actions in a marriage, most likely their spouses—as the receiving agents—are acutely aware and provide a storage place in their memories for all the negative comments and behaviors endured. Perhaps it would be wise to start establishing a reservoir of good deeds right from the beginning of a relationship. One could compare it with the establishment of a nest egg that would come in handy at some time of need and would also accrue interest in the form of the partner's goodwill in the meantime.

The Time Factor and Memory

Several decades ago, the then widely accepted notion of Helson's (1964) *adaptation level theory* was that although the impact of significant changes in life circumstances is temporary, organisms react more strongly to changes than to stable conditions. The fact that they are most sensitive to new conditions indicates that changes command the organism's attention to a higher level than would be required for existence in stable conditions. It is not surprising that change elicits strong reactions, but over time it gradually ceases to produce a reaction and eventually will be taken for granted. In other words, habituating to the change, the organism eventually returns to a calmer state of being.

Walker, Skowronski, and Thompson (2003) have taken exception to the notion that bad is stronger than good. Evaluating experimental data, particularly autobiographical memory information, they have suggested that when looking at the frequency of the events in question and the durability of the affect associated with them, negative affect is outlasted by positive affect. They argue that, in general, people perceive life events as pleasant and the pleasant emotions associated with them fade more slowly from memory than unpleasant emotions, and they conclude that people's memory systems do not treat positive and negative affect equally. Thus, the differential fading of emotional memories with time can be seen to provide individuals with a heightened sense of positivity or psychological well-being, sometimes referred to as "the psychological immune system" that assists in dampening the effects of negativity (Gilbert, Pinel, Wilson, Blumberg, & Wheatley, 1998).

The hypothesis that human development proceeds as an interactive process of person, context, and time was the basis for the theory of life span development proposed by Bronfenbrenner (1995). According to theory, the impact and general perception of an event not only are influenced by personal variables and the context in which it occurred but also are modified by the passing of time.

Developmental researchers have proposed that the process of maturation occurs in stages, phases, or periods of time when certain age-related changes in behavior, thinking, emotion, and personality take place (Erikson, 1963; Levinson, 1990). During childhood, one can think of sensitive periods—a span of months or years during which children may be sensitive or particularly responsive to specific experiences or to their absence. An example of a sensitive period could be considered a child's age from 6 to 12 months, a period that is significant for the development of parent–infant attachment. In adulthood, a concept related to timing is the notion of *on-time* and *off-time* events (Neugarten, 1979). The underlying hypothesis suggests that those experiences that occur at the expected times for an individual's culture or cohort will be less difficult to adjust to than experiences that occur unexpectedly (at off-time). An example here would be that a person widowed at age 70 would experience less serious life disruption than an individual confronted with widowhood at age 30.

Focusing on adulthood, Levinson (1990) proposed the concept of *life structures*. These include all the roles individuals normally play and all their relationships, as well as the conflicts and balance that are operating among them. Upon entering a period in adulthood that requires a new life structure, there is a period of adjustment—the *novice* phase—followed by the *mid-era* phase, during which adults become more competent at handling new challenges through reassessment and reorganization of the life structure constructed during the novice phase. Eventually, the *culmination* phase brings about a return to stability when individuals have succeeded in building a life structure that facilitates the management of the new challenges with increased confidence and reduced stress.

Many lifestyle changes require a new life structure. Those that are expected, such as marriage, allow for various degrees of preparation, which will facilitate the transition. For those that come unexpectedly, the challenge of creating new life structures will be experienced as significantly more complicated. Many lifestyle changes also involve changes in people's roles. Retirement reduces or eliminates the role of worker or employee. Reorganization within one's employee role could bring on a change from a supervisory position to a line position and vice versa. Divorce and widowhood permanently, or sometimes temporarily, eliminate the role of spouse while perhaps emphasizing that of parent because now there is only one parent to be responsible for the couple's offspring.

Larry, the suddenly widowed father of two children, was faced with the need to create a new life structure at the time of an unpredicted forced lifestyle change. With his wife and children, Larry had moved to the city about 2 years earlier to follow his professional development plan. His new work situation was very promising, confirming to him that he had made the right decision. But the death of his wife confronted him with the options of moving with his children back to their hometown, where they would have the help of his mother and his parents-in-law; letting the children move back and live with their grandparents while he remained in the city; or trying to develop a life as a single father while having to work fulltime to provide for their needs.

Whichever option Larry would adopt, he would have to build a new life structure and his role configuration would be different in each option. If he sent the children back to live with their grandparents, he would essentially be a single man again. If he moved with his children, he would be a single parent but, most likely, members of the extended family would be significantly involved in his life. On the other hand, if he decided to keep the children with him in the city, again, he would be in the role of the single parent but without frequent and direct assistance from and interaction with other family members. Each of the choices would be very challenging and each would have its own opportunities built in. Larry's struggle and final choice will be described in detail in a later chapter.

"Meaning Making" and Constructive Alternativism

To accept the notion that the psychological effects of bad events outweigh those of good happenings might seem pessimistic, but it might provide an explanation for why so many people feel threatened by, or at least uncomfortable with, major changes in their lives. If indeed the impact of bad events on the human mind is so much more powerful than that of good events, not much mental and emotional energy might be available to ponder any possible advantageous outcomes. Precious opportunities might be lost needlessly; after all, not every major change contains life-or-death situations.

George Kelly's formulations of a psychology of personal constructs based on the concept of constructive alternativism (1963) can be seen as offering a more positive outlook. Humans possess the creative ability of "meaning making"—giving meaning to the world rather than just responding to it. The idea of constructive alternativism presents us with the notion that there are always alternative constructions available to choose among in dealing with the world. No one needs to paint himself into a corner; no one needs to be hemmed in by circumstances; no one needs to be the victim of his biography. (Kelly, 1955/1991, p. 11)

According to Kelly, constructs provide the channels for mental processes. At the same time, constructs function as controls that individuals place upon lives. Intellect is the essential controlling feature of the human mind and the intellect is involved in formulating communicable constructs. It was Kelly's suggestion to think of constructs as pathways to movement; each pathway included a series of dichotomous choices. In reconstructing, individuals can either rattle around in their old slots or they can construct new pathways for themselves that previously had not been accessible or perceptible.

The perception of an event and the meaning given it by individuals are shaped by previous experience and as such influence individuals' reactions to an event or a crisis situation (Collins & Collins, 2005; James & Gilliland, 2005). What meaning individuals assign to an event can be learned by assessing their affective, behavioral, and cognitive reactions in the situation (Myer, 2001). Four different *life dimensions* seem to be impacted in a crisis event: physical, psychological, social, and moral/spiritual. For instance, there may be a difference in the way a repeatedly divorced person and the individual who divorces for the first time experience the event of divorce. Additionally, divorce will be perceived differently in families with several divorced members than it will be in families with no divorced members.

To assist in understanding the impact of a crisis event on individuals and organizations, Myer and Moore (2006) developed a crisis in context theory (CCT), which is based on an ecological model. The premises of the model state:

1. The impact of crisis events is experienced in two layers, dependent on the physical proximity to the disaster and individuals' reactions, which are moderated by their perception and meaning attributed to the event.
2. There is a reciprocal effect that occurs among individuals that are affected by the event.
3. A time factor influences the impact of the event in at least two ways. The amount of time that has passed since the event occurred and special occasions, such as anniversary dates of the event, both produce effects.

Growth Through Adversity

Combining influences from earlier humanistic-existential theorists with the thoughts expressed by proponents of positive psychology, Joseph and Linley (2005) proposed a social–cognitive model of growth based on organismic valuing process theory. The authors attempted to expand on already formulated descriptive theories of growth through adversity by establishing criteria for explaining and accounting for the phenomenon characteristic of growth. As growth consists of positive changes in people's evaluation of their self-perceptions, relationships with others, and philosophies of life, the theory needs to be able to explain why some people experience long-lasting negative effects from traumatic events, such as is often cited in the large body of explorations dealing with post-traumatic stress disorder (PTSD).

Within the relevant literature one can find various terms used in descriptions of growth or increased psychological well-being following the experience of traumatic events. These terms have been used interchangeably and have been applied to many different types of traumatic events. The use of numerous terms to explain the same or similar situations can be confusing. Perhaps it is simply a matter of resilience—a normal human process people express in extreme situations, as some proponents of positive psychology think (Masten, 2001). "Resilience refers to a class of phenomena characterized by good outcomes in spite of serious threats to adaptation or development" (p. 228). According to Masten, resilience is not the result of interactions of rare and special qualities, but it comes about through the everyday magic of ordinary, normative human resources in minds and bodies.

Following these lines of reasoning, investigators from the positive psychology movement stress the importance of positive emotions in the dynamics of psychological resiliency (Fredrickson, 2001). On the basis of several studies, it appeared that positive emotions might actually fuel psychological resilience and thus trigger upward spirals toward improved emotional well-being. Observing that psychological resilience is an enduring resource in people, the author proposed that over time the experience of positive feelings might not just reflect psychological resilience, but might actually build it. In the face of adversity, by finding positive meaning in ordinary events during the adversity itself, people may experience positive emotions. Positive meaning and positive emotions are considered to follow reciprocal relationships (Fredrickson, 2000).

According to research reported in the literature, in testing possible solutions to a current problem, a person will usually choose the solution that elicits the best, most pleasant feeling. Even in cases where people are presented with different types of solutions to a problem, one of which is the most sensible and another that elicits a better feeling, people will choose the solution that gives them the better feeling (Denes-Raj & Epstein, 1994). This is in contrast to when people follow habitual activities. These situations do not require decisions about novel stimuli and therefore feelings do not influence the choice of habitually made solutions.

In general, growth-through-adversity theories have some aspects in common with theories of PTSD, but they emphasize the process of positive change instead of focusing on the development of psychopathology. Some models center on the notion of effortful activity toward meaning making (e.g., Calhoun, Cann, Tedeschi, & McMillan, 2000; Hager, 1992; and as mentioned by Kelly, 1963, previously). Tedeschi and Calhoun (1995, 2004) proposed a functional-descriptive model that described how traumatic events act as seismic challenges shattering previous goals, beliefs, and ways of managing psychological distress. When pretrauma schemas are erupting and broken, people try to make sense of what has happened to them and attempt to handle their emotional responses to the trauma.

Nora, a widowed mother of three whom we will meet in a later chapter, found herself in the unthinkable position of having to lock up food from one of her children. This was a defensive measure on Nora's part in response to the child's regular raids on the contents of the family refrigerator. Nora felt devastated. Her role as wife and mother was shattered after her husband's death. Her parental authority was challenged severely, but she had the responsibility to provide for her family in day-to-day living. "The day I decided to lock up the food, I felt terrible. It was worse than losing a baby when I had a miscarriage; it actually felt worse than having my husband die," Nora reported. Perhaps the miscarriage and her husband's death affected her differently because she was not responsible for those events. "To keep food from my child made me feel like a murderer. But the next morning my daughter looked just as healthy as she ever had. She was pouting while she ate her breakfast, but she ate it," Nora continued.

Nora was surprised by her own positive feelings at that breakfast, even though her husband had died recently and she had had to expand her job from part- to fulltime due to financial stresses. Her children were just as challenging as before, but Nora got a glimpse of having taken control over her situation. She had made a good decision in a daily routine. What surprised her most was that she did not even have to scream or plead; she just did what was necessary to continue running her family. The need to plan for and problem-solve through daily events prevented Nora from immersing herself in grief over her husband's death. She had to face harsh realities on a daily—almost hourly—basis.

Returning to Joseph and Linley's organismic valuing process theory, it is stated that people are intrinsically motivated toward rebuilding their assumptive world in a direction consistent with new trauma-related information, which in turn leads to greater psychological well-being. Individuals tend to assess the meaning of the event and its existential implications, searching for paths for growth and actualization. The process of growth through adversity occurs gradually over a period of time, as it takes time to adjust mentally and emotionally to the adverse event and accommodate and interpret the new trauma-related information. The outcomes of the psychological resolution of the difficulties connected to the adverse event can be one of assimilation—that is, returning to the pre-event baseline—or the experiences can be evaluated and accommodated in either positive or negative directions.

Joseph and Linley assume that assimilation will be the most common outcome; most people will want to forget about a trauma-related event and will attempt to continue with their lives pretty much as they did prior to the event, perhaps with the development of more rigid defenses. Of course, some of the lifestyle changes people choose or are subjected to may not allow a return to the pre-event status and people are forced to accommodate in one way or another. Evaluations and accommodations that proceed along positive lines would include the search for opportunities to increase one's competence and psychological well-being. For most people wanting to achieve a positive accommodation, some cognitive restructuring is essential.

For Karen, the young mother of a little girl, return to pre-event status was not possible. In the residential treatment center for chemical dependency where she worked as a nurse's aid, she had met Joe, a patient trying to overcome his cocaine addiction. Karen developed romantic feelings for Joe; they got married and temporarily moved in with Joe's mother. Joe was in jail when Karen discovered that she was pregnant. She was searching for options. In a little more than 2 years, Karen had encountered a series of adverse events and there was a moment when she nearly gave up. As will be seen in a later chapter, however, Karen was able to grow psychologically to the point where she made herself independent and able to provide for herself and her daughter.

Memories of Momentous Events

When presented in autobiographies, momentous events often appear as significant and life-altering events (Pillemer, 2001). These memories provide emotional or intellectual landmarks in people's lives; memories that are associated with life transitions are especially vivid and long lasting. People who experience a major life change usually lack familiar routines or scripts to guide their behavior in the changed circumstances. They attend more closely to stimuli in the new environment because these events often contain critical information about how to succeed in this environment. New events, like those that present challenges, are thought about more often and those memories serve directive functions, providing lessons for the new life.

Individuals may trace the beginning of a life path to a particular defining event, which becomes linked to long-term goals and plans of action. Strong emotions originally experienced in life-altering events, such as embarrassment, fear, pride, or extreme helplessness, among others, become reactivated repeatedly in the individual's memory and thus continue in guiding and motivating the individual. Many of our actions occur because we want to feel better and, if we become aware of any problems, we set about solving them in order to feel better than we currently do or to avoid feeling worse (Overskeid, 2000). Thus, a person who has felt embarrassment or fear connected with a lifestyle change will work hard to avoid getting into a similar situation again because he or she wants to avoid experiencing that unpleasant feeling.

As there are many explorations about how people react to changes that uproot or alter significant parts of their lives, researchers in the field have offered various explanations. Comparing these explanations or hypotheses, some seem compatible with some others, while different proposed explanations appear to be in contradiction to the rest. However, something can be learned from most of them. For instance, applying Myer's (2001) explanation in the case of an individual contemplating moving in with a romantic partner without being married, the individual can expect strong attempts of persuasion to avoid cohabitation at all costs from his or her family of origin if there has been no previous example of cohabitation within the family background.

It would also be helpful to remember that, in general, people tend to choose the solution that elicits the most pleasant feelings, even if another available alternative would appear more logical or sensible, as described previously. Being drawn by the wish to feel good, the individual may justify the choice with, "Even though choice A makes some sense, I have this strong positive feeling about choice B; that must mean that B is the better option. My (gut) feelings couldn't be that wrong."

At the transition point from one lifestyle to another, it is the individual's choice whether to exclusively focus on the negative aspects of the challenge, to attend to the more positive aspects of options inherent in the change, or to let his or her feelings determine the choice. Often, the tendency to focus on positive or negative aspects of life events develops as early as in childhood. Betty remembers having liked chocolate as a young child. She had voiced her preferences but when her mother came home from shopping trips, the treats she brought for the children invariably were Snickers bars for Betty. Hoping that her mother had misunderstood, Betty voiced her preference one more time, as she remembers. She was disappointed again when she received another Snickers bar. That was the time when Betty decided not ever to tell people what she liked because, if they knew, they would present her with something quite different.

This experience taught her that she was one of the unlucky people who did not get what they wanted in life. Instead of the glamour of the chocolate, she was doomed to be given common Snickers bars for the rest of her life. Her generally negative attitude developed at that point; changes and choices represented negatively charged events for her. She tried to avoid them as much as she could. It seemed impossible for her to get what she wanted, and her suspicion that others, once they knew what she really wanted, would make sure that her desires were not met led her to feel victimized. Thus, her generally negative attitude about her choices in life was emphasized by the victim stance she adopted due to her suspicion of the intentions of others. Not surprisingly, Betty struggled with depression for many years until she finally decided to seek treatment.

Ambivalence About Choices

Like Betty, people may resist the very idea of options about how to feel and how to behave; they may consider events in their lives to be predetermined. Unlike Betty, who avoided making choices in an overt manner, others are not always aware of the fact that they have alternatives that they can choose from. And still others may reject the idea of choices because of feelings of anxiety they experience when decisions are requested of them. While focusing on the uncomfortable experience of anxiety, they do not realize that attentiveness to the existence of choices brings with it an invitation to decide—to select among the different options. Additionally, awareness of the various factors interacting and influencing one's opinions is of tremendous value in determining the most advantageous option.

Situations of choice among options involve elements of uncertainty. Sniezek and Buckley (1993) made a distinction between subjective uncertainty—the individual's personal experience of not knowing the outcomes in a given situation—and environmental uncertainty—the reflection of objective reality and its predictive probability for certain events to occur. Contributing to subjective uncertainty are several factors. For instance, the individual making the choice may not have access to or be aware of all available information, leaving the individual with an incomplete set of data about a particular event.

The characteristics of the decision makers shape decision-making situations in various ways. The degree of confidence that decision makers have in their ability to arrive at sound decisions varies greatly, from extreme confidence to serious underestimation. Furthermore, people's comfort with taking risks ranges from those who thrive on the excitement of "living on the edge" to those who insist on guarantees before considering any decision. As with many other behaviors, decision-making skills can be improved over time as the individual learns which important elements and probable consequences to include in the selection process. Also, levels of confidence in decision-making capabilities improve as a function of increased decision quality over time and situations.

Choosing among options carries with it a certain degree of stress. However, it is in the individual's power to determine the level of stress or anxiety associated with a given decision. The decision can be viewed as a bridge between wishing and acting (Yalom, 1980). It requires the individual's commitment to a specific path. When a person selects one alternative, the other options are lost, at least for the time being. Another source for stress comes from the decision maker's demand that the decision to be made be the correct or absolutely best choice. Accepting the responsibility for possibly having chosen the wrong option leaves some individuals paralyzed and unable to move in any direction. In situations of acute stress, they may attempt either to ignore the existence of choices or to manipulate others to decide for them. It becomes more important to avoid experiencing post-decisional regret than to have chosen well.

Lori, a young, divorced mother of two sons who will be introduced in the chapter on divorce, is a case in point. During her marriage, her husband's criticism of her had greatly weakened her self-confidence. In particular, he ridiculed Lori for making poor decisions. Not surprisingly, she avoided decisions because of the high level of anxiety she experienced when contemplating making a less than perfect decision, which would be followed by her husband's sarcastic remarks. Even after the divorce, Lori was deeply affected by his criticism.

As can be seen from the various case histories, external aspects of lifestyle changes, such as whether to live by oneself after years of marriage or changing professions or job settings, are easier to cope with than the deeper, hidden aspects of modifying one's concept of self that had been affected to some extent in the situation prior to the transition from one lifestyle to the next. Lori's mental and emotional divorce from the influences of her husband's opinion and treatment of her took much longer than the actual physical separation from him.

For an individual's transition from one lifestyle to the next a process of personal self-reevaluation or reconceptualization would often be beneficial.

In the shift from single to conjoint lifestyle, there is a tendency for parts of the individual person to become forgotten or misplaced or replaced with personality aspects that seem to be required by the particular lifestyle as, for instance, described by Dalma Heyn (1997) in her book, *Marriage Shock: The Transformation of Women Into Wives*. Similarly, when facing a single life after years of marriage, different personality traits may need to be emphasized now for successful adaptation. Relationship breakups may leave one or both partners with bruised egos and fractured self-confidence.

Reconceptualizing the Self

According to self-verification theory (Swann, 1983), individuals tend to have others view the self in ways that are consistent with their own pre-existing self-perceptions. This tendency of confirmation by others holds for both positive and negative aspects of an individual's view of self. Although initially people want to make good impressions on those around them, with time it seems that a desire for consistency of one's own self-concept with the view of others takes over. This phenomenon appears to function in a way similar to the concept of confirmation bias, where preference of evidence supporting existing beliefs or opinions has been observed (Nickerson, 1998).

A study concerned with the connection of self-verification to depression included, as part of a larger study, 138 married women and 258 undergraduate females who were involved in dating relationships (Katz & Beach, 1997). It was hypothesized that self-verifying feedback would result in increased stability of the participants' self-views. Furthermore, it was expected that for individuals with high self-esteem, the self-verifying feedback would lead to decreased depression while, conversely, for individuals with low self-esteem, self-verifying feedback would bring about increased depression. The results demonstrated that in both married and dating women, self-esteem and depressive symptoms were more strongly related among women who received self-verification from their partners than in women who did not experience self-verification.

The authors explained that self-verifying feedback functions to intensify the degree of influence of self-esteem on depression. While high self-esteem individuals' positive self-views will be reinforced by the feedback, for those who experience low self-esteem, the levels of depression will increase as a result of self-verifying feedback. Instead of defending the threatened self-view by engaging in self-promoting behaviors, the individual may experience depression, as happened with the women in the preceding study; for others, anxiety will join the already negative emotions. Acute feelings of depression and anxiety are not conducive to the calm and rational considerations necessary for responding in an enlightened self-interested manner to threats to one's self-concept. Considering the detrimental impact that confirmation bias or desire for consistency between self-concept and self-verification can have on an individual whose self-concept is already poor, encouragement to overcome the maladaptive behavior is of extreme importance.

People's beliefs and expectations about their ability to achieve desired goals and their ability for effective handling of obstacles that may stand in the way of those goals generally determine the degree and duration of efforts engaged in for reaching the goals. The person's estimate of the efficiency of a certain behavior resulting in a given outcome is the person's notion of an outcome expectancy. But there is also the degree of the person's conviction about being able to successfully perform the behaviors necessary to yield the outcome. This is considered as an efficacy expectation. These two expectations are part of the cognitive processes that mediate the acquisition and regulation of human behaviors. But the fact that they are performance based makes them especially powerful in effecting psychological changes (Bandura, 1997).

These expectancies are not the same as a person's personality traits because they are cognitive considerations that can only be defined in relation to specific actions in specific situations. However, self-efficacy expectancies are related to people's self-evaluations, such as the notions of self-esteem and self-concept (Maddux, 1991). It can be readily understood that individuals' self-efficacy expectancies are significant determinants in the manner in which people handle changes and whether they conceive of change as a welcome challenge that can be successfully negotiated or as one more setback that carries with it losses and failures.

CHAPTER 2

Marriage

A Multitransitional Process

After reading seven essays from a symposium on marriage and its future, cultural anthropologist Ellen Lewin (2004) responded with the question, "Does marriage have a future?" According to some researchers, a "process of deinstitutionalization—a weakening of the social norms that define partners' behavior" (Cherlin, 2004, p. 848), has occurred over the past few decades. As a public institution through the apparatus of state, marriage functioned to shape the gender order. "Molding individuals' self-understanding, opportunities, and constraints, marriage uniquely and powerfully influences the way differences between the sexes are conveyed and symbolized" (Cott, 2000, p. 3).

Even as the social basis of childrearing, marriage has become less important than it has ever been (Whitehead, 1996). Changes in the meaning of marriage and parenthood have turned socially defined roles into individual pursuits. Marriage and parenthood are no longer socially required functions of adulthood. Both the emergence of same-sex marriages and the increasing number of cohabiting unions are viewed as examples of the weakening of social norms—a weakening of the institution of marriage.

Transitions in the Meaning of Marriage

According to Cherlin (2004), two transitions in the meaning of marriage occurring in the United States during the twentieth century provided the social context for this deinstitutionalization. A transition from the institutional marriage to a companionate marriage was followed in time by another transition to the individualized marriage, emphasizing personal choice and self-development. In companionate marriages, spouses regarded each other as friends and companions with similar goals for their union but still adhering to the traditional division of labor within marriage. When romantic love and emotional satisfaction were added as important criteria for marriage, the increase in the level of intimacy the spouses experienced with each other may have been instrumental in the development of individualized ambition and significance.

The developing trend toward a "postmarriage" society incorporates a conceptual change from marriage as a childrearing institution to a more voluntary system of family relationships with limited commitments and ties that are easily dissolved (Whitehead, 1996). This change renders relationships in the postmarriage society more fragile and less permanent, with greater instability of family life. More open-ended and contingent commitments allow for greater freedom and opportunity for adults to seek satisfying relationships and, as such, these changes may not necessarily be undesirable. A marriage without emotional satisfaction can be abandoned when it becomes difficult or disappointing.

However, marriages are still popular in some places. Each year, an amazing number of marriages are performed in the city of Las Vegas. In its "Welcome to Las Vegas: Weddings (Always and Forever)" column, the *Las Vegas Guide* (2006) informs visitors that, within Clark County, 122,259 marriage licenses were issued in 2005. Although one of the most popular wedding days is Valentine's Day, getting married is easy here on any day. For the amount of $55.00 in cash (checks, casino chips, or credit cards will not be accepted), marriage licenses can be obtained at the downtown Clark County Marriage Bureau. The welcoming article includes exact address and opening hours. Blood tests and waiting periods are not required.

Once in possession of the license, couples can get married at the Office of Civil Marriages or they can do it elsewhere. The license is valid for a period of 1 year. Very thoughtfully, a telephone number is supplied for additional information. For the celebration of the new marital status, a wide range of wedding packages is available to the couples, ranging from the basic plan for $385 to the most elegant version for $1,510. Again, a telephone number is conveniently provided. And if the license was used in haste, Nevada has always been helpful in rectifying such mistakes.

If, indeed, the context of marriage has changed, what is the current meaning? Is it the symbolic significance that makes it a status marker with the wedding itself as a symbol for individual achievement, as Cherlin proposed? If so, what criteria do individuals apply now when considering marriage? If they are searching for greater self-fulfillment and increased intimacy and emotional closeness in their marriages, does that mean that today's marriages are more durable than those of the past?

Durability of Marriage

In a given year, the ratio of divorces to marriages is usually cited as 50%, meaning that there is one divorce for every two marriages. By 2003, the divorce rate had declined to 3.8% (National Center for Health Statistics, 2004). When viewed on a longitudinal basis, researchers found that the actual likelihood of divorce in the United States had reached a peak of 22% in 1988 and then leveled off to 18–20% toward the end of the twentieth century (Raschke, 1987; U.S. Bureau of the Census, 1997). The leveling off of the divorce rate is seen as partly due to a decrease in the marriage rate and an increase in the number of cohabiting couples whose breakups are not included in the divorce statistics.

The decision to divorce does not necessarily mean that people do not like to be married. Actually, it appears that the average length of the waiting period between divorce and remarriage is shrinking from 5 to 3 years (Mackey & O'Brien, 1995), although a large number of those who remarry divorce again, indicating that divorce is not the guaranteed path to happiness.

Marital Satisfaction

Too little is known about establishing and maintaining a sufficient degree of marital satisfaction to avoid marital failure. Most research about marital satisfaction has explored simple linear relationships between several variables without encompassing the complexity of marital dynamics and interactions (Rosen-Grandon, Myers, & Hattie, 2004). Characteristics such as anger, jealousy, or infidelity are thought to be significant predictors of divorce (Amato, 1996). Similarly, personality variables and interaction styles are thought to be influential in marital happiness and marital separation (Gottman, Coan, Carrere, & Swanson, 1998).

Factors such as marital satisfaction, marital quality, and marital discord have been linked to spouses' personal well-being in both cross-sectional and longitudinal studies (Christian, O'Leary, & Vivian, 1994; Cox, Paley, Burchinal, & Payne, 1999). Identification of the role of potential moderator variables was the goal of a meta-analysis of 93 studies that examined the association between marital quality and personal well-being (Proulx, Helms, & Buehler, 2007).

The findings showed that the dependent variable of personal well-being was linked to higher levels of marital quality. However, several moderating effects for sample, study, and design characteristics were also significant and the investigators concluded that future research would benefit from using sample populations that are homogeneous in the length of marriage because longitudinal effects are more easily detected with the use of standard measurements.

Overall marital functioning is frequently impacted by the stresses the spouses experience. This has been referred to as *stress spillover* (Bolger, DeLongis, Kessler, & Wethington, 1989). With increasing external stress, partners become more negative in their interpersonal behaviors at home. Furthermore, stressors acting on one of the spouses may reverberate beyond that spouse's own relationship evaluation and may impact the emotions and judgments of the other partner—a situation referred to as *stress crossover* (Larson & Almeida, 1999). To examine stress crossover and conditions that may facilitate crossover, a recent study followed a sample of 169 newlywed couples over a period of 3.5 years (Neff & Karney, 2007). The husbands showed a significant crossover effect, which was moderated by the couples' observed conflict resolution skills. The wives showed a significant stress interaction effect depending on their own stress levels.

In other words, in situations where wives are coping with greater levels of external stress, both husbands and wives are experiencing lower levels of marital happiness. However, when the husbands are the ones experiencing greater external stress, the husbands are less happy, but their wives' happiness is lower only if the wives too feel higher levels of stress. The couples' behavioral skills served a moderating function on crossover stress for husbands. Thus, better conflict resolution skills may improve couples' resilience in coping with the impact of stress on their marriages.

To assess differences between husbands and wives in changes on various aspects, such as psychological distress, spousal interaction, social support, and marital satisfaction, as well as the strength of intraspouse and cross-spouse links, 526 couples were followed over the first 4 years of their marriage (Kurdek, 2005). The findings of this study did not indicate significant differences between spouses.

An initial sample of 522 married couples was involved in a longitudinal study to determine predictors for marital satisfaction and timing of separation. It was observed that the measured variables of love for partner, liking of partner, and trust all declined significantly over time for both spouses, but somewhat more so for wives than for husbands (Kurdek, 2002). For husbands, only the variable of psychological distress showed decline over time. Not surprisingly, for both spouses, high levels of psychological distress and low levels of liking and trust at the beginning of the marriage predicted quick separations as well as low levels of marital satisfaction at the eighth year of the study for those who were still married.

When comparing married and divorced couples on their evaluations of their own and their partners' ability to love and communicate, it was found that both married and divorced persons regarded their partners as having less ability to love than they did themselves, even though they saw themselves and their partner as experiencing the same problems in the relationship. However, the factor that really distinguished the married couples from the divorced was the tendency to see the (ex-)partner as a less able listener than oneself (Skaldeman, 2006). In congruence with past social cognitive research showing that people perceive themselves as more trustworthy and able than others (Sedikides, Campbell, Reeder, & Elliot, 1997) and with Heider's (1958) concept of the self-serving attribution error, which implies that success tends to be attributed to the self while failure is explained in terms of circumstances or the behavior of other persons involved in the situation, the investigator expected similar patterns with a general positive self-bias to emerge in the study.

Describing marriage in terms of an adulthood developmental process that results in the establishment of various interaction processes, Mackey and O'Brien (1995) in their study of "lasting marriages" suggested that partners' behaviors evolve in the relationship and the nature and dynamics of these behaviors within marital interactions have a significant effect on the spouses' marital satisfaction. Among the marital interaction processes identified by the authors were communication quality, mutuality in decision-making, conflict containment, sexual and psychological intimacy, and relational values of trust, respect, empathic understanding, and equity.

It is commonly believed that interaction styles that demonstrate positive behaviors between partners are reflections of their satisfaction with the relationship, whereas negative behaviors are expressions of their dissatisfaction with the relationship (Rusbult, Johnson, & Morrow, 1986; Stafford & Canary, 1991). A longitudinal study demonstrated that mutual patterns of negative interactions have the strongest impact on relationships (Levenson & Gottman, 1985).

In fact, Gottman (1994) developed a diagnostic index for evaluating relationships, which indicated that in order for relationships to succeed, positive interactions must outnumber negative ones by at least five to one because the negative or bad interactions are so much more powerful in destructiveness than the good interactions are in soothing or healing influence.

Another conceptual model identified love, loyalty, and shared values as three distinct factors of marital characteristics, suggesting three paths to marital satisfaction (Rosen-Grandon, Myers, & Hattie, 2004). The most important characteristics of loving marriages were identified as respect, forgiveness, romance, support, and sensitivity. However, the presence of the markers for a loving relationship was not sufficient for the achievement of marital satisfaction. Loyalty appeared to be the necessary factor on the path to marital satisfaction. In those relationships where it was a priority, loyalty was described as a devotion to one's spouse independent of sexual activity and despite possible disagreements concerning expression of affection. Shared values in relationships include ways of managing conflict, agreement on (mostly traditional) gender roles, and high priorities on parenting and religiosity.

Overall, marital satisfaction according to this model proceeds along different interaction processes—those of affectional expression, consensus, and sexuality and intimacy, mediated through the importance and satisfaction of the loyalty factor. Sexual satisfaction was indicated as an important ingredient in loyal relationships regardless of possible disagreements over the expression of affection in the relationship. As additional factors of interest for future explorations the investigators suggested the consideration of the premarital context for relationship and personality variables that likely have an impact on marital satisfaction.

Premarriage Characteristics Leading to Marital Distress

Focusing on the transition from single life to being married, couples were asked at the time of their marriage and 1 year later to identify characteristics conducive to marital satisfaction (Kurdek, 1991). When comparing the couples that stayed together during the first year to those who did not, three personality variables were identified as related to marital satisfaction: motives to be in the relationship, satisfaction with social support, and psychological distress.

Following 162 newlywed couples over a period of 4 years showed that only 53 of the couples were still married, 24 couples had separated or divorced, and the remaining couples did not respond or could not be located after the study's duration (Bentler & Newcomb, 1978). The investigators used personality questionnaires and found that the still married couples were more homogeneous in their personality traits than the divorced or separated couples. Furthermore, it appeared that wives' personality traits were more frequently predictive of future marital quality than were husbands' traits.

In testing the hypothesis that for many couples the seeds of marital distress and divorce are sown before the spouses' official commitments, Clements, Stanley, and Markman (2004) followed 100 couples for a period of 13 years from the premarital phase through the primary risk period for divorce. With a sample of 135 couples planning marriage, the Denver Family Development Project started in 1980. The 35 couples that ended their relationship before marriage were excluded from the study. Ten assessment points were scheduled during the observation period. The participating couples were predominantly European American.

Marital status and satisfaction over time were used to categorize the couples into groups. The divorce group consisted of 20 couples and, depending on their marital satisfaction, the remaining 80 couples were differentiated into either the married but distressed group or the happily married group. Forty-one couples remained continuously satisfied through the whole observation period. In addition, one or the other partner out of 17 couples had been distressed at some time in their marriage, but had recovered to the point that the couple did not significantly differ from the continuously satisfied couples. Twenty-two couples remained married but were distressed.

Husbands' and wives' scores were recorded for eight variables: premarital satisfaction, religiousness, age, problem intensity, exchange orientation, problem-solving facilitation, emotional invalidation, and communication effects. Data analysis showed that premarital interaction and conflict aspects played a key role in differentiating marital outcomes.

As indicated in other studies (Gottman, Coan, Carrere, & Swanson, 1998; Matthews, Wickrama, & Conger, 1996; Rogge & Bradbury, 1999), interaction patterns play a pivotal role in the development of marital dissatisfaction. Negative interactions (with emotional invalidation being a key example) prior to and early in the marriage lead to erosion of positive aspects over time. Spouses experience significant distress and disappointment of their expectations about the spouse being their best friend (Markman, Stanley, & Blumberg, 2001). Negative interactions, such as emotional invalidation, during conflict situations lead to defensive or accusing behaviors in one or the other partner and result in a shift to pervasive negative attitudes, even in a previously positive or neutral emotional atmosphere.

As found in the studies mentioned earlier, spouses' interaction patterns play a significant part in the quality of marriages. Individuals have established these patterns long before the potential spouses meet and therefore they should be observable prior to committing one's future life to a partner. But how many people pay attention to those patterns? In the glow of early infatuation, individuals see and hear what they wish to see and hear. Only with the dimming of the glow does reality slowly make its entry.

Family Background Influencing Marital Stability

Economists and sociologists emphasize the impact of economic factors, such as the couple's financial situation and wives' labor-force participation, upon marital stability (Brines & Joyner, 1999). Additionally, sociodemographic factors and family background characteristics, such as intergenerational transmission of marital stability, are thought to be indicative of successful marriage foundations.

Focusing on these aspects, demographers have found that parental divorce increased the odds for marital instability by 70% for daughters (Bumpass, Martin, & Sweet, 1991). Similarly, another study (Amato, 1996) showed that the odds of marital disruption were increased by 69% in cases where the wife's parents had been divorced and jumped to 189% if both spouses' parents had been divorced. Additionally, parental divorce has been suggested to have an impact on individuals' relationship characteristics. If, while divorcing, parents model poor interpersonal styles, their offspring may develop personality characteristics that lead to interpersonal behavior problems.

Examining connections between parental divorce and young adults' certainty about their romantic relationships, Jacquet and Surra (2001) studied a sample of 404 individuals (87 women and 75 men from divorced families and 120 women and 122 men from intact families). Examining their findings, the investigators reported that parental divorce plays a part in shaping the experiences of young adults, but this was more evident for women than for men, especially regarding feelings of love and trust in a partner.

Women with divorced parents were less inclined to trust their partners' goodwill than women from intact families. Women from divorced families reported more conflict and negativity in their own relationships than was found for women with intact families. For men, regardless of the marital status of their own parents, they seemed to be hesitant to trust women who were ambivalent about trust. Men from divorced parents who paired with women from divorced families showed significant lack of trust in their female partners' honesty.

Other interesting aspects regarding the risks of marriages between spouses from disrupted families of origin were revealed in interviews involving 199 Black and 173 White couples as part of the "Early Years of Marriage" study (Timmer & Veroff, 2000). Analyses of the study's data showed that among all spouses, but especially among wives from divorced families, an increased closeness to their husbands' families was predictive of increased happiness in their marriages and reduced risk of divorce.

Generally, a family's cohesiveness (the closeness of relationships in family networks) brings about psychological and behavioral consequences in offspring (Rossi & Rossi, 1990). But it is the wife's preferences that influence both the size and degree of cohesion of the network because women function as the connecting links or "gatekeepers" within the family constellation (Reiss & Oliveri, 1983). These considerations would indicate that the wife's ability to establish links with the extended family would have greater impact on the marriage than would the husband's ability to do so.

The findings in the Timmer and Veroff (2000) study revealed that husbands and wives reported feeling less emotionally close to divorced families than to intact families; however, spouses from divorced families did not report being any closer to their spouses' families than was reported by those with intact families. Regarding the happiness and stability of their marriages, the data indicated that the couple's closeness to the husband's family had beneficial effects on the marital happiness and reduction of divorce risk. The closeness was especially significant if the wife came from a divorced family. This effect apparently was not linked to the presence or absence of children in the couple's marriage. One implied lesson from this study points to awareness of the importance of the lifestyle change when parents become parents-in-law—especially parents of sons as they welcome a new daughter into their family.

Searching for additional explanations for the intergenerational transmission of marital instability, Amato and DeBoer (2001) examined national, longitudinal data from two generations. The investigators designed their study in such a way that they could measure explanatory factors that preceded the divorces of adult offspring as well as the divorces of their parents. The factors explaining transmission of marital disruption from parents to offspring seemed to be relationship skills and marital commitment.

Poor relationship skills that can jeopardize marital stability include unclear communication; inattentive listening; expression of negative emotions; a tendency to criticize, which will lead to defensive behaviors in the other spouse; and avoidance of problem-solving discussions. Thus, children observing their parents' disturbed interactions prior to the parents' divorce are at risk to learn interpersonal behaviors that undermine intimate relationships and increase their own marital instability in adulthood. Indeed, when studying the behaviors of dating couples, it was found that partners with divorced parents demonstrated more communication problems than those with continuously married parents (Sanders, Halford, & Behrens, 1999). Through their parents' divorces, children learn that the commitment to a marriage can be broken when the marital relationship is unsatisfying.

According to the investigators, the data obtained from the 17-year longitudinal study suggested that the association between parents' and children's marital instability is of a causal nature. Parental divorce approximately doubled the odds that their offspring's marriages would also end in divorce. For those parents who experienced marital distress but remained continuously married, their children's marriages were not impacted by an increased risk of divorce. Therefore, it is not necessarily the spouses' poor relationship skills but their level of commitment that accounts for the dissolution of marriage. In the authors' opinion, the primary mechanism in the intergenerational transmission of marital instability can be seen in the undermining of commitment to the marriage.

Leisure Activities and Marital Satisfaction

In the search of factors that predict marital satisfaction, leisure time activities have been linked to marital quality and satisfaction for more than 60 years (Burgess & Cottrell, 1939) and research since has followed this notion to assert that marital companionship is the most significant aspect of married life in America (Blood & Wolfe, 1960; Lee, 1977). However, one study using a diary method to collect data found that companionship and marital satisfaction were unrelated (Huston, McHale, & Crouter, 1986).

Just how much companionship is needed for the marriage to be satisfactory? If spouses share most of their leisure activities, there may not be much opportunity for outside stimulation to occur and without fresh ideas the mental and emotional atmosphere may become tedious. Spouses who engage in shared leisure activities, such as going out together, having friends in common, and spending a good portion of their income on collective rather than individual consumption, practice what is referred to as a joint lifestyle. While joint lifestyles tie couples together, they also create certain degrees of dependency. The more time and activities the spouses share, the more their enjoyment and well-being are dependent on the partner.

Couples' lifestyles can be conceived of as falling somewhere along a continuum from almost completely joint to almost completely separated, based on the degree to which the spouses engage in joint leisure activities. The degrees of joint lifestyles change for individual couples over the course of the marriage according to the stages of the relationship and the birth and presence of children. Similarly, the spouses' work schedules influence the degree of the joint lifestyle.

A survey study with 1,523 married and cohabiting couples in the Netherlands explored the effects of different variables on couples' joint or separated lifestyle (Kalmijn, 2001). The factors of interest included the life cycle of the couples, their work life, their social and cultural homogamy, the degree to which partners resembled one another, and their value orientations. The results demonstrated that life cycle factors are important determinants of separated lifestyles. The roles of homogamy and the couples' value orientations showed modest effects. Although time constraints resulting from work schedules and the presence of children had an impact on the couples' ability to realize a joint lifestyle, it was found that dual-earner couples generally did not demonstrate a more separated lifestyle than other couples.

Kate and Ken were married for almost 5 years. Although they were strongly invested in their respective careers, it did not keep them from enjoying several shared activities. They enjoyed outdoors activities as well as visiting with friends. The birth of their children drastically changed their lifestyle. Apparently, they had not discussed their future roles as parents before actually becoming parents. Ken believed—as had been the case in his family of origin—that the children were Kate's responsibility. He occasionally played with them in the evening but he believed their existence need not impact his fishing and hunting weekends with his friend David. The children were too young to be taken along and Kate naturally had to stay at home with them. A year's lease on a cabin located about 180 miles from the town they lived in was too tempting for Ken and David to pass up.

Kate was left stranded at home with the children for significant periods of time, a situation she did not enjoy. Whenever she brought up the subject for discussion, Ken withdrew. He did not see any sense in discussing something that, according to him, followed the laws of nature. But their marriage could not survive the resentment that developed in Kate about the neglect and disrespect she felt from Ken.

Had Kate and Ken decided to seek marital therapy to assist with the adjustment from marriage to parenthood, Ken might have been able to realize that his short-term hedonistic attitude was not conducive to a happy marriage. Instead, assuming the responsibilities of a partnership would have been a better investment for him in the long run. Even better, premarital therapy, where both Kate and Ken could discuss in detail their ideas and beliefs about marriage and parenthood, seemed indicated in this case.

Another option might have been for Kate to engage in single-sided relationship therapy, where the focus is on the client's relationship with a particular person—the other person in the relationship dyad. That person's reactions and responses are anticipated by the client who is familiar with this person's interaction style and are considered within the session as if the other person were present (Maass, 2007). "Knowing the interaction style of the other allows the client to evaluate the estimated responses of the absent person and helps the client formulate his or her next step" (Maass, p. 179). In this framework there are opportunities to rehearse and modify one's behavior for achieving the most advantageous outcomes.

In a longitudinal study that followed a cohort of couples for over a decade, investigators collected data at two different times (Crawford, Houts, Huston, & George, 2002). At Time 1 the couples had been married for about 2 years; data collection at Time 2 occurred when couples had been married about 13 years. It was hypothesized that the more compatible couples are in their leisure interests, the more couple-centered their leisure would be and the more they would participate in these activities together. They would also pursue leisure activities that both of them liked. A third hypothesis stated that the more compatible couples are, the more they will pursue leisure activities together that one partner likes even though the other does not share the liking.

Based on interdependence theory, the investigators assumed that couples select each other partly due to common leisure interests. Therefore, spouses are not very likely to engage in many leisure activities without the partner. Congruent with this assumption, they formulated another hypothesis suggesting that the more couples pursue activities apart, the less satisfied they are with their marriage. Considering the results, the investigators thought that one of the most interesting outcomes of the study was the link between leisure compatibility and the time the spouses spent engaged jointly in those leisure activities that both of them liked at Time 1. It appeared that compatibility in preference of leisure activities did not necessarily draw spouses together and encourage joint participation; rather, it seemed to have suppressed spouses' inclination to engage in leisure activities independently.

Overall, the findings of the study indicated that the link between companionship and marital satisfaction is less strong than previously believed. How often spouses pursued activities of their own and their partner's liking seemed important. Leisure activities preferred by husbands but disliked by wives, whether they participated as a couple or the husbands were involved alone, seemed to result in wives' dissatisfaction.

Longitudinal analyses revealed interesting patterns. Comparing participants' responses from Time 1 to Time 2, spouses pursuing husbands' preferred leisure activities that were disliked by wives seemed to cause and result in wives' dissatisfaction. Thus, their joint participation in these activities at Time 1 predicted wives' marital dissatisfaction at Time 2. When husbands engaged alone in their preferred activities at Time 1, it was also predictive of wives' dissatisfaction. In other words, those leisure activities that are enjoyed by husbands but disliked by wives—regardless of whether husbands engage in them alone or both spouses participate in them—are a crucial factor in wives' contentment. If, indeed, as the investigators suggested, this factor precipitates and produces wives' unhappiness in the marriage, it would be worthwhile for spouses to give this topic serious consideration both prior to and early in their marriage.

Jenny and George: Skiing Into Marriage

Jenny and George loved to ski; in fact, they had met each other on the slopes of the White Mountains in New Hampshire. They both lived in New York City and continued their relationship, finally leading to marriage. They arranged most of their vacations around their interest in skiing and found many places they enjoyed until Jenny developed back problems and pain in her hips due to a severe condition of arthritis. Her mother had suffered from it but Jenny, who was so physically active, never thought that she would have to face this disabling condition herself. Their young marriage was put to the test; skiing had been important to both of them. The activity they so much enjoyed together was now impossible to participate in for one of them. They had hardly time enough to adjust to their new marital status when this sad development required additional adjustment to Jenny's impaired physical condition. How the young couple coped with this misfortune will be seen later in the book in chapter 8.

Leanne and Walt: Competing Leisure Activities

Leanne, like many women, believed in the importance of maintaining the closeness she and Walt experienced during their dating and honeymoon time. Maintaining emotional intimacy requires time spent together. Both of them held fulltime employment and their free time was precious. Leanne's first choice for joint leisure activity was taking long walks together a few times a week. They could talk about their wishes and hopes for the future while at the same time investing in their physical fitness. It worked for a while until Walt complained about the weather. He was not enthusiastic about walking in the rain and wind occasionally presented by the autumn season.

Listening to his colleagues at work, he became interested in golf. Leanne agreed; they joined a country club and took golf lessons. Walt seemed to have a natural disposition for it, but Leanne's progress was not what she might have hoped for. She came to dislike golf, especially as, due to the difference in their abilities, they were not spending as much time together as originally planned. With the birth of their first child Leanne discontinued her activities on the golf course; Walt, however, enjoyed his Sunday mornings and whenever possible a Wednesday afternoon with his golf buddies.

Walt did not think Leanne would mind; she was busy with the baby anyway, so she would not miss him. Walt's logic was flawed, however. Leanne would have liked some help or, at least, his company. But she did not want to nag. The exercise was healthy for Walt and as soon as the baby was a bit older, they could explore leisure activities as a family. Leanne's intentions were good, but she was torn by the belief that now as a family it would be appropriate to become regular members of a church.

Walt was not inclined to trade his golf activities for church attendance; instead, he suggested that Leanne and the baby attend church while he was out on the golf course and on Sundays that the weather did not allow for golf, he would attend church with Leanne. For a while this compromise seemed to work until members of the congregation made remarks about Walt's sporadic church attendance. Leanne felt she needed to defend him but her own resentment stifled the defense.

By the time their second child was born, the early emotional closeness between Leanne and Walt had evaporated. When their second child was about a year old Leanne committed herself to a part-time job. Most weekends were spent in performing chores around the house and yard on Saturdays. On Sundays, weather permitting, Walt headed to the golf course while Leanne and the children went to church. Leanne's resentment slowly eroded her loving feelings for Walt and Walt, sensing Leanne's covert dissatisfaction, became disenchanted with their marriage but considered it as a more or less normal development that occurred with time between marriage partners.

Leanne and Walt's story appears to confirm the findings of Crawford et al.'s study discussed before. At the points in their relationship when changes occurred, such as shortly after their wedding, in searching for leisure activities that both spouses could enjoy, Leanne probably settled too early for golf when she did not know yet whether she would enjoy it. When they realized how much Walt enjoyed playing golf, perhaps Leanne could still have searched for an activity that would bring her equal pleasure. And even though they did not perform these activities together, they could have shared their pleasure by discussing their interests with each other. This could have provided content for stimulating conversations as well as learning about the other's hobby without necessarily having to participate in it.

Instead of evaluating the situation as a loss of time and attention from Walt, Leanne could enrich her life with an interest of her own and communicate it to Walt during the time they spent together. Furthermore, one could reason that while she was taking time for her own interests she would be less inclined to build up resentment toward Walt for his involvement with golf. Another critical point of change in their relationship occurred with the arrival of their children. This is a crucial time in a couple's marriage as their roles change from lovers and spouses to include those of parents. If they have not done so already in preparation, this is the time to seriously discuss the sharing of tasks and responsibilities that will be necessary for the well-being of their family.

Transition to Parenthood

Reviews of studies about the effects of parenthood on adults' lives are mixed. There are pictures of joy and personal growth that children provide and there are accounts of the costs and problems they create for the parents (Bird, 1997; Ross & Van Willigen, 1996; Umberson & Gove, 1989).

The role of parent can be expected to increase stress in people's lives, leading to overload and marital conflict. Parenthood changes one's life insofar as former identities, such as worker or spouse, shift in level of significance in order to accommodate this new commitment that places daily demands on adult individuals—especially on women, as they are generally the primary caretakers in childrearing.

The increased stress and strain on marital relationships among new parents has found attention in the literature. The birth of the first child changes the marital relationship in many ways; there is less time for the two spouses to spend together as there is less time for individual recreation and enjoyment. In addition, division of housework and child care may introduce conflicts between the parents (Demo & Cox, 2000). On the other hand, other studies have demonstrated that nonparent couples reported just as much strain on their relationship and were just as likely to break up as those couples that had made the transition to parenthood (Cowan & Cowan, 1992).

To explore how new parents differ from their childless counterparts in social and psychological well-being, Nomaguchi and Milkie (2003) used data from a nationally representative sample of 1,933 adults who were childless at the first interview and several years later compared those who had become parents and those who remained childless. Indicators for costs and rewards of parenting included measures relating to social integration, self-esteem, self-efficacy, hours of housework, and marital conflict. Marital conflict was measured by frequency of disagreement with spouse.

It was found that new parents reported higher levels of social integration than childless couples. When focusing on gender differences, the investigators observed that, among women, married mothers' lives were marked by more housework and marital conflict but less depression than the lives of childless married women. New mothers also reported more disagreements with their husbands than did their childless counterparts. Hours of housework were collected as the sum of time spent on nine household tasks per week, such as cleaning, meal preparation, grocery shopping, lawn work, laundry, etc., without inclusion of direct activities with the child.

Analysis of the data showed that new mothers spent 9.07 hours per week more in housework than women without children, while new fathers were spending only 1.04 hours per week more than nonfathers. The data indicated little effect of parental status on the lives of married men.

The investigators explained that the dependent variables in their study did not include indicators that directly evaluate parental experiences connected with the hours of child care; nor did they assess the nature of spousal disagreements whether or not they were child related. They further cautioned that changes in marital status between the two interviews, one of their primary independent variables, might not have been unrelated to another independent variable, the presence of children. Therefore, it is possible that those couples that experienced greater marital conflict due to the new parenthood status might have separated before the second interview.

Thus, the question about the impact of children on marital dissatisfaction and dissolution has not received an answer with this study and remains open for conjecture. As with any other significant change in one's lifestyle, when considering parenthood there are options in the way to approach the changes. A consideration of losses might include loss of financial resources, of independence, and of time for other pursuits. But the way children bring meaning and joy to one's life as well as the aspect of social integration that was observed in the Nomaguchi and Milkie study can be counted as gains.

Pattern and Timing of Parenthood and Marital Quality

Over the past decades the pattern of family building has changed dramatically. Although about one third of all women in the United States give birth to their first child before age 25, many couples have delayed parenthood until the wives are in their 30s and even 40s. Becoming first-time parents in their early 20s is significantly different in many ways from new parenthood for people in their early 30s. The relative success of transitional stages in peoples' lives depends largely on the timing of the transitions. As, for example, in teenage pregnancy and consequent childrearing, transition to motherhood occurs at a time when the transition from childhood to young adulthood has not been completed and developmental tasks for each stage have not been mastered. Thus, a couple's early parenthood might occur before the transition from young single adulthood to conjoint living with a spouse and adjustment to the new responsibilities of this stage has been established with sufficient strength to withstand the stresses of this phase of life.

Education, emotional maturity, and financial security are only some of the factors that account for a sense of readiness for parenthood in those who wait. Findings of explorative studies have indicated that couples who delay parenthood until they are in their late 20s or 30s are more likely to share tasks more equally than those couples who have children earlier in their marriage. In addition, studies looking at the links between the timing of parenthood and the division of household chores suggest that couples who start their families at younger ages may subscribe to a more traditional lifestyle than those who delay the event of parenthood (Coltrane, 1996).

In accordance with the findings of those exploratory studies, Helms-Erikson (2001) proposed a connection between couples' timing of parenthood and the marital quality, based on the couples' family roles, as expressed in their division of housework. Information about marital status, family relationships, and psychological well-being of 180 dual-earner couples of diverse socioeconomic status was collected through home visits and a series of telephone interviews.

For the timing of parenthood, wives were divided into three groups according to their ages at first childbirth. Mothers who had their first child at age 24 or younger were classified as "early" parenthood, those who became mothers first between the ages of 24 and 28 years were designated as "on time," and the women who became mothers at age 28 or older constituted the "delayed" group.

The first group consisted of 62 parent couples, whereas the other two groups each included 59 couples. It was found that the timing of the transition to parenthood alone is not a predictor for marital well-being 10 years later. Considered to be "at risk" for negative marital evaluations were early first-birth couples, who divided tasks in a less traditional manner, and delayed first-birth couples with traditional task division.

Analyses revealed that husbands and wives in "risk" groups evaluated their marriages more negatively, suggesting that congruence of behaviors, background, and attitudes is important for marital quality. In addition, early first-birth couples rated their marriages more poorly than did the "on time" or "delayed" couples. Wives' gender-typed attitudes emerged as a significant covariate in the analyses but did not account for the effects of "timing of parenthood" and the interactions of "timing of parenthood" and "division of housework."

For couples with early parenthood experiences and a less traditional division of household labor marital discord was shown; however, when childbearing was delayed with couples of the same pattern, the marital outcomes were more positive. Couples who start early with family building and divide chores equally may be in greater marital conflict than those who delay parenthood. Whether couples subscribe to traditional or egalitarian lifestyles is not a predictor for marital happiness. What is important for the marital well-being of dual-earner couples is the congruence of their behaviors, beliefs, and backgrounds into and through the childrearing years, not just immediately after the birth of their first child.

Although it is not mentioned much in the relevant literature, contrary to Nomaguchi and Milkie's (2003) study mentioned earlier, therapists in the field of marriage therapy often hear husbands complain about feeling neglected by their wives after the children's birth. They view themselves at times as nothing more than "sperm donors."

The Effects of Infertility on Marital Satisfaction

Just as the presence of children impacts the marital quality in some ways, so does the involuntary absence of children affect the marital relationship. For many couples this can mean years of uncertainty as they pursue various options that could possibly lead to pregnancy. Until couples finally abandon treatment, there is still an element of hope present. The actual transition to acknowledging permanent biological childlessness occurs only after infertility treatment is terminated and pursuits of achieving pregnancy are stopped (Deveraux & Hammerman, 1998).

Most of the burden of fertility treatments falls upon women; they tend to assume more of the responsibilities and guilt feelings about the state of their childlessness. Men's emotional responses seem to be less strong than women's (Daniluk, 1997; Domar, 1997; Pasch, Dunkel-Schetter, & Christensen, 2002). Men also tend to agree readily with their wives assuming the responsibility for the infertility—even in cases where the underlying diagnosis was related to male rather than female factors (Gibson & Myers, 2000).

The question of how spouses adapt over time to the transition to biological childlessness was the focus of a study that followed 38 women and their male partners in several Canadian cities for a period of 3 years (Daniluk & Tench, 2007). The participant couples, mostly Euro-Canadian, had been trying to conceive for a mean of 6.92 years and the mean length of time they had spent in following medical treatment options for infertility was 5.91 years. Termination of treatment efforts was activated by 95% of the couples rather than by the physicians. Emotional exhaustion was the most frequent reason stated for the termination. About 55% of the couples indicated that they would pursue the option of adoption.

In contrast to other studies mentioned earlier, there were no significant gender differences in psychological distress reported by the couples. Associated with poorer adaptation to biological childlessness over time—when compared to more successful adaptation—were more symptoms of psychological distress as evidenced by lower levels of marital satisfaction, less sexual satisfaction, less life satisfaction, and lower self-esteem. Of particular significance in these findings was the continued and persistent decrease in sexual satisfaction reported by the participating couples. The intense focus on achieving pregnancy during the infertility treatment process eliminated aspects of pleasure and spontaneity and changed the meaning of sexual activity from pleasure to work for procreation.

When conception becomes more important than the spouses' feelings for each other, they reduce or eliminate their previously experienced enjoyment in sexual activities and turn it into a demand performance or chore. Thus, with the loss of opportunities for biological parenthood, the spouses may also face the loss of their positive feelings for each other and the enjoyment of the other's presence (Maass, 2002/2006). When goals are impossible to attain, in successful adaptation individuals can move on by abandoning them or they can progress by finding an appropriate substitute. And in doing so, they search for new meanings while reappraising their options and coping with the stress of the event.

Marital Sexual Life: Effects and Consequences

The literature on assortative mating indicates that partners choose each other on the basis of similarity along different dimensions (Watson, Klohnen, Casillas, Simms, & Haig, 2004). One of these dimensions seems to be partners' prior sexual experience, particularly the number of intercourse partners (Garcia & Markey, 2007). Investigating 106 couples who were dating, cohabiting, or married about the number of sexual intercourse partners they had prior to the initiation of their current relationship, it was found that, with the exception of cohabiting couples, romantic partners showed a significant level of matching in the prior number of intercourse partners. For married couples, similar numbers of prior intercourse partners between men and women were related to higher levels of love, satisfaction, and commitment in the marriage.

Sexual attraction and sexual activities are significant aspects of marriage. Previous research has reported that the frequency of marital sex declines with the duration of the marriage (Blumstein & Schwartz, 1983; Call, Sprecher, & Schwartz, 1995; Masters, Johnson, & Kolodny, 1992). Some of this decline is undoubtedly related to the physical aspects of aging (Udry, Deven, & Coleman, 1982), but that is not a complete account for the phenomenon. A frequently cited reason for divorce has been the occurrence of extramarital sex (South & Lloyd, 1995). Extramarital sex has significant disruptive potential for marriages and presents lifestyle changes within the marriage as well as being a likely marriage-terminating force.

Evolutionary theorists offered explanations for the decline of sexual activity with marital duration by citing trade-offs in the allocation of resources between mating efforts and parental responsibilities: More time, money, and other resources will be used for childrearing efforts than for sexual endeavors (Lancaster, 1994; Posner, 1992). While this may be correct for many families, it does not explain the occurrence of extramarital sex. Furthermore, the declining marital sexual activity with increasing marital duration has been observed in childless marriages as well (Call et al., 1995).

Another theoretical approach considered declining frequency of sexual activity in marriages within the context of diminishing marginal utility

(DMU) and human capital investment (Liu, 2000). Initially, sexual activity between spouses is thought to result in high levels of satisfaction and sexual activity increases. But with the increase of sex, the level of satisfaction decreases and, in turn, the frequency of sex decreases. But people make rational choices and being married generally means being involved in a long-term relationship where both partners have incentives to invest specific human capital, such as the provision of empathy, companionship, sexual pleasures, and many other benefits. Thus, the human capital investment effect functions in slowing the rate of declining frequency of marital sex over time.

To answer the question about the relationship between marital duration and extramarital sex, Liu (2000) proposed two hypotheses. As the marital utility (MU) of sex with an old partner is lower than that of sex with a new partner, MU continues to decline with marital duration. Furthermore, for those couples who work harder to make their sex life new and stimulating, the investment of the additional effort becomes far greater than the effort involved in having sex with a new partner, whose sexual behaviors will be new for at least some time. In other words, while the investment in sex with a long-term partner tends to be greater than the pleasure derived, the opposite would be true for the investment in the sexual relationship with a new partner.

Additionally, Liu (2000) considered previous research findings about men's greater investment in their careers than in relationships (England & Farkas, 1986) as well as the notion that physical pleasure in a sexual relationship is more important to men than to women (Masters et al., 1992). In contrast, for women, emotional attachment and satisfaction are expected to be more important than physical pleasure in a sexual relationship (Buss, 1994; Masters et al., 1992). Thus, for men, the likelihood of extramarital sex would be expected to increase with marital duration, whereas with women the likelihood of extramarital sex is expected to decline because their relationship-specific human capital investment accumulates with the duration of the marriage.

However, because of the importance of the emotional relationship aspects, the woman's human capital investment is likely to decline as the man's interest and involvement with extramarital partners becomes apparent, and her physical and emotional interests will decline, independent of the duration of the marriage. While it most often is the woman's wish for intimacy that prompts her sexual actions, if the wish for intimacy remains unfulfilled in the sexual relationship, her sexual desire and human capital investment in the marriage will plummet (Maass, 2007).

The preceding discussion most likely constitutes an oversimplification because of the multitude of other factors involved in human relationships. Several of these factors and their effects are explored in other parts of this book. Suffice it to say that the complexity of intervening variables in marital relationships provides for many changes over the duration of the marriage and each change in itself presents opportunities for reducing losses and amplifying gains for the individual spouses.

Setting Priorities: Career or Marriage

For many women the transition to marriage involves decisions that influence another life area, that of their careers and employment. It is much more common for a woman than a man in our society to change a career path to accommodate married life. Additional changes in career goals can be expected during the transition to parenthood. The various aspects of women's employment during motherhood will be explored in the chapter on career changes; the focus of discussion here is primarily on the marital relationships.

Some women make the momentous decision of choosing between a career and family life much too early in their lives when they have insufficient information about themselves and the future. Melanie, a young woman mentioned in a different context (Maass, 2002/2006), is a case in point. Melanie's plans of a future career in archeology came to a premature end when she met Ted, a history and prelaw student aspiring to a future in politics. A career in archeology seemed impractical for the wife of a politician. Melanie dropped out of college and obtained an office job to be a support for Ted. They married while Ted was finishing law school. It would take years for Ted to establish himself professionally. Melanie continued working part-time while raising their two sons. (Let us call the development to this stage "Point A.")

For several years Melanie's life was filled with the care for her family and her part-time job. Her oldest son decided to become an architect. Melanie was fascinated by his studies. She read his textbooks and helped him with his papers and design work. Then she learned that Ted had been involved in a brief extramarital affair. Melanie's trust in Ted and her confidence in herself were shaken. She realized that she had maintained a lifestyle designed for a world that no longer existed. Acknowledging the fact that she had no valid permanent basis of existence as an individual, she entered a brief period of therapy to sort out her options (Point B).

With the therapist's guidance, Melanie explored current interests that could lead to a meaningful occupation. There was her interest in architecture, but was that a realistic goal? It was too early to tell; besides, she had never finished her bachelor's degree. Her first step was to fulfill this requirement. Melanie obtained information from a local college. Her old credits could not be applied toward current studies, but there was a possibility of testing out of some of the core courses, provided her scores were sufficiently high. Furthermore, the "general studies" program offered by the college was tailor-made for people like Melanie. Parts of her work history and life experiences could be applied towards college credits. With a lot of effort on her part, it seemed possible (Point C).

Melanie was excited when she told Ted about her plans. In expressing doubts over her ability to test out of some of the core courses after having been out of college for so long, he jokingly added that her spelling skills seemed to focus mainly on the letters a, r, c, and h. Melanie was not amused. She confided in her older sister for another opinion. Her sister's advice was to focus all her energies on working on her marriage to overcome the impact of Ted's affair rather than to think about college and a career (Point D).

Sample Process of Exploration

Applying the process of exploration of lifestyle changes to Melanie's case, what were her challenges and options at Points A, B, C, and D? At Point A Melanie terminated her career plans (loss) and started the process of building a family (gain). It appears that she traded one for the other—a simple exchange, but was there another option for her? Even after deciding that archeology was not a practical career choice in view of Ted's goals, she could have shifted the focus of her studies to another field.

Having made the decision of attending primarily to raising a family, what factors were operating at Point B? Ted's affair had destroyed a part of her trust in him (loss). Along with her loss of innocence or naiveté, her self-confidence plummeted (another loss). She did not seem to gain much at this point, but what were her options? Divorcing Ted (loss), living single life (gain freedom, but likely financial loss). Remain married and return to school (likely gain of future independence). At Point C Melanie's situation had not changed much except for increased anger over Ted's response to her wishes, perhaps immediately adding weight to a decision of divorce. At Point D, Melanie's sister and her advice strengthened the "remain married" position (gain) while rejecting the plan to attend college (loss of emotional support as well as future independence).

After a lot of soul searching and with the guidance of her therapist, Melanie made the following decision at Point D: Considering that Ted's extramarital affair could not be counted as an asset in his political ambitions, obtaining a divorce would not improve Ted's prospects either and it would not be to Melanie's benefit. She decided that it would be in her best interest if she placed her own well-being over that of Ted—if they had to be rank-ordered. This decision was the reversal of the one she had made at Point A. Also, realizing that Ted's judgment was not infallible stressed the importance of looking out for her own interests while simultaneously increasing her self-confidence. Melanie decided to remain married to Ted with the attempt of putting their relationship on a mentally and emotionally closer basis. She made her return to college with the goal of embarking on a career a condition of staying married. That was a promise to herself she intended to keep.

Conceptual Models of the Stability of Marriage

The question of what determines the stability of a marriage has been of interest to investigators, especially when it appeared that the risk of marital distress and the duration of the marriage share a positive correlation. About 30% of divorces occur within the first 4 years of marriage (Clarke, 1995). To understand the process involving the variables of time and marital satisfaction, information from couples at the beginning of their marriage as well as information gathered at various follow-up assessments would seem to be important.

This was the approach Bentler and Newcomb (1978) used when they administered personality questionnaires to 162 newlywed couples, as mentioned earlier in this chapter. Four years later the still married couples showed a more homogamous pattern of personality traits than those who divorced. Not all of the 162 couples entered their first marriage at that time, which introduced another variable that was not controlled for in the study.

Differences between spouses in the areas of personality traits, attitudes, and socioeconomic status have been linked to high rates of marital tension and union dissolution, especially in African American marriages (Ruggles, 1997). Using data from three waves of the National Survey of Families and Households, it was found that African American marriage partners showed high levels of dissimilarity in traits that may result in incompatibility (Clarkwest, 2007). Linking the level of dissimilarity to the higher divorce rates in African American marriages, the researcher proposed, referring to a subsample of newlyweds, that the higher levels of differences might be a result of lower rates of resolution of spousal differences during the initial relationship stages rather than stem from differences in assortative mating. According to the investigator, African American couples' higher levels of dissimilarity in the measures used in this study can be linked to about one fifth of the divorce gap between African American couples and those from other populations.

Different conceptual models regarding the path from the beginning of marriage to the existence of marital distress have evolved. The *enduring dynamics model* explains marital distress as the end result of problems that existed from the beginning of the marriage. These problems may derive from different sources, such as stemming from personality traits or problematic interaction styles, but whatever their source, they were in existence from the start, even during the courtship phase (Huston & Houts, 1998).

On the other hand, both the *disillusionment model,* focusing on decrease of positive aspects (Murray, Holmes, & Griffin, 1996), and the *emergent distress model,* emphasizing increasing negative aspects (Gottman, Coan, Carrere, & Swanson, 1998), propose that marital distress is the end result of changes in marital functioning. Usually, at the beginning of their relationship spouses have idealized pictures of their partners and the relationship. At this time of their union they express affection freely and frequently and seem to agree on most important decisions. Over time, they view each other and the relationship more realistically. Differences in attitudes and limitations in the partner are not overlooked as easily as was the case at the start of the relationship.

In their study with 146 newlywed couples in first marriages Huston, Caughlin, Houts, Smith, and George (2001) tested the applicability of the three models. The couples provided information at the beginning of their marriage and in at least one of two follow-up assessments over the first 2 years of marriage. The outcome variables were determined as marital stability, timing of divorce, and level of marital satisfaction at 13 years.

The investigators found that marital stability was consistent with the disillusionment model. Changes in love, responsiveness, affectionate acts, and ambivalence distinguished couples in the still married group from couples in the divorced group more clearly at the 2-year point in marriage than at the beginning of marriage. This is not surprising, as one would generally assume that at the beginning of a marriage infatuation combined with hope for change would have a beneficial impact on the spouses' feelings about their marriage.

Considering the timing of the divorce, couples with early divorces (between 2 and 7 years of marriage) were different from those with late divorces (between 7 and 13 years of marriage) by values of love and responsiveness more so after 2 years of marriage than at the beginning, thus being congruent with the enduring dynamics model. Regarding the variable of marital satisfaction, the findings again were consistent with the enduring dynamics model, as spouses from happily married couples were better distinguished from unhappily married couples by values of love, responsiveness, and ambivalence at the beginning of the marriage than by changes in these values over the first 2 years of marriage.

Spouses' Relative Power in Marital Conflict and Health Consequences

Research efforts directed at investigating the effect of marriage on the spouses' health have generally documented physical and psychological beneficial effects in married individuals when compared with their unmarried counterparts (Gordon & Rosenthal, 1995; Kiecolt-Glaser & Newton, 2001). But there are also potential risks in marital relationships, resulting mainly from negative interactions between spouses, which impact cardiovascular, endocrinological, and immunological functions.

For instance, an increase in wives' blood pressure as a result of hostile spousal interaction has been noted (Ewart, Taylor, Kraemer, & Agras, 1991) and increases in wives' norepinephrine and cortisol levels were associated with husbands' withdrawal during conflict situations (Kiecolt-Glaser et al., 1996). These findings raise the issue of a gender-related effect on individuals' physiological conditions. What aspects in the marital relationship could account for such effects? Why would conflictual spousal interactions affect women more than men?

Spouses' endocrinological responses when dealing with conflict in association of power in marriages were the focus in a study of 72 newlywed couples (Loving, Heffner, Kiecolt-Glaser, Glaser, & Malarkey, 2004). The investigators considered different theoretical approaches that have been linked to defining and delineating marital power. Resource theory has associated marital power with the spouse who has the greater fund of resources (Blanton & Vandergriff-Avery, 2001; Kulik, 1999), whereas gender-role theory suggests that men are usually the power holders, regardless of the resources (Trentham & Larwood, 2001). Personality characteristics, such as dependency, were suggested by Rusbult, Arriaga, and Agnew (2001) because dependent individuals generally have less power in relationships and during conflicts are more concerned about the loss of the relationship.

Considering these theoretical approaches, Loving and coworkers (2004) conceptualized marital power as closely connected to perceptions of dependence and control within a marriage, which are tied to levels of emotional involvement. The partner who is less emotionally involved in the relationship holds the greater power in the relationship. The partner with the greater power also is the one who can exert more control, leaving the less powerful spouse at a greater risk for psychological distress and illness (Fowers, 1994).

Following this line of thought, Loving et al. (2004) hypothesized that increased levels of the stress hormones adrenocorticotropic hormone (ACTH) and cortisol would be found in less powerful spouses following a discussion of conflict with the more powerful spouse. Both ACTH and cortisol are released through activation of the hypothalamic-pituitary-adrenal (HPA) axis during periods of stress. In this study, determination of marital power was based on comparisons of the spouses' reports of their dependent love for one another. The connection between marital power and problem-solving behaviors of spouses was explored with the use of the

Marital Interaction Coding System-IV, an instrument developed by Weiss and Summers (1983) that provided data on problem-solving activities during 30-minute marital conflict resolution activities.

The results showed that for less powerful spouses there were relative increases or sustained elevations in ACTH at the end of a conflict discussion. For instance, in couples where the wives were more powerful than the husbands, the wives' ACTH levels did not change related to the conflict. But when their husbands held more power, the wives' ACTH levels were higher after the conflict situation than prior to it. In the more powerful husbands, the ACTH levels showed significant declines following the end of the conflict, whereas the less powerful husbands' ACTH levels did not decrease until 30 minutes after the end of the conflict situation. On the other hand, in couples where both spouses shared power in the marriage, the ACTH responses for both followed the pattern seen when the wife held the power.

Examining cortisol levels in relation to marital power, it was found that wives' cortisol levels declined when they were the power holders as well as when power was shared between the spouses. Cortisol levels follow a diurnal rhythm and tend to normally decrease during the morning hours. Thus, the wives with shared or greater power demonstrated the normal cortisol action, but wives with more powerful husbands did not show this natural diurnal cortisol pattern. Husbands' cortisol levels followed the normal diurnal pattern when the husbands held greater power and when their wives were more powerful, but when marital power was shared, the husbands' cortisol levels did not decrease until 30 minutes after the termination of the conflict discussion. The investigators interpreted the husbands' responses in the shared power condition as indicating that shared marital power presents a unique challenge for husbands during conflict discussions.

What might be the long-term implications of these hormonal responses? Stressful actions or perceptions of stress can lead to ACTH or cortisol increases and could thus have health repercussions. As explained earlier, both ACTH and cortisol are released through activation of the hypothalamic–pituitary–adrenal (HPA) axis and chronic HPA activation may result in immune system dysfunction (Lovallo, 1997; Rabin, 1999).

As people enter into marriage and change their single lifestyle to that of a marital partnership, how many individuals seriously consider the possible health effects that may result from the combinations of personality characteristics and power status within the marriage? During the early phase of passionate love individuals naturally focus on the gains that marriage will bring to them. There is the daily presence of the loved person, the companionship, and the parenthood and, for women, perhaps financial security and protection. However, these gains are often offset by losses in independence, power, control, and possibly health risks. Individuals may ask themselves before they enter into this type of commitment, "Will this union be a fair trade for me or am I going to give up more than I will gain?"

Myra did not ask herself that question when she accepted Jeffrey's marriage proposal and discontinued her studies. Jeffrey was in his last year of medical school and there were still years of training ahead for him. They could not afford tuition for both of them, so Myra dropped out of college and went to work as an administrative assistant. They postponed parenthood until Jeffrey had completed the medical residency requirements. The years of Jeffrey's training had determined the location of their residence; now he was ready to accept a position at a hospital in a different town, requiring the family's relocation.

At this point Myra's balance sheet has the following entries: First, Myra traded her college studies for an office job and the opportunity to have Jeffrey as her husband. Then, when they moved to another town, she relinquished her job for the possibility of motherhood. It is too early to tell how the balance of Myra's commitment will turn out, but Myra's story will continue in a later chapter.

What are people's reasons for getting married? Love; sexual attraction; companionship; parenthood; financial benefits; sharing of responsibilities; and cultural, social, and religious values are just a few—or, more simply stated, to get something they value but over time they devalue that something. They may lose it by not taking care of it and then they focus on what they have paid or given up for what they pursued—the freedom to do what they wanted. Marriage feels like a big loss then. This raises the question: "If it was worth pursuing and achieving it, would it not be worth nurturing it and turning it into a permanent value?" Analyses of recently collected data from the Toledo Adolescent Relationships Study regarding adolescents' expectations about marriage and cohabitation showed that three quarters of them had *definite* or *probable* expectations to marry in the future (Manning, Longmore, & Giordano, 2007).

These findings seem to provide an answer to Lewin's (2004) question at the beginning of this chapter. They also emphasize the relevance of the discussion of the many different factors that affect marital relationships, a discussion that is expected to increase individuals' awareness of and sensitivity to ongoing changes as they occur in the life of a marriage. Each one of them amounts to a lifestyle change—however, less drastic than that coming about through divorce due to marital dissatisfaction. Each one of these smaller lifestyle changes presents the possibility of loss as well as the likelihood of options. In situations of marital disillusionment, losses can be felt as reduction in loving feelings, trust, ideals, spontaneity, excitement, and companionship—among others. When aspects of marital disillusionment threaten survival, as might be interpreted by a less powerful spouse when engaged in conflictual interactions with the more powerful partner, the fear of anticipated losses may lead to health-related losses such as damage to the person's immune system, as was discussed earlier in the studies relating increased levels of stress hormones to interchanges of marital disharmony.

Options for lifestyle changes relating to the overall marital satisfaction may include engaging in extramarital affairs, temporary withdrawal without extramarital affairs, focus on different aspects of the relationship, and—best of all—improvement of the relationship through improved communication, attention, and affection.

CHAPTER 3

Cohabitation
Prelude to Marriage or an End in Itself?

The decision to live together without the formality of marriage is a decision made by an increasing number of people these days. Today, in the United States about 5.5 million heterosexual couples live together without being married (Schneider, 2003). This number represents a 72% increase in the number of unmarried couples living together in the decade between 1990 and 2000 (Simmons & O'Connell, 2003). Ever since the 1960s, cohabitation has been on the increase. What was once frowned upon has gained widespread acceptance and has become less of a moral issue. Currently, many parents, relatives, and friends of those who cohabit seem to be less concerned than they would have been 50–60 years ago.

People tend to think that living together without the formalities of marriage allows for an easier exit if things do not work out as hoped. But whether legally married or not, the decision to part can be just as painful as it is in an actual divorce. When individuals have pooled their resources, whether married or not, it can be quite distressing to sort out which part of the financial responsibilities belongs to which partner. A purchase made together may acquire a special emotional value for one of the partners because of the memories that are connected with it. How to tell one's family that the live-in relationship is over can entail the same emotional distress as informing one's family and friends about a divorce. Of course, if there are children involved, the situation becomes even more complicated whether it is a cohabiting situation or a marriage that is ailing.

Who Are the Cohabiting Partners?

Many of the partners living together have been married and divorced or widowed before they made the decision to cohabit. According to the U.S. Census Bureau (2000a, table 58), cohabitation is more frequent among the divorced than among never married individuals. Living together as an alternative lifestyle—temporary or permanent—has been chosen by people from all social, educational, and age groups (Smock, 2000).

Although about 75% of people living together are under age 45, the number of middle-aged cohabitors has increased over the past two decades, with about 5% being 65 years or older. In comparison, among those 60 years and older, the rate of increase has tripled during the period from 1980 to 1990, whereas the rate among unmarried people living together under 40 years of age has almost doubled (King & Scott, 2005). Living together without being married has become a popular way of life for people across all ages.

But is it that simple? Is it just a matter of "shacking up"—as some people call it? Scholars in the field of family studies have debated whether unmarried living together is a prelude to marriage, like simply an inversion in the timing of events—moving in together first, marriage second—or whether cohabiting is an alternative to marriage; in other words, it is a decision *not* to marry (Heuveline & Timberlake, 2004).

On the average, cohabiting couples seem to delay childbearing longer than married couples do (Manning, 1995); however, in the early 1990s, births to cohabiting mothers amounted to more than 10% of all births and to almost two fifths of out-of-wedlock births (Bumpass & Lu, 2000). Other investigators have come up with even higher numbers, stating that the proportion of previously divorced and later cohabiting women giving birth has reached almost 20% (Brown, 2000a).

The presence of children may have brought cohabiting more into public focus, encouraging public policymakers to think about incentives that would persuade unmarried partners to proceed to marriage (Smock, 2000). To complicate matters further, some researchers found that unmarried live-in partners in the United States resemble single dating people in many of their characteristic behaviors (Rindfuss & VandenHeuvel, 1990) and proposed that cohabitation was not an alternative to marriage but to being single. Others (Casper & Bianchi, 2002) have proposed as many as four types of cohabitation: (1) alternative to marriage, (2) precursor to marriage, (3) trial marriage, and (4) co-residential dating. This classification divides the range of cohabiting types into two categories: those that include the expectation of marriage (2 and 3) with the third option—while including the possibility but also uncertainty—about marriage, and those that exclude expectation of marriage (1 and 4). The duration of the relationship is generally expected to be longer in situations 1 and 2, while it may be relatively short in the co-residential dating situation and of uncertain length in the trial marriage.

One could imagine situations where the two partners believe they share the same expectations for their relationship, yet they are actually in different types of cohabitation. Partner A may see himself or herself to be in a type 2 relationship (precursor to marriage) while partner B is closer in conception of the relationship to any other of the categories, but definitely not 2.

An example of this came to life in the conversation of two male friends over lunch as overheard by a neutral observer. Person A (let us call him Ralph) told Person B, "Tim," about some of his difficulties with his live-in female partner. Ralph valued the comfort and convenience of the living arrangement. Tina, his partner, was a caring person who did many things for Ralph. Although Tina's daughter from a previous relationship lived with them, Ralph paid half of the rent and utilities. Tina took care of all the cooking, cleaning, laundry, and shopping—not a bad arrangement for Ralph.

Recently, while on a business trip, Ralph had met Karen, an attractive and interesting career woman. They hit it off and decided to take another trip together. How could Ralph explain this second trip to Tina, who had become a bit concerned lately about the fact that their relationship did not progress to marriage as fast as she would have liked? Ralph was in a quandary: He wanted to get to know Karen better and this trip seemed to be a great opportunity, but he did not want to sacrifice the convenience of living with Tina. Tim asked what the poor guy was to do. Ralph had the answer: an engagement ring! And he showed it to Tim. Was the ring for Karen? Tim wanted to know. No, the ring was for Tina, Ralph explained. It would buy him time for up to about 2 years. The ring would alleviate Tina's suspicion that Ralph might not be serious about their relationship. She would trust him and continue to take care of him as before while he could plan brief absences to search for what else or who else might be available to him.

Recovering from his surprise over Ralph's intention of giving an engagement ring to a woman that he was not sure he wanted to marry, Tim asked Ralph what he would do if he decided that he liked another woman better than Tina. "Well, of course, we would break up," Ralph answered. But in the meantime the ring would vouch for Ralph's sincerity and in the end he would probably have to let Tina keep the ring. That was why the ring should not be too expensive—just enough to ensure him 2 years of convenience.

Analyzing this story in terms of the different cohabiting categories, one would guess that Tina was believing—or at least hoping—to be in category 2, precursor to marriage, while Ralph viewed the relationship as being in category 3, trial marriage, at best, but more likely in category 4, co-residential dating.

If children are being born and reared in a cohabiting relationship, the situation becomes even more complex, and scholars have expanded the range to include six ideal-typical ways of cohabitation. Learning about the different viewpoints and opinions might be confusing to many. All the more important it is to know one's expectations and—as much as one can—those of one's partner while in the process of deciding whether to enter the prelude for marriage, live in an alternative to marriage, or embark on an alternative to a "singlehood" situation.

The existence of children from previous unions adds another dimension to partners' expectations. If the female partner has a child from a previous relationship, her expectations regarding marriage with the current cohabiting partner will be somewhat reduced because the male partner might not be invested in parenting another man's child. On the other hand, if the male partner is financially responsible for children from his previous union, the female partner might not want as readily to make a commitment to marriage as if there were no such obligations on her partner's side.

Individuals' expectations are good predictors about the transition of relationships. If partners hold similar outlooks and similar expectations for the future of their relationship, they most likely achieve their goals because they perceive themselves as a team striving for the same objective. On the other hand, partners who entertain different expectations have not formed an identity as a couple and may already have begun to separate from each other—if not yet physically, then at least mentally or emotionally.

Sexual Attitudes of Unmarried Couples

Information gained from the National Health and Social Life Survey (NHSLS) (1992) showed that cohabiting people engage in sexual activities more frequently than do married couples and the majority of the cohabiting partners reported to never have cheated sexually. Of the cohabiting persons, 75% had sex only with their partner during the prior year. These findings could be interpreted to mean that, overall, cohabiting partners treat each other well and believe in sexual monogamy.

Other investigators, however, using the same 1992 NHSLS data, found that cohabitors were more likely to engage in infidelity than married people (Treas & Giesen, 2000), even when factors for permissiveness of personal values regarding extramarital sex were controlled for. This finding would indicate that the greater risk of infidelity was not a function of cohabitors' holding less conventional values but of a lower investment in their unions. Cohabitors who entered marriage had similar demands on sexual exclusivity as the married people who had not cohabited before marriage.

Treas and Giesen (2000) admitted that data quality is a concern with sensitive matters like extramarital sex. Expressing confidence in their findings, they suggested that the results of the two investigations might have been affected by different operational definitions of sexual infidelity.

Gender Differences in Level of Commitment

The group most likely to have engaged in extradyadic sex (32%) consists of unmarried men between the ages of 42 and 51 who have lived with a woman for a period of 3 years or less (Laumann, Gagnon, Michael, & Michaels, 1994). This statistic might indicate that the levels of commitment in living-together arrangements are somewhat different for women and men, with men taking the commitment less seriously. In situations with cohabiting partners, the link between expectations and future marriage often depends on the power differential in the relationship. Men's expectations usually carry more weight toward the transition to marriage than women's expectations.

Denise, an attractive professional woman in her early 30s, had dated Randolph, a distinguished looking, professionally highly respected man, for almost half a year when Randolph suggested that she move in with him. Denise was delighted; to her it meant the prelude to marriage. Randolph had been married and divorced three times and, as he stated, he wanted to make sure it was the right relationship before he made that commitment again. Because Randolph had joint custody of his two children from his second marriage, he argued that they needed to remain in the house he had lived in with his third wife. The children usually spent one week with their mother and the next week with their father.

In order to buy out his third wife's part in the house, Randolph had to take on a second mortgage. Denise was expected to contribute a certain amount as rent for her use of the house and almost half of their living expenses. This arrangement stripped Denise of the majority of her paychecks, but she considered it to be her home and an investment into marriage. She did the cleaning, shopping, and cooking and worked in the yard. During the weeks that Randolph's children lived with them, Denise was the one to drive them to school before she went on to her job downtown. It was a 45- to 50-minute excursion one way, but again, she did not complain.

What should have alerted her was the differentiation Randolph made between his and her friends. When his friends came to visit Denise was expected to be the perfect hostess and support him in entertaining them. When they visited her friends, Randolph would appear in garments that one would consider inappropriate at first visits. For instance, on warm days he would be dressed in shorts, a shirt, and wearing sandals without socks. It was almost as if he had worried that her friends could not afford air-conditioning in their homes and that he would be uncomfortable. On cooler days he dressed in warmer but similarly informal attire.

In conversations Randolph demonstrated an interest in educating Denise's friends on various topics. On those occasions that Denise's friends came to visit her and Randolph, Randolph would put in brief appearances and fade out to other parts of the house or even leave without an explanation.

The demonstration of the power differential between the two sets of friends could have been an indicator about her position in this relationship. But Denise explained it away by telling herself that Randolph felt more comfortable with her friends and therefore he dressed and treated them more casually. As Denise continued to work on the house and yard, taking care of his children in addition to her own full-time work, she saw less and less of Randolph. Many evenings he came home late from meetings; on the weekends he played golf or spent hours in the country club's gym.

Five years into their relationship Randolph became increasingly more critical of her and after almost 6 years he told her that their relationship was not what he had hoped for; in fact, he had already started dating another woman. Denise was told to find a place of her own and move out of the house. With no savings over those 6 years, Denise had to move back in with her parents for a while. She had no furniture to worry about—most of what she possessed prior to moving in with Randolph had been discarded for not matching the décor of the house.

Denise's story serves as a reminder for those who are considering moving in with a partner: Clarification at the outset about the level of commitment that one expects to give and receive is an important step in the process of deciding on an alternate lifestyle. Of course, honesty about expectations concerning the level of commitment does not entail a guarantee that indeed both partners will be committed to the same degree but, at least, there has been an attempt to communicate the inclusions and limits of the commitment. The commitment might not include *blind* trust and if future observations indicate reasons for doubt, a closer look at the situation would seem to be appropriate.

Denise worked hard and long in explaining away the reality of her situation. Within a therapy framework she would have been prompted to challenge her own statements regarding Randolph's differential behavior between his and her friends. Taken in context with his general behavior and requests of her, would her explanations follow a logical trend or would they be indications of denying the reality of her position in the relationship? Did her relationship with Randolph resemble that of a partnership built on cooperation or on competition? Prior evaluation of the conditions under which she was about to enter the cohabiting situation would have revealed that she was about to embark upon a venture that would leave her without resources should the relationship deteriorate. Under a therapist's guidance she would most likely have been encouraged to challenge her wishful thoughts about investing in a marriage under these circumstances.

Ethnic and Racial Differences in Living-Together Lifestyles

In general, unmarried couples are less homogamous than married couples; they may come from different sociocultural or educational backgrounds (Jepsen & Jepsen, 2002), they are twice as likely as married couples to be interracial (Fields & Casper, 2001), and they are more likely to endorse nontraditional attitudes (Axinn & Thornton, 1993; Booth & Amato, 1994). These findings might signal greater overall open-mindedness in cohabiting couples, but they also reflect situations that potentially include more opportunities for disagreements between partners and stress impacting the relationship.

Important considerations in culturally different unions include the awareness of ethnic culturally determined values held by the partners in these relationships. People tend to assume that their own values are similar to those held by their partners and later find themselves surprised and dismayed by the difference in values and beliefs. Although we may think we know what cohabiting or living together means, different attitudes toward this phenomenon can be found among people of different backgrounds.

For instance, analysis of data from two large national studies concerned with the effects of pregnancy on the cohabiting couples revealed some interesting findings (Manning & Landale, 1996). Considering the influence of pregnancy on subsequent marriage of the cohabiting partners among mainland Puerto Rican, non-Hispanic Whites, and African Americans revealed that pregnant non-Hispanic Whites were more likely to get married than premaritally pregnant White women who were not living with a partner. On the other hand, pregnant Black women living with a partner were no more likely to marry than if they had not been cohabiting. Finally, pregnant Puerto Rican women were less likely to marry if they were cohabiting than if they had not been living with a partner at the time of conception.

The investigators believed that the different results were partly due to cultural differences. For many non-Hispanic Whites, cohabitation may constitute a transitional stage between dating and marriage, whereas African Americans do not necessarily hold the same view of cohabitation. Furthermore, Puerto Rico has a history of consensual marriages in which heterosexual conjugal partners live together without having undergone a legal marriage ceremony. This tradition of consensual marriage may have started due to a lack of financial resources required for marriage licenses and weddings.

Among college students who have decided to share their lives, one generally finds more interracial couples than within other populations. One would hope that these young people avail themselves of the study of the values held by individuals of different ethnic and cultural backgrounds.

An interesting difference was reported between cohabiting women in relationships with partners who had less than or as much education as they did and women in marriages where the husbands were likely to be better educated than their wives (Blackwell & Lichter, 2000). Apparently, the stronger commitment as reflected in marriage—if we want to interpret it this way—fosters more restrictive and traditional requirements for a partner than individuals are willing to accept in cohabiting relationships.

Age Differences Influencing Relationship Patterns

More recent investigations have shown that most cohabiting couples are adults in their mid-20s; about 25% of individuals in this age group are living together (Waite & Joyner, 2001). Both heterosexual and homosexual couples living together in a committed relationship without being legally married are now included in the term "domestic partnership." Some states are developing rights for access to benefits, such as health insurance, for partners in domestic relationships.

There are differences between older and younger cohabitors. Older couples do not view living together as a way to test compatibility before marriage. They are more likely to think of their relationship as an alternative to marriage. Younger individuals, on the other hand, often regard their living-together situations as a prelude to marriage (King & Scott, 2005).

Examining data from the National Survey of Families and Households (NSFH), the authors attempted to identify distinguishing characteristics of older cohabitors. A number of differences emerged. For instance, male cohabitors represented the larger percentage of the oldest cohabitors. This finding confirms the similarity of some selection criteria in choosing a mate: whether it is in marriage or in just living together, individuals choose along an age gradient where men pair with women of younger ages.

Not surprisingly, the oldest cohabitors were least likely to have children living with them in the same household. This fact might be a major contributing factor to the reported higher quality of their relationships when compared with those of younger cohabitors. Another reason for reduced stress in the unions of older cohabitors may be that they are not considering marriage as the next logical step. With older individuals, concerns about the views of their adult children and questions about inheritance may rule out the possibility of remarriage. Additionally, there may be financial advantages in cohabiting with regard to taxes, pensions, and Social Security benefits.

By not expecting marriage to occur, tension between partners is less likely to build up than it might in cohabiting unions of younger people where one or both of them view marriage as the logical outcome of their partnership.

Teenage Cohabitation

Some couples decide to live together despite significant risk factors within their relationship. Perhaps teenage couples are the ones facing the greatest difficulties when they decide to cohabit because of an unexpected pregnancy. The list of their risk factors includes immaturity due to young age, insufficient level of formal education, and, with that, lack of stable employment and insufficient financial resources—all in addition to the stress of the responsibilities and demands of the pregnancy.

Jeanne Warren Lindsay (1995), who started a program for teenage parents in a school district in Los Angeles County, interviewed 80 young people who at the time were living or had lived with a partner. Of the 80 interviewees, 31 were married; 18 of them did not live together prior to marriage while 13 did cohabit. Twelve of the young people—although still dating each other—were no longer living with their partners.

Out of the total group of 80 interviewees, 65 had lived with one of the partner's parents and half of the whole group was still living with parents at the time of the interview. To avoid misinterpretations, it needs to be clarified here that these 80 teenagers did not constitute 40 couples. The group of interviewees consisted of 26 males and 54 females, ranging in age from 14 to 21+ years, with a mean age of 17.6 years. The ethnic constitution of the group was 28 Hispanic, 30 White, 12 Black, 7 Native American, and 3 Asian. Only 4 of the interviewees had no children, 7 were pregnant, 58 were parents of one child, 10 had two children, and one of the young people acknowledged three children.

The author provided details on one of the more successful couples as example of the struggles and hurdles these young people had to overcome. Both partners, now age 25, had been living together for almost 10 years at the time of the interview. Although they have three children, with the oldest being 9 years old, both are working. Simple arithmetic reveals that both parents had been 15 years old when the pregnancy occurred. At first, they had to live with his parents until they graduated from high school. They made the decision to get married after their second child was born. According to the author, these two young people have worked hard to get where they are today; they have overcome many of their struggles and are emotionally close as a family. But the young woman reported, not surprisingly, that after having three children and the responsibilities associated with that, her sex drive has gone down.

Today, would the two young people make the same decisions as they did 10 years ago? The author did not explore this question. And perhaps we do not need to know the answer. The reason for including this study and the particular story here is to highlight the extreme difficulties that arise when people at this young age decide to make commitments and take on responsibilities that seem much too heavy for the stage in life that they are in. These young people need more in the way of suggestions and resources than this chapter is designed to provide.

Duration of Relationship as Reflection of Level of Commitment

As cohabitation resembles in many ways the pattern of marriages, its main difference is thought to be the level of commitment and, perhaps connected to that, the relatively short-term living arrangement found in many cases. About half of cohabiting relationships last less than 1 year (Bumpass & Lu, 2000); others may end their relationship within 2 years either by breaking up or by marrying each other. After about 5 years only 10% of cohabiting couples were reportedly still living together without being married (Brown, 2003).

Longer duration of cohabitation was found to be linked to the partners' reduced interest in marriage and children; individuals whose cohabiting relationships had dissolved reported an increased acceptance of divorce (Axinn & Barber, 1997). As cohabiting relationships may involve more autonomy than interdependence, individuals' attitudes may change to become less conventional, thereby reducing their commitment to lifelong romantic relationships (Schoen & Weinick, 1993). Another national survey reported that 19% of unmarried couples remained together after 5–7 years of cohabitation (Bianchi & Casper, 2000). For many, the duration of the cohabiting relationship is a reflection of the risks involved and that is the compelling reason for seriously considering all aspects of the decision to move in with a partner.

As people advance in age, the likelihood of having been involved in marriage, divorce, or widowhood or the breakup of previous relationships increases, making the quality and stability of future unions seem less certain. Individuals who have experienced a marital dissolution tend to shy away from committing themselves to another marriage with a cohabiting partner. Furthermore, prior cohabitation seems to be associated with poorer relationship quality and stability in subsequent cohabiting unions. Some research has revealed that cohabiting relationships become more unstable and unhappy—often due to increasing lack of interaction—as the time of living together increases (Brown, 2003).

This development seems quite similar to what often happens in marriages over time. Does that mean that people are not so much different after all or that it takes just as much effort to maintain a happy relationship while cohabiting as it does while being legally married? It is a point for serious consideration at the outset of any relationship and can be an impetus for exploring the various options for being happy in either type of relationship.

Other investigators have reported similar findings among cohabiting couples, such as the involved individuals admitting to being less happy and finding their relationship less fair compared with married couples (Skinner, Bahr, Crane, & Call, 2002) or they are less willing to pool their finances (Heimdal & Houseknecht, 2003; Kenney, 2004). Higher incidence of depression (Kim & McKenry, 2002; Lamb, Lee, & DeMaris, 2003), increased frequency of sexual activity outside the relationship (Treas & Giesen, 2000), and greater evidence of domestic violence (Brownridge & Hall, 2002; DeMaris, 2001) have been found in cohabiting couples as compared to married couples.

The various aspects about why living together does not work for some while it works for others are worth attending to when considering the option of cohabiting. Learning from those facts and experiences can prove to be less costly—financially as well as emotionally—than starting with a blank slate and proceeding with an uninformed mind.

Reasons for Cohabiting

Most of the available statistics do not disclose much information regarding the reasons for the general instability of cohabiting unions. The reasons that challenge the stability of cohabiting unions are many; often the very reasons for deciding to live together have significant built-in risk factors for instability. More obvious reasons for failure of relationships include dishonesty, immaturity, unrealistic expectations, clashing personality characteristics, power imbalances, lack of financial resources, and children from previous relationships, among others.

An examination of the reasons for cohabiting may reveal that the two partners do not necessarily make the decision to live together for the same reasons. Breakups often result from lack of communication or from mis-communications between the partners. In some cases, partners may not have been as forthcoming with the real underlying reasons for wanting to live together and there are cases where the reasons for moving in together become reasons for divorce later on, as in the case of Jim and Judy, who decided too late in their relationship that they needed marriage counseling.

They had been married less than 3 years and had lived together before that for about 3 years. What had gone wrong? In their first conjoint session Jim complained about Judy's lack of interest in lovemaking. After the birth of their daughter, things seemed to deteriorate between them. Jim thought that Judy was angry most of the time and her anger seemed to be directed at him. Judy's response was evasive; she mumbled something like being under a lot of stress and not getting enough sleep. The therapist realized that Judy was not going to disclose much at this first session and decided to schedule individual sessions for each spouse.

What emerged in Judy's individual session was the following. When, almost 6 years ago, Jim suggested they move in together Judy was dis-appointed. She had hoped Jim would propose marriage. But then she reasoned with herself that it would be better to cohabit than not because at least they would be together all the time rather than just be dating. It seemed to her like some kind of a commitment and she did not perceive another option. After 3 years of living together Judy got pregnant. Did she purposefully forget to take her birth control pills regularly? The answer would not have been helpful at this time.

Jim was not in favor of an abortion and decided they should get married. Now Judy should have been happy, except she was convinced that Jim's only reason for marriage was her pregnancy. She explained that—except for the baby—she was not good enough for him to marry. The baby was the main reason. Every time she thought about it, her anger increased until not much of her earlier love for Jim remained.

Unfortunately, Judy's angry feelings also affected her relationship with her daughter; Judy felt like she was competing with little Megan for Jim's affection. Jim had become a devoted father. It is perhaps not so difficult to understand that when Judy observed Jim and Megan's loving interactions she experienced the pain of jealousy, which only fueled her anger more.

During one of their fights Judy admitted that she had been disappointed when Jim had proposed cohabitation rather than marriage and she had felt taken for granted. Jim responded by accusing her of not having been honest with him. The argument escalated to a point beyond repair. The outcome of this sad story can be found in three unhappy people. Jim pain-fully misses his daughter, little Megan is deprived of the daily loving care of her father, and Judy is just as angry and jealous as before.

At the point when Jim and Judy entered therapy a lot of damage had occurred in their relationship. Jim might have been willing to continue working on the marriage; however, Judy was so entrenched in her anger that she was not willing to let go of what she thought was her protection. Like many people, she regarded her anger as an armor that kept her from becoming weak. While the therapist attempted to focus on Judy's wishes and goals for herself and to determine the real sources of the pain, Judy put a higher priority on punishing Jim than on reaching a happier space for herself within the family.

Among the list of stated reasons for moving in together, many declare it as a period of trial marriage. It would give them and their partners the opportunity to find out whether they are compatible, insisting that within the intimacy of living together, the partners would get to know each other much better than if they continued dating. Others stress the economic benefits for the partners when they exchange the cost and maintenance of two residences for one; still others point to the reduced pain and expenses when comparing the possible breakup of the cohabiting union to a divorce. Then there are those who view themselves as independent spirits who reject any authority to determine their lifestyle for them—all of these have been named as reasons for moving in together. Or, as explained by one college student, going home in the morning after having spent most of the night at his girlfriend's place was too much bother (Macklin, 1983). Moving in with his girlfriend in part became a time-saving contemplation.

Moving in Together to Get to Know Each Other

Many of the reasons have the ring of logic to them. It stands to reason that one would get to know another person better with all of his or her habits and quirks on a daily basis while living together than by observing him or her with best behavior out on a date. Or one can make the case for the durability of blind love; it can work 24/7 for maybe up to 3 years or until one of the partners runs out of excuses behind which to hide the other partner's bad habits or behaviors.

According to investigators in the marriage and family field, many young people living together believe that this will help them more in their selection of a good partner for marriage than dating would (Bumpass, Sweet, & Cherlin, 1991; Thornton & Young-DeMarco, 2001). Most individuals in cohabiting arrangements express plans to marry their partners (Manning & Smock, 2002), which confirm the common view of cohabitation as a step in the process leading to marriage (Seltzer, 2000; Smock, 2000).

However, when subscribing to this common view, it is important to realize that—according to some research—live-in partners who marry each other within a 1- to 2-year period of moving in together make up a relatively small percentage of cohabitors (Brown, 2000b; Sassler & McNally, 2003). In fact, there is evidence that recent cohorts of cohabitors are less likely than living-together couples in the past to marry their partners, even if pregnancy comes about (Bumpass & Lu, 2000) and many are now living together for longer periods of time before marrying or breaking up. Thus, the decision to move in together as a reason to get to know one's future spouse better deserves serious investigation and thought.

On the other hand, some relationship experts make the distinction between event-driven commitments, which are the result of immediate or external occurrences, and relationship-driven commitments (Surra & Gray, 2000). For instance, if one of the partners has been evicted from his or her place of residence or there has been a change in the job situation, the suggestion of moving in together may be based on that partner's need for a place to live. This type of event-driven commitment would generally be considered as less stable than a commitment made based on the value of the relationship as experienced by the partners.

Moving in Together Because It Is Cheaper

According to the preceding considerations, deciding to live together for financial advantages would amount to an external, event-driven commitment. Sharing the rent and utility payments for one residence instead of assuming the sole financial responsibility for one's living quarters can be a tempting proposition. Amounts of money that can be saved immediately jump into many individuals' minds. Another line of thought might be that two people together can afford more spacious or more comfortable living quarters. A word of caution would, however, suggest not to agree on moving into a place where half the rent is more than one partner would be able to afford by himself or herself—even if the other partner promises to take on more than half because his or her income is greater.

Actually, it would be wise to consider the possibility of becoming responsible for the whole amount of the rent. One obvious reason for this suggestion is that if for whatever reason one of the partners exits the relationship, leaving the other with the responsibility for the whole amount—lease or no lease—the remaining one will not be stranded. In the case where everything works out well with both partners and one pays less than half for half the space, that partner will be entering some kind of obligation. That partner gives up some standing in the equity and may end up performing a heavier load of the chores, such as cleaning, cooking, laundry, or shopping. Over time this person may come to feel that he or she is contributing more than a fair share.

If partners share all the expenses down the middle but they are more than one of them would be willing or able to pay when living independently, that partner may end up saving nothing and having nothing to fall back on if the relationship does not work out and he or she wants to leave. With no money for a down payment or the security charge—usually an additional month's rent—it becomes difficult to find another place to live. The case of Denise discussed earlier serves as an example of such a distressing situation. By paying more than one can afford in a cohabiting arrangement, one endangers one's independence; by paying less than one's half, the person surrenders a degree of control over his or her destiny.

The Convenience of a Built-in Sex Partner

Of course, people generally do not move in together so they can have someone for sex at any time they want. But the expediency of an easy sexual relationship—along with other conveniences—can be tempting. It can be considered an all-purpose relationship, pooling financial resources for economical advantages and sharing maintenance chores like half the workload in laundry, meal preparation, and cleaning, compared with living by oneself where the whole apartment needs cleaning and the whole laundry is waiting. In addition, there is a certain amount of protection in living with another person in case one has an accident while exchanging the light bulb in the ceiling light fixture. Having a ready-made sex partner can just be the icing on the cake.

That is what Paul thought when he suggested that Pat move into his apartment. They both worked for the same company and found each other attractive. While out on a date one evening, they were discussing how far Pat had to drive to make it to work every day. She lived in the suburbs with her divorced sister and her sister's two daughters. While she saved on rent and enjoyed being around her sister and her little nieces, her sister's house was about 35 miles from Pat's place of work. Besides she felt awkward entertaining her friends, especially male friends, in her sister's house.

Paul's apartment was within walking distance of their office, which meant she would not even have to use her car every day. There would be significant savings in time and money if she lived with Paul. The fact that she was strongly attracted to Paul made the decision easier. Pat insisted on paying her half of the rent and utilities up front before moving in; she did not want to abuse Paul's generosity. Paul proposed to pay for the groceries in exchange for Pat's meal preparation. That sounded reasonable until Pat found out that Paul liked more elaborate meals than the snack-like foods she was used to. Also, to Pat's surprise, Paul's definition of meal preparation included cleaning the dishes. Although Pat appreciated Paul's generosity— he often supplied a bottle of excellent wine along with the groceries—the obligation to whip up a meal worthy of the wine was at times more than she would have liked to do.

Whether it was Pat's physical beauty or the atmosphere created by the exquisite wine, Paul demonstrated a strong sex drive. In his opinion, having sex five to six times a week was the absolute minimum. At first, Pat felt flattered by Paul's sexual advances but she did not like his reactions when she was not readily responsive. Headaches were not something Paul took seriously. After about 8 months of their cohabiting relationship Pat looked for another job and moved back into her sister's house.

If Pat and Paul had continued to date, their attraction might have grown into love, which might have been strong enough to open the door for discussions and negotiations. With moving in together as fast as they did, Pat had placed herself in a position of dependency. As her resentment over Paul's frequent requests for sex and her obligation to prepare meals worthy of the wine selected by Paul developed, there was no space in which to negotiate. At the same time, Paul developed anger and resentment over being turned down with his initiations for sex; he was in no mood to negotiate either. The hasty decision to live together eliminated the option of getting to know and appreciate and respect each other.

When You Live Together You Are Already There

For some individuals, such as students who also hold jobs, time to go out on a date is difficult to afford when they have to study in their limited free time after work. Yet they crave close relationships with another person just as most other people do. Living together with a romantic partner makes this possible because it cuts down on travel time from one residence to the other and to the restaurant, ball game, etc. As mentioned earlier, it becomes a time-saving as well as money-saving arrangement.

A risk factor in this arrangement can arise when a partner with less stringent time constraints may feel neglected, even though the other partner spends most of his or her time in the home when not working or at school, but for all practical purposes may not be accessible because it is now studying time. Although they could hold hands while one is reading a textbook, after a while this arrangement may become less exciting.

Lynn and Pete had such an arrangement. Pete loved Lynn but always seemed to be hassled for time. He worked the afternoon/early-evening shift in a big audio/visual equipment store. The mornings until noon he spent in classes to pursue his college degree. Lynn held a full-time position at a bank. Her evenings were free for meeting with friends and other recreational activities. At the beginning of their live-in relationship Lynn felt sorry for Pete, who had to work so hard and needed all his time to keep up with his studies. She quietly took care of all the household chores, allowing Pete to study in the evenings and hoping that there would be a little time for her on the weekends.

After about a year Lynn got tired of this lifestyle. Her life was like that of a working married woman; she had all the duties of being married without many of the benefits. Their sex life had dwindled down to brief encounters. She began to resent the fact that Pete did not help around the house although she reminded herself that she had allowed him to use all his time for his studies. She had invited him to be selfish because she had cared so much about him. But now she felt taken advantage of. Pete could be a bit more sensitive to her needs and could either take the initiative and perform some chores on his own or spend more time paying attention to her.

One evening after having been out with her girlfriends, Lynn came home to find food on the countertop and dirty dishes in the sink. Pete had fixed himself something to eat and then left everything pretty much where he had used it. Lynn blew up; this was too much! Pete was stunned but defended himself by stating that he thought Lynn knew and was in agreement about his efforts to improve his career by going to school so that they could have a better life in the future. He apologized meekly, expressed his hurt feelings, and assured Lynn that he loved her. To convince her of his love for her, he proposed that they get married. And they did. Lynn got a small wedding band and a new last name; that was all that changed. Almost 4 years later Lynn got a divorce and Pete received his MBA degree.

Analysis of Neglected Issues

Analyzing their situation, it can be seen that Lynn had set a pattern for their relationship that was difficult to break. Once a person has received special treatment (in this case Pete), the recipient has no vested interest in changing it. The person who has volunteered to do the pampering (Lynn) will appear in a negative light when she wants to reverse the roles or just get a fair trade in the work assignment. Furthermore, because she had let enough time go by to build up anger and resentment while she was hoping that Pete would become aware of her sacrifices and do his part, her communication when she finally confronted the situation likely contained a measure of hostility.

By agreeing to marry Pete, Lynn had made an even stronger commitment to the situation as it was, which had not been pleasing to her from the beginning. Thus, she not only condoned Pete's actions, but also committed herself on a deeper level that eventually required more emotional and financial pain to get out of.

When they had decided to move in together, neither Pete nor Lynn had clearly stated individual reasons for making that decision. Most likely, those reasons were not exactly the same for both of them. They also had not communicated their expectations for the relationship, an issue that will be pursued in more detail in another chapter. For instance, Pete apparently believed that Lynn had as much interest in his career goals as he had. Lynn clearly had expected more from Pete—if not in financial or household-maintenance support, then at least in terms of companionship. Additionally, they had not defined the range of their commitments. There may have been hidden agendas that one or the other of them did not want to disclose, but more likely, they were not even aware of the need for exploring their commitments. Certainly they did not look at the practical aspects of living together.

And probably most dangerous of all were the background issues. Lynn did not have sufficient self-knowledge; she did not know how much she was able and willing to give without building up resentment. If she had been aware of this basic knowledge, she would have avoided taking on the major part of the responsibilities in maintaining a home. As it happened in her case, when she finally realized she contributed more of her energy to the maintenance of their household and their relationship, she was perceived as complaining and nagging, which in return gives rise to defenses and accusations from the other person rather than significant change.

The example of Pete and Lynn does not mean that they were doomed to spend years in a relationship that went nowhere. It does not even mean that Lynn's situation was hopeless when she realized she was giving more than she could afford to do in good graces. There were options she could have exercised. Being a fair person, Lynn could have acknowledged that she had set the stage for her own disappointment. After she had calmed down her angry feelings about being taken advantage of, she could have decided that this was not a way to continue. She could have sincerely explored what she was willing to contribute and what, under the circumstances, Pete could do to help. Once she had reached those conclusions, she could carefully consider how to communicate to Pete that change was necessary—not as an ultimatum or a form of blackmail—but with indications on how this would be in his best interest, too.

Lynn might have educated herself about successful communication styles or even have sought the help of a counselor or therapist, or coach—as some of them now call themselves. Under no circumstances should she have agreed to Pete's proposal to get married, unless she had had plenty of time to observe behavioral changes on Pete's part and with sufficient time and opportunity to determine if these were indeed lasting changes. Lynn might even have reasoned to herself that if Pete was using all his time to get ahead in his career, so could she. In fact, that might be one way he would have understood that she was not willing to sacrifice anymore and she could come out ahead personally and professionally.

She could also have moved out, telling Pete that she would be happy to date him and discuss their future options as they got closer to his goal of receiving his MBA degree.

The case histories of Jim and Judy, Pat and Paul, and Pete and Lynn indicate that people have a tendency to move in together more suddenly than they would proceed into a marriage—perhaps because they feel the decision to cohabit does not entail as strong a commitment as that of marriage. However, the pain of these six people was significant during their periods of cohabiting and following the termination. Careful examination of their wishes and goals, their expectations and willingness, their beliefs and attitudes prior to committing to this type of partnership could have paved the way to a more satisfying destination.

The Legal Side of Unmarried Living Together

In Sweden about 30% of couples sharing a household are not married, but they have all the rights and obligations of married couples. Unlike Sweden, in general, there are no firm or consistent state or federal legal guidelines to follow for people who decide to live together without being married in the United States. Cohabiting partners and children born outside of marriage, as well as other relationships between parent and minor children who live apart, are families or unions without formal recognition by state laws, except those state laws that regulate child support. State laws vary from one state to another in the availability of domestic partnership registration, and the rules, responsibilities, and benefits under such registration (Seltzer, 2000). Often the courts serve as arbitrators in cohabitation-related disputes with their distinct approaches to making decisions in these cases (Seff, 1995).

Cohabiting individuals, particularly women, are at a disadvantage when it comes to long-term wealth accumulation, a fact that was demonstrated in Denise's story discussed earlier. These negative aspects can be avoided if partners pool their incomes and sign written contracts that delineate the distribution of property in case the union dissolves. In reality, however, most cohabiting unions are characterized by low levels of economic consolidation and a more egalitarian division of labor (Batalova & Cohen, 2002; Heimdal & Houseknecht, 2003).

Examining the effect of premarital cohabitation on household labor in 22 countries, Batalova and Cohen (2002) found that in all countries women perform more routine housework than men. But married couples with a history of cohabitation prior to marriage demonstrated a more equal division of housework. Another finding was that in those countries that had higher levels of overall gender equality, cohabitation rates seemed to influence the equalizing effects of cohabitation. It could be concluded here that the increasing cohabitation trend might be a part of a broader social trend toward a more egalitarian division of housework.

For their own protection, partners in a cohabiting situation need to familiarize themselves with some of the risks they may encounter in these living arrangements. For instance, when looking to rent a house or an apartment, who is going to sign the lease? Some landlords require signatures from both partners. But, as discussed earlier, in cases where only one of the partners signs the lease, that individual may be financially responsible for the whole amount when, at a breakup of the relationship, the other partner moves out. On the other hand, the other partner may become homeless after a breakup of the relationship. Similarly, how fast the leaving partner has to vacate the premises is another question.

Different situations and questions arise when the partners buy a home together and later separate or one of them dies. Insurance policies may contain legal pitfalls for cohabiting individuals. If children are born to unmarried couples, who is responsible for their support and what are the custody rights? Other complications can arise from guardianship issues and consent to the children's medical treatment. Another question is concerned with when cohabitation turns into a common law marriage. Some states recognize common law marriages and the period of time required varies from state to state.

Children in Living-Together Households

It has been estimated that one in four American children "will live in a family headed by a cohabiting couple at some point during childhood" (Graefe & Lichter, 1999, p. 215). Children under age 18 are part of more than 40% of cohabiting households (Simmons & O'Connell, 2003). Although the majority of them were born in marriages that preceded the cohabiting relationship (Wineberg & McCarthy, 1998), about one sixth of these children originated in the cohabiting unions. Of the children conceived in cohabiting unions in the early 1990s, 27% were born into marriage, 65% were born into the cohabiting unions, and 8% were born outside any union (Raley, 2001).

It is generally expected that conception will have a positive effect on relationship stability because it gives an impetus for cohabiting people to transition into marriage. This effect is assumed to be strongest for Whites because of the higher rates of marriage among pregnant, cohabiting White women (Manning, 2001, 2004).

According to previous research, about three quarters of cohabiting partners in the NSFH were *planning* to marry their partners (Bumpass,

Sweet, & Cherlin, 1991). A similar proportion of cohabiting mothers in the National Survey of Family Growth reported their *expectations* to marry their partners (Lichter, Batson, & Brown, 2004). It has been suggested that if partners consider cohabitation as a transition to marriage, moving in together before the birth of a child may constitute a stronger commitment to the relationship than if the partners remained living apart; it would make early separation less likely to occur (Waller & McLanahan, 2005).

Because the majority of cohabiting couples are less likely to stay together than married couples, the children will be subjected to significant changes in the family environment (Graefe & Lichter, 1999; Raley & Wildsmith, 2004) and some investigators have voiced concerns about the consequences for the children living in cohabiting families (Booth & Crouter, 2002; Brown, 2004). Others have emphasized the importance of attending to both the marital status and biological ties in this context (Manning, 2002).

Is the family context for children living in cohabiting families similar to that of children who live with their two married parents because in both cases the children live with both biological parents? Or is there a greater similarity for children living in cohabiting parent families with those who live in cohabiting stepfamilies since they both lack the marital link? A study examining the well-being of children in cohabiting families with two biological parents, cohabiting stepfamilies, married stepfamilies, and households with two married biological parents used data collected from kindergarten children and their parents from the Early Childhood Longitudinal Study—Kindergarten Cohort (Artis, 2007).

Almost 20,000 children were included in the sample. The focus within the collected data was on direct assessments of the child's cognitive development and on parents' assessment of the child's psychological development. It was found that the indicators of child well-being showed great similarities for the cohabiting family situations without significant differences between families with cohabiting biological parents and those with cohabiting stepparents. There were no significant differences for children in cohabiting families and married stepfamilies when compared to their counterparts in families with two married biological parents.

However, an exception was observed for reading skills. In reading competency, children in cohabiting families lagged behind the children in families with two married biological parents. Children in cohabiting, families with two biological parents scored significantly lower on cognitive tests and demonstrated less self-control than children in families with two married biological parents.

Because of the complexity of the various interacting variables the investigator admitted that it could not be clearly determined whether the observed differences in cohabiting and married families were associated with characteristics correlated with selection factors for marriage, such as persons who marry possessing characteristics different from those who cohabit, or if marriage itself exerted a beneficial effect.

Expectations About Living Together (Expressed and Unexpressed)

People do not always express their expectations clearly; perhaps the expectations are not well formulated in their minds as yet or they are afraid that they might scare away their partners. Or they might take it for granted that everyone holds similar expectations about living together and therefore one does not need to discuss them in detail. However, living-together situations present more space and occasions for unexpressed expectations than marriages (see Table 3.1).

When two people decide to get married, they usually tell their families and best friends about their decision and plans. They even send out printed invitations for selected people to witness the big event. Most people who decide to move in together do not send out formal announcements about the event beyond informing their friends and magazine subscription managers about the change in their address.

For example, two young people who had been dating for about 6 months decided to live together. Tom, the young man, told his parents about it, hoping that they would accept the decision without disinheriting him. Excitedly he told Leslie, his partner, that his parents had invited both of them for next Sunday dinner, adding the question, "How did your parents respond when you told them about us living together?" Leslie's answer, "I did not tell them about it; I don't want them to know yet," elicited mixed feelings in Tom, a young graduate student. To him, it seemed that his girlfriend considered him not good enough for her parents to know that she was living with him. His angry feelings were based on believing that Leslie must really be ashamed of him.

Although some young people enter marriage after a brief courtship, most allow more time to get to know the families and friends of their future spouses. They have some knowledge about each other's attitudes, habits, beliefs, opinions, and preferences. In many cases of deciding to live together, as in the case of Leslie and Tom, they may not even have met their partner's parents and siblings or other relatives.

Another difference when comparing married life with cohabiting life is that people have a general idea about the roles they assume in a marriage; it may be what they are familiar with from their family of origin or—if they did not like that situation—the exact opposite to how their parents arranged their marital life. This is not necessarily so in cohabiting situations. Tom had assumed that he and his girlfriend would spend all their

Table 3.1 Questions to Ask When Considering Cohabitation

(1) Reasons for cohabiting

    (a) To get to know my partner better

    (b) To save money

    (c) To save time

    (d) To be able to interact spontaneously whenever we feel like it

    (e) Hidden agendas

    (f) Other (please explain)

(1a) What are my partner's reasons?

(2) What type of cohabiting situation do I want?[a]

    (a) Alternative to marriage

    (b) Precursor to marriage

    (c) Trial marriage

    (d) Co-residential dating

    (e) Other (please explain)

(2a) What are the range and depth of commitments made for chosen situation?

(2b) What type does my partner want? What are the range and depth of my partner's commitments?

(3) Expectations about living together (expressed and unexpressed)

    (a) Type of partnership: 50/50 (equal)

        (i) Sharing finances, how?

        (ii) Time together

        (iii) Spending time with friends, relatives

        (iv) Decision making

        (v) Communication, how?

    (b) Different ratio, which?

        (i) Sharing maintenance chores, how?

        (ii) Individual time

        (iii) Sexual activities

        (iv) Honest feedback from partner

        (v) Other (please explain)

(4) Control issues

    (a) Promises kept/broken

    (b) Respect for one's decisions/privacy

    (c) "Forgetfulness" about responsibilities

continued

Table 3.1 (continued) Questions to Ask When Considering Cohabitation

    (d)   Partner's treatment of my friends

    (e)   Prolonged silences, refusal to talk

    (f)   Other (please explain)

(5) Background (self-knowledge) issues

    (a)   What **must** I have to be happy?

    (b)   What am I willing and able to give without feeling resentful?

    (c)   What can I compromise on for a limited time without feeling resentful?

    (d)   Other (please explain)

(6) Suggestions: precohabitation agreement

    (a)   Written contracts that delineate the distribution of property in case the union dissolves

    (b)   If one partner has to vacate the premises, what is the agreed-upon time frame?

[a] This classification divides the range of cohabiting types into two categories: those that include the expectation of marriage (b and c), with (c) including the possibility of but also uncertainty about marriage, and those that exclude expectation of marriage (a and d).

time together. When she had plans to go out with her friends, he was ready to go along. She told him that he was not invited. Similarly, when she invited some of her friends she encouraged him to go to the movies by himself. And, of course, on the rare occasion that one of her parents was invited, the young man had to find another place to study for a couple of hours. This came as another disappointment—one that he did not quite know how to handle, although he could have anticipated that something like that might happen when Leslie informed him of not wanting to tell her parents about their live-in situation.

In fact, it would have been appropriate for Tom to ask how they would handle situations like that before they decided to share living (and sleeping) space with each other or, at least, after Leslie admitted not wanting to let her parents know about it. Tom could have protected himself from surprises or disappointments like these by taking the time to first define his expectations about the living arrangements and then clearly communicating this in detail to Leslie.

Visits from the partners' friends and relatives are important issues to discuss prior to actually moving in together. Does one of the partners have to walk the streets in the rain if the other has visitors? Stating expectations about the way to handle situations like these is not necessarily sufficient for the smooth navigation of the cohabiting couple; the partner's feedback and opinion regarding those events are extremely important. Just declaring one's intentions without receiving feedback does not guarantee a trouble-free life after having moved in together.

Tom and Leslie discussed their situation with a therapist because they wanted to prevent further deterioration of their relationship. To help clarify their situation, the therapist asked them to complete a questionnaire about their individual considerations regarding cohabitation. Leslie's parents divorced when she was a junior in high school, a fact she never resolved for herself. Leslie was very critical of her mother and overprotective of her father. Although Leslie communicated little with her mother because she was punishing her for leaving her father, Leslie did not want to admit to her mother that she herself might be engaging in behaviors—such as cohabiting—that were not socially acceptable. In addition, she also wanted to be perfect in the eyes of her father.

Regarding the situation with their friends, Leslie admitted that, with the exception of her best friend, her other friends did not like Tom, while Tom's friends were happy or indifferent about Tom and Leslie living together. In this period of transition for them and their friends, Leslie and Tom were beginning to think of themselves as the foundation that unites the two groups of friends. This issue was certainly worth working on, but before that they had to resolve two significant individual issues: Leslie had to come to terms with her relationships to her parents and Tom had to learn to recognize and respect Leslie's independence. He had assumed that because they lived together, they had to do everything together, a situation that resulted in many of their arguments.

Tom and Leslie were able to resolve their individual issues while continuing their option of living together. Having to face those issues at the beginning of their cohabiting relationship spared them the development of resentment and angry feelings. Actually, they were able to laugh about some of their differences in the way they began their journey together.

Other, more obvious expectations when people move in together may center on chores that need to be done to maintain the apartment or house. Again, when two people get married, they usually have an idea about their roles in the marriage as they have observed their parents. Of course, it does not need to be any different in a cohabiting situation, but, then again, people have different ideas about the types of commitment—including their roles—in the two living arrangements. One partner might think living together is not binding as much as marriage would be and therefore the level of care that is extended to the partner may not be as deep or involved as it would be in a marriage.

For instance, in a traditional marriage, the woman often assumes the responsibility that the husband and children are well fed, well clothed, and live in a relatively dust-free environment. In a live-in arrangement, one might assume that one's partner is capable of finding the way to the fast-food place and to the cleaners without particular assistance.

Investigation of the effects of cohabitors' own relationship assessments and expectations for the outcomes of their unions yielded some interesting findings (Brown, 2000b). Couples in which the female partner reported happiness but the male partner did not were not more likely to separate than were couples in which both partners were happy. In fact, in unions with one happy and one unhappy partner, the effects on future marriage and separation were dependent on gender. For instance, although a union of an unhappy male and a happy female was less likely to end in marriage, it was no more likely to end in separation than that of a very happy couple. On the other hand, an unhappy female and a happy male were especially likely to separate but no less likely to marry.

In sum, it seems that an unhappy male is unlikely to move in either direction—separation or marriage—and an unhappy female partner is likely to move in opposite directions. It would be interesting to know how the female cohabiting partners assessed their options. Perhaps they were resigned to remaining unhappy either way they decided.

The "Cohabitation Effect"

Some people believe that cohabitation will improve their ability to select a more appropriate marriage partner than marrying without prior cohabitating experience (Hall & Zhao, 1995) because cohabitation offers better opportunities to really get to know the prospective spouse. For those who decide to live together in order to find out about each other's habits and turn this arrangement into a trial situation for marriage, some of the reported research might come as a disappointing surprise or—at least—lead to confusion, given the conflicting results expressed in the relevant literature.

Research literature has shown that spouses who cohabited prior to marriage have higher rates of marital separation and divorce than spouses who did not cohabit before marriage (Bennett, Blanc, & Bloom, 1988). The positive relationship between marital instability and cohabitation has been called the "cohabitation effect."

Various hypotheses have been proposed to explain the cohabitation effect. One of the hypotheses suggested that the link between cohabitation and marital instability may be an artifact of union duration and the normative decline in marital satisfaction during the early years of marriage (Kurdek, 1999). This explanation will be discussed in more detail later.

Another explanation suggested that the association between divorce and cohabitation can be accounted for by selection effects. Individuals who decide to cohabit may be more likely to possess characteristics that in themselves represent risk factors for divorce (Bumpass & Sweet, 1989; Teachman & Polonko, 1990). Although it was observed that younger adults with lower religiosity and greater acceptance of divorce were more likely to be in a cohabiting relationship (Axinn & Barber, 1997), no demographic characteristic that had been explored as possible selection effect has consistently explained the cohabitation effect (Cohan & Kleinbaum, 2002).

A third explanation for the cohabitation effect suggested that the experience of cohabiting itself produces negative effects within the ongoing relationship, lowering partners' assessment of value as well as lowering their threshold for leaving a relationship—even if it has become a marital commitment by then. Increased acceptance of divorce and decreased rates of religious participation have been reported by cohabiting individuals when compared to their precohabitation attitudes (Axinn & Thornton, 1992; Thornton, Axinn, & Hill, 1992).

Almost two decades ago Bennett and colleagues (1988) investigated the link between premarital cohabitation and subsequent marital stability. Their data, obtained from couples in Sweden, indicated that after the first 8 years of marriage, there was no difference in the divorce rates between those who had cohabited and those who did not live together before marriage.

Another study about cohabitation in the United States (Teachman & Polonko, 1990) revealed that when, for all couples, marital duration was counted from the beginning of the marriage, those who had lived together prior to marriage seemed to have a greater likelihood of divorce than those who had not lived together. However, when marital duration was counted for the cohabitors from the beginning of their co-residential union, the odds of dissolution were not significantly different between cohabitors and noncohabitors, except for those who had cohabited more than once before marrying. In other words, if the beginning of the cohabiting union is counted as the actual start of the transition to married life, cohabitors have been "married" longer when compared to noncohabitors at any given marital duration, at least according to this study.

On the other hand, DeMaris and Rao (1992) found that cohabitation in the United States is associated with a greater likelihood of dissolution, even after counting the time spent in unmarried cohabitation as part of the marriage. Similarly, according to more recent investigations, couples who lived together before getting married seemed to experience more difficulty in their marriages and faced an increased risk of divorce (Amato, Johnson, Booth, & Rogers, 2003; Cobb, Larson, & Watson, 2003), with 50% of the marriages likely to end in divorce.

There was an interesting exception to this high likelihood of divorce for couples where the woman lived with the man she married but never had a sexual relationship with any other man (Teachman, 2003). This may be an indication of the seriousness that women apply to their first significant sexual commitment. It would also confirm the earlier discussion about gender differences in levels of commitment.

Cohabiting as a Cost/Benefit Model for Marriage

Before committing efforts and financial resources for a wedding and honeymoon, does it make sense to obtain an accurate estimate of the costs and benefits of married life? If so, cohabitation would provide a reasonable testing ground. This cost/benefit exploration would also provide other than financial information. For instance, how much time would be spent together with the partner, how much time would be left for individual endeavors, how much time would be available to enjoy the company of family and friends, and how much time would be required for performing maintenance tasks?

Noncohabiting dating couples are usually somewhat removed from several of these issues and their estimates might be more positive or more negative than the reality they will be confronted with after entering marriage. Furthermore, the perceptions of costs and benefits of marriage might be different between cohabiting partners and noncohabiting dating singles in ways that would influence the likelihood of their entry into marriage (McGinnis, 2003). In the past, the body of relevant research did not provide much information on this issue, except that as long as 20 years ago, cohabiting women were found to hold more negative attitudes about marriage than noncohabiting single women (Tanfer, 1987). In a comparison of married and cohabiting individuals, it was found that women and men in pre- and postmarital cohabiting unions perceived fewer costs and more benefits to breaking up (Nock, 1995b).

More recently, McGinnis (2003) proposed a model of courtship where partners' decisions to enter into marriage are largely determined by the perceived (through intentions and expectations) costs and benefits of marriage. The investigator also hypothesized that a couple's cohabitation will have a significant influence on their perception of costs and benefits. Again, potential costs or benefits are not limited to the economic situation but include one's personal freedom, one's sexual satisfaction, and one's relationships with family and friends, among other things.

Because negative information is generally weighed more heavily than positive information, it was expected that potential costs would be a more powerful predictor than potential benefits in the overall considerations in deciding about marriage. Based on this rationale it appeared likely that the effect of cohabitation on marriage intentions should be positive.

To test the proposed model, data for the analyses were taken from the NSFH, a national longitudinal probability sample of American households. Respondents provided information through interviews and a self-administered questionnaire at two time periods, first in 1987/1988 and again in 1992/1993. The findings indicated that the factor of cohabitation significantly reduced both cost perceptions and benefit perceptions related to marriage. With that, the cohabitation effect increased the likelihood that respondents intended or expected to marry their partners.

Contrary to previous findings that cohabitors have less favorable views of marriage than noncohabitors, the results showed that cohabitating individuals are less likely to see costs as result of marriage than do steady daters. This effect may well be due to the difference in relative standing of the cohabitors and noncohabitors. In many ways—although by no means all—individuals engaged in living-together situations are closer to married couples and any *additional* cost through marriage would be perceived as less than the costs inherent in the transition from single-dating status to that of being married.

The findings of the preceding study demonstrate the need for considering many suboptions while in the process of deciding among the main options of a situation. When continuing singlehood, cohabitation, or marriage are options confronting the individual, each of these options carries with it a framework of smaller but not less significant options to explore and select or reject.

The Possibility of a Fundamental Change in General Expectations

The commonly assumed expectations of cohabitation functioning as transition into marriage may not be as realistic anymore and plans for marriage may not be a principal reason for entering cohabiting relationships (Sassler, 2004). An increasing number of cohabiting unions do not progress to marriage. For instance, among young people in Canada, the nonmarital union disruption rate is about twice the divorce rate (Statistics Canada, 2002).

This high termination rate of cohabiting relationships might indicate a preference for serial cohabitation rather than for marriage, and repartnering might occur faster after cohabiting than after divorce. Indeed, based on a national probability sample of 10,749 Canadians, it was found that 56% of women and 62% of men reported ever having formed a second cohabitational union within 20 years of disruption of the first union, while only 16% of women and 20% of men formed a marital second union (Wu &

Schimmele, 2005). Furthermore, the second union choice was affected by the type and exit status of the first union. Out of the group of individuals who had cohabited, 71% chose cohabitation as a second union, while only 8% directly entered into marriage as a second union. Individuals exiting a marriage as their first union opted mainly for marriage as a second union.

Divorced individuals who had been cohabiting prior to their marriage predominantly (86%) chose cohabitation as a second union. When the factor of timing in repartnering was explored, it was found that 56% of former cohabitors repartnered within 5 years of relationship termination, whereas 41% of the divorced (without premarital cohabitation) and 20% of the widowed individuals committed to a new partner within this time period. Overall, the divorced (with premarital cohabitation) had the shortest timing of repartnering: 63% of them entered into a new cohabiting union within a 5-year period. In terms of gender differences, it was observed that men tend to repartner in higher proportions than women and more rapidly.

Conclusion

It is not so much a question of whether cohabitation is right or wrong, good or bad; rather, it is important to explore all the options inherent in the situation and select the best one for the right (healthy) reasons. More so than marriage, cohabitation can be seen as an ongoing period of options and opportunities for gaining self-knowledge along with getting to know the partner and for practicing negotiation skills to achieve a set of circumstances that is advantageous for both partners. Cohabitation can be an option that provides space for continuing growth before making the next commitment. And if—contrary to expectations—partners decide to separate, it would have been a learning experience about what to search for and what to avoid in future relationships.

CHAPTER 4

Until Divorce Do Us Part

Factors contributing to the breakup of marriages make up a long list; several of these factors were discussed in chapter 2. Prior to marriage, not much attention is paid to the physical and emotional adjustment required when people share their lives on a day-to-day and night-to-night basis. There are resource materials educating people on the sexual aspects of married life—at least for the beginning—but how two different individuals with their personal wishes, habits, and goals are supposed to fit neatly into one lifestyle pattern is largely left unexplored.

With the advances of medicine and technology, people live longer lives and that includes longer periods of sharing their life with a partner. Over long periods of time individuals likely develop interests along different paths—even while they are sharing the same environment with a spouse. As they grow in different directions and strive for different goals, they may find it more difficult to continue living together than to separate.

When state legislatures reformed divorce laws, the judgment regarding the viability of a particular marriage was left to the spouses in that marriage. Beginning in the mid-1960s, the adversary principle in divorce was in the process of elimination, with the state of California adopting "no-fault" divorce in 1969. Within the next 4 years at least 36 states accepted it as an option and by 1983 every state offered similar provisions.

In the past, divorce petitioners had to demonstrate that the other spouse failed to fulfill state-defined marital obligations, but no-fault divorces eliminated the state's judgment on the spouses' performance within an ongoing marriage. The decision about living up to each other's expectations remained with the spouses. Without requiring proof for any wrongdoing or offensive behaviors of one of the partners, divorce has become much easier to obtain.

About four out of five divorced people remarry, and most of them do so within 3 years of the divorce (Lown & Dolan, 1988). This would indicate that one of the most frequently used cures for an ailing marriage in our society is divorce, often followed closely by remarriage. On the surface, this process may appear logical, but many of the people involved in it have found it to be a temporary cure. Divorce may be the termination of an unhappy situation; it is not, however, a guarantee for future happiness. Evidence demonstrates that second marriages are more likely to dissolve into another divorce than first marriages, even though many remarried people consider their second marriage to be better than their first (Ganong & Coleman, 1989; Lown, McFadden, & Crossman, 1989).

Negative Affect in Marital Interactions as Seeds for Divorce

Among the correlates of marital dissatisfaction, negative affect (O'Leary & Smith, 1991; Weiss & Heyman, 1990), hostile behaviors (Matthews, Wickrama, & Conger, 1996; Pasch & Bradbury, 1998), and withdrawing or avoidant behaviors (Heavey, Layne, & Christensen, 1993; Raush, Barry, Hertel, & Swain, 1974) have been identified.

In a study about hostile and distancing behaviors between spouses that might allow prediction for marital distress and divorce, Roberts (2000) focused on three types of withdrawing or distancing responses: intimacy avoidance, conflict avoidance, and angry withdrawal. Intimacy avoidance was seen as the lack of responsiveness to a partner's needs for care and closeness and was expected to produce effects over and above hostility and other conflict-based forms of interactional withdrawal. Participants in the study were part of a sample of newlyweds who had been involved in the Buffalo Newlywed Study (BNS; Leonard & Roberts, 1998; Leonard & Senchak, 1996). All spouses were in their first marriage and had been married an average of 1.5 years when they completed a questionnaire, the Marital Adjustment Test (MAT; Locke & Wallace, 1959). Close to the time of their third anniversary, the couples were contacted again for information on marital stability.

Reporting the results of the study the investigator stated that, for wives, the primary predictor of marital outcomes was hostile responsiveness from their partners, but for the husbands it was their wives' withdrawal. It was further found that for wives, in the context of high husband hostility, husbands' conflict avoidance provided a buffering effect and wives' intimacy avoidance added unique variance to the prediction of husbands' marital distress. The findings regarding wives' intimacy avoidance seem to be in contrast to the generally reported wife-demand–husband-withdraw pattern in the literature, as described later and in the chapter on marriage, unless distinction is made between emotional and sexual intimacy in the case of the wives.

Roberts (2000) suggested that the role of gender in the relationship between marital distress and rates of both hostile and distancing partner behavior is significant. Wives may complain about their husbands' withdrawal but in reality it may be the husbands' hostile responsiveness that wears away wives' satisfaction. In a similar vein, it may be the husbands who complain about their wives' hostility but it may be the wives' intimacy withdrawal that erodes husbands' marital satisfaction. Further research is needed to explain or reconcile these different outcomes. A determination of either one of the reported findings as the relevant one goes beyond the scope of this book.

Partner Violence and Divorce

The occurrence of partner violence as a predictive factor of divorce is not surprising; most people would want to escape from such situations. Yet in a follow-up study of 100 women who had resorted to a shelter for battered women, after 1 year only about one third of the women had not returned to their partners (Rusbult & Martz, 1995). Two thirds of the women did not take the opportunity to escape future violence directed at them.

Clinicians and mental health professionals who were involved during the early stages in the provision of shelters for battered women would not be surprised at the high number of victims returning to the violent scene. In those days, frequent relocation of the shelters was necessary because some of the abusive husbands had managed to learn the location of the shelter. Thus, the promise for the women's safety and protection was compromised in the previous location (Maass, 2002/2006).

Court records, police files, and shelters for victims of batterers document numerous cases of "patriarchal terrorism," a severe form of violence against women carried out by men who seem to be motivated by the desire for total control over the partner (Johnson, 1995). Frequent and severe beatings with escalation of the severity of the beatings characterize this type of domestic violence. Another type of violence that tends to erupt occasionally during interpersonal conflict but does not escalate in severity over time involves both men and women.

In an effort to determine the extent to which physical and verbal conflicts are connected to relationship dissolution, DeMaris (2000) used data from a 5- to 7-year follow-up of 3,508 married and cohabiting couples in the National Survey of Families and Households. Couples' risk for disruption apparently was elevated by male violence, but the expected difference in the effect of male violence on the stability of the union between married and cohabiting couples was not observed. The data seemed to indicate that verbal conflict in itself was not predictive of disruption, but the style of the conflict resolution was significant. In couples with a more positive attitude toward argumentation there was a lower risk for disruption. This finding would be congruent with the indications of other studies that the emotional atmosphere surrounding conflict is of greater impact than its sheer amount (Gottman, Coan, Carrere, & Swanson, 1998; Matthews et al., 1996).

Consequences of the Complexity of Sexual Interactions

Issues of sexuality are a major area of adjustment in marriages and they present major areas for problem development, as already mentioned in a previous chapter. In fact, sexual problems have been reported as the main cause leading to divorce during the first 3 years of marriage.

In our sex-satiated culture, where everybody is expected to love sex, it is difficult for people to admit that they are not that interested in sex (McCarthy & MacCarthy, 2003). While a decrease in sexual interest is expected to occur in people who have been married for 20 years or longer, it is more surprising to learn that desire problems are also experienced by newlywed couples as well as unmarried couples. Problems of sexual desire are not limited to the experiences of boredom or advanced age; these difficulties can occur among couples of all age groups.

Considering the complexity of human sexual attitudes and behaviors within the framework of the reason–emotion dichotomy as discussed in a previous chapter, communication—or the lack of it—can open the door to a wide range of marital difficulties confronting spouses and ultimately leading to divorce. Except for the purely physical aspects, the underlying dynamics that operate in this area of life often remain unexplored before significant commitments are made by partners who believe that sex is a natural function that will take care of itself once the selection and commitment aspects have been exercised.

Lynette was raised in an affectionate family. Her mother and two sisters were emotionally expressive and, at times, Lynette's father seemed overwhelmed by the emotionality in the female-dominated household. Actually, it worked well for him because they all tried to lavish their affection on him. In her early 20s, Lynette met Ron, her future husband. Ron pursued her ardently and she took that as a sign of his love for her. Their dating progressed well and Ron did not seem to mind Lynette's hugging and kissing him, although he did not verbalize his feelings for her beyond simple "I love you" statements.

They started making plans for the future. Lynette drew verbal pictures of the kind of life they would lead. How great it would be waking up together in the morning after a night of lovemaking and cuddling. Ron talked more about plans on where they would live, what type of house they would look for, what cars they would buy—it all seemed to fit into his goals for his professional future.

It was a wonderful wedding; everybody said so. Returning from their honeymoon they moved into an apartment in the building Ron had previously been living in. It was less convenient to get to Lynette's job but this was not a permanent situation. Ron did not have much trouble moving his belongings into the larger apartment and they would decide in a year or so where to settle for starting a family. Their love life was passionate—at least, considering their sexual interaction. Lynette would have liked to talk more about what their embraces meant to her, but Ron was not in a talking mood during sex or after their lovemaking. Lynette's questions about his feelings seemed to irritate him. If she asked him to, he would cuddle up with her after sex, soon to drop off to sleep.

Lynette began to feel lonely and thought she did not know as much about her husband as she thought she did. Her inquiries about his feelings for her evoked in him irritation and a loss of what to say. In his opinion, their being married and living together was proof that he loved her. Was that not obvious? What else did she want? In a raised voice he accused her of not trusting him while his facial expression displayed his irritation. Over time, irritation escalated into anger. Lynette feared being confronted with Ron's anger. She was not afraid of physical harm; he was not a violent person. It was an emotional coldness and isolation that she experienced in those interactions. Soon sex was no longer the enjoyable activity that had fostered emotional closeness along with the physical intimacy. Lynette's sexual desire plummeted. This was just another reason for Ron to feel bad because his needs were neglected.

Lynette found consolation in the arms of an understanding male coworker who was married to a wife who failed to understand him. Ron and Lynette were one of those couples who divorced within the first 3 years of their marriage, as found in the McCarthy and MacCarthy (2003) study mentioned earlier.

Prediction of Divorce

As stated in the chapter on marriage, divorce is not a guarantee for happiness. Studies have shown that people who have experienced separation or divorce from a spouse reported higher levels of psychological distress than those who remained married (Booth & Amato, 1991; Coombs, 1991; Mastekaasa, 1994; Ross, 1995; Waite, 1995).

Logically, these studies could be interpreted to mean that the psychological distress of the divorced individuals even after the divorce was still a remainder from the unhappy days spent in their marriages, while the still married individuals' distress levels were not of the same magnitude as those of the divorcing ones and—in their opinion—did not necessitate as drastic a step as separation or divorce. Another reason for the prolonged unhappiness of the divorced individuals could be seen in the possibility that they might have recognized having made a hasty decision regarding the divorce and were now in a state of regret over that decision. This explanation finds some confirmation in studies discussed later in this chapter.

Has the psychological distress experienced by the divorced individuals been a contributing factor in the dissolution of their marriages? Some investigators seem to think so when they suggest a social selection explanation according to which individuals with high psychological distress and mental disorders are found in disproportionate numbers among divorced people and those are also less likely to remarry (Aseltine & Kessler, 1993).

Additional explanations for the higher levels of distress among divorced people when compared to married individuals include answers based on crisis theory (Booth & Amato, 1991) and role theory (Ross, 1995). Crisis situations involve life event stressors that are discrete, observable events with beginnings and ends determining their course (Wheaton, 1999). In addition, stressful role transitions, such as those related to divorce or separation, also can be conceptualized within the framework of crisis theory. The process of role transition, similar to a crisis situation, is marked by a beginning—the dissolution of the relationship—and, once the transition is completed, the psychological distress can be expected to return to pre-transition levels, thus representing the end of the process (Booth & Amato, 1991; Wheaton, 1999).

In contrast, a relatively constant and enduring conceptualization of stresses and strains emerges when divorce or separation is considered within role theory. As the stress is linked to the roles the individuals are functioning in, it can be expected to endure until the individuals' roles are changed again (Pearlin, 1999). The role configurations of divorced persons are different from those of married individuals regarding economic and social situations and often introduce long-lasting stressors into the everyday life of the divorced person (Avison, 1999). The stressors of the divorced person are linked to the changed role and therefore may remain active as long as the person is in that role. Entering a new conjugal relationship could be seen as reducing the chronic stressors of "singlehood" and single parenthood and increasing the levels of available emotional and social support. Of course, a lot depends on the nature and quality of the new relationship.

Contrary to the belief that most divorces result from a deterioration of the marital relationship due to high levels of distress, evidence has been presented that many couples do not experience high levels of discord prior to divorce (Amato, 2002; Amato & Booth, 1997; Booth, Amato, & Johnson, 1998). In a recent study, longitudinal data from Waves 1 and 2 of the National Survey of Families and Households were examined to identify high- and low-distress marriages that end in divorce (Amato & Hohmann-Marriott, 2007). A cluster analysis of 509 couples that divorced during that time revealed that, regardless of marital quality and sharing many risk factors, the couples were about equally likely to have been in high-distress or low-distress relationships. Additionally, members of both divorce groups seemed to have had opportunities for having contact with alternative partners.

Not surprisingly, those who had been in high-distress marriages reported increases in life happiness after the divorce. But those leaving low-distress marriages admitted declines in happiness following divorce. These findings point to the existence of two distinct groups of divorcing couples. In the high-distress group many risk factors for divorce were combined with an unhappy, conflicted relationship, whereas in the low-distress group, similar sets of risk factors combined with a moderately happy, low-conflict marital relationship.

As divorce motivation in the low-distress marriages did not seem to be driven primarily by the couples' relationship quality, marital happiness and conflict—standard indicators of marital quality—are not predictors for divorce among the low-distress marriage group. Instead, the construct of relationship commitment seems to be a relevant factor in this group. In about three fourths of the divorcing low-distress couples, one or both partners were involved with partners outside the marriage at the time of divorce.

The end of a marriage still constitutes a major life change for many people and research has focused on identifying factors that are operating in marriages and eventually are leading to breakup. Identifying those factors would be beneficial to the work of marriage therapists in their attempts to help clients improve their marriage or, in those cases where marriage therapy comes too late in the development, to learn from the sad experiences of the past in order to avoid future relationship breakups.

Predicting the Timing of Divorce

There are two time periods that appear to be the most critical for the survival of marriages; half of all divorces occur during the first 7 years of marriage and the second critical period comes at midlife, about the time when the first child reaches the age of 14 years. To find out if the same predictors for marriage dissolution are operating at both critical times, Gottman and Levenson (2000) followed a cohort of couples for 14 years with periodic assessments of marital stability. Four years after the beginning of the study 8.8% of couples had been divorced after having been married for an average of 5.2 years; by 1996, 27.8% of the sample had divorced. The average length of marriage was 16.4 years.

Most distressed marriages are characterized by a wife-demand–husband-withdraw pattern, meaning that in conflict situations wives issue demands but husbands withdraw either emotionally or physically (Christensen, 1990; Christensen & Heavey, 1993; Heavey, Christensen, & Malamuth, 1995). The wife-demand–husband-withdraw pattern seems to be of particular risk to marriages. As was discussed in the chapter on marriage, during couples' conflict situations an increase in wives' cortisol levels was observed at husbands' withdrawal (Kiecolt-Glaser, Dura, Speicher, Trask, & Glaser, 1996) and husbands' withdrawal behavior was followed by the wives' expression of hostility in another study (Krokoff, 1991, 1992).

In the Gottman and Levenson (2000) study, the wife-demand–husband-withdraw pattern was found to be predictive of both early and later divorcing. However, the results also indicated the existence of a nonconflict development in these patterns. Along with the hypothesis that wives start discussions in marital conflict (Ball, Cowan, & Cowan, 1995) and are more critical than husbands, this may leave husbands to create or maintain this pattern.

There was a difference in the variables that predicted early divorcing and those that predicted divorce later in the marriage. Spouses' negative affect during conflict situations was instrumental in predicting early divorce but not later divorce. The lack of positive affect, rather than the presence of negative affect, in discussions of events of the day and conflict predicted later divorcing. In a similar vein to the lack of positive affect, the findings in Skaldeman's (2006) comparison between married and divorced persons discussed in the chapter on marriage are relevant here. The views that the spouses had of themselves and the (ex-)partner regarding their listening skills were the main difference in this study between married and divorced persons. The divorced individuals viewed their former spouses as worse listeners than themselves. This was interpreted that the ex-partner was less motivated to take time for an empathic approach in listening and understanding the other.

Initiation of Divorce

Conflicting evidence can be found in the literature regarding wives' economic resources and risk of divorce. Some research reported a positive association between wives' financial resources and risk of divorce (Heidemann, Suhomlinova, & O'Rand, 1998), while other researchers stated a negative association between the risk of divorce and wives' economic resources (Conger et al., 1990). There are also research reports that have found that the risk of divorce is highest when husbands and wives possess similar economic resources (Heckert, Nowak, & Snyder, 1998; Nock, 1995a, 2001) and the opposite, lowest risk of divorce in situations where husbands and wives have similar resources (Ono, 1998; Risman & Johnson-Summerford, 1998).

Setting aside for the moment the conflicting findings about economic resources and impending divorce, the focus could be turned toward the question, "Who initiates the divorce?" The perspective of economic independence would predict divorce initiation by wives, whereas the equal dependence perspective, based on research on commitment and dependence in marriage (Nock, 1995a, 2001), would expect that either spouse might initiate divorce.

Focusing on participants of the Marital Instability Over the Life Course study (Booth, Amato, Johnson, & Edwards, 1993), Stacy Rogers (2004) contacted and re-interviewed 1,592 individuals in 1983, 1,341 in 1988, 1,189 in 1992, and 1,047 in 1997. Responses were grouped into three categories: divorce discussed by wife first, divorce discussed by husband first, and continuously married. Analysis of the results revealed that the highest risk of divorce occurred when wives contributed 50–60% of the total family resources. Not surprisingly, marital happiness was found to be a significant context, as the highest odds of divorce were found in situations of low to moderate marital happiness and spouses' equal economic resources. Additionally, in situations of equal economic contributions, both spouses, not just wives, were likely to initiate divorce.

The context of termination of marriage is poorly described by statistics usually found in the literature on marriage and divorce. We think of the wedding as constituting the beginning of a marriage and divorce as the end. However, much that influences the marriage has occurred between the spouses long before the wedding day. And, similarly, much of what determines the breakup has happened over time, just as on the day that the divorce is granted the relationship between the now ex-spouses is not always completely cut.

For some spouses the decision for divorce takes the form of a process that can go on over many years. It is a developmental process in which the seeds of disenchantment are germinating over years and it is not a straight line either from beginning to end. Along the way, there are points of evaluation and reevaluation; options may be explored and discarded and decisions are reached and changed.

Generally, when spouses realize that the bliss of marriage is not all that they expected, they do not schedule an appointment with a divorce lawyer right away, especially when children are involved. Spouses may deal with marital disenchantment by looking at other areas in life to give them a sense of meaning or fulfillment. It could be an activity that has served as a hobby for some time or it could be the introduction of a brand new involvement.

Monica, for instance, felt neglected by Paul, her husband and the father of their children. While the children were at a young age, Monica, a medical technician, worked part-time in a physician's office. Paul put all his energies into establishing his own business; he wanted to be independent. Monica would have liked Paul's help and support with the children, but he was too busy. His lack of involvement with the children undermined Monica's authority in their eyes. When the children were grown, Monica worked fulltime and shifted all her energies into her job. She was very efficient and soon became the backbone of the expanding physicians' practice. Her employers made her feel important and for a while she derived the meaning for her life from her work. The appreciation from her employers had to make up for the emotional support she missed from Paul. She still loved him but she began to worry about the time when retirement became a reality.

In the meantime, younger and more ambitious employees made their presence felt in the doctors' office. Monica became less indispensable; her hours were reduced. Monica felt at a loss. She used the extra time to plant flowers and some vegetables in their garden, but while it took up time and made her feel useful, it did not give her life personal meaning. Monica could not quit her job and embark upon another career. With her job, she carried the health insurance for both of them. Monica felt trapped. Her story is not an isolated case; often the wives of men who proceed to build their own business are left with the responsibility for obtaining health insurance benefits through their jobs.

Fathers who accept the provider role but refuse to participate in family activities on a regular basis place a heavy burden on their wives. Except for the financial aspects, Gina carried the full responsibility for the household and their two children, one of whom was a special-needs child. All the negotiations with schools and community agencies were left to Gina, including disciplining the children. Gunther, her husband, left for work in the morning and came home in the evening to watch TV or to leave for his exercise regimen at the local YMCA. There was no opportunity for discussions or intimate conversations. Gina, a passionate woman, had to resign herself to the weekly perfunctory sexual encounters with Gunther.

In her youth she had been a gifted student in college and enjoyed debates and sociopolitical discussions. Now she felt isolated and empty. Motherhood was important to her but she wanted more. She wished for an adult, mentally stimulating and emotionally caring relationship. Gina's thoughts wandered to imagine how life could be with a different type of husband. However, she did not seriously consider divorce. But she needed something to make her feel alive. Returning to school by taking classes at the local university appeared to be the answer.

Gunther was not in favor of it. He did not think Gina needed more education and the money for tuition would be better placed in a college fund for their children. In response to Gunther's concern about the money, Gina found a part-time job in a bookstore and set out to enroll in one class. She was excited, and the challenge and stimulation distracted her from the disappointment of her marriage. Gunther grudgingly gave in and she continued taking classes until it was suggested by one of her professors that she seriously consider becoming a writer.

Gunther's reaction was even more negative at this point. He accused Gina of flirting with the professor and said that the suggestion of becoming a writer was probably a result of the flirtation more than an acknowledgment of Gina's talents. Shortly thereafter Gina received a small inheritance from her uncle. It was her hope that the money would get her started on entering the graduate program at the university, but Gunther had other ideas. He determined that at least half of the inheritance belonged to the family, just as he had been contributing his salary over the years.

This was one of the reevaluation points: Should Gina leave the marriage because Gunther wanted to prevent her from doing what by now had become important to her? How would her children be affected by that decision? Would the children's lives benefit or be hurt by a divorce at this time? Was there another option? As Gina applied for acceptance into the graduate program she also applied for available scholarships and assistantships. It was a happy day when she was also awarded an assistantship with her acceptance. This meant she had to make time available to perform the duties that were required by the assistantship. In addition, she maintained her part-time work at the bookstore and she deposited half of her inheritance into the family bank account.

Gunther changed jobs and spent the work week in another town, returning home on weekends. He did not insist on moving the family to the different town because he wanted to see if the new position was what he had expected it to be. It would be unwise to uproot the family and interrupt the children's schooling at this time. This arrangement worked well for both Gunther and Gina. Gunther had even less responsibility for the children and Gina could organize her time more efficiently around the children, her studies, and the work necessary to maintain financial resources for her studies.

After 1 year, Gunther tired of the weekly commute and found a more comfortable place to live. He rented a house with the option to buy and with enough space to accommodate Gina and the children on occasional visits. At the same time, the older child left the family home. It seemed reasonable to sell the family home and find a smaller place for Gina and the younger child to move into until the child's graduation from high school.

Although the new living arrangements made it easier for Gina to pursue her studies, the relationship between the spouses did not improve. There were fewer arguments but there was also even less emotional connection than before. Gina initiated the conversation about divorce; Gunther was not in favor of it, but as weeks passed his resistance grew less strong. Gina had second thoughts; she worried that she might have given up too soon on the marriage. There were times when she wished that Gunther would have rejected the idea of a divorce more strongly. After all, marrying at a young age, she had never been on her own before. Would she be able to survive? It took almost another year until she initiated the divorce proceedings. There were periods of recurring doubts after that. If she had done things differently, would the marriage have survived? If she had not insisted on going back to school, would Gunther eventually have involved himself more in her life after their children were grown? These are haunting questions that can be expected to enter her mind periodically.

Through many years of their marriage, Gina had attempted to build a bond between her and Gunther, a bond that would extend in meaning beyond the necessities of the daily routines and the raising of their children. Faced with the lack of success of her attempts, she looked for other areas from which to derive a sense of fulfillment for her life without leaving the marriage. It was this search, however, that eventually enabled her to let go of her fears and transition to a life on her own. Throughout those years where the family lifestyle changed from conjoint family life to varying degrees of separateness, for Gina there were periods of increasing emotional detachment followed by intense strivings for reconnection, turning again to detachment. But the timing was finally right; her youngest child would graduate from high school and embark upon a college career within the year. There were enough years ahead for her to start a whole new life.

The Wide Range of Effects of Divorce

Being married means that spouses share mutual goals and plans. When they divorce, their mutual plans are destroyed, their mutual goals are lost, and, with that, the emotional and physical investment made in them so far has become void. The termination of a union of two individuals is more than the simple physical separation of two people. As they entered this particular union, each of them had ties to others, such as their families of origin, friends, and relatives. Some of these ties will be cut when the union disintegrates while some others may remain functional—although perhaps on a different level, or different premise, than before. The dynamics of such relationships can be viewed as shifting from a family-oriented to a person-oriented basis.

Although in widowhood similar shifts in the relationship nature can occur, these shifts are often not as pronounced as in divorce. In widowhood the focal point of the relation does not exist anymore, whereas in divorce the original focal person may still operate within the circle of family and friends but now with a different attachment by virtue of having formed a new union. Thus, the premise and the terms of relationships change. "It is as if I have to prove myself all over again" was how a young divorced woman described the situation with her former sister-in-law, whom she values as a friend.

> When I married John, the reason for the relationship was the fact that I was her brother's spouse. With the divorce that position does not exist for me anymore. In the future, another person may occupy the position of sister-in-law. Now I am looking for acceptance on the basis of my personal characteristics.

As in many other instances of lifestyle changes, individuals can immerse themselves in the painful depth of the losses that occur as by-products of divorce or they can choose to renew a predivorce relationship in a meaningful way by placing it in a different context and assigning it new functions and goals. It would be unrealistic to expect inclusion in family holiday get-togethers as in the past, but the contact could be much more rewarding because the previously related-through-marriage individuals would now spend time together based on their liking for one another rather than because they were part of the same extended family. One critical aspect of this type of relationship is to refrain from ex-spouse bashing. Even the most objective person would not want to take sides against her own brother or son. It would be best not to test those family loyalties.

This is what Myra, briefly introduced in the chapter on marriage, learned in the aftermath of her divorce from Jeffrey, her busy physician husband. Myra and Jeffrey had joint custody of their four children, who resided with Myra, but Jeffrey had visitation rights on every other weekend and some holidays. Jeffrey did not take the visitation schedule seriously and demanded that Myra deliver and pick up the children when it was his turn to have them. Also, he did not allow her to make other plans because at times he would be too busy to keep the children for the whole time of their scheduled visits.

After having complied with Jeffrey's demands for several frustrating months, Myra, with the help of a therapist, decided a change in her approach to the visitation schedule was necessary. She informed Jeffrey that the children would be ready for their visit with their father at a certain time at her home. Myra gave Jeffrey the choice whether he wanted to pick them up or deliver them at the end of their visit with him. She was still willing to cooperate in sharing the transportation, but the rest was up to Jeffrey.

Jeffrey tested her determination on the next scheduled visitation by arriving about 2 hours late for collecting the children. Myra had made alternate plans and after waiting for more than 1 hour, took the children to a visit with a friend of hers. Jeffrey was furious but had to accept the situation. From then on he engaged the help of his mother. If he could not adhere to the schedule, he asked her to collect the children and more often than not she actually kept them for a major part of their visits. What seemed at first like Jeffrey's selfish manipulation, however, brought rewards to the other family members.

The children came to value the company of their grandmother. It was during their visits with her that they discovered their talents for storytelling and illustrating, and it was their grandmother who channeled their activities into producing children's books as birthday and Christmas gifts for friends and relatives. The children remembered the bedtime stories Myra had told them over the years. While they were at their grandmother's they wrote them down and included some aspects from their own imaginations; John, the oldest one, added drawings and cartoons to illustrate the stories.

During the week their grandmother would call and remind the children not to forget to think more about the bedtime stories so they could continue with their production on the weekend visits when their father was not available. Myra was grateful to her former mother-in-law for the self-confidence the children developed while in her care. Recipients of the children's books were delighted and asked for more. Grandmother encouraged the children in their activities of illustrated storytelling. She had the time and resources available for organizing the work in a way that could be presented to a publisher. Grandmother's efforts paid off: She found a publisher who used their early booklets to introduce a new children's book series.

The relationships between Myra and her former mother-in-law and between the children and their grandmother had changed dramatically following the divorce. By making their business venture the primary focus of their relationship, they had less time to ruminate about their father's frequent absences and it distracted them from the complaints they may have had otherwise. In a way, they placed the responsibility for the father–child relationships on their father. Grandmother became a person in her own right, independent of their father. To Myra, Grandmother was not just someone she could ask for a favor if she needed someone to supervise the children; their relationship became one of equals in their small business. As Myra reported to her therapist,

> The other day I overheard my oldest son talking to a friend about being away from home that weekend. The other boy said something like, "You are going to be with your father and grandmother again." My son answered, "Yes, but we are also working on our business. My grandmother bought a new computer for the business and we all have to learn to operate it. She is not just a grandmother; she is a business manager." I was so proud of my children and my mother-in-law, too. I had to tell her about it. (Maass & Neely, 2000, p. 82)

Regarding her former mother-in-law, the role of a business partner removed her from the close connection of being Myra's ex-husband's mother; they had more important issues to discuss now than to indulge in complaints and defenses about a third person.

The importance of family members' linked lives as they are embedded in sociohistorical context has been a focus of life course theory (Elder, 1998). The lives of grandparents and grandchildren, like those of parents and children, undergo transitions throughout the developmental course. Expecting a change in the nature of some grandparent–grandchild relationships during the grandchildren's transition to higher education, Crosnoe and Elder (2002) have compared reports of grandparent and grandchildren about aspects of mentoring and relationship quality over time. According to the concept of generational stake, tension can develop as grandparents accentuate continuity of their mentor role in the relationship while the young emphasize autonomy and may distance themselves from the older generation.

Another aspect of this investigation focused on the degree to which the grandparent–grandchild relationship is modified by the quality of the grandparent's relationship with the grandchild's parent. Family systems theory states that any relationship is inseparable from the larger family system and the middle generation functions in the gatekeeper role that links young and old and has a significant impact on the quality of the relationships (Cox & Paley, 1997; King & Elder, 1995; Rossi & Rossi, 1990).

Looking at Myra's situation in terms of the theoretical ideas mentioned before, one would expect the quality of the grandparent–grandchildren relationship to remain at a satisfactory level as the grandchildren approach transition to higher education because their relationship has a solid basis in educational and cooperative working dynamics. As the grandchildren's educational growth progresses, so will the quality of the content of their working efforts with the grandmother grow, due to the underlying mutual respect inherent in their relationship. The business approach, unique to this particular situation of the grandparent–grandchildren relationship, will protect the generational stake for the grandmother as the association continues and she remains in the position of guiding business manager.

In addition, despite the fact that the parents are divorced, Myra has successfully assumed the gatekeeper role by developing a connection between her children and her ex-mother-in-law that is qualitatively different from the previous connection they had when the children's father had been the natural link between them. Myra's gatekeeper role may decrease as her children reach maturity and are able to restructure their relationship with the grandmother in a more direct framework. However, Myra's continuous participation in their joint venture may provide for a different position in the family constellation.

Prediction of Adjustment to Divorce

The distress individuals experience at the time of divorce or following the dissolution of a marriage depends on both pre- and postdivorce conditions and varies from individual to individual. As revealed in some previous studies, the pattern of distress associated with divorce may be different for men and women (Horowitz, Raskin White, & Howell-White, 1996). Compared with men, for many women their standard of living is likely to decline; because they are more likely to have custody of the children, they experience higher stress levels (Avison, 1999).

Another gender difference seems linked to the age at divorce. Women who are younger at the time of divorce have a greater likelihood of marrying again than those who are in their middle 50s and beyond, while for men, this difference is not as pronounced (de Jong Gierveld, 2004). On the other hand, studies have shown that middle-aged women demonstrate greater resilience than younger women in managing life transitions such as divorce (Marks & Lamberg, 1998). As stated earlier, another marriage might be just a temporary aid in adjusting to the effects of divorce, while resilience is generally considered to be a valuable attribute no matter what the situation is and it would be of benefit to individuals whether or not they enter another union following a divorce.

Considering the various stressors that confront divorced persons, it is not surprising that they generally experience lower levels of psychological well-being than married persons. Recently separated or divorced adults reportedly have more automobile accidents, lose more days at work due to illness, and are more likely to become depressed and suicidal (Bloom, White, & Asher, 1979; Menaghan & Lieberman, 1986; Stack & Wasserman, 1993). In addition, they experience strong feelings of failure and report a loss of self-esteem and feelings of loneliness (Chase-Lansdale & Hetherington, 1990).

Although many of the stressors, such as financial hardship, moving to a different location, and reduction in the size of social network and emotional support among others, may be the same for many divorcing persons, people vary in the extent to and time in which they adjust to the divorce-related stress. For some, it takes a significant period of time to recover from the disappointment of a failed relationship, while others are restored to their earlier level of psychological well-being in a relatively short time. In general, younger individuals can be expected to recover from the stress faster than older individuals. The poorer adjustment of older divorced people may be in part related to the lower probability of finding a new partner at their age.

Considering marital disruption a serious life challenge that stresses those involved in it, crisis theorists tend to view divorce as a life crisis that temporarily changes the mental health of the divorced (Booth & Amato, 1991; Mastekaasa, 1992). As a temporary event, a crisis would be expected to have an end as well as a beginning, and linked to the notion of a crisis would be the concept of transitions—a transition in roles from married to newly divorced to adjusted to divorce. The role transition period may initially introduce additional distress, but it would be characterized by gradually reducing stress levels. Indeed, it has been reported that individuals' psychological stress increased prior to the crisis and then, 2 years after the marital disruption, returned to levels comparable to those of married individuals (Booth & Amato, 1991).

As mentioned earlier, there are strains and stresses inherent in the roles individuals find themselves in and these stresses are of a relatively enduring nature (Pearlin, 1999). As family theorists offer different explanations for the ways people experience and cope with the consequences of distressing life events such as divorce, others are interested in the efficacy of the explanations when applied to real-life data. Exploring the application of three different theoretical frameworks in a pooled time-series analysis of a four-wave panel of married persons that were followed over a period of 12 years, Johnson and Wu (2002) reported that, according to their analysis, the higher stress levels of divorced individuals are primarily reflecting the stipulations of role theory. The crisis theory and social selection approaches that were also applied to the data showed only small effects.

While overall the roles that divorced persons occupy are fraught with stress, they are not all at the same level due to the many differences within the roles of divorced persons. Divorced parents usually experience more distress and encounter more problems than divorced individuals who are single. And even within the divorced parents group there are differences in stress levels, depending on the number of children or perhaps even due to the gender of the single parent—topics that will be explored in more detail in the chapter on single parenthood in this book.

The wide variation of stressor constellations among divorced people makes it difficult to fit them neatly into any one theory, as investigators continue to search for answers. Within the framework of stress and coping theory, Wang and Amato (2000) collected data from 208 individuals who divorced during a 17-year longitudinal study. It was hypothesized that adjustment would be linked to variables reflecting resources, stressors, and individuals' definitions of the divorce. The need to adapt to several negative life changes in a short time was thought to overwhelm individuals' coping ability and lead to reduced levels of psychological functioning and well-being. Resources such as higher levels of education were considered of help in coping with divorce-related stress.

Additionally, people's definitions of the event were thought to be a likely factor in the adjustment process. For instance, people who have negative attitudes about divorce in general might view their own divorce in more negative terms than those with less negative attitudes. Also, those spouses who wanted the marriage to end would probably think in less negative terms about divorce.

The investigators were surprised to find that stressors such as decline in financial resources, the loss of friends, or relocating did not affect divorce adjustment significantly, except for those who were not employed. It was speculated that participants might not have evaluated these negative changes as part of the divorce itself. The formation of new intimate relationships facilitated individuals' adjustment to divorce, as would be expected. Adjustment for those who, while still married, held positive attitudes about divorce was less stressful and they also reported less attachment to the former spouse than did people with negative and rejecting attitudes about divorce.

Overall, adjustment was found to be more difficult for older than for younger individuals. Similarly, the duration of the marriage affected individuals' adjustment. Those who had been married for a longer time had more invested in the relationship than those who divorced earlier and, with the greater investment, they experienced more pain and distress, which slowed the adjustment process.

Long-range effects of divorce can be observed in the way it impacts the sequence and timing of family roles. For divorced women and divorced men, remarriage expands the number of years of childrearing, either through conception of offspring in the new union or through becoming stepparents (Lampard & Peggs, 1999; Norton, 1983). This extension of the childrearing years would shorten the time period remarried couples would have between the departure of the youngest child and the time when their elder parents might need financial or physical assistance. Each of these changes requires a new period of adaptation, accompanied by significant upheaval. There are fewer opportunities for stabilizing life structures and more periods of transition or crisis to face.

Time Factor for Healing and Adjusting

On the surface it seems reasonable that the formation of a new romantic relationship or remarriage to a new partner would be of great benefit in the adjustment to divorce. However, the time factor is of concern. If the new relationship develops soon after the divorce, it may be just a temporary cure, forging a new connection while on the rebound. Involving oneself deeply with a new partner reduces the time and concentration available for contemplations of the real underlying reasons for the failure of the previous marriage. If individuals do not devote the time to explore past mistakes and misunderstandings, they deprive themselves of opportunities to learn from the past. And what is perhaps even more important, they do not allow themselves the time to investigate different options that might be available to them.

This concern is especially relevant to women who might have married early without sufficient time for contemplation about their future. For women, marriage is still an opportunity and a temptation for trading their individual goals for mutual goals or, more precisely, their husbands' goals. Most men start early in life on a predictable path to achievement, while women may be distracted by thoughts of marriage and motherhood and their dreams may remain dormant for some time. For divorcing women, this would be a time to search for what has been forgotten rather than to mourn for what is lost with the dissolution of the marriage. What about the childhood or young-adulthood interests and dreams that appeared so magical at the time and seemed to have been stashed away in an old shoe box in the attic a long time ago? Perhaps now it feels like those dreams belonged to another person, a person who was familiar once and has since moved far away. But now can be the time to revive the dreams and the dreamer.

Turning-Point Episodes and Personal Event Memories

Within the psychology of life stories, childhood recollections can be understood and interpreted (McAdams, 2001). Episodes remembered from the past that mirror specific events, occurring at a particular time and place, become self-defining or personal event memories (Pillemer, 1998). At the time of recollection, these memories evoke in the person sensory images that contribute to the feeling of "reliving" the event and connecting the details to particular moments of phenomenal experience.

Individuals possess many varieties of personal event memories, but those that are influential in self-determination hold symbolic messages that the "rememberer" interprets as generating or affirming an interest or vocation. When the original event occurred at the time of encoding, the memory selection was determined by goals inherent in the interest or "dream." The originating events can remain dormant for long periods of time until suddenly a turning point episode in the person's life arouses the self-defining memory and may function to redirect a life plan (Pillemer, 2001).

During the period of adjustment to a divorce or bereavement, such a turning point episode could make its appearance. When Carole's friend Jennifer requested her help, it became a turning point episode for Carole that triggered personal event memories in her. In a few months, Jennifer was going to get married and Carole had agreed to be her maid of honor. The two women had been friends since childhood and both had married soon after graduation from high school before they knew much about life. Both had given birth to daughters within months of each other and both were single mothers now. Jennifer and her husband had divorced, while Carole had been faced with sudden widowhood. Carole admitted that her marriage had not been happy and eventually would have led to divorce, but her husband's fatal accident while driving under the influence of alcohol eliminated the need for divorce.

This was going to be Jennifer's second marriage. Her mother's physical health was impaired and she spent most of her time in a wheelchair, making it too difficult for her to undertake the wedding preparations. Her older sister had volunteered to take over the planning for her niece's modest second wedding but had been recently diagnosed with pancreatic cancer. Initially, Carole hesitated to assume the responsibility for her friend's wedding celebration, but what is a friend for if not to step in when needed, she thought. Jennifer gratefully hugged her friend, laughingly asking, "Remember when we had our little tea parties as kids and you set the most beautiful table? You made such pretty decorations and party favors. We had so much fun then with your grandmother watching us and making sure we would not get into trouble."

For a moment Carole stood motionless, her eyes filling up with tears as she remembered her grandmother's voice, telling her that if people had parties every day, parties would not be special anymore. Carole had lost her parents at an early age and was raised by her mother's parents, a gentle, loving couple. Her grandmother had taught Carole to make crafts, knit, crochet, and sew. She also learned to cook and bake. Carole loved to invite her friends to ice cream or tea parties. Her grandmother encouraged her but insisted that she do as many of the tasks that she was able to at her age. Setting the table was her favorite task because she could make everything look pretty.

Those happy days seemed a lifetime ago. Her grandfather died soon after Carole's wedding and her grandmother followed a few months after the birth of Carole's daughter. There was not much money left and soon after her husband's death Carole and her daughter had to move in with her parents-in-law, who needed assistance and offered her a home in exchange. She managed to enroll in a community college on a part-time basis and upon graduation she secured employment as administrative assistant with a small local company. With working, raising her daughter, and providing care for her parents-in-law, who required more time and effort over the years, Carole had little time left to think about the good times of her childhood. She did not spend much thought on how the table was set for meals, as long as it was clean.

Carole felt guilty when she realized how little she had cared about her surroundings. She could have made life a bit more pleasant for the two older people who had opened their home to her, and what legacy was there for her daughter? Where had her ambition to make everything pretty gone? It was lost in the daily struggle for survival.

Recently, her father-in-law had to be moved into a nursing home because he needed more intensive care than the two women could provide. When they returned from one of their visits to the nursing home, Carole's mother-in-law thanked her for never having complained about the way her son had treated Carole and her daughter. She added that it would have broken her husband's heart to realize that their son had not fulfilled his family responsibilities as his parents expected him to. Carole quietly promised herself to renew her focus on the beautiful, cheerful, and pleasing aspects that she could add to their lives.

Her friend's request for help and the recall of old childhood memories became the turning point episode in Carol's life. The wedding celebration was splendid; everybody talked about the wonderful decorations, the little personal favors at each setting, the flower arrangements, music, and the food display. Instead of a sit-down dinner at the reception, Carol had suggested a buffet, which with its artistic arrangement added to the décor.

Keeping her friend's limited budget in mind, Carole shopped for bargains and with the help of her daughter created much of the decoration and many of the little gifts. As she worked feverishly, she experienced some of the excitement she remembered from the past. She was giddy with the surge of creativity she felt inside herself. It was exhilarating and intoxicating; she did not want to let go of what she now perceived as a gift. It was the beginning of a small-scale event-planning business.

For Carole, as for many other young women, the struggles of adolescence and young adulthood often displace earlier memories into hard-to-get-to compartments of the brain. When confronted with concerns about marriage and motherhood, young women may abandon parts of themselves as they abandon precious memories. Most often they are not aware of this process, as they are also not aware of what would trigger the reappearance of displaced or forgotten materials.

Strictly speaking, Carole was not divorced and her story would normally be discussed in the chapter on widowhood; however, her marriage had not been a happy one and probably would have ended in divorce had her husband not died in an accident. Due to the relevance to this part of the book, her experience of forgotten memories is included here.

Discovering those forgotten or misplaced memories can be a rewarding process for the individual. In the midst of hectic schedules, divorced as well as widowed persons might experience a feeling of emptiness, even while busy with activities of daily living. Amid activity and anxiety about making time for necessary but not intrinsically rewarding tasks, they may feel mentally bored. Although their time is occupied, they remain insufficiently challenged, as though something meaningful is missing. But between boredom and anxiety, an optimal state of "flow" can exist where both time and skills are engaged in a meaningful challenge (Csikszentmihalyi, 1990).

For instance, considering artists who for many hours are immersed with great concentration in their activities of painting or sculpting or composing, for them nothing else seems to matter. From his study of artists, Csikszentmihalyi (1990) concluded that such joyful absorption in meaningful activities is a major source of happiness and well-being that lies within individuals. Those individuals who, in one way or another, become aware of the existence of this optimal state of "flow" within themselves can fall back on their skills and talents to help them in the adjustment to distressing events such as divorce.

However, a degree of self-confidence would be required for the person to consider his or her skills or talents as important enough to devote time and energy to the involvement in them. If the creative urges are not very strong, they may be displaced by a focus on immediate, more pressing demands. Other, less obvious needs for adjustment to divorce that a person might face may surface at a later time in the divorced person's life. Needs for changes as result of role reduction or role modification are expected and frequently reinforced by the divorced person's environment. Socialization with friends will often be different for the newly single person. In the case of single custodial parents, more responsibilities than before will be waiting to be handled by the single parent.

Bruised Egos and Eroded Self-Confidence

Many people regard divorce as a personal failure, a failure to do what is necessary to build and maintain a successful marriage. It is not difficult to imagine that a divorced person's ego might be a bit bruised. Additionally, the notion of failure might have been emphasized in the relationship with the spouse while still married. In other words, having been married to a critical partner may have already eroded what self-confidence the person had to begin with. The actual divorce decree is just the official stamp on the person's damaged self-concept, legally determined and affixed for all to see. Divorced individuals, especially divorced women, report their impression that they are being treated differently after their divorce. Married friends seem more hesitant to invite them; the stigma of divorce can still be felt.

Lori, the divorced mother of two young sons, reported on the difference she observed in behaviors of people in her church congregation. One member's wife had died of cancer, leaving him a widower in charge of their two little daughters. The congregation's support of him seemed to be in stark contrast to the indifference Lori thought they offered her following her divorce. The experience of the divorce and her troubled marriage had long-ranging effects on Lori's concept of herself, as reflected in her therapy case history (Maass & Neely, 2000).

During her marriage to Walt, Lori had not worked outside the home. She devoted her time and energy to her husband and their two sons. Prior to her marriage, Lori had pursued a bachelor's degree in fine arts but did not consider herself sufficiently talented to be a successful artist. However, her background in arts prompted her to do volunteer work at a local art museum. Walt, an ambitious account executive with a growing company, occasionally made fun of Lori's volunteer work. His teasing of her volunteer work fit in with his generally critical attitude of Lori and her shortcomings. He especially ridiculed her decision-making attempts. When faced with the need to make a choice, Lori was also confronted with Walt's critical remarks about not having considered the most advantageous option. Thus, situations that involved any type of decision making became filled with stress and anxiety for Lori.

Over time, his criticism became incorporated in Lori's concept of herself. She developed significant anxiety, which impaired her concentration and also affected her interest in sex. She found it difficult to relax and enjoy their lovemaking as she had done in the past. Instead, she became a vigilant spectator in their sexual encounters, losing all aspects of fun and spontaneity. Sex became a task whose performance she dreaded.

Lori's lack of sexual desire resulted in increased criticism and sarcasm from Walt. Whenever Lori tried to defend herself, Walt countered with statements like "we both know that you are not capable of doing a good job with…." After the divorce, Lori obtained a part-time position as sales associate in an upscale department store to supplement the child-support payments from Walt. Because she derived enjoyment from her volunteer work at the art museum, she continued with her monthly schedule. Another volunteer who had produced a monthly newsletter for the museum's volunteers fell ill and Lori offered to help out. It turned out to be an opportunity to get in touch with her creativity. For the first time in a long time, Lori received praise and encouragement for what she did. It felt good but she could hardly believe it.

Lori's newsletter came to the attention of a professional in the commercial arts department where the museum brochures were produced. The woman thought Lori showed strong talent in the area of graphic design and she encouraged her to take classes in graphic design and computer artwork application. Both classes were offered at the local art school on the same evening because one built on the other. Lori could not afford to pay the tuition for the classes and the fee for a babysitter for the evenings she attended the classes. In her excitement she thought that Walt might be able to change his visitation night with the boys to the night of her classes. This simple switch would eliminate the cost for the babysitter.

Instead of being willing to trade his visitation evening with Lori's evening of classes, Walt scolded her for thinking of spending money for such frivolous and useless activities. He had to work hard enough to make the child-support payments. Lori would be better off looking for a fulltime job in order to help provide for their sons. As usual, Lori had made a silly decision in considering the possibility of improving her skills. Lori fell back into her defensive mode, telling Walt about the encouragement she had received for her work on the newsletter. Walt had an explanation for that: The people at the museum were paying her compliments only to get more work without pay from her. They were using her, and Lori, as usual, was too incompetent to realize that they were taking advantage of her and him, too, because his financial support made her volunteer work possible.

Walt succeeded in rattling Lori's self-confidence. Whether it was out of habit or out of conviction, Lori believed Walt's evaluation of her competence.

After all, he had known her for a longer time and was probably more accurate in his assessment than the people at the museum. She was ready to bury the short-lived excitement of her dreams. Even though the divorce had occurred more than 2 years ago, Lori was still under the influence of her ex-husband's judgment of her. She still perceived her own competence through his critical eyes and came up short. How long would it take to erase this perception and replace it with a realistic account of her abilities?

Lori had first consulted a therapist because of her disabling anxiety. She could not afford regular therapy sessions but was able to remain in contact with her therapist on an as-needed basis. When Lori told her sister about the sad ending to her plans, her sister offered to take care of Lori's sons during the time it would take her to attend classes under the condition that Lori discuss the situation with her therapist. Under the guidance of the therapist, Lori explored events in her marriage and after the divorce to examine the validity of and evidence for her beliefs about the correctness of her husband's knowledge of her competence or lack thereof.

With her lack of self-confidence Lori had ascribed predictive quality to her husband's criticism of her, as the therapist pointed out, without challenging the validity of his pronouncements. According to Lori's knowledge, how many times had her husband's predictions regarding her competence been accurate? Before adopting his negative statements into her own belief system, it would be wise to look at evidence for the correctness of her husband's predictions.

As the therapist pointed out, Lori was still vulnerable to her ex-husband's criticism of her; therefore, as a completion of her divorce adjustment process, it was her responsibility to achieve mental and emotional independence and neutrality. And if, with the help of her sister, she could afford the investment in the art classes, she could engage in studying as a future-oriented goal-directed activity that would enable her to observe her progress and apply the outcome in building a self-concept that was grounded in reality.

Several years later in a visit with her therapist, Lori took stock of her life. Since taking the two classes after her divorce, she had continued with her studies, resulting in the recent achievement of her MFA degree. She admitted that progress had been slow because of her financial and time restrictions. However, her instructors had agreed that she had a good eye for composition and the necessary patience to complete her designs, no matter how painstaking the task was. Her connection to the museum proved to be a valuable one as she continued with her volunteer work. Her loyalty was rewarded when she was offered fulltime employment as graphic designer. During her years of study, the professional who had first recognized Lori's talent remained an encouraging influence and it was her recommendation that was instrumental in Lori's getting the job. She terminated her job as sales associate but has been working occasionally as a freelance designer for the store's advertising department.

In her personal life, Lori has become more outgoing, probably as a result of her increasing confidence. She enjoys her friends and an occasional date. Walt has started a new family and is complaining about the money he has to pay for his two sons. He is fond of his new family but, in his opinion, the money he has to hand over to Lori in addition to the financial output for his new family is due to Lori's shortcomings. If she had been a more competent wife, they would not have divorced and he would not have to support two families.

Lori feels that as sad as it was to experience the family disruption, the divorce from Walt has set her free to explore her talents and stretch her skills and imagination. Her concept of herself is finally independent of Walt's judgment. She has learned to assess her skills and competencies realistically by looking at the evidence of her work rather than listening to the prejudiced criticism of others. For Lori, the opportunity to fill her life with meaningful and rewarding activities has been a growing process that started with the loss of her marriage. Lori is not complaining.

Divorce may be made easier by the presence of an extramarital partner, as in the case of Lynette and Ron, or the decision to divorce may come as the result of a more complicated process of establishing one's independence and significance as a person, as demonstrated in Gina's and Lori's stories. In either case, contemplating such lifestyle changes within a therapeutic environment puts the emphasis on arriving at the decision based on the best interest of the client as much as possible under the circumstances.

Few divorces are granted to two people who are in agreement about ending the marriage. Frequently, one of the partners wants the termination more than the other and it is usually the one who would rather stay married who has the more difficult adjustment to face. Aside from the bruised self-esteem resulting from having been left—often to be replaced by a younger, more attractive, richer model—there are other setbacks to cope with, such as dealing with loneliness or handling financial impediments. But even for those who are involved in a divorce against their will, what they will face in the future can indeed include exciting new developments, as long as they do not remain preoccupied with the losses that accompanied the divorce.

CHAPTER 5

Lifestyle Changes due to Widowhood

When sharing substantial parts of one's life with another person, many significant decisions have become joint ventures rather than individual selections. Over time, considerations of the opinions of one's partner turned into stable habits in decision-requiring situations. Responsibilities that were once shared suddenly become individual responsibilities for the one left single through widowhood.

In widowhood, much like in divorce, individuals face something like an identity crisis: Previously they were part of a couple, part of a team; now, as newly single people, they may see themselves as "half" of something that becomes difficult to describe and identify. Not being married anymore requires the creation of a new image of oneself that can be presented to the world. Some friendships may have been based on a "couple framework" and may be awkward or difficult to continue for the single person.

The adjustment to the loss of a long-term emotional relationship in addition to meeting daily responsibilities that once were shared with a spouse, are difficult tasks for the newly bereaved person to manage. Widowed members of traditional couples, who adhered to rigid gender-typed division of labor in their households, may be especially ill prepared for the new responsibilities facing them. Coping with behavioral and psychological readjustments, widowed persons may seek a spousal substitute to fill the void or they may withdraw into loneliness and depression.

Some research has demonstrated that the problems individuals are faced with in bereavement are different for men and women (de Ridder, 2000; Porter & Stone, 1995), with men reporting more work-related problems and women focusing more on difficulties relating to the self, parenting problems, and problems involving others. These differences between men and women can be understood as a consequence of the particular focus on the stressor. Men may bring their personal distress into the work environment while women tend to concentrate on personal or relational aspects connected with the loss.

In general, though, women's psychological distress over widowhood is seen as related to financial strain, reflecting women's dependence on their husbands for financial stability while they were married. For men, the psychological distress over the loss of a spouse seems to be linked to their dependence for emotional support and aspects of homemaking tasks (Carr et al., 2000; Lee, DeMaris, Bavin, & Sullivan, 2001). However, as current and future cohorts of couples adhere to more flexible divisions of household labor, the evolving roles of spouses may bring about different patterns of adjustment experiences for bereaved adults.

For healthy adjustment to loss, it is necessary to address both the emotional consequences of loss and the concurrently occurring life changes due to widowhood. Preoccupation of one of these aspects to the exclusion of the other delays the adjustment process. In other words, coping orientations directed toward the task of loss and those directed toward restoration are required for resolving the grief over the loss of a loved one (Stroebe, Stroebe, & Schut, 2001).

The Risks of Seeking and Giving Advice in Widowhood

It is tempting for a widowed person to approach friends or family members for advice in some life areas that have changed as a result of widowhood. Often people are happy to come to their friends' aid with advice, but there are some risks to the relationship (Watzlawick, 1983). One can expect one of two outcomes of a helper and help-seeker relationship. If the advice is not successful in alleviating the other person's difficulties, the advice giver will become tired and will withdraw. A similar outcome results when the advice seeker does not apply the offered advice; the provider will build up resentment about having not been taken seriously and will withdraw.

On the other hand, if the advice has been instrumental in resolving the difficulties, there will be a change in the relationship. As the advice receiver is no longer in need of advice, he or she will slowly withdraw from the relationship. In either circumstance, the relationship between the two individuals will be changed. Negative feelings such as resentment or guilt are likely to develop in the first scenario, as the advice recipient may judge the advice not good enough to help and the advice provider feel offended because the advice was either not followed or ineffectually applied. In the second scenario the relationship had been temporarily unbalanced with the advice seeker in a one-down position. Having applied the advice successfully, both sides seem to be on an equal footing, a condition that the relationship may not survive.

Handling relationships that had developed prior to widowhood becomes a challenge for the widowed person as well as for the friends. Often the easier path is that of slow and subtle withdrawal leading to disintegration of the relationship. Adding to this, the function of giving and receiving advice can complicate those relationships even further.

Nora, the widowed mother of three children mentioned in chapter 1, was in her early 40s when her husband died after years of illness. Vernon had a congenital heart condition that had killed his father at age 40. At age 45, Vernon felt like he was on borrowed time. He was still employed by the company he had started with in his younger years, but due to his illness he had chosen a less competitive position than he had originally aspired to. Avoiding stress became the overriding goal in his life.

Unfortunately but not surprisingly, the children—except for the youngest one—learned to use the situation to their advantage. Unacceptable behaviors that previously Nora had tried to keep under control by reprimanding the children and applying consequences, resurfaced when the children complained to their father, who would remove the consequences to keep his peace. Thus, Nora's authority with her children was steadily undermined.

Vernon's death placed Nora in the role of primary disciplinarian and decision-maker, a role for which neither she nor the children were prepared. It did not help when, in a well-meaning attempt to distract Nora from her grief and guide her toward more future-oriented thinking, her uncle told Nora that now she had to be both mother and father to her children. Some of the friends she had turned to for advice echoed her uncle's sentiments and added that it was time for Nora to implement strict disciplinary behaviors. Nora tried to fulfill the responsibilities of a single parent. However, the children, traumatized by their father's death, resisted and rebelled against her new authority. Financial stress required Nora to expand her previously part-time job into fulltime employment, leaving her less time for child supervision and household maintenance.

Nora's oldest daughter Jenny was in her second year at college. Jenny's grades had deteriorated and Nora attributed that to Vernon's death. With the bill for next semester's tuition came a note informing Nora that Jenny had been placed on academic probation. Nora asked Jenny about any difficulties she might be experiencing besides the loss of her father. Jenny shrugged her shoulders without answering. Nora did not know how to interpret Jenny's response and told her if her grades did not improve, there would not be any money paid for college tuition. This time Jenny had an answer. In an angry voice she told her mother that her father had promised her a college education and it was now her mother's duty and responsibility to fulfill her father's promise. Nora was too shocked to respond.

Ron, Nora's son, was a senior in high school. Since his father's death he seemed to have withdrawn from the family. He did not say much; sometimes he became a bit bossy, especially with Tina, the youngest child, but also with his mother. Perhaps he saw himself now as the man in the family. Tina had become very clingy since the death of her father. She was trying to be with her mother at all times. Nora sought advice from her friends again. They suggested different discipline approaches. For a while they still included Nora in their social activities, but they felt awkward having a single female in their circle of coupled friends; besides, Nora seemed so needy. One of her friends recommended a therapist.

At the time of her appointment with the therapist Nora was desperate. She had just found out that Jenny had charged to the maximum amount on the credit card that she had given Jenny for emergencies. In addition, Jenny had run up their phone bill with long-distance calls. Nora saw herself forced to sell a piece of the property that she and her husband had bought for their retirement. But that would take time and Nora needed money now for food, gasoline, utilities, and mortgage payments.

Jenny was home for the holidays. Upon her return home from work Nora had noticed that parts of the meat and other ingredients for the family's evening meal had disappeared out of the refrigerator despite the notes she had left not to take them. Nora mentioned the disappearance at dinnertime. Ron denied having touched it; Jenny, without admitting that she had helped herself to parts of the family's dinner, said she had been hungry. Nora explained to her children that with the debts incurred through credit cards and long-distance phone calls, in addition to the normal financial responsibilities, her income was not sufficient to cover such expenses and feed the family. Jenny suggested she file for bankruptcy. Ron agreed that was a good idea. Nora rejected this as an option; they all had to do with less from now on. A few days later the main ingredients for the evening meal had again been drastically reduced. Jenny was not home for dinner but left a message that she was at a friend's house.

With the guidance of the therapist Nora explored her options how to handle the situation. One option was to shop daily just enough for the evening meal, but that would be highly inconvenient and more costly, too. Another option would be to invest in a small refrigerator that she could lock and keep in her bedroom. The expensive food items for the family's meals could be stored there. Nora rejected this option. How could she lock up food from her own children? People would condemn her if they found out.

It took one more food disappearance and Nora was ready to do the unthinkable. She accepted that as a single parent she was in a lonely position without the luxury of having the support of a spouse. Thinking back to the past when her husband was still alive, she realized that she did not have his support either when it came to disciplining the children. Although the reason for the change in her role was sad indeed, she decided she might be able to handle the responsibility—as long as she did not insist on the approval of others.

This was only the beginning of the changes Nora made in her life. When Ron was ready to enter college, Nora decided she wanted to trade the long and harsh winters of the Midwest for a warmer southern climate. With the help of a friend she was able to get a job lead and after some exploration she found a pleasant affordable condominium for herself and Tina with a guestroom for Ron or Jenny. Prior to the move she discussed the possibility with Tina and then took her along on trips to check out the area in which they wanted to settle.

Looking back on her life from the time her husband died, Nora could hardly believe how many changes she had made based on her own decisions. She admitted that if she had not had to take care of the daily crises and responsibilities after Vernon's death, she might have indulged in her grief over his death and feeling sorry for herself.

A final confrontation with reality occurred when the friends she and Vernon had spent time with slowly disengaged from her. Nora recalled:

> That's when I realized that the only person I could count on is myself. At times it still makes me feel lonely but there is an advantage to it, too: If anything, I have become a bit more adventurous, such as leaving my home and starting over in a different location. There are activities that I am considering now that I would not or could not have thought about before. In my decision making now the first consideration is my welfare and that of my children. I am not looking for approval from others. It would be nice to have people agree with my decisions but they are not living my life.

In cases of prolonged illness, partners can prepare themselves emotionally and mentally for the inevitable, but in situations of sudden widowhood through accidental death of a spouse, there is no time for preparation and the change in one's circumstances is immediate. The change to widowhood is even more challenging in situations where the remaining spouse is left with dependent children, as in Nora's case. Whereas in divorces the absent parent can be requested to assist in some areas of childrearing, in widowhood, there is only one parent left to cope with all the demands and responsibilities. Having the full responsibility for dependent children is extremely stressful for the single parent and the chances for finding a suitable second spouse or partner are usually greatly reduced.

Horizontal and Vertical Loyalties

Over the life span, individuals develop as part of families, extended families, friends, communities, church congregations or interest groups and different degrees of loyalty are formed within different relationships. According to David Seaburn (1990), people build up vertical and horizontal loyalties.

Vertical loyalties extend over generations and connect the individual with previous and future generations, including parents and grandparents at one end of the continuum and children and grandchildren at the other. Horizontal loyalties connect the individual to siblings, spouses, friends, and peers. These are connections that tie individuals within one generation.

At times of widowhood (and divorce, too) horizontal and vertical loyalties can contribute to conflicts. Loyalties previously experienced toward one's ex-parents-in-law can become problematic for the single parent who may have less contact with them, although as grandparents of the single parent's children, they are still much involved in the family constellation. On the other hand, loyalties to previous siblings-in-law may deteriorate (Maass & Neeely, 2000).

Larry: Conflicting Loyalties

Larry, the suddenly widowed father of two children mentioned in chapter 1, was confronted with significant conflict over loyalties to his former parents-in-law when they insisted that he return the children to their home-town and into their custody. Especially, Larry's mother-in-law threatened to sue for custody of her grandchildren on the grounds that Larry was morally not a competent parent to single-handedly raise teenage children.

About 2 years before his wife died, Larry had left his job with the local newspaper and moved the family to the city to accept an editorial position with a promising future in a publishing company. His wife, Kathy, was involved in a fatal automobile accident. Larry was able to arrive at the hospital while she was still conscious. Kathy asked him to promise that he would move the children back to their hometown. Larry hesitated, partly because he did not want to accept his wife's imminent death and partly because he was not sure that he wanted to make that promise. Kathy died before he responded. Now he felt troubled and guilty as he approached therapy. Larry's conflict involved difficulty with his horizontal loyalty toward Kathy and the requested promise and his vertical loyalty concerning his children and his parents-in-law.

What were the loyalties to himself? Larry had not thought about that question. In fact, he had actually rejected that aspect when he responded to the therapist's question about keeping the children with him in their new environment. Larry believed that would be not only impossible but also selfish. At the time he accepted this new position, he realized that he had put his own career goals ahead of the family's goals. Having a supportive wife by his side allowed him to make the change that seemed beneficial for his future without neglecting the welfare of the family. Now he had to put the children's welfare first and, in order to do that, he had to suppress any thoughts about his own wishes and desires. As much as he would miss being with his children, he thought he had to disregard his feelings.

To be of assistance to Larry, the therapist needed to understand how Larry perceived his situation and the main forces of the difficulty or challenge. The different loyalties Larry was struggling with had already revealed themselves as Larry described his reason for contacting the therapist. But what were the feelings associated with the struggle and how did Larry perceive the sources of the challenges—beyond the death of his wife? In other words, how much of the struggle was due to forces inside Larry and how much did he attribute to external forces? The more he attributed to outside influences, the more helpless he would likely feel and the fewer options for solution he would be aware of.

Larry's resistance to discussing emotions within the context of the challenge led the therapist to approach him with a brief questionnaire to learn about Larry's cognitive style, to see how Larry approached problem solving and decision making (see Table 5.1). Emotions are also briefly explored in the questionnaire. The answers to the different items make up a mini-profile about the individual's approach to a given challenge. Does the individual's approach reflect a passive acceptance or a more actively questioning and taking-charge approach? The answer to that question provides the therapist with an opportunity to develop a framework that facilitates the therapy process with the individual client.

Several emotions were circled on the questionnaire, such as anger, resentment, guilt, shame, depression, and anxiety. Larry was also asked to construct a list of options that he perceived as relevant to his situation (see Table 5.2). In addition to the ones that were obvious from the content of the first session, Larry had added the option of staying in the city and keeping his children with him. Although he still did not think it was a feasible option, he wanted to let the therapist know that his employer had shown great understanding for Larry's situation and had suggested that Larry could divide his workdays by being in the office in the mornings and working from home in the afternoons to be available to his children.

What were Larry's reasons for determining that this was not a feasible option, the therapist inquired. After hesitating for a moment, Larry admitted that he was intimidated by his mother-in-law's threat of suing for custody of the children. Her reason for labeling him a morally unfit parent was the fact that Kathy had been pregnant when she and Larry

Table 5.1 Cognitive Style

Identification of the problem

1. *The current problem was caused by*
    - a. _×_ A disastrous external event
    - b. ___ Responses to others
    - c. ___ My own decision
    - d. ___ The situation I was in

2. *I intend to solve the problem by*
    - a. _×_ Accepting it, making the best of it
    - b. ___ Changing my approach to it
    - c. ___ Finding out why it happened
    - d. ___ Moving away from it, forgetting it

3. *To solve the problem, I have to*
    - a. _×_ Support family members' feelings
    - b. ___ Allow for friends' and colleagues' feelings
    - c. ___ Act on how I feel about it
    - d. ___ Just do it—get it done

4. *When I think about resolving it, I feel*
    - a. _×_ Anger, resentment
    - b. _×_ Guilt, shame, depressed
    - c. ___ Anxious, I want to avoid it
    - d. ___ Relief, when I think it will be over

5. *Where do the feelings come from?*
    - a. _×_ When I act against family beliefs
    - b. _×_ Promises I make and do not keep
    - c. ___ When others do not do as they promise
    - d. ___ When people do not care about me

6. *This problem happened because*
    - a. ___ I didn't know until it was too late
    - b. ___ It is in my genes—it is who I am
    - c. ___ I am impulsive, cannot control it
    - d. ___ It is a habit—since I was a child

Source: Modified from Maass, V. S. and Neely, M. A. (2000). *Counseling Single Parents: A Cognitive–Behavioral Approach.* New York: Springer Publishing Company.

Table 5.2 Exploration of Options

Larry is suddenly widowed with two children: In this situation

What are his options?	Likely outcomes
O.1: Return to hometown with children	Larry: career setback
O.2: Return children to grandparents in hometown	Children feel abandoned
O.3: Keep children with him in new town	Lack of supervision
O.4:	

Which option has the greatest appeal? O.3 (impossible); the least appeal? O.2
Steps/actions to take for

Preferred option	Next preferred option
1) Find reliable help; arrange schedules	Return to previous job
2) Overcome mother-in-law's objections	Find housing for family
3) Need help from children, chores, etc.	Dissolve and move household
4)	
5)	

Is he able to take these actions? (yes/no) Is he willing to take them? (yes/no)
What are the obstacles for

Preferred option	Next preferred option
1) Mother-in-law's threats	Disappointment in career
2) Not enough time in the day: job, household	Delay on writing (book)
3) Children's safety	Stuck in small town
4)	

got married. Although Larry realized that the courts would probably not declare him an unfit parent on those grounds, he did not want his children to learn of their mother's premarital pregnancy.

How could Larry handle the situation if indeed his mother-in-law was serious in taking him to court? The anxiety over wanting to protect his children from the disappointment about their deceased mother paralyzed Larry's thinking process. The therapist wondered about Kathy's knowledge regarding sexual facts in general and her own sexuality in particular. Larry remembered that Kathy was pretty naïve at the time; her sex education was nonexistent. Her mother had never talked to her about sex. Larry's eyes widened in surprise, "Do you think I could use the fact that Kathy's mother had not prepared her in that area of her development as an indication that my mother-in-law had not been a fit parent to her daughter?" he asked excitedly. "I still don't want my children to know, but by sharing my thoughts with Kathy's mother, she might see the unreasonableness of her intentions," he continued.

Based on that insight Larry decided to discuss the issue of where to live with his children and inquire about their preferences. His daughter wanted to continue living in the city. She liked her new school and the opportunities available to her. Larry's son was undecided; he still missed his friends from his hometown, but under no circumstances did he want to live without his father and sister. Following the family discussion, Larry confronted his mother-in-law, calmly informing her that if she acted on her threats, he was prepared to let it be known how poorly she had prepared her own daughter for her future life. He added that for the sake of her grandchildren he hoped she would reconsider her position.

His next step was to gratefully accept his employer's offer of modifying his work schedule and to set up housekeeping with the help of his mother, who agreed to spend several months with him and the children to establish a household routine. Larry took on the role as sole parent and head of household of his family.

Prior to his mother's return to her home, Larry made appointments for the family to meet with the therapist. He wanted to establish an atmosphere in the therapist's office where the children would feel comfortable to talk and seek guidance without Larry's presence. Especially with his mother leaving them, he thought it was important for his children to have an outside source for help and guidance.

Their new lifestyle brought more work and more responsibilities for all of them. For the children, some of the carefree atmosphere of childhood had given way to more serious planning and thoughtful decision making. There was less playtime and more goal-related efforts were expected of them. Overall, however, the children were proud that their father had considered them mature enough to embark with them on their new family journey instead of handing them over to live with their grandparents. The trust their father placed in them inspired both children to assume new responsibilities.

The option Larry chose for himself and his family opened opportunities for all of them. The flexible work hours allowed him to continue writing the novel he had started long ago. Through the program in her new school, his daughter was able to apply for a pre-internship experience in her field of interest, and his son, who seemed to follow his father's footsteps in a writing career, appreciated the chance to work for his father's publishing company during the summer months.

As he realized that the option he had finally decided on worked out well for the family, Larry was able to resolve his guilt feelings toward Kathy. He learned in therapy that even in the most harmonious marriage, spouses are not always in complete agreement on every decision that confronts them. Usually there is time for discussion and compromises while working together on the resolution of challenges. There is also time to conjointly modify decisions if they turn out differently from what the spouses had expected and there is time to reconcile differences of opinions and disagreements. In Larry's case that time was not available, but he learned to look at the situation in terms of how they would have handled it if Kathy had not died. He was convinced that the welfare of their children would have been more important to both of them than to give and keep a promise.

Resolving conflicts with horizontal or vertical loyalties can be a difficult task for both male and female widowed individuals. Traditionally, the ties from one generation to another affect women in more fundamentally different ways than men. In women's connection to the home, they are the main generational links not only in their responsibility for the family's offspring but also in the care of and consideration toward their parents and parents-in-law. In their role as "kin-keeper" within the family, women are the ones who maintain relationships by writing letters and arranging gatherings of families and friends (Moen, 1996). In this role, they have more frequent contact and establish loyalties with members of two to four generations within family constellations. In widowhood (as in divorce) some of the ties dissolve, while others may become even stronger than before.

Judith: Playing Second Fiddle

Vertical loyalties became an issue soon after Norman, Judith's husband, died. Norman and Judith had a close relationship to his parents, partly because of Melinda, who was their only grandchild, and partly because Judith and her mother-in-law had formed a close emotional bond on their own. Norman's older brother, Thomas, and his wife were deeply involved in their careers and their marriage remained childless. Soon after Norman's father retired, his parents moved to Florida into their condominium. During the winter holidays they rented another condominium for their sons and their families. They also spent part of the summers visiting with Norman and his family. Melinda was a junior in high school when her grandfather died. Although Judith encouraged her mother-in-law to move closer to her two sons' families, the older woman chose to remain in Florida.

Norman's unexpected death was difficult for Judith. Most of her life had revolved around him and Melinda. As a young girl Judith had studied music. She became an accomplished pianist with a pleasant voice matching her attractive appearance, but her teachers discouraged her from pursuing a career as a concert musician. Judith managed to obtain an entry-level position in a publishing company where she met and fell in love with Norman, a young and talented illustrator and cartoonist for a popular magazine.

Encouraged by Norman's parents, Judith left her job at the publishing company when she and Norman got married. Taking care of Norman and Baby Melinda was a fulltime job. Judith knew from Norman's mother that he needed periods of uninterrupted time to nourish his creativity. It was Judith's job to keep the household running smoothly. Norman, as the younger and obviously talented of two sons, had led a sheltered life while growing up and he continued to live with his parents until his marriage to Judith.

With Melinda's entry into kindergarten, Judith had decided to give music lessons to some of the children in their community, hoping to kindle an interest in Melinda who only reluctantly attended to her piano lessons. Melinda seemed to have inherited her father's talents and was more interested in drawing. Later Judith joined a women's barbershop harmony group. It felt good to practice her musical skills and she enjoyed the company of the other women. They were serious in their pursuit and became known in their town. Judith became good friends with Helen, one of the other women. Their voices were complementary and Judith's piano skills helped them develop their own program in addition to their performances with the barbershop harmony.

With Norman's death Judith's financial situation changed drastically. The music lessons would not be sufficient to provide for her and Melinda. Judith did not want to dip into the savings that were earmarked for Melinda's college education. Judith's mother-in-law invited her and Melinda to live with her in Florida; they could all more or less frugally live on her income and Judith could leave her savings untouched. Norman's brother and his wife strongly encouraged Judith to accept her mother-in-law's offer. They were even willing to donate a small monthly amount of money to ease the transition for Judith and Melinda. Judith's brother-in-law had a good reason for the encouragement; if Judith moved to Florida to live with his mother, she could take care of her as the mother got older and her health declined. This would free Norman's brother and his wife, who were both busy with their careers, from taking care of the mother.

For Judith, the decision was a difficult one. Her feelings for her mother-in-law tested her vertical loyalties in the situation. Besides, in little more than a year's time Melinda would enter college. They had already focused on two out-of-state educational institutions to which Melinda would apply. At that point it would not make a great difference where Judith lived; Florida seemed as good a choice as other places. On the other hand, her involvement with the barbershop harmony and the musical bond with her friend Helen, representing horizontal loyalties, gave her great pleasure as well as the feeling of returning to something that was important to her. After so many years she had finally focused on her own satisfaction and fulfillment. What would happen to her if she gave up on herself again and moved to Florida?

Judith decided to invest in herself for 1 year. She had to find some fulltime employment to survive financially, but if she could manage that, she would have not only the emotional support from her friends but also the opportunity to pursue her musical activities. If in a year's time she could not make ends meet financially and could not see any prospects for developments in her musical endeavors, she would reconsider her situation and agree to move to Florida. Judith talked to her mother-in-law, thanking her for the offer and explaining how she felt about her own prospects and goals. Her mother-in-law's understanding and acceptance of Judith's decision came as a pleasant surprise. Judith felt good about the respect with which her mother-in-law responded.

People might criticize Judith's decision on the grounds that her musical talents had not been great enough from the beginning to suggest a career on the concert stage, so what great things could she possibly expect now? In fact, her brother-in-law and his wife adopted that stance. They thought Judith had nothing to lose because she did not have much to begin with.

The question of whether Judith could become a famous and successful musician was not at the basis of Judith's decision. She knew better than to expect miracles. She loved her music without demanding recognition as a virtuoso. What was important to her was the possibility of becoming financially self-sufficient in whatever modest way in her current environment and with that the option of practicing and performing with the friends who had similar aspirations. Widowhood had robbed her of the life with her husband but it did not have to render the rest of her life without meaning.

Widowhood as the End of Two Lives

The biography of Oona O'Neill Chaplin, whose life was determined by two men, describes a woman who chose the presence of a male protector over her own independence (Scovell, 1998). Born to a famous playwright father whose love and acceptance she craved but never obtained beyond early brief moments of attention, she found her place beside another male genius—perhaps even more famous than her father.

In him she found a lover, a father, a provider, and a protector. She immersed herself in her role as Charlie Chaplin's wife and the mother of their eight children. Her husband required her undivided attention, admiration, and devotion. They lived for each other to the exclusion of outside influences—even their children remained outside the intimate bond between the spouses.

Observers described Oona as always composed and unwavering in her devotion to her husband. They thought she had a natural talent for writing but she kept it hidden. There was no competition; Charlie was the undisputed genius. During the later years of her marriage, Oona resorted to drinking, which became more noticeable after her husband's death. When the alcohol loosened inhibitions, underneath her calm exterior she seemed to harbor a tremendous smoldering anger—anger directed toward men.

As Oona had not attempted to supply meaning to her being, life without Charlie was meaningless, in spite of the existence of children and grandchildren. She embarked upon several affairs, but she had nothing within herself to hold onto. Replacing her father with her husband, she had never stood on her own. She did not devote time or energy to developing an inner significance that would provide meaning and strength to go on after her husband's death. Too well had she learned the lesson from her parents: Total and complete devotion to the male genius was the path to prevent abandonment. And in following that path she abandoned herself.

Oona O'Neill's story could have been the model for Judith's life if it had not been for the interest in music. Judith was accustomed in her marriage to give priorities to her husband's life and career. True, her relationship with Melinda was probably different from Oona's with her children, but it was really her way of practicing her skills and talents, even though it was for the benefit of others, like her daughter, that preserved something meaningful for her and that she had already expanded on by the time her husband died. Her life did not have to end with his. Even with Melinda starting on her own path soon, a meaningful part remained in Judith's life with her music and how it connected her to her friends.

Widowed Persons' New Mates and Their Adjustments

The widows, widowers, and children are not the only ones whose lifestyles change drastically through the death of a spouse. Less thought is usually given to those who over time take the place of the deceased mate. Perhaps because they have a choice whether or not to marry a widowed person, less attention is focused on them. Unlike divorce cases, where there are usually some bad feelings or at the least some disappointments, in widowhood the deceased spouse can achieve saint status through the lingering memory of good times. Probably the most difficult scenario develops for the woman who marries a widower with children, especially daughters.

Widowed men tend to marry sooner after the spouse's death than widowed women consider remarriage. One reason for this is the fact that single women seem to outnumber men. Another factor is that if the previous marriage had been a harmonious or happy one, men usually prefer to reinstate that type of lifestyle. Often, they are looking for a woman with personality traits and values similar to those of the deceased wife. That type of choice automatically opens the door to comparison, more so than if the two women were completely different in their characteristics and behaviors. The new woman may feel like an intruder when she moves into the widower's home.

Furnishings and decorations that have been chosen by the first wife cannot be changed or replaced, in order to avoid additional trauma to the children. To spare the children's feelings, pictures and portraits of their mother cannot be removed, often leaving the second wife with daily reminders that she is a trespasser. Her lifestyle changes from that of a single woman to wife and stepmother of children she does not know and who may resent her presence. For the woman, it feels like walking on eggshells; in many cases she has to prove herself and her value to the family on a daily basis.

The tension existing in these situations often makes open communication and expression of feelings difficult. During her daily trips through the house, the new wife may pass repeatedly objects of memory of the first wife, trying to remind herself it would be selfish and damaging to the children if she insisted on making changes in their home. These reminders may work for her in the general part of the house, but a photograph or other reminder of the previous wife, perhaps forgotten by the husband and left in the bedroom he now shares with his new wife, might trigger an emotional outburst or emotional withdrawal in the second wife.

Heather: Feeling Like an Intruder

Heather, a successful artistic director at a local museum, had married Richard, a college professor and widowed father of two teenage daughters. Although Heather owned a beautiful home in a desirable part of town, the couple decided to live in Richard's less spacious home to avoid uprooting the girls. Eileen, the older girl, was ready to graduate from high school in less than a year and Susan had just started her second year in the same high school. Richard and Heather's plans were to remain in the house until both girls were in college.

Heather put her house up for rent. An important part of her job involved designing sceneries and stage settings. Heather loved this aspect of her work. She felt that her creativity allowed her to make meaningful contributions. Unfortunately, Richard's house was too small to provide her with a studio for her work. But it was only a temporary situation, she told herself. Her job required frequent traveling, which she appreciated under the circumstances because it gave Richard more time to spend with his daughters and required less intense initial involvement on her part.

Heather was able to accept her living conditions, although there was no doubt that it still was the first wife's home. Keeping her stepdaughters' welfare in mind, Heather refrained from making any changes except for claiming space for her personal needs in the master bedroom and the tiny bathroom. She had hoped that Richard would be sensitive enough to remove all traces of his first wife's existence from their bedroom without a request from her. There was, however, one picture of the original family left on top of the dresser. Heather passed the dresser at least twice daily. The sight of the first wife's smile in Heather's bedroom did nothing to improve her sexual interest in her husband. It was bad enough that the girls' bedrooms were close by in this small house and noises traveled easily among the upstairs bedrooms.

Why did Heather keep silent instead of making her wishes known? A few changes could have been accommodated, especially in the couple's bedroom. Heather believed that changes had to be initiated by Richard; if she made changes, she felt like an intruder. Because of the couple's deteriorating sex life they sought therapy. Richard had not been aware of the reason for Heather's developing resentment. He apologized for not having removed the old family picture and he set to work on soundproofing their bedroom.

Richard admitted that he and Heather were actually better matched than he had been with his former wife. Heather's professional life had opened many opportunities for her, which in Richard's opinion made her an exciting companion. In fact, he had looked forward to their life together after the girls' departure for college. In his second marriage Richard had wanted to be more adventurous than he had been in his first marriage. His hopes had been for a different lifestyle with his new marriage but he had not realized that, before setting out on a new voyage in his life, he needed to finish the old business and—except for the relationship with his daughters—close the previous chapter of his life. Without open communication about their feelings, expectations, and hopes, Richard and Heather would most likely have missed the opportunities that were available to them within their relationship.

Heather's silence was based on the *belief* that Richard had wanted to keep the reminder (picture) of his first wife in their bedroom. Perhaps he had not completed the grieving process yet. But why not ask? When her therapist inquired, Heather responded that she had been afraid to hurt his feelings or appearing demanding. People often act on their beliefs as if they were true, even if the action is not in their best interest. Sincerely held beliefs often do not require questioning in the person's mind and a certain path of action will be pursued without exploring other possibilities. Encouraging clients to apply a reality check to their beliefs instead of silently accepting them can provide clients with additional—and perhaps more beneficial—options for action.

Seeing and Experiencing for the Lost Partner

At a holiday bazaar Ann, an attractive, late-middle-aged woman, picked out a few items she wanted to purchase. Looking at them while holding them in her hands, she said, "I am going on a European cruise next spring." Tears welled up in her eyes as she spoke but she held them back, explaining that her husband had recently died of a heart attack. They had so looked forward to this particular cruise, which they had to cancel several years before due to the 9/11 terrorist attacks. Now seemed to be the right time, but Ann was a widow. She refused to bury herself in grief. They had been happy in their marriage and Ann was going to do and see what they had planned to do together. "My eyes will see Europe for him," she said. "It will be like a living memorial and I will talk to him as if he were by my side."

The prior evening had been something of a rehearsal for her as she decided to take a ride downtown in a horse-drawn carriage, something she and Jim had talked about doing but never got around to. "I am not putting off things anymore" was Ann's resolution. It was a bittersweet experience; she allowed herself to shed a few tears in the dark before returning home to the condominium they had looked at shortly before Jim's death. They had discussed that a condominium would be perfect for them at this time in their life. They would not have to worry about it while traveling. After Jim's death Ann went to see the condominium again; as she looked around, it felt like home. She bought it and moved in by herself.

Widowhood was not the first major change in Ann's life. Her family of origin lived on the East Coast, where she had met her first husband. Bertram was a businessman who traveled a lot. They moved to the Midwest. For the next 4 years Ann was a housewife but felt lonely during Bertram's absences. She found herself a job as bookkeeper/administrator and made friends in her new environment. However, she missed a husband's companionship and suggested divorce. As she stated, having an affair while married was not congruent with her values and her view of herself. She and Bertram remained friends after the divorce; he never remarried. In her own way Ann still loved him. She now realizes that her impatience with Bertram's absences was an expression of her own immaturity.

After the divorce, as a newly single-again woman, Ann dated several men but she was careful about getting to know them well before making a commitment. She observed the men she dated, noticed how they treated other women and the men's relationships to their own mothers. Some of the men made her cry instead of laugh; they would not be good partners for her. Then she met Jim and they dated for about 14 years before getting married. Their marriage lasted 7 years. Less than a year ago Bertram, now retired, had died—also of a heart attack. Ann admitted that she would probably have returned to Bertram after Jim's death, but now she had lost the two important men in her life.

How does she see her future? In spite of her losses she has a passion for life. She needs to continue to work. She has friends she likes to be with. The memories of her two husbands and her life with them will remain with her. After her return from the cruise she intends to add some volunteer activity to her busy life. There are so many older people who need assistance and encouragement; many have no children to care for them. Ann wants to share some of her passion for life with them. Her own mother suffers from Alzheimer's disease. Ann's younger sister lives close to the mother and so does her brother, who is married to a nurse. They are engaged in the care for the mother and have assured Ann that she need not worry about relocating to the East. Her employment opportunities may not be as good for her there as the secure job in the Midwest, which she has been enjoying.

For the time being, Ann's part in the caregiving is limited to financial assistance and semiannual visits. She reasons that as long as there are people in need, she might as well help them in the area of her residence. Her mother's illness has progressed to the point where she does not recognize Ann as her daughter. Why not exchange caregiving efforts for someone who has no family or whose family members do not live close by? Perhaps there could be some kind of caregiving agency that would organize, schedule, and supervise efforts that could be traded among relatives who do not or cannot reside in the vicinity of their needy elderly or impaired loved ones.

Would she marry again? Yes, if another good man came along, she would seriously consider entering another relationship. In fact, she sees her openness to another commitment as a testimonial to her dead husbands. If they had not been good men and good husbands, she would most likely be rejecting any thoughts of giving marriage another chance.

As Ann is looking at places and experiencing events in the memory of her dead husband, such as seeing by herself the places they had planned to visit, other widowed persons apply different coping tactics to confront and deal with the void that was left by the dead spouse. It would seem natural that novelist Joan Didion would turn to writing in response to the losses of her husband, novelist and collaborator John Gregory Dunne, and her daughter. After 40 years of life together he suffered a massive coronary that took him away at the time when their recently married daughter was hospitalized with a life-threatening illness (Matousek, 2007). In her memoir of loss and mourning Didion described the physical and mental effects of loss as she experienced them in ways different from what she might have thought about death and illness and life. *The Year of Magical Thinking* received the 2005 National Book Award and Joan Didion will be working on the adaptation of her book for a Broadway theater production. Writing about those experiences was her path back to life and sanity, as she admitted in a recent interview. Interestingly, she added that she did not see any option other than to go on. Out of responsibility to her daughter and her husband she could not let herself go.

On the other hand, John Leonard, the former editor of *The New York Times Book Review*, said in his introduction to Joan Didion's book of collected nonfiction, *We Tell Ourselves Stories in Order to Live* (2006), that her readers should not be surprised by *The Year of Magical Thinking* because she has been writing about loss all these years: "She has been rehearsing death. Her whole career has been a disenchantment from which pages fall like brilliant autumn leaves and arrange themselves as sermons in the stones" (Leonard, 2006, p. x). So, when all was said and done, perhaps she was right when she thought she could not do other than she had done all along.

Carrying on with life after tragedy may at times look like the only option available because another option, that of giving in and committing suicide in one way or another, is not an acceptable path and therefore not an option. When people disapprove of an action or find it unacceptable, that action or behavior may appear not to exist for them—what does not exist cannot be an option. This might have been the circumstance that Elizabeth Cabot Cary Agassiz found herself in when both her husband and a daughter-in-law died within days of each other (Schneider & Schneider, 1993).

Elizabeth grew up in Boston and was educated at home. In 1850, at the age of 28 years, she married the Swiss naturalist Louis Agassiz. Her life was devoted to him and his children from his first marriage. The lecture notes Elizabeth wrote became the basis for some of his publications. She was also knowledgeable enough to write introductory guides to marine biology. To supplement the family income she started a school for girls on the third floor of their house with her husband the instructor and Elizabeth acting as counselor and school administrator. Her support of her husband's lectures and expeditions continued as she accompanied him and kept notes and records of his discoveries.

After 23 years of marriage, Louis Agassiz died and the death of her daughter-in-law a few days later left Elizabeth with the responsibility for raising three foster-grandchildren at the time she was writing the biography of her husband. During her widowhood Elizabeth promoted the foundation of Radcliffe College, which opened in 1879 as the Harvard Annex and incorporated in 1882 with Elizabeth Agassiz as president. She resigned from that position in 1903 at the age of 81 years, 4 years before her death. Educating women for education's sake as well as to train women as teachers was her objective.

Widowhood in Later Years

Analyses based on the Changing Lives of Older Couples study including 210 participants (Carr, 2004b) indicated that, for men, an interest in dating and remarriage depends on the amount of social support they receive from friends. Looking at a period of 6 months after loss of a spouse, men with low or average levels of social support from friends are more likely than women to express an interest in remarrying at some future time. Emotional support rather than economic stability or instrumental support may be a primary reason for seeking late-life romantic relationships.

Turning to another aspect of widowhood among people aged 65 and older in the Changing Lives of Older Couples study, Carr (2004a) compared men and women who had been dependent on their spouses prior to widowhood and their adjustment to late-life loss. Carr's particular focus was on the widowed persons' self-esteem and possible gender differences. Analysis of the data seemed to indicate that women who had been most emotionally dependent on their husbands had poor self-esteem during their marriage but that, following bereavement, their level of self-esteem was higher than before. Similarly, men who had been dependent on their wives for homemaking tasks and financial management demonstrated the greatest psychological growth following the loss of their wives.

The investigator reported a surprising—although weak—trend, as the data seemed to suggest that women's personal growth showed a negative relation to the receipt of emotional support from friends. Strong support networks might be less encouraging for women to tackle new tasks and increase their self-sufficiency, as it may be tempting to rely on the assistance of their friends. These findings "suggest that widowed persons who were once highly dependent upon their spouses reap psychological rewards from the recognition that they are capable of managing on their own" (Carr, 2004a, p. 220). The story of Nora, discussed earlier in this chapter, reflected those dynamics.

Some studies have reported that depression and suicidal thoughts are more common in widowers than in widows (Byrne & Raphael, 1999; Chen et al., 1999); however, some of the depression may be linked to increased alcohol intake among widowers when compared to married men of similar age (Byrne, Raphael, & Arnold, 1999).

On the more positive side, enhanced creativity has been observed in older adults. Leading gerontologist Gene Cohen (2000) developed a four-stage theory of mid- to late-life creativity to describe the potential for creative work in the later years. According to Cohen, at around age 50, creative individuals enter a *reevaluation phase,* when they reflect on past accomplishments and formulate new goals. An increased sense of time limitation leads to increased desire for production. During the following *liberation phase,* individuals in their 60s become freer to create because they have retired from their fulltime work. In their 70s, in the *summing-up phase,* creative people may feel compelled to tie together their accomplishments into a cohesive meaningful entity. Finally, during their 80s and beyond, individuals may enter the *encore phase* with a desire to complete unfinished works or fulfill desires that they did not gratify earlier.

Cohen's proposed theory points to the possibility of meaningful options inherent in the challenges of even late-life experiences. He explained that "aging and creativity intersect in distinctly different ways at different times to produce new opportunities for personal growth and discovery" (2000, p. 117) and he distinguished between different categories that coincide with aging. There is a type of creativity that first becomes apparent in later life, perhaps arising from greater attention to the inner life. For others, creativity continues as something that had been started earlier and might even have been dormant for a time. And there is a type of creativity that develops in response to a loss or adversity.

Completing One Life and Building Another

Some people's life span is long enough to accommodate more than one distinct lifestyle. Anna Mary Vernonson Moses was born in 1860. Her life as a farmer's wife, mother, and homemaker lasted until 1927, when her husband, Thomas Moses, died and her children had become adults (Kallir, 2001). During this first part of her life she had learned and practiced all the domestic skills and had been creative with her embroidery. Arthritis made it difficult to continue with her needlework but, following her sister's suggestion that painting may be less painful, Anna Mary started on a painting career.

By then she was in her late 70s. Self-taught, with very little schooling of any kind, she belonged to a long tradition of American folk artists. Her extreme success placed her in a class by herself and as "Grandma Moses" she enjoyed a level of fame denied many other female artists. Every American president from Truman through Kennedy paid homage to Anna Mary Vernonson Moses. By the time of her death in 1961 at the age of 101, she had produced more than 1,600 works.

Creativity as Distraction From Loneliness

The life story of Nellie Mae Rowe contains similar elements. Nellie Mae was born in 1900. Her artistic talents came to the surface after the death of her second husband, as a remedy for loneliness (Kogan, 1999). In order to pass the time and distract herself from the loneliness, she decorated her house and yard with vibrant, color-saturated creations, constructing what she called her playhouse. Initially, some of her neighbors reacted in negative ways. They threw things at her house and destroyed some of her decorations. Eventually people's reactions changed. The assaults stopped and visitors came to look at her playhouse. In the years between 1973 and 1975 more than 800 people—among them folk art curators and collectors—signed her guest register.

In 1976, a group exhibition organized by the Atlanta Historical Society, "Missing Pieces: Georgia Folk Art 1770–1976," featured Nellie Mae Rowe's drawings. Two years later Atlanta contemporary art dealer Judith Alexander started to represent Rowe and provided her with high-quality art supplies. Nellie Mae Rowe was able to earn a stable income as an artist from then on. Her works have been shown regularly in solo and group exhibitions throughout the country.

Although the stories of both Anna Mary Vernonson Moses and Nellie Mae Rowe describe a creativity that became apparent later in life, we could also understand them as demonstrations of a type of creativity that developed in response to a loss. Both women tried to fill the void left by the deaths of their husbands with a meaningful activity that was at the same time uplifting and focusing away from losses and the end of life.

Not everyone can afford to wait for latent talents that might come to the rescue when needed. Constructing as early as possible a well-rounded life with many rewarding interests and activities can serve a preventive function in maintaining independence mentally and emotionally as well as providing stimulating aspects throughout the individual's lifetime.

When Leonard Sidney Woolf started to write his autobiography in 1960 he was 80 years old. It was an undertaking that encompassed five volumes, the last of which he wrote at age 89 in 1969, the year he died. As a publisher, he and his wife, the writer and novelist Virginia Woolf, had founded the Hogarth Press. Virginia had drowned herself in 1941 at the age of 69. After a lifetime of giving voice to the thoughts of others whose works he published and almost two decades after Virginia's death, he finally spoke out about his life and his ideas.

Different Types of Creativity

The word "creativity" often induces thoughts like, "Oh, that's for the great artists or musicians, or inventors, but not for ordinary people like me" in some of us. Yet, creativity is not something that has been reserved for the famously talented only. Since the beginning of the twentieth century, psychologists studying the phenomenon of creativity have widened and expanded its definition.

For instance, Howard Gardner (1993), an expert on human development, distinguished between two types of creativity: There is the type of creativity with a "big C" that would be the type of creativity ascribed to the extraordinary accomplishments of unusual people like Albert Einstein, Vincent Van Gogh, Pablo Picasso, Wolfgang Amadeus Mozart, Ludwig van Beethoven, and many, many others. But there is also creativity with a "little c"—a type of creativity that is based on the realities of everyday life comprising the interests and skills people embody as they go about their life. A person's expression of the "little c" creativity may never become publicly acknowledged because the person's strivings are relatively small and directed at less ambitious goals than the strivings of people with "big C" creativity.

The "big C" type of creativity has been likened to a kind of public creativity represented by creative acts that are acknowledged and celebrated by the public, whereas the "little c" creativity is more of a personal nature, perhaps a new idea or a fresh perspective that an individual developed for himself or herself but that has not come into public awareness (Cohen, 2000). A comprehensive discussion about creativity is outside the scope of this book but it is important to mention here because of the significant difference it can make for the person who is faced with a dramatic life change such as widowhood.

Lena, retired from her career as a registered nurse, has been widowed for 2 years. Her husband had been in ill health for the past 5 years and Lena was the primary caregiver. It was a natural transition for her from nurse to caregiver. Megan, her only daughter, lived about 300 miles away with her husband and their three children. Her husband's death made Lena think about the legacy she could leave for her grandchildren. Beyond material things, she looked for something that would in a meaningful way remind them of her and would also transmit what guidelines she could pass on to them. Of course, it should not have the appearance of advice because that would not be intriguing enough for them to look at.

One of her friends suggested Lena keep a journal; this would enable the grandchildren later to get to know Lena through her daily thoughts and reports of activities. It sounded like good advice, but Lena had never been disciplined enough to keep a diary or journal. In fact, she felt it was too rigid an undertaking for her to sit down every evening and strain her mind about the happenings of the day.

However, something about the suggestion resonated in her. Perhaps something like a scrapbook might work. From time to time she had cut out articles from magazines and newspapers that discussed a topic she was relating to on an emotional level. She had kept those clippings and sometimes wrote her own opinions about them in the margins. Lena retrieved the envelopes with the old clippings and spread them out on the kitchen table. An idea formed in her mind: Some of the articles along with her comments could give an impression about her thoughts, beliefs, and attitudes. Her comments could also function in opening other ideas parallel to or springing from the discussions in the clippings. How could she organize the materials to compose a picture of her mind and her relating to the world, a picture that her grandchildren could comprehend of her as a human being?

Lena decided on a system of loose-leaf binders with transparent pockets. Photographs and other delicate items could be placed inside the protective pockets, along with some notes Lena wrote about her responses to the pictures. If she found brief passages in books that resonated with her, she copied them along with her responses and placed them in the binder. Magazine articles that held a personal meaning for her would find their places in the binder. At times, she would scribble a personal message to one of the grandchildren in relation to a particular article. If, on a given day there had been a specifically meaningful event or interaction with others, she would record that, adding her own feelings and interpretations. All entries were arranged in chronological order, but there were days for which she made no entries.

When the first ring binder was almost filled, Lena showed it to her friends. They thought it was a marvelous idea and asked her if she would be willing to get them started on their own binder projects. Word got around and Lena was asked by senior citizen centers to introduce her idea to their members and conduct monthly group meetings around the "Legacy Binders" project.

The project would not qualify as an earth-shaking invention and that was not what Lena had in mind. Lena had never considered herself to be talented or creative. As she searched for a solution to her wishes of leaving to her grandchildren a meaningful reflection of her life, she evaluated available options and modified one according to her intentions. It is an example of the "little c" type creativity described earlier (Gardner, 1993) that is often operating outside the limelight of the "big C" type creativity but contributes so much to the daily lives of those who practice it.

CHAPTER 6

The Challenges of Single Parenthood

Whether through divorce or through widowhood, single parents face double difficulties and responsibilities. They are required to handle twice the strain with half the resources usually available in two-parent families. In traditional families, both parents assume responsibility for children's health, education, behavior development, and emotional adjustment. Concerns over job-related difficulties, finances, disappointments in friendships, and other setbacks can be shared. In single-parent families, all responsibilities fall upon one who is already stressed by emotional adjustments to the loss or absence of the other spouse. Single parents face the challenge of combining several roles as they confront financial and nurturing responsibilities that in most cases previously were shouldered by two parents.

The Disappearance of the Traditional Family

The so-called traditional family, dating back to the 1940s, seems like a myth today. Single-parent families are now considered to be significant components of society. Since 1970, there have been fewer than 20% of American families with the father being the traditional provider, the mother being a homemaker, and their two children attending school. Family statistics showed that in 2005, of all children in the United States younger than 18 years, 23% were living with a single mother and 41% of those were living in poverty (U.S. Census Bureau, 2005).

Lack of financial resources is not the only challenging change in the transition to single-parenthood; additional responsibilities result in a drastic reduction of free time for rest or personal development as the task load increases. A single parent's social life is virtually nonexistent. The fact of being unable to physically and mentally withdraw from the children for any significant period of time greatly increases the level of stress the single parent is experiencing. And it is not surprising to find that stress undermines parenting efficiency more in single-parent families than in two-parent homes (Conger, Patterson, & Ge, 1995). The increased stress without opportunity for relief might well be a contributing factor in the often cited finding that single parents are more likely than parents in two-parent homes to use harsh discipline measures (Simons & Johnson, 1996).

In dissolved marriages or in families with an absent spouse, direct parental childcare suffers when single parents work outside the home in order to pay the bills. And when parents are ill prepared for family breakup, their bitterness and acrimonious behaviors lead to troubled children. These factors increase the level of difficulties single-parent families face.

Another factor contributing to the rising numbers of single-parent families can be seen in the significant number of births to unmarried women in the United States. About one in three births in the United States occurs outside of marriage (Ventura, Martin, Curtin, Menacker, & Hamilton, 2001). Discussions of unmarried motherhood have generally focused on teenagers; more recently, though, an increase of births among unmarried women aged 20 years and over has been observed. Examining the increase of birth rates among unmarried women since 1980, 61% have been recorded for teens, 69% for women aged 20 to 24 years, 67% for 25- to 29-year-olds, and 82% for women 30–34 years of age.

Analysis of data from the Panel Study of Income Dynamics (PSID), describing a total of 2,613 births to 1,615 women for the 10-year period from 1980 to 1990, revealed that the economic status of older, single mothers was closer to that of teenage mothers than to that of married child-bearing women their age (Foster, Jones, & Hoffman, 1998). Despite this difference in economic status, studies have reported that about half of recent births to unmarried women were the results of planned pregnancies (Abma, Chandra, Mosher, Peterson, & Piccinino, 1997).

Similarly, data from the 1995 National Survey of Family Growth regarding correlates of planned and unplanned childbearing among unmarried women showed that although nonmarital births were less likely to be planned than marital births, nearly half of all births to unmarried women were planned. Of those, 54% occurred among cohabiting women and 39% among single women. Overall, college-educated mothers made up a very small proportion (less than 5%) of all unmarried births (Musick, 2002). As hypothesized, Blacks and Hispanics had higher rates of planned and unplanned unmarried births than Whites.

Factors that make childbearing outside marriage more acceptable relative to other options include low marriage expectations, nontraditional attitudes about family life, and poor career prospects. However, statistics about nonmarital childbirth are misleading because a significant percentage (almost 40%) of recent unmarried births occurred within cohabiting couples (Bumpass & Lu, 2000) and—strictly speaking—these would not fall into the category of single-parent families.

"Welfare Motherhood"—A Self-Fulfilling Prophecy?

Selena, a bright, beautiful girl, grew up in a small Midwestern town. She did not remember much of her father, who had died when Selena was almost 3 years old. Her mother remained a widow and applied for public assistance in order to provide for her son, Lester, and for little Selena. The Aid for Dependent Children (AFDC) program supplied the basic necessities of life but did nothing for the self-esteem of its recipients. The "welfare mothers" and their children faced the judgmental attitudes of their communities and expectations of teachers and others that predicted trouble. Those expectations—whether overtly or covertly expressed—serve as self-fulfilling prophecies, generating or exacerbating the anticipated difficulties (Amato, 1991).

Although Selena was bright and diligently completed her homework assignments, her teachers did not encourage her to excel. She did not have many friends, perhaps because she was beautiful—but she was also part of a "welfare family." To compensate for the lack of friends, Selena immersed herself watching television in her free time. Life was confusing to Selena; there seemed to be two distinctly different parts to it. Life in her small community had little connection or transition to life on television. The television shows became real life to her, waiting for her to explore. After high school graduation, at the age of 18, Selena packed her few decent-looking clothes along with her meager childhood savings and took off for New York City. She told her mother that she was going to be a model.

Her mother, no longer being eligible for AFDC assistance, moved to a larger town about 60 miles from home. She managed a meager existence for herself by performing manual labor, such as cleaning stores and offices. About 12 years after she had left for New York City, Selena returned to her mother's home—pregnant and without a husband. Selena did not offer much information about her years in the big city. However, she insisted that her pregnancy was a planned one. She had decided to have a child and out of the group of people she was acquainted with she had chosen a good-looking man with above average intelligence to be the father of her child. The man did not know about her pregnancy and she refused to give his name to anyone. After the birth of her baby daughter Selena applied for AFDC. One of the self-fulfilling prophecies of her childhood had come true: She had become a "welfare mother," just like her mother had been.

Studies using data from the National Longitudinal Survey of Youth (NLSY) collected over a period of 14 years focused on a sample of 594 women, for whom detailed information regarding AFDC and non-AFDC income was available. Five years after they left AFDC, great diversity in the economic status of the young women was observed (Meyer & Cancian, 1998). Some of them did not continue receiving welfare payments during the 5 years, but nearly four fifths of the women received a means-tested transfer at some time and almost one fifth of the women remained poor.

These and other studies "appear to support the dire prediction that the destiny of a significant portion of single-parent families headed by mothers is one of persisting poor socioeconomic and distress-ridden existence, unless the mother enters into [another] marriage" (Maass & Neely, 2000, p. 16). But Selena was determined not to be one of the fifth that remained poor and she did not want her daughter to repeat her own childhood experience despite her situation. She and her daughter lived with her mother, living on her mother's small income and Selena's welfare payments. With Medicaid assistance, she availed herself of counseling and applied for education grants. Selena's daughter was not yet 5 years old when Selena proudly started her job as paralegal in a local law firm.

As Selena's story demonstrates, single mothers do not have to succumb to the pessimistic outlook but can explore alternative solutions that will lead to increased independence and self-sufficiency. Rather than look for marriage as the solution, for many single mothers additional education or job-skills training represents opportunities for future independence (Sandfort & Hill, 1996).

Single Fathers and Their Psychological Well-Being

The great majority of fathers live with their biological children for some period of time following birth, either in marital or cohabiting unions (Bumpass & Lu, 2000). In a longitudinal study of data from the PSID, a sample of 1,388 men who became fathers throughout the period from 1968 to 1997 were followed from the start of their co-residential relationships with their children to the termination of that co-residence (Gupta, Smock, & Manning, 2004). The sample also included 100 fathers who were cohabiting at the time their first biological children were born. The transitions from co-residential to nonresidential father occurred in three stages: the 1970s showed little change, but from the late 1970s through the late

1980s, a sustained increase in transitions was observed, with a leveling off during the 1990s.

The investigators observed that the probability of nonresidence decreased significantly with the fathers' and mothers' increase in income. Thus, larger incomes appeared to decrease the risk of family disruption. In addition, women's incomes also seemed to have a stabilizing effect on the family structure. If the stress of limited financial security is associated to some degree with family disruption, the resulting single parents are likely to experience a double load of distress.

In most single-parent families the mother is the head of household; however, the number of single fathers in the United States has grown by about 25% during the years from 1995 to 1998. This increase in the number of single-father households appears to be a reflection of the changes in attitudes of courts and society in general (Bart, 1999). In the past, fathers could assume custody only in cases where the mother had been declared unfit to mother. Now fathers may seek custody of their children for other reasons. They may want to maintain their family or the children might prefer to reside with them (Greif, 1995).

Because, traditionally, mothers were considered to be primary caregiver to children and fathers took on the provider role for the family, each one as a single parent has to shoulder new responsibilities and learn new skills. In addition to their job skills, single fathers have to add homemaking and childrearing skills to their repertoire. Similarly, single mothers, whose career orientation may not have been strongly developed in the past, may now have a need to acquire job skills in addition to their homemaking responsibilities. Research has shown that men, once they have assumed physical custody of their children, are quite able to adapt to the tasks of the primary parent role (DeMaris & Greif, 1992).

The burden of carrying out the duties and responsibilities of a single parent can be eased by being connected to and making use of support networks. A study of network support among a sample of married and single-parenting mothers and fathers showed that men were more likely than women to make use of the offered support (Heath & Orthner, 1999). Divorced, middle-income custodial fathers are also more likely to date, to cohabit with intimate partners, and to remarry than custodial mothers are. One of the reasons for this difference can be seen in the fact that middle-income men have greater chances in the dating and marriage market than custodial mothers. Another reason may perhaps be that men, although taking their fatherly responsibilities seriously, may not be involved to the same degree of intensity in the lives of their children as custodial mothers are. The fathers may be more willing to delegate some of the parenting tasks to helpful others.

Exploration of the meaning of fathering to men and the effects of it on their lives and their children's lives is linked to the men's motivation for fathering (Marsiglio, Day, & Lamb, 2000). The way a man sees himself in the position of father influences his behavior. His role identity as father determines his parental actions and involvement. According to some evidence, instead of conceptualizing themselves with multiple identities related to the father role, fathers hold a generalized concept of "self-in-role" (Futris & Pasley, 1997). Men see themselves as fathers, not as nurturers, caretakers, and so on. They do not perceive nurturing and caretaking behaviors as distinct from the generalized concept of being a father.

Interesting results were obtained in a study using data from the National Survey of Families and Households involving 844 fathers who were married and had at least one biological child below the age of 19 years in the household at Time 1 (1987–1988). At Time 2 (1992–1994), 729 fathers were still married, but 135 fathers had divorced or separated (Shapiro & Lambert, 1999). Out of this group, 33 fathers had the child living with them while 82 fathers' children had a different residence.

The findings at Time 2 showed that—as would be expected—fathers whose children were not living with them reported significantly poorer relationship quality than fathers who resided with their children, regardless of marital status. An unexpected finding was that divorced fathers who had their children living with them reported a better relationship quality with them than fathers who had remained continuously married. However, the psychological well-being of the fathers who had sole responsibility for their children was more compromised than that of any of the other fathers. While those fathers were rewarded with a better parent–child relationship quality, they paid for it with increased depression.

Brad, a 37-year-old separated father of two sons, was referred to therapy by a friend and coworker. Brad's depression interfered with his work performance. His position of foreman with a 12-man mechanics crew carried significant responsibilities. Brad's first words were: "I want you to help me get my wife back." Brad and Shirley had been married about 10 years but had separated 2 months before. Although Brad's job was in the city, they had decided to raise their two boys in the country, which amounted to more than 2 hours' driving time each day for Brad. With that his workdays stretched to 10 or 11 hours and he was tired when he arrived home. Not much time was left for the family, although he tried to make up for it on weekends, spending time with his sons.

Shirley started to work part-time at a restaurant when the boys were in school. Most of her work as waitress was during lunchtime, but she had to commit herself to working two evenings a week. One of the evenings had to be on the weekend, the owner of the restaurant insisted. Brad agreed to take care of the boys on those evenings. Things settled into a routine; the restlessness or boredom Shirley seemed to experience prior to her work at the restaurant resolved and her mood was more even now than before.

Occasionally, Shirley had mentioned that their sex life was not all she had expected but during the last couple of years she appeared calmer and did not complain about anything that Brad could remember. Then, on her birthday, she asked for a divorce. Brad was stunned; he tried to promise her that he would do whatever she wanted to improve the marriage. But Shirley was determined; as she said, he had neglected her earlier requests for change, and now it was too late. She wanted Brad to move out of their home. Brad complied, hoping that dating and courting Shirley would make her change her mind. He thought therapy could help him in his pursuit to romance his wife.

But his hopes were not based in reality. Shirley was not only determined to divorce him, but also had become engaged in an affair with a somewhat younger man she had met at the restaurant. Brad was angry; he had temporarily moved in with his parents, which meant he was about 45 minutes away from his sons. But he was closer to work and he thought his parents' home was a better place for the boys when they came for their weekend visits than the tiny place he could afford to rent in the small town near their home.

After the divorce Brad decided to look for a small house near his sister, who with her family lived much closer to the city. This would also be closer to his place of work. It would be helpful to have family close by. Brad's parents were planning to move to Florida for their retirement. During his marriage to Shirley, Brad did not have much contact with his sister beyond the yearly Christmas holiday visits and similar family get-togethers. Shirley was not one to keep close contact with the family. But if he moved closer to his sister's family, Brad could help them out when they needed somebody to babysit their children in the evening and his sister's children could be playmates for his sons during their visitation. This move would be beneficial for all.

About 6 months later Brad received an urgent phone call at work from his older son, informing him that he had called 911 when the two boys found their mother passed out in the living room. The ambulance was on the way. Shirley had been drinking; her relationship with the young man had not proceeded the way she had hoped. It was not the first time that she had been intoxicated but it was the first time she had passed out. Brad and Shirley decided it would be best if she entered a residential treatment facility and Brad would temporarily move back into the house, to take care of their sons.

The essential skills for functioning in the role of primary caretaker can be developed by female or male parents. Studies have compared single mothers and single fathers regarding time spent with their children and spent in performing household tasks. In situations where mothers were absent, fathers showed increased levels of involvement (Hall, Walker, & Acock, 1995). As part of a larger study, investigators looked at different categories of family structure for effects of fathers' time spent with their children and the children's grades (Cooksey & Fondell, 1996). The data showed that single fathers were quite involved in their children's lives and they engaged more in a variety of activities than did fathers in more traditional family settings. However, in this study, children from single-father households seemed to achieve poorer grades in school despite the higher level of paternal involvement.

In Brad's case, he got to spend more time with his sons than originally anticipated. Although he returned to his house after Shirley's release from the treatment center, there were several relapses over time. On recommendation of his attorney, Brad filed for temporary sole custody of his sons and moved them to his new home. Shirley agreed that they needed to sell the house they all had lived in. Her treatment episodes had been expensive and Brad could no longer maintain two households. When Shirley approached him with suggestions for reconciliation, Brad returned to his therapist to discuss his decision of remaining single and filing for custody of his sons.

More than a year passed. Brad's decision to move close to his sister's family had been a wise one. The children got along well together and the support from his sister was appreciated when Brad had to be at work. At the same time, his presence helped his sister and her husband get away occasionally. Brad had enrolled in some cooking classes and was now able to prepare nutritious meals for his family. Actually, he enjoyed the cooking class because it made him feel creative. He had progressed from just strictly following the recipes to allowing himself to experiment. He also made some friends among his classmates. One of his male classmates was interested in photography and had given Brad some tips about taking pictures of his sons. Another development was that Brad had started dating a young widowed mother of four children. Cindy was as "cute as a button," as Brad described her, and they got along well.

Brad seemed to handle everything quite well, so why did he return to therapy at this time, his therapist wondered. The relationship between Brad and Cindy had progressed to a point where a commitment was indicated. In preparation for this session, Brad had listed and rated his concerns about the situation, as he had learned to do in his earlier therapy. Brad explained some of his problematic ratings in the areas of children, money, vacation, meals, and responsibilities.

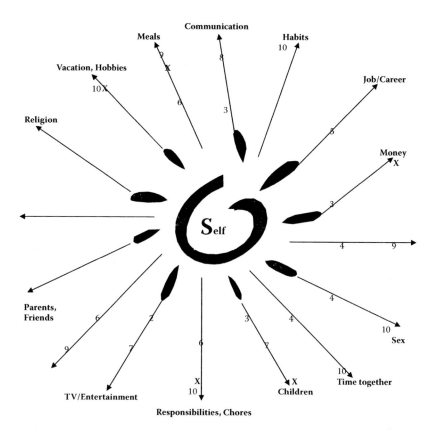

Directions: Please rate [X] the life areas on the scales above according to the level of difficulty or stress they impose on your relationship. Consider "1" as light (hardly any stress) and "10" as severe (hardly bearable). "5" or "6" are points where you would want to start doing something about it. Please add any areas that are important in your life but are not named on any of the scales.

Figure 6.1 Interpersonal growth scale (IGS).

From discussions with Cindy, Brad had understood that she was not considering moving her family in case she was to get married again. One of her children was a "special-needs" child and she felt that he was currently in an optimum placement for his condition. Also, an expansion of living space in her house could be accomplished by converting the basement into additional bedrooms or family recreational space. On the other hand, Brad did not think another move to a different area and different schools would be advantageous for his sons; they had—with the help of his sister's family—adjusted to the move from their original home. And although it might be a minor setback, the drive from Cindy's home to his job site would take about the same time it took him to commute from his previous home to his work. Brad still remembered the toll it took on his first marriage. He doubted that Cindy would reconsider her decision of remaining in her house.

With a somewhat sheepish grin, Brad added that Cindy was the absolute ruler of her kitchen. Now that he had found pleasure in creating meals, Brad was afraid she would not be happy sharing her domain with him. Money and vacation were items that would be problematic with the size of the resulting family; they would have six children to think of. Although he felt guilty about his concerns, Brad thought he knew himself well enough to hesitate in shouldering that financial burden at this time in his life. Aside from his concerns for the well-being of his sons, Brad considered many of the reasons against a commitment to Cindy as selfish on his part; yet he felt relieved that he could express his thoughts, doubts, and feelings to somebody neutral and nonjudgmental.

The therapist thought there might be a hesitation about commitment on Brad's part because he was afraid of losing his view into another world. Brad agreed that even with the increased responsibilities as a single parent, he felt younger and more curious about things. He and his sons had explored activities at the local community library and they were excited about the options for learning and entertainment available to them. Because of the responsibilities both he and Cindy had, Brad was afraid that the toll of survival within a commitment to Cindy would stifle his newly found curiosity. Brad knew that under the impact of the complexity of their combined families he would succumb to the pressure and his life would be much the same as before—even though Shirley and Cindy were entirely different women.

As clients attempt to expand the range of application of their newly learned problem-solving skills, their focus may shift to various areas. Brad, the client discussed here, remembered that in the past he had encountered difficulties addressing the most significant problem area. With the new situation demanding decisions, Brad avoided repeating his earlier detour by applying previous learning to prepare himself for the current decision-making process. Remembering achieving desired results in earlier problem-solving attempts, clients have a tendency to return to the same therapeutic relationship when other parts of their lifestyles require attention.

Single Mothers and Their Psychological Well-Being

Similar to single co-residential fathers, single mothers are also considered to be at greater risk for psychological problems and for ineffectual parenting practices than are married mothers. A Canadian study, based on interviews with 518 single mothers and 502 married mothers in Ontario, revealed that single mothers were almost three times more likely than married mothers to have suffered from a major depressive disorder (Davies, Avison, & McAlpine, 1997).

This finding seems to be in contradiction to an earlier observation (Brown, Andrews, Harris, Adler, & Bridge, 1986) that single mothers with children were less likely to state that they were depressed than married women with children. The investigators explained that in their study the single mothers had effective supportive networks in the community. This might indicate that the actual presence of a spouse is not sufficient to buffer the effects of a stressful situation, especially since some spouses might be ineffective in reality.

Although most people would initially think that the adjustment to being a single parent would be easier for women than for men, at times single mothers feel that they are judged more harshly than single fathers for their children's deprivation of the other parent. Single mothers also feel they receive less support from others than single fathers do. As Lori, a divorced mother of two young sons remembered, the people in her church congregation were very supportive of the widowed father of two little daughters. The man's "wife had died of cancer and the whole congregation rallied to his side, especially the women. They all wanted to help and comfort him and invited him for dinner....After my divorce, nobody seemed to want to comfort me" (Maass & Neely, 2000, p. 215).

Temporary Single Parenthood

Perhaps even more difficult is the adjustment to temporary single parenthood, as can occur in families where one member is deployed in a military mission, or where a parent is institutionalized for some time due to a serious, long-term illness or because of incarceration. Although officially still married, the parent remaining with the children struggles with many of the difficulties that other single parents are confronted with. In such cases two periods of adjustment may be involved as the family members are looking forward to being reunited at some point in the future. Attempts at discipline and family management by the remaining parent might occur in an uncertain or ambivalent manner while waiting for the return of the temporarily displaced spouse. The case of Brad before is an example of temporary single parenthood, such as Brad experienced when Shirley, the mother of his sons, was confined to a residential treatment facility. In his case, what were periods of temporary single parenthood eventually took on permanent status.

Karen, the young mother of a little girl, also believed that her situation was a temporary one. Karen had been employed as a nurse's aid in a residential treatment facility for chemical dependency when she became emotionally attached to Joe, a patient. She thought she could help him overcome his addiction. A few months after his discharge from the treatment program they were married. Joe was unemployed and Karen's salary from her job was not sufficient for the two to live on, which led to what Karen hoped would be a temporary residence with Joe's mother. Karen was not suspicious that Joe spent so much time in what she thought was "job hunting." And even though Joe did not obtain employment, he did not seem overly concerned about that.

One day Karen was confronted with the fact that Joe had been arrested for armed robbery and possession of cocaine. That explained his lack of concern about not finding employment. Joe was in jail when Karen discovered that she was pregnant. Searching for options she turned to her mother-in-law. Karen's first impulse had been abortion or possibly giving the baby up for adoption. Joe would be devastated, his mother responded; he loved children and having a child would motivate him to straighten out his life.

After her daughter was born, Karen returned to her job at the treatment center. Scraping together the money for gasoline to visit Joe in prison about 180 miles away was difficult. In addition, there were outstanding debts in Joe's name for which she, as his wife, was now responsible. On her next visit to the prison Joe informed her that she needed to make a payment of $1,000 to an attorney as retainer. After discussing his case with another inmate who was to be released soon, Joe saw a possibility for filing an appeal on his conviction. But a smart lawyer was needed and the fellow inmate knew of one who would be willing to take Joe's case. Karen tried to tell him that she had no money left over and there were already debts of his that needed to be repaid. Joe refused to listen; he told her it was her responsibility to help him.

While driving home, Karen thought about how cold Joe's behavior toward her had been. He did not even inquire about their daughter. All he was interested in was her obtaining the money for the attorney. It was a rainy evening and Karen felt the anxiety mount in her. In order to make the visit, she had unofficially traded her shift with a coworker and needed to be back for the night shift. She started to cry as she realized the hopelessness of her situation. She was trapped; there was no way out for her and her little daughter. How long could they stay with Joe's mother, who would start resenting them if Karen could not get enough money together for Joe's lawyer? It was all Karen's fault, first for believing in Joe and then for confiding in and believing his mother when Karen was pregnant. Not only had she made a mess of her own life, she had ruined her child's life as well.

Karen woke up in a hospital bed. Apparently, her car had skidded off the road and hit a tree. She was not seriously hurt beyond a broken shoulder, but she seemed to be in a state of shock because she did not respond to questions except for her name and address. The hospital personnel considered the possibilities of a panic disorder or even suicide because her injury did not seem to explain her unresponsiveness. A psychotherapist was called in for consultation.

When Karen realized that the hospital was on the outskirts of her hometown, she decided to communicate with the therapist. They did not discuss directly the possibility of a suicide attempt then and, as it turned out, Karen did suffer from panic attacks. She disclosed her thoughts as she remembered them while driving to the therapist. There was especially one recurring thought she remembered: She did not want to drive up to the prison to see Joe anymore, not ever! But how could she continue living with his mother? The therapist agreed to continue seeing Karen on a pro bono basis until her situation was resolved in some way.

Karen's situation did not improve for quite some time. She had lost her job because she had not informed anybody about trading her shift. Karen realized that, perhaps due to her panic disorder, she tended to make decisions fast, in order to relieve the anxiety without weighing the possible consequences. Now, exploring her options with her therapist, Karen temporarily moved with her daughter into a homeless shelter for women with small children. She was determined to divorce Joe and therefore could not remain with her mother-in-law. Her next step was to contact vocational rehabilitation services, which enabled her to obtain financial assistance for studies at a vocational college and for continuing therapy.

For living expenses Karen applied for help to the Temporary Assistance to Needy Families (TANF) program that determined lifetime limits of about 5 years' maximum on welfare payments. The majority of recipients in this program were obviously single mothers, who still felt society's stereotypical attitudes about welfare mothers being able-bodied but lazy persons receiving welfare benefits.

A study examining how women on welfare interpreted their own and others' welfare use revealed that the respondents were aware of their stigmatized status and tended to blame the social structure, the welfare system itself, or fate for their reliance on welfare benefits (Seccombe, James, & Battle Walters, 1998). Interestingly, when discussing the reasons for other women's dependence on financial aid, the respondents were in agreement with the opinions of society at large.

Unlike the women in the preceding study, Karen accepted the full responsibility for her predicament and, as she discussed with her therapist, felt obligated to make the most of the opportunities society was offering her so that, in turn, she could help others with the taxes she would pay in the future as an income-earning citizen. Her therapist had used the word "dignity" in one of their sessions and Karen had looked it up in the dictionary for the correct meaning. Karen wanted to have the sense of being worthy and to conduct herself accordingly. That was her goal for herself and for inspiring her daughter. After graduation from a 2-year program in secretarial and bookkeeping training combined with data entry skills, Karen was able to secure an entry-level position with a progressive local pharmaceutical company that provided childcare services for its employees.

Another decision point arose for Karen when Joe, her now ex-husband, asked her to relieve him of all child support payments in exchange for staying out of her and her daughter's life forever. Within 1 year he would be eligible for parole and he wanted to be relieved of financial obligations from the marriage. Karen was tempted to agree immediately to Joe's request. There was nothing she wanted more than to be rid of him and with her training she could provide for herself and her daughter in a very modest way. Besides, judging by Joe's previous behavior, he would probably never pay anything toward their daughter's living expenses anyway. But did she have the right to make that decision? What would happen to her daughter if Karen could not work for some reason or died before the child was independent? At the least, she would have a legal right to help from her father. "I would not want to relinquish my child's rights to assistance" was Karen's reasoning for rejecting Joe's request and risking his bothering her again in the future.

About a year later Karen took another step in her process of exploring and sorting out options. During her training she had been especially interested in the area of bookkeeping. Now she was considering the possibility of working toward a degree in accounting. In fact, her employer would even reimburse her for part of her tuition, provided her grades were acceptable.

Karen demonstrated significant progress in her willingness to make her own decisions and accept the responsibility for the consequences. She had learned to overcome her haste in decision making and instead considered alternatives and their possible outcomes. For individuals who have difficulty making decisions and also tend to experience anxiety, situations that require them to decide on important issues are fraught with rising anxiety. Deciding implies a commitment to a specific path. By choosing one alternative, the individual rejects or loses the other options.

The self-imposed pressure of having to make the correct decision increases the anxiety level with every back and forth until people pick one possibility, just to get it over with and end the state of anxiety. But once she had overcome her anxiety reaction toward decision making, Karen could accept that there was not just one solution to a problem; most situations present several options for consideration.

Parenting Styles

Most people's parenting styles are influenced by the type of parenting they experienced in their childhood; they could be in total agreement with their parents' practices or they might be in opposition to the type of parenting they received. As parenting beliefs are transmitted across generations, they influence the childrearing practices of generations. But, as mentioned previously, in some cases, parents employ parenting styles that are quite different from those that their own parents demonstrated. Whether this change is an expression of rebellion against their parents' way of raising them or not, it is at times perceived by the older generation as a rebellious act and they may feel offended when observing this difference.

Wanting to explore how parenting beliefs and practices are associated with adolescents' beliefs regarding effective discipline and the impact of parenting on child development, Simons and colleagues (Simons, Beaman, Conger, & Chao, 1992) contacted 451 two-parent families with sons and daughters attending the seventh grade in public or private schools in North Central Iowa. One of the requirements for inclusion into the study was that the family contained a sibling within 4 years of the age of the seventh grader.

Measures used by the investigators focused on mothers' and fathers' supportive parenting behaviors as well as on supportive and harsh discipline practices the parents had experienced from their parents while growing up. Expectations that socialization of parenting beliefs varies by gender of the child were supported: Boys seemed to be attuned more to discipline and girls more to the consequences of parental involvement. However, expectations that boys derive their discipline beliefs mainly from the behaviors of their fathers and girls obtain their beliefs about the impact of parenting from the behaviors of their mothers were not confirmed. It was found that discipline beliefs of boys were linked to harsh disciplinary behaviors of both parents. Similarly, girls' beliefs were associated with supportive parenting behaviors from both mothers and fathers.

These findings indicate that different aspects of their parents' roles may influence adolescent boys and girls, but in constructing their own parenting beliefs, they use both parents as sources of information. Applying these findings to situations where a previously two-parent family has been transformed into a one-parent family, children's parenting beliefs may become confusing to them and the now single parent may need to perhaps modify existing parenting practices.

Parenting styles are important in two-parent families but even more so in single-parent families because the effects of the ways the one parent directs the family are not buffered or diffused by the parenting approach of the other. In general, for adolescents as well as for younger children, an authoritative parenting approach has been associated with more positive outcomes than other parenting styles, especially with regard to the children's self-concept (Dekovic & Meeus, 1997) and development of internal locus of control (McClun & Merrell, 1998).

Authoritarian parenting styles, on the other hand, have been linked to children's poorer grades in school and negative self-concept (Steinberg, Darling, Fletcher, Brown, & Dornbusch, 1995; Steinberg, Lamborn, Darling, Mounts, & Dornbusch, 1994). Children raised by permissive or indulgent parents also show negative outcomes, as they are less likely to assume responsibility, are less independent, and at times exhibit more aggressive behavior.

The most consistently negative outcomes are linked to the patterns of uninvolved or neglecting parenting style. The "psychologically unavailable" parent, perhaps due to being overwhelmed by other problems or due to disinterest in the child, may be confronted with impulsive or antisocial and less competent children who are less achievement oriented in school (Lamborn, Mounts, Steinberg, & Dornbusch, 1991).

Another aspect of parenting, parental involvement in education and extracurricular activities, is important for children and the lack of this involvement has been associated with children's conduct problems (Frick, Christian, & Wooton, 1999). For the already stressed single parent, this is an area that often becomes neglected due to conflicting time demands.

Parents who are looking back on their own happy childhood might adopt their own parents' parenting styles, as mentioned earlier. It seems logical to implement philosophy and skills that have worked well in the past and apply them to the present. Yet, today's children are not necessarily carbon copies of their parents.

Sarah's expectations for parenthood were based on her own childhood. She patterned her parenting skills after what she remembered from her parents. As hypothesized by some investigators (Simons, Beaman, Conger, & Chao, 1993), parents who themselves had been raised by supportive parents will most likely adopt their parents' supportive style; Sarah followed this trend with her adopted daughter, Grace. In her childhood, Sarah had been a cheerful girl who liked to please her parents and others around her. Her school grades were quite good and she demonstrated no behavior problems. During her college years Sarah succeeded in a field of studies that was traditionally occupied by men.

Sarah's marriage to Tim remained childless and they decided to adopt a child, Grace, a beautiful little girl. Sarah's beliefs that trust and acceptance were the best techniques to raise a well-adjusted child were combined with Tim's more authoritarian approach. Although Grace seemed to be more headstrong than her mother may have been, no major difficulties emerged. During the marriage, however, Sarah discovered some aspects about Tim's sexual attitudes that she could not accept and that led to divorce when Grace was about 11 years old. Tim moved to another state and Sarah became the custodial parent. Sarah's liberal parenting style was not counterbalanced anymore by her husband's authoritarian approach; this resulted in a degree of freedom for Grace that she was not ready and mature enough to handle. Minor difficulties developed, but Sarah still wanted Grace to develop responsibility on her own.

Sarah started to date again and shared some of her experiences with Grace. The boundaries between parent and child became vague. Grace became more of a friend and confidant to her mother than a daughter. Their enmeshed relationship assumed a psychologically and emotionally intrusive nature. At 15 years of age Grace felt entitled to the privileges of adulthood without assuming its responsibilities. Sarah realized that her parenting style was ineffective and she sought advice from friends. The situation escalated to crisis proportions when Sarah attempted to integrate her friends' advice into her own practices. Grace rebelled in confusion and anger. Finally, the court system stepped in, the recommended counseling came too late, and Grace's placement by the court was inevitable.

Years later Sarah and Grace had another opportunity for rebuilding their relationship. Grace was ready to enroll in college and Sarah—with some help from Tim—assumed the financial responsibility. Sarah was remarried to a widower with grown children. The time was not ripe for conjoint residence with Grace, but they were able to spend holidays together and slowly built a relationship that did not resemble the close mother–daughter connection they may have hoped for or reflect their previous enmeshed family style.

It was a slow process, learning to abstain from blaming, to respect each other, and let go of unhealthy interaction habits. Grace had become a registered nurse. Sarah completely respected Grace's professional choice and judgment. Grace continued to work after getting married and giving birth to a baby daughter. She allowed Sarah to be the grandmother she would have been if their relationship had progressed more smoothly and Sarah happily accepted her new role in her daughter's and her granddaughter's lives.

Opportunities for Growth and Reduced Ambiguity

The impact of family dissolution on the children has been explored, evaluated, and reported in numerous studies. It is not surprising that children suffer the consequences of separation from a parent in various ways. The dissolution of a traditional family unit and the stress associated with that affects all members of these families—parents as well as children. As vulnerabilities develop as result of the family transitions, so can growth opportunities present themselves, which may promote an increased sense of competence and creativity for parents and children.

With the assumption of exclusive responsibility for the care of their children, single parents have an opportunity for reduced ambiguity and contradictions regarding behavioral rules and consequences resulting from the violations of such rules. In intact families, children are often able to use the difference in the parenting styles of two parents to their own advantage. In single-parent families, depending on the parenting style of the main care provider, discipline systems can be established in exact terms where rules and consequences are spelled out clearly, leaving little room for ambiguity and unnecessary arguments. Nora, the widowed mother of three children (see the chapter on widowhood), demonstrated how the ambiguity in their parenting style when her husband was still alive had undermined her authority with the children and made it difficult for her to function as a single parent until she established herself as the head of her family.

The Impact of Values and Beliefs on the Perception of Options

When considering various options, judgment about the feasibility or practicality of the different choices might become clouded by conflicts of underlying values. Individuals might hold some conflicting values within themselves and, in addition, if their beliefs and values are in con- tradiction to those held by significant others in their environment, the decision-making process can become very complicated, indeed. And even when decisions and actions are congruent with the values and beliefs held by the person, the outcome may not be in the person's best interest if beliefs are based on incomplete or misinterpreted experiences.

Curt was shocked when he learned that his wife, Steffi, had been involved in an affair with another man. Infidelity was offensive to his value system and he filed for divorce immediately. There was no possibility for recon- ciliation in his opinion. On the other hand, he also strongly believed that children, especially girls, needed to be in the care of their mothers. Against his attorney's advice to seek sole custody of his two daughters, and even though he missed them deeply, Curt decided that the girls should live with Steffi and be with him every other weekend and on some holidays.

About 2 years later Curt received a call from Child Protective Services, questioning him about the sexual abuse of his older daughter. He was furious;

at first he thought the caseworker was accusing him of the abuse. But apparently the perpetrator was Steffi's boyfriend, who frequently stayed at the home. The caseworker just wanted to know if Curt had any suspicion or knowledge of the situation. Curt vaguely remembered that some time ago the girls had asked him if they could live with him. According to his firm belief that they needed their mother, he had rejected the idea, not even inquiring about the reason for the request. Now, Child Protective Services recommended that Curt take the children to live with him, at least until this crisis was resolved. Steffi had betrayed him twice, Curt ruminated; how was that going to affect his life? It seemed that everybody was trying to take advantage of him.

Recently, he had become attracted to a woman in her mid-30s. Pamela, a divorcée, seemed hesitant about dating. Perhaps she had been hurt in her marriage, Curt reasoned. He told her about Steffi and her infidelity. He also mentioned that he had just undergone a vasectomy, declaring that two children were all he could afford. It was Pamela's birthday; they had dinner in a nice restaurant and later had some champagne in Pamela's home to toast her birthday. It led to sex and Pamela, remembering Curt's vasectomy, did not use any precautions to avoid pregnancy.

Pamela was shocked to find out she was pregnant. She confronted Curt and he admitted that his urologist had not cleared him yet when they had sex. He still had to submit another sample of ejaculate. Pamela tried to discuss the option of abortion. According to his beliefs, Curt told her that abortion was a crime. Preventing conception was one thing, but abortion was murder. Instead, he suggested they get married. His daughters would be excited about the baby. Pamela, however, accused him of deception regarding the status of his vasectomy and blamed him for not considering her feelings. She walked out and wrote him a note, stating that she could not imagine herself living with someone who was so judgmental and inconsiderate of others' opinions and feelings. She refused to see him again.

Weeks went by while Curt tried to contact Pamela without success. Months later he saw her in a department store. When she saw him she put down the item she had obviously been considering purchasing and briskly walked away. It was almost summertime and under her lightweight clothing Pamela looked as slim and trim as he remembered her. Did she have an abortion, Curt wondered. He went to a nearby coffee shop to think. He had wanted to marry her and protect her from committing the sin of aborting the child, but she was too stubborn and probably did not trust his knowledge about raising children. They could all have been a happy family. Pamela could have supervised his daughters along with taking care of the baby.

His thoughts were consumed with what had happened to him—what the two women he had loved had done to him. He never considered the possibility that he could have chosen different actions. Curt was not ready to make the shift from conceiving of himself as a victim of circumstances and of the decisions of others to being an active participant in the events as they occurred in his life. Opportunities for growth can evolve from reconstructions of family systems, as could have occurred in Curt's life. Perhaps out of need in response to the many demands individuals face, their focus may shift to the conception of self, asking, "What are my strengths?" Instead, Curt was still focusing on outside forces for explanations to his disappointments.

Over the period of these events Curt had sporadic interactions with the same therapist. Learning about Steffi's infidelity, Curt decided on a divorce, leaving custody for his daughters in Steffi's hands. Later, when he found out about his daughter's victimization, he returned for another visit to the therapist. Each time as Curt described the situation, the therapist tried to guide Curt toward exploration of Curt's beliefs and how they might have influenced his decisions and the outcome in each of these situations. Although apparently representing strong family values, when applied in a rigid manner to complex situations, these beliefs may not lead to the most desirable outcomes for Curt. But Curt was not about to consider even the slightest change. At the time of his disappointment in Pamela's leaving the relationship, Curt again returned to the therapist, attempting to enlist the therapist's help in contacting Pamela and persuading her not to have an abortion. The therapist explained that professional ethics would not permit approaching an unknown person on behalf of a client and trying to interfere with that person's belief system.

Progressing Beyond the Victim Stance

When family systems disintegrate, in the adjustment to the new circumstances a situational loss can be turned into a learning experience that will eventually lead to other opportunities. Intense focus on losses carries with it the risk that people will view themselves as victims of outside forces and attitudes of victimology might erode the notion of responsibility (Seligman, 1999). People who consider their difficulties to be caused by outside forces tend to expect solutions to come from outside themselves. But progressing beyond the victim stance helps individuals to recognize their strengths and to stretch their abilities in the search for solutions.

Beth's history was one of unfairness, misery, rejection, and helplessness. She grew up as the only girl with two brothers who were favored by her mother. All the attention was focused on them. At an early age Beth had to help with household chores while her brothers were free to roam around their tiny town. Although she did well in school, there was no praise for her good grades. Her grades were unimportant because any funds available for higher education were earmarked for her brothers. When she was old enough to work in the local café during the summers, the money she earned was deposited into the education fund. Beth believed that her father loved her in his own way, but he never stood up to his wife on Beth's behalf.

The café was located on the main highway going through town and truck drivers stopped for snacks or coffee. They were the best source for tips, Beth learned. One of them seemed to arrange for stops along his route repeatedly at the café. Beth was self-conscious when she waited on him because he paid so much attention to her and tried to engage her in conversation. It was flattering to have someone be attentive to her. One day he asked her to marry him. Beth thought he was joking but he meant it. She had just turned 18 and graduated from high school. Beth's mother disapproved; timing was bad for a wedding. Beth's older brother had dropped out of college in the middle of his second year. The money for his tuition had been wasted and soon money for the younger brother's college would be needed. In her first act of open rebellion, Beth eloped with the young man.

They returned to the small town and rented an apartment from the owner of the café. Beth continued to work there even after the birth of her daughter while her husband was on the road. Less than a year later her husband did not return from one of his trips. Beth was afraid he might have been in an accident and contacted her husband's employer, who informed her that her husband had terminated his employment. Beth was pregnant with her son. She never saw or heard from her husband again and finally divorced him.

Beth was forced to apply for public assistance. Her mother told her how embarrassed she was to have a "welfare mother" as a daughter, but she suggested that Beth and her children move into a small bungalow on her parents' property. Beth could help with cleaning and cooking chores in exchange for rent and leftover food for her children. This time Beth was too afraid to rebel; as a victim she could not afford rebellion. She also did not trust her competence in making decisions.

What made the situation difficult for Beth was the way her mother treated her daughter, Mona. Beth's mother found chores for Mona to do and she scolded Mona when she found her playing or sitting with a book, trying to read. Beth's mother displayed less harsh treatment toward Mona's brother. This was a replay of Beth's childhood and youth.

There were times when Beth encouraged Mona to read and spend time on her schoolwork only to encounter her mother's criticism. Her mother reminded her that whatever Beth studied had been a waste. She could have worked more around the house or in the local store to contribute money toward the family funds. Instead, Beth got married to a "no-good" man and had children. If they let Mona have time to read and play, she would end up as Beth did—or worse. In her mother's opinion, the women's movement from long ago stood for a "bunch of nonsense."

When Beth looked at Mona she was filled with guilt feelings. It did not seem possible to raise her daughter in this environment without harming her. Beth was a frequent visitor at the town's small public library; it was her sanctuary. Although she did not have much time to spend there, she always felt better just being in the presence of all those books. She confided in the female librarian, telling her how she and her children were financially unable to live on their own because Beth had no training beyond high school. The librarian introduced Beth to college catalogues and information about scholarships and entrance exams.

In her limited spare time Beth studied materials relevant to the Scholastic Aptitude Test (SAT). It took her about a year until she felt ready to take the test. The next step—applying for a scholarship and college admission—was to be determined by her test scores. If her scores were very low, she would try to find fulltime employment or some kind of job training. In the case that her scores were good but not outstanding, Beth would allow herself to retake the test one more time. With very good scores she would be ready to explore how to go about taking the next step.

Beth's scores were indeed outstanding and with the help of the librarian she embarked upon the next steps. She was awarded a scholarship and with the aid of student loans and hope for part-time work, Beth and her children—against her mother's threats of not taking them back in—set out for another town to carve out a meager but stimulating existence. There were hardships to overcome and it took almost 7 years to reach her goal of becoming a librarian. At her graduation, Beth was surrounded by her proud children and the librarian from her hometown. Her mother, widowed by now, did not attend the graduation ceremony and did not respond to Beth's invitation.

Beth marveled at the turn of events. If her husband had lived, she would not have considered a career although secretly, she always wanted to go to college. Being a single mother, she had the option of remaining with her children in her parents' house as her mother's servant, unable to provide her daughter with better opportunities. The other, then seemingly unlikely, option was the one she chose.

Single-Parent Families With Live-in Grandparents

Many single parents rely on their own parents to assist with the tasks of raising children. In fact, 13% of children living with a single parent also have a grandparent living in the household (U.S. Census Bureau, 2005). Reports in the relevant literature seem to focus mostly on single-mother families with live-in grandparents.

By merging data from mother–child files collected during the 1979–2002 waves of the NLSY, information about children living in three-generation households was evaluated with regard to cognitive stimulation effects on the children (Dunifon & Kowaleski-Jones, 2007). The results showed that for White children, living with a single mother and a grandparent increased cognitive stimulation and higher reading recognition scores were obtained, compared to children living alone with a single mother. For Black children, however, co-residence with a grandparent was associated with less cognitive stimulation.

There are many factors in grandparents' co-residence with a single parent that have beneficial impact, such as an increase in the family's financial resources, assistance with the children's supervision, and sharing other family responsibilities. However, studies that have investigated these three-generation living arrangements have mainly focused on the effects of the grandparents' co-residence on issues of child development. Less is known about the effects on the single parent.

When the single parent is considered, the initial focus is on the benefits to the single parent. While the single parent is engaged in the workforce, the grandparent is available for the supervision of the child. The parent is relieved of childcare worries and also does not need to be overly concerned when the job situation requires overtime work. There will always be a responsible adult present to care for the child. But there are occasions for the single parent's reduction in authority in the child's eye; grandparents may seize the opportunity to move into the family nucleus and may compete with the single parent for the position of head of household.

Soon after Sue's father retired from his position, he and his wife sold their house, planning to move into a condominium. This was about the same time that Sue and her little daughter Kara moved back to their hometown. Sue's marriage had ended in divorce after a few years. Her employer valued her intelligence and hard work and offered a significant promotion along with a geographic transfer. Her new place of work was in her hometown. It seemed like a good solution when Sue looked for a house for herself and Kara that her parents were willing to change their plans and move into a small apartment in Sue's house. The space allowed for the parents' privacy while they were also at hand to take care of Kara as needed.

Sue's job required frequent traveling and with this living arrangement she was able to leave on short notice without the need for elaborate planning. Kara was doing well in school and seemed popular among her friends, but Sue observed a shift in authority as Kara interacted with her mother when compared to interactions with her grandmother. Kara seemed to view Sue in the role of an older sister. That was not the only change, however. As a still young and attractive woman, Sue dated several young men. During the times that she was working in town, her parents acted much like they had when Sue was a young girl going out with a boyfriend. Sometimes Sue was annoyed by her parents' questions and suggestions, but she decided that having reliable care for Kara during her absences was more important than being turned into an adolescent again in her parents' eyes.

After the death of Sue's father, the home situation underwent another change. The relationship between Kara and her grandmother increasingly resembled that of a mother–daughter relationship, with Sue existing on the periphery. At the same time, the frequency of her travels increased and she needed her mother's presence in the house even more. Kara was now in high school. Although Sue would have liked to remarry, finding a suitable partner was difficult. Some men were intimidated by her income; others were reluctant to take on three generations of women. In addition, Sue's mother became critical of Sue's dating, insisting that she set a good example for Kara by staying home in the evenings when she was not traveling instead of going out with different men.

The tension between Sue and her mother increased when Sue's younger brother returned to town. Sue knew that Hank had always been her parents' favorite. He was good-looking and charming and everybody forgave him that he did not put much effort into making a living. There had always been situations in which his interaction skills had helped him find jobs. Now he was between jobs, returning from California to make a fresh start in the Middle West. Sue's mother expected her to make space available for her brother. It was only natural that he would stay with them until he had established himself.

Sue was shocked. All her life she had worked hard, wanting to gain her parents' praise but never receiving it while there had been no dearth of praise for Hank. Now her mother put her in a position to provide room and board for her brother for what seemed an indefinite time. She realized she had let the transition from single mother to dependent daughter go on for too long. But her loyalty to her mother required that Sue be careful in her responses to the situation. What options did she have now? There was no immediate solution. Sue sought the help of a therapist to explore with an objective person the various possible solutions to the situation and to choose the one that would be best for her and Kara in the long run.

The therapist started the process of exploration with asking Sue how long in her best estimate she would be able to accommodate her brother. Sue's answer indicated that if she knew it would come to an end, she could go as long as a year, unless unforeseen difficulties arose on Hank's part. One option would be to wait and see how long her brother intended to stay and make decisions then as needed. Another option would be to prepare the circumstances in such a way that Hank's visit could not extend beyond 1 year. "What changes might occur within that time period?" the therapist asked.

Sue replied that Kara would be graduating from high school in a little more than a year; most likely she would attend college away from home. Sue could consider selling her house around that time and possibly invest in a small condominium for herself and Kara's visits during semester breaks. There would have to be a bedroom with bathroom for her mother, which could function as Sue's study or a guest room should her mother decide to retire somewhere else. The money from the sale of the house would be needed for Kara's college expenses, she would explain to her mother and brother.

The plans for putting her house on the market in the relatively near future also would serve as a good reason for Hank to obtain storage space for his belongings in one of the self-storage places around. Whatever he brought with him, there would only be enough space in Sue's house for those items he would need on a daily basis. Sue needed to obtain different estimates for rent spaces and to contact a real estate agent, who would assist her through the different phases of her plan.

An additional option Sue considered was a job transfer to another region of the country. She could inquire within the company about possible openings at the level of her position in other territories the company served. If a suitable opening developed, she could rent the condominium to her brother and mother or, if they did not need it, it could be sold. Perhaps her mother would prefer to move into a retirement place or keep house for Hank until he settled down to start a family. Sue and her therapist knew it would take a while for these options to develop. But they were entirely within reason. A lot depended on Sue's skills and her ability to remain patient for the next year.

Of course, all single parents with live-in grandparent situations are not the same. Probably the single-father family with grandparents would be quite different in the constellation of authority. Parents are more reluctant to take over the rules when living with sons than they are when it is the daughter they are residing with. The case of Larry in the chapter on widowhood is an example. After Larry's wife's sudden death Larry and his two children were on their own. His widowed mother came to live with them for several months until the family was settled in new routines. Larry's mother never intended to stay with her son's family indefinitely and returned to her home at the point when they could manage their lives.

As in many of the other lifestyle changes considered in this book, a situation of single parenthood incorporates many aspects leading to distress and disappointments while there are—perhaps less obviously than in other circumstances of change—also options for increased independence and self-fulfillment.

CHAPTER 7

Caregiving
Putting One's Life on Hold

During the adult life course, situations evolve for many people where they are required to become a caregiver for a spouse or a family member with a disabling physical or mental health condition. The likelihood of this condition to occur is increasing for both men and women. An estimated 44.4 million Americans, age 18 and older, are involved in providing unpaid support to an adult age 18 or older and more than 34 million of the caregivers are taking care of people 50 years of age and older, according to information from the National Alliance for Caregiving (2004). More and more stories appear in the popular press about persons who are faced with the decision of taking care of an impaired family member or placing him or her in a nursing home. A recent account in the AARP Bulletin by Oscar-winning actress Olympia Dukakis (2007) described how, after caring in her home for her mother, who had developed Alzheimer's in her late 80s, she finally came to the decision that her mother would receive better care in a nursing home than Dukakis and her family could provide.

Almost half of all caregivers report spending 8 hours or less per week in caregiving activities and about 17% report providing more than 40 hours of care per week. The average length of caregiving has been estimated as 4.3 years. Interestingly, the number-one place that caregivers consult for information about caregiving is the Internet.

The most likely candidates for the role of caregiver are daughters and daughters-in-law, although the sex of the frail elder makes a difference in the sex of the caregiver. Daughters are four times as likely as sons to care for an older mother but only 40% more likely than sons to help a frail father

(Lee, Dwyer, & Coward, 1993). In general, women live longer than men, which means that there will be more women (mothers and mothers-in-law) requiring help as they age. Therefore, based on the adult children's tendency to provide more help to same-sex parents, it is not surprising that for women there is a much greater likelihood of becoming responsible for such care.

Almost four out of ten caregivers are men, but male caregivers are more likely to work on a full- or part-time basis. Men do become involved in the care of an elder parent, especially if they are unmarried. In cases where both a son and a daughter are sharing the responsibility for older, frail parents, the son's contribution is likely that of financial assistance or instrumental support (home repair or mowing the lawn) while daughters provide physical assistance of daily living, such as dressing, bathing, cleaning, and cooking meals (Stoller, Forster, & Duniho, 1992). But just as women are more likely to be the caregiver with children, they are more likely than men to be in the role of caregiver to aging parents. Overall, female caregivers provide more hours of care and give more intense personal care.

Almost six out of ten caregivers work while providing care, with 62% having had to make adjustments to their work life, such as coming late, leaving early, taking a leave of absence, or terminating their jobs. And a significant number of caregivers are forced to do so from a distance. As people move to different areas in the country where their jobs take them, the elderly parents may be hundreds of miles away. Finding appropriate care from a distance can be a frustrating and often guilt-inducing project. There are organizations that can assist with information and can name resources on a national level. Many of these organizations are accessible on the Internet. For instance, geriatric care managers (GCMs), who are generally nurses or social workers, can assess the needs of an elderly person, make recommendations, and assist in coordinating the level of care needed (Mitchell, 2007). Geriatric care managers in the area of a distant elderly parent can be found through local agencies or through the National Association of Professional Geriatric Care Managers. Perhaps in the future, there will be agencies that coordinate caregiving services with others in different locations.

Those who cannot travel frequently to the location of their elderly family member in need of services might be able to provide services to needy persons in their geographical neighborhood in exchange for coupons in various numbers of service units that can be redeemed toward services provided to their distant elderly parents or relatives. This notion is reminiscent of thoughts and ideas formulated by Ann, introduced in the chapter on widowhood, who lost her two husbands and whose mother was in need of care many hundreds of miles away.

Another aspect in the area of family caregiving can be seen in the growing number of grandparents who take on the responsibility of providing care for grandchildren, who may depend on the elderly to assume the parenting role because of a variety of reasons, such as their parents' death or inability, divorce, military service, or incarceration. For those who have raised one generation, entering the late life period may just be a transition to do more of the same rather than to enjoy a qualitatively different period of life.

Caregiving situations involve relationships that are characterized by dependence, restriction of choices, demands for commitments, and elements of entrapment. These are characteristics that introduce feelings of ambivalence in the participants. As the balance of power and dependency shifts, the level of ambivalence increases and the changes bring forth both gains and losses for all involved. The work entailed in providing for the needs of another can be energy draining but it can also be an expression of love and a way of connecting with others.

Ideologies About Assisting Older Persons

Fundamental elements in the decision of providing assistance to older people are the underlying beliefs individuals subscribe to regarding the responsibility for the welfare of the older population. People who believe that persons are responsible for their own welfare and taking care of their own needs express an ideology of individualism. Needs are regarded as individual problems rather than as social problems in this ideology (Hooyman & Gonyea, 1995; Weiner, 1995).

But not all families with individualistic ideologies adhere to the assumption that providing for the needs of the elderly is the sole responsibility of the needy older person. Familism is the ideology of those who believe that as private, emotionally close units, families have the obligation for the care of their members without outside involvement. Familism in the United States is consistent with the notion that the nuclear family is the ideal. In the good family system, family members, especially women, are able, available, and willing to assume the responsibilities of assisting needy family members (Cowart, 1996). The underlying belief here is that people who are related by blood or marriage are bonded in special, natural relationships (Stein et al., 1998).

Another type of ideology is that of collectivism, which is in agreement with a definition of a good and just society as one that provides for the needs of all its members. Public assistance is viewed as allowing people to age in dignity (Holstein, 1997). Assistance to the elderly and the needy proceeds as a function of the beliefs of individuals who are instrumental and involved in caregiving.

Information collected in interviews from 270 adult residents in the state of Missouri indicated that ideological beliefs were better predictors of normative obligations than were contextual variables (Killian & Ganong, 2002). The participants' age range stretched from 40 to 86 years; half of them were women. The task for the participants was to respond to short vignettes describing older persons in need of assistance and to indicate their level of agreement or disagreement with seven items on a 9-point scale. The items were reflective of beliefs based on the different ideologies.

It was found that participants' adherence to any one of the ideologies did not exclude adherence to the others. Furthermore, judgments regarding the obligation to help were not mutually exclusive. These observations indicated that a higher level of complexity operates at the basis of the investigation than had been expected.

Models of Caregiving Research

Research traditions within the caregiving literature have addressed the processes through which the nonhousing needs of aging parents are resolved by adult siblings. One such approach is the principle of the "shared-functioning kinship system" (Litvak, 1980).

The *shared-functioning kinship system* is a model of caregiving that assumes, as a functional unit, the family members' cooperation and sharing of the caregiving responsibility. This research tradition reveals evidence of gender differences in the amount and type of care provided by the family members. Sons are more likely to provide more infrequent and sporadic assistance, restricted to a few specific tasks, whereas daughters typically are the ones who render regular, predictable services such as transportation, housework, and personal care—termed *routine* assistance (Dwyer & Coward, 1991; Stoller, 1990).

Similarly to the shared-functioning kinship system, another research tradition, the *principle of distribution* (Shanas, 1979) also supports gender differences in parent care. However, this model implies that rather than family members as a unit, one individual maintains the responsibility for the majority of elder care. In other words, much of the needed support is single-handedly provided by one individual, the identified primary caregiver. Within the family network, one individual, most frequently an adult daughter, disproportionately takes on the role of main caregiver; other family members may pitch in with additional support on a regular or occasional basis.

Another research question has focused on how *lineage* may affect decisions of family caregiving allocations (Shuey, & Hardy, 2003). The primacy of consanguineal ties in caregiving relationships may represent a factor less studied in the past. Because caregivers are typically women, in some instances, the husband's parents may be less likely to receive the same degree or quality of care as the wife's parents. Inconsistent results have been found when comparing the effects and relationships in caregiving situations to parents and providing care for parents-in-law (Ingersoll-Dayton, Starrels, & Dowler, 1996; Peters-Davis, Moss, & Pruchno, 1999; Spitze, Logan, Joseph, & Lee, 1994).

Using a sample population from Wave I (1992) of the Health and Retirement Study (HRS), Shuey and Hardy (2003) observed that of couples with surviving parents 11% provided financial assistance to at least one parent and most of them assisted parents only on one side. Furthermore, personal care assistance was given to a parent or parents on one side only—in particular, disproportionately to a parent on the wife's side. It was of interest to note that the majority of couples contributed either one type of help or the other—not both. Financial assistance only was provided by 52% of the couples compared with 38% who supplied personal care assistance only. Overall, the results indicated a matrilineal advantage in the provision of assistance.

When Mothers and Mothers-in-Law Need Help

Marian, an attractive, lively woman in her early 50s is a fulltime professional in the medical field. She and her husband had been married for about 28 years when her husband's widowed mother required assistance after having suffered a stroke. Previous to this Marian's mother-in-law lived on her own in a town several hours driving distance from Marian's home. Marian drove down there to visit once a month. Just about a month after the youngest of Marian's three children left for college, the mother-in-law sustained a hip fracture and temporarily had to move in with Marian and her husband. As Marian stated, she did not even have time to develop an "empty nest" syndrome.

Following rehabilitation from her stroke Marian's mother-in-law moved into an assisted-living facility. Marian spends 3–4 hours weekly, visiting her twice a week to keep her company and check with her needs. There is a daughter living in New York City. She cannot do much for her mother because she is involved with her career. At times, she feels left out but she cannot afford to move back home.

When asked about the impact her mother-in-law's impairment has made on her own life and her plans for the future, Marian thinks for a moment before responding to the question. Marian is familiar with the impact a family member's illness has on the rest of the family. Her brother died of Lou Gehrig's disease and the family was closely connected in the care and concerns for him. Marian's own parents still live independently in her hometown several hours away. How long will they be able to maintain their independent lifestyle? When the time comes that they need assistance, how is Marian going to respond to the situation? Will she have to curtail the time and effort she gives to her mother-in-law in order to provide for the needs of her own parents?

Marian sees herself as a person who follows as life takes her on its journey. She is not a busy planner; she reacts to what life dishes out. There are moments when a little bit of resentment sneaks into her thoughts. Her husband could do more for his mother and thus ease the burden on Marian. But then she reminds herself that she is giving time and care to her mother-in-law because she likes her. Her mother-in-law has been a gracious and loving lady and Marian wants to help her for her own sake and for the feelings she has for her mother-in-law.

During her visits, Marian at times encounters another older lady in the assisted living facility who tries to catch Marian's attention. This lady is the mother of two married sons. She feels neglected because she rarely has visitors. Her sons are too busy with their jobs and their wives do not have a close emotional bond with their mother-in-law, mainly because the mother-in-law had not welcomed them warmly into the family when they married her sons. Some mothers of sons have a difficult time accepting any woman as a wife for their sons; no woman seems to be good enough to take on the part of the mother in the care for her son. When the mother regards her new daughter-in-law negatively as replacing her, she may risk the goodwill of the young woman, which much later might come back to haunt her.

Sally and Andrew had just packed the next to youngest of their children off to college when Andrew's mother, who lived in the same town, needed temporary care after discharge from the hospital for a broken hip. Sally moved her mother-in-law into their home for this convalescence period. She, who worked part-time as cook in a local restaurant, had looked forward to having some time for her quilting pursuits, but since it seemed to be a temporary adjustment, she did not mind. Her mother-in-law's condition improved and she was able to return to her own home with frequent visits from Sally to check on her well-being. There were a few phone calls from the mother-in-law complaining of some moments of unsteadiness, but they passed. However, Sally and Andrew proactively decided to explore various living arrangements for the elderly that provided different levels of care.

It was a wise decision because they could afford to explore the options without the stress of an immediate need. They arrived at a list of acceptable places and rank-ordered them according to the benefits. Then Sally's mother, who lived in another state about 5 hours' driving time from them, needed hospitalization for a back ailment. Sally traveled to be with her mother. Surgery was required to be followed by a period of stay in a convalescent home. However, the physicians doubted her mother's ability to live independently, even after recovery from the surgery. Sally's mother had many friends and did not want to leave her familiar environment. While her mother was in convalescent care, Sally searched from home through various channels for an appropriate placement for her mother. After all, there was still one child to be loved and taken care of. Andrew did what he could to look after their daughter and his mother in addition to his job responsibilities.

As the events developed, both mothers needed to be placed in nursing care within 6 months of one another. The explorations of suitable places done previously by Andrew and Sally paid off. Placement into an acceptable living arrangement could be handled relatively smoothly for all concerned, although it still required a lot of Sally's time and efforts. Her own mother's situation, however, turned out to be quite different. From a distance, her search for an appropriate placement had not been as successful as in her mother-in-law's case. Sally observed on one of her visits that her mother's care left a lot to be desired, which prompted her to renew her search for a more suitable place.

For years it seemed to Sally that she was spending most of her time visiting one or the other nursing home, trying to make both mothers comfortable in their environments. For her own mother, there were several moves necessary to find an adequate place. This, of course, was stressful for her mother and Sally felt guilty about not being able to provide the level of quality care for her mother that she had found for her mother-in-law. Sally described her feelings of that time and the time following both mothers' deaths as an onslaught of anxiety, worry, panic, sadness, guilt, relief, and deep sorrow.

Many caregivers experience relief when their loved ones' pain comes to an end through death and, in turn, feel guilty over having felt the relief in addition to experiencing guilt feelings in connection with the fear of perhaps not having done enough for the comfort of the ailing person. One cannot take on the care and responsibility for another person's well-being without going through these emotions. In Sally's case, she admitted to a double load of guilt feelings. When she was unable to provide for her mother as well as she had for her mother-in-law, there were fleeting moments of resentment toward her mother-in-law, only to be followed by guilt—in addition to the guilt she felt over having let her own mother down by not having provided well enough for her.

Adjustment to the death of the person one had looked after for a significant period of time becomes more complicated for the caregiver than the normal grieving process one expects following the death of a loved one. Irritations and brief moments of resentment experienced and perhaps acted upon during the period of caregiving might come back in the form of guilt feelings to haunt the caregiver.

As mentioned, daughters and daughters-in-law are most generally the caregivers of parents and parents-in-law, even when they work fulltime outside the home and have their own children to raise. The sons who have been the recipients of their mothers' love and pampering do not necessarily reciprocate when it comes time for mothers' eldercare. What happens when the adult children of aging parents divorce? Perhaps the daughter-in-law has provided assistance to her husband's parent or parents. With the divorce, will her caregiving efforts end? As with other caregiving responsibilities, women are not only expected to perform family labor, but they are also supposed to enjoy the act and the closeness it provides (Connidis & McMullin, 2002). The question arises: Where and when do these expectations transition into demands?

It is worth considering that daughters-in-law often feel they have less authority than biological children in the care of their parents-in-law. Even in families where the relationship to mother-in-law is upgraded to "second mother," daughters-in-law still do not consider themselves to have the same decision-making prerogative as biological children have (Merrill, 1997). At the time of transition from mother to mother-in-law there are opportunities to either feel the partial loss of a son or to enjoy the gift of having a daughter who will share the burden of caring for the son and who will provide the connection to the next generation.

Modification of Care-Receiving Expectations

When the need for care of elder family members arises, family expectations and interactions often change in some ways. Parents may modify their global expectations of caregiving activities from their children to reflect the specific realities of their adult children's lives (Peek, Coward, Peek, & Lee, 1998). For instance, parents realize that adult children who have not achieved age-related norms for adult status, such as having secured a reliable position in the work field, marrying, having children, or being financially independent, will be less likely able to provide care for their elderly parents (Bumpass, 1990). On the other hand, caregiving children and grandchildren have to address the requirements for working out a balance between the needs of their dependent elders with those of the whole family (Piercy, 1998).

Caregiving responsibilities arise at different times in the lives of adult children. They can occur when aging parents need help from a son or daughter at a time when their own children are grown or the need may become apparent because of a temporary impairment at a time when the son's or daughter's children are still young and require intensive parental supervision. Whether the existence of children fosters or undermines their parents' caregiving efforts was the question addressed by Gallagher and Gerstel (2001) in a study of household interviews involving 179 married women and 94 of their husbands.

On the factor of wives' employment, 65% of the women were employed and 35% were not employed and not seeking employment. The women's median age was 41 years, ranging from 24 to 89 years. Of the women, 64% had one or more children living in the home, 64% had living parents, and 63% had living parents-in-law.

Evaluating their data to answer the question whether children serve as connectors or as constraints in the caregiving scenario, the investigators found that, overall, for homemakers more than for employed women, their children were more likely to connect than to constrain caregiving. The caregiving efforts of employed women were less affected by the presence of children, but the trend was still more in favor of children's presence as connecting parents into networks of care than as constraining them. Differing effects were observed depending on the characteristics of the child, such as age and gender; however, for the content of this book these details are of a lesser degree of relevance.

Division of Caregiving Responsibilities Among Siblings

How do siblings decide on and divide caregiving responsibilities to their help-requiring frail parents? And how do they perceive the equity of their own assistance and that of their siblings provided to the parents? The deteriorating condition of an aging parent can be a contributing factor in the changes of sibling relationships. A shift in focus from individual life situations to that of a partnership in shouldering the responsibilities for a parent common to all of them can introduce tension among brothers and sisters that have previously related on an emotionally calm basis. Based on their individual goals and temperament, siblings within a given family do not interact with each of the others in exactly the same ways and do not feel the same degree of emotional closeness to each of their siblings. They also do not perceive duties and responsibilities in exactly the same way as the rest of the siblings do.

In previous generations, the role of the caregiver to an aging parent could be the fate of a spinster among the siblings. Today's spinsters, however, may be unmarried not because they have not found a suitable husband but because they value their own career more than marriage. While pursuing their career on a fulltime basis, they can ill afford to spend the time and effort on the care for a frail elderly parent. Thus, the challenge of having to provide parent care may affect the sibling relationships in significant ways and may signal a different phase of relating to one another. It is probably fair to say that many siblings do not assume an equal share of the caregiving responsibilities and instead leave a greater burden for another sibling to shoulder. Siblings who are more involved in the caregiving aspects often experience frustration, anger, and resentment toward the less involved siblings, who, in turn, may feel guilty and defensive. Some of those who are less actively involved in the caregiving process may blame their more involved siblings for "taking over" and making themselves more important in the eyes of their aging parents.

Attempts in Achieving Equity

Using equity theory as a framework for analyzing the processes siblings may employ in their attempts to restore balance in the combined responsibilities to their parents, investigators in a study with 40 group participants focused on two approaches to resolve the conflict (Ingersoll-Dayton, Neal, Ha, & Hammer, 2003). According to equity theory, individuals who experience distress over the unbalanced relationships will attempt equity restoration either by changing their own behaviors and those of the other involved persons (actual equity) or by modifying their perceptions of the situation (psychological equity).

To emphasize the ways caregivers adopt in their attempts to change the behaviors of their siblings or to modify their own perceptions of the caregiving situation, Ingersoll-Dayton and colleagues applied the concept of *forging* equity. Almost two thirds of their sample population described their situation as an imbalanced distribution of labor among siblings. The remaining third regarded their situation as equitable. Some of the individuals who felt they provided more care than their siblings attempted to forge the actual equity by asking their siblings to increase their share or change some characteristics of the caregiving load. Others tried to forge psychological equity by modifying their own perception of the caregiving relationship.

In the process of forging psychological equity, individuals focused on specific factors, such as gender, proximity, employment status, other family responsibilities, and personality characteristics of the siblings. Not surprisingly, siblings tended to assign caregiving tasks to women's domain of expertise, placing higher expectations on sisters than on brothers to provide parent care and especially so if a sister was not married. Employed siblings most often used their work status as an explanation why another, unemployed sibling should be more involved in taking care of the elder person's needs. Siblings who lived in places distant from the needy parents were not expected to be as helpful and those with significant family responsibilities of their own similarly were excused—although more reluctantly than the long-distance siblings.

Another way of forging psychological equity can be seen in individuals' attempts to explain the lower level of other siblings' involvement in parent care with ascribing certain personality characteristics to their siblings. These siblings may be described as irresponsible or immature or self-centered. On the other hand, the less involved sibling may also use personality traits as explanation for the more involved sibling's motivation for care.

As can be seen, many variables factor into the complexity of sibling accountability for the care of their aging parents. Each one, however, is responsible for his or her own part and the impact of his or her involvement on his or her personal life and on how he or she regards this impact: Is it a situation mainly characterized by losses or are there possible positive aspects?

Of course, there are different levels of caregiving, ranging from spending as much as 3 hours per week helping an older person to providing complete daily care in one's home. Also, the intensity of caregiving may change over time for individual caregivers, starting perhaps with a lower level of assisting a few hours a week to more intense care as the parent's frailty increases and reverting again to a lower level after the older person has been placed in a nursing home or similar facility with professional caregiving.

Whatever level of caregiving falls upon an individual, emotional and financial drain can have severe consequences for the individual's functioning in the workplace and in the home, according to psychologist Dolores Gallagher Thompson of Stanford University's Older Adult and Family Center. Psychologists and other researchers are aware of the need to reduce caregivers' stress and anxiety by developing programs like caregiver family therapy (Stambor, 2006). Another way of alleviating the stress of caregivers is through adult daycare programs.

Transitions in the Process of Caregiving

Some investigators have hypothesized that the transitioning into caregiving would constitute the most distressing phase of caregiving (Aneshensel, Pearlin, Mullan, Zarit, & Whitlatch, 1995). Data collected in a study examining the effects of transitioning into activities of caregiving for kin and nonkin care recipients showed that the transition into providing care for primary kin, such as a child, spouse, or biological parent, was associated with an increase in depression. However, beneficial effects were observed in some women who began to provide nonresidential care to a biological parent and reported an increase in purpose in life compared to noncaregiving women (Marks, Lambert, & Choi, 2002).

Psychologist Sara Honn Qualls at the Gerontology Center at the University of Colorado in Colorado Springs (UCCS) has developed a program for helping caregivers make the transition. Using trained therapists, the program coordinates the power of entire families to care for an ailing member. Over the course of several weeks, the therapists aid caregivers in the reevaluation of their role, identifying caregiving tasks, and assigning tasks to different family members. The program's goal is reduction in the primary caregiver's burden by coordinating the whole family's support through the impairment of the needy family member (Stambor, 2006).

On the basis of longitudinal data, some researchers have found that about a quarter of women provided significant levels of care for their own parents or parents-in-law at some point in their middle adult years (Robinson, Moen, & Dempster-McClain, 1995). Furthermore, there has been a steady increase in the likelihood of filling a caregiver role from generation to generation during the twentieth century, indicating a further rise in caregiving responsibilities as life expectancy continues to increase.

Many caregivers fulfill these responsibilities in addition to meeting the needs for their own immediate family as well as the requirements of their jobs. The caregiver role carries with it risks for depression and marital tension as consequences of the *caregiver burden*. And, again, evidence indicated that women experience more of the burden and psychological distress than men do in the caregiver role (Yee & Schulz, 2000). There also seems to be a difference in the caregiving role relationship. Providing care for a spouse apparently has more negative effects on the caregiver than providing care to a parent (Seltzer & Li, 2000).

Affective Changes Between Terminally Ill Spouses and Their Partners

Past research on cancer patients and their spouses has mentioned transitions in the relationships of these couples. An increase in the expression of affection was noted (Rait & Lederberg, 1989), along with an increase in relationship problems due to the stress of the illness and the care given to the ill spouse (Meyerowitz, Heinrich, & Schag, 1983; Pederson & Valanis, 1988).

Another variable operating in situations of a terminal illness is that of anticipatory grief. While the caregiving spouse is still emotionally involved with the dying spouse, there is also a process of emotional detachment occurring, a tendency to withdraw and reinvest intrapsychically (Knott & Wild, 1986; Rando, 1986). Others have challenged this notion of anticipatory grief and argued that the terminal illness of a spouse intensifies the bonding between the spouses (Parkes & Weiss, 1983; Schuchter, 1986). Some research findings (Swensen & Trahaug, 1985) have shown an increase in expression of love accompanied by an increase in commitment.

To explore the contradictions around this issue, a study was designed involving a group of 114 cancer patients with their spouses and a comparison group of 100 healthy couples (Swensen & Fuller, 1992). Married couples, after one of them had been diagnosed with cancer, were expected to report greater expression of love than they previously did, according to their memory. In addition, they should also be more expressive with their loving feelings than a matched comparison group of healthy couples. Furthermore, the couples with a spouse suffering from cancer were expected to report experiencing more problems in their marriage now than prior to the diagnosis and more problems than the noncancer couples. The spouses in the cancer-diagnosed group were also thought to report greater commitment to one another now than prior to the diagnosis.

Over 90% of the patients in the cancer group had undergone surgery and chemotherapy and had been in treatment for about 1 year. The cancer patients were in an advanced stage of their illness and their medical professionals had not recommended other than palliative treatment for them. The measures obtained by the investigators showed that significantly more expressions of affection were reported by the cancer patients and their spouses after the diagnosis of cancer than they remembered prior to the diagnosis. Of this group, 65% stated that they had become closer in their relationship to each other, while 28% recalled no change, and 7% rated their relationship as worse now than before the cancer diagnosis. Neither group reported any difference in the existence of marriage problems. For the cancer patient group, the commitment scores showed a shift in focus from spouse to other-than-spouse in their commitment from the time of their marriage to the time of investigation. No commitment scores were obtained from the control group.

According to the investigators, the shift in focus of commitment in the cancer group spouses from the personal qualities of the spouse to other-than-spouse considerations following the diagnosis of cancer seem to lend support to the notion of anticipatory grief described by Rando (1986).

The amount and degree of caregiving was not a focus in this study; neither were personality aspects of the couples. However, both are of interest here because of the factors of emotional closeness and anticipatory grief that are part of many situations where a spouse is the primary care provider for a terminally ill partner. If indeed there are processes of reinvesting intrapsychically occurring while the spouse of the terminally ill partner is caring for but also preparing for the inevitable event of death, that might explain the observation mentioned in the chapter on widowhood that some widowed persons enter a new relationship relatively soon after becoming widowed.

Christian and Patrick were men in their middle 70s when they became widowed due to their wives' terminal illnesses. Both women had been diagnosed with advanced stage cancer and were given less than a year to live. There were adult children in both families but Christian and Patrick, being retired, assumed most of the care for their wives, except in Christian's case, when one of his daughters came to help from time to time.

As Patrick remembered his experience of the last year of his wife's life, Margaret's temperament did not change much; she had always been a strong-willed woman. Although she could no longer perform most of the chores around the house including some of her personal care, she was able to let Patrick know exactly what to do. He learned to prepare meals the way she had done for the family. She instructed him in doing the laundry and some cleaning between the visits from outside help. Margaret had even worked out the arrangements for her own funeral. Their marital relationship changed into almost a mother–son relationship at this point.

After the deaths of their wives both men remained independent; they did not move in with their adult children. And both found new relationships within a year. Patrick's children encouraged him to attend Parents without Partners or other single groups, where he met Linda, a woman in her late 60s. They both commented on the fact that they were older than the majority of the participants. Neither one had young children like the other people, but Linda was actually raising her daughter's children while her daughter served in the Armed Forces. Patrick and Linda liked each other and started dating seriously.

When Marianne, Christian's wife, died of pancreatic cancer they had been married for 52 years. Although it had not been a happy marriage, divorce was not an option in Christian's mind. It seemed that he had always taken care of Marianne. They had met at a school dance and Marianne looked so pretty in her blue polka dot dress with a bright red sash. But it was not a trouble-free period of dating; soon after their meeting Marianne's family kicked her out of the house. Christian found her a place to live and a job. They got married in 1943 and Christian had to join the Armed Forces just shortly before the birth of their oldest daughter.

Christian claims that Marianne's personality changed when he returned from the war. She was at times difficult to get along with and seemed to be looking for something else. There was an invisible wall between them. Christian had a rich work history, making it up the ladder from service station attendant to district manager at Standard Oil. He likes people and gets along well with them. People trust him. The family moved many times, but both daughters were able to graduate from the same high school.

In preparation for retirement, Christian and Marianne took trips to different parts of the country during their vacations in search of the perfect place. They preferred a warm climate and took two trips to Hawaii but finally settled in Arizona. They moved to Phoenix in 1980.

After Marianne's death Christian felt lost for a while. Taking care of his wife had taken a toll and he was not in the best of health himself. Over time he had undergone seven heart bypass surgeries. During the summers he explored the state of Utah, enjoying the different landscape.

Attending a rehabilitation program for his heart condition Christian met Pat, a nurse who had never married. A deep friendship developed and after dating for about a year, Pat moved closer to Christian's residence. They had 4 wonderful years together before Pat became ill. During the last 3 years of their relationship, her condition grew worse but nobody knew what was happening to her. Finally, she was diagnosed with cancer of the bladder. In spite of her illness, those 7 years were happy years; they had found a deep love. Christian could not let her stay in a hospital; he took her to his home and put her in the biggest room with a splendid view. He took care of her until she had to be placed in a hospice. In addition to the bladder cancer, Pat was suffering from Parkinson's disease and Alzheimer's disease.

Twice death took a partner from Christian after he took care of them. There were differences in the way Christian responded to the deaths of the two women. His relationship with Marianne had become that of housemates; emotional intimacy had eroded over the years, but he took care of her because it was his duty and responsibility. With Pat, there was a more pronounced tenderness in his feelings and his behavior toward her. He protected her in a way that he might have used for a small child, perhaps intensifying the bonding between them, as suggested earlier (Parkes & Weiss, 1983; Schuchter, 1986).

Widowhood had opened the door to a whole new life for Christian. He would not have wanted to miss it, but he is not looking for another involvement; the pain is too strong. His thoughts are with Pat, the woman he found and loved late in life. He knows that for her he was the completion of her life. "I finished her life out," Christian says softly, and he wonders where he will spend his summers. He cannot bear returning to Utah without Pat; there are too many memories. The first summer after her death he visited his home state and spent time with some friends and his older daughter. Then it was time to go back to Phoenix and start another life, one without Pat.

While both men had different experiences after their wives died, they both may have reinvested emotionally and mentally in their own personal lives while attending to the care of their terminally ill wives, as suggested earlier in the work of Knott and Wild (1986) and Rando (1986). In cases where the caregiving responsibilities stretch over several years and the spouse recovers from the illness, the effects on the marital relationship can be quite different. The increased feelings of love and strengthened sense of commitment observed by Swensen and Fuller (1992) earlier may develop in the beginning but might not last after the major impact of the illness has subsided.

Michael and Libby, also discussed in the chapter on chronic illness, had been married for 7 years when Libby was diagnosed with breast cancer. Michael, in addition to his fulltime job, assumed the responsibilities for their two children and their household. It took about 3 years for Libby to regain her strength, to assume some of the chores, and to return to her part-time job. Michael's sense of relief when Libby's condition improved did not last long; his emotional state changed from the numbness during Libby's critical stage to anger and depression. The family physician explained Michael's response as delayed stress response and prescribed antidepressant medication for him.

While she was critically ill, Michael could not allow the resentment to surface, so he blocked it out by feeling "numb." Upon her recovery, he expected not only to be relieved from the heavy load, he felt entitled to a "vacation" from household responsibilities as a reward for his previous good behavior. But Libby was not ready to release Michael to the vacation condition and instead criticized him for not performing his part. One could interpret Michael's period of "numbness" as representing the phenomenon of withdrawing and reinvesting intrapsychically as discussed earlier in the cases of Christian and Patrick, especially in view of the knowledge of Michael's extramarital affairs.

Furthermore, at the time of Libby's diagnosis of breast cancer the couple had been married for 7 years, which is one of the two most critical times for the survival of marriages; half of all divorces occur during the first 7 years of marriage, as mentioned in the chapter on divorce. It is thus possible that their marriage had already entered a critical phase and Libby's illness may have prolonged it but also weakened it beyond repair.

Caregiving situations have two sides: that of the caregiver and that of the care recipient. For both, lifestyle changes confront them with the various aspects of losses and gains or opportunities. Those who are on the receiving end may—if they can—want to learn to give to the caregivers, to make it easy and desirable for them to be of help rather than to expect or even demand assistance.

The Chronic Stress of Caregiving

It is not all about the sick person, reminds Andrew Weil, M.D. (2007); too often the caregiver is overlooked when it comes to healing. Unfortunately, nobody has the official responsibility to take care of the caregiver. The tendency to consider one's own strength unlimited is great when the caregiver is confronted with the need and the helplessness of the ailing person, the patient. Another aspect adding to the stress is the possibility of feeling guilty when considering a rest period for oneself. "What if something happens to the helpless person while I am taking a nap? I could never forgive myself" are thoughts that keep caregivers at the side of the care-receiver long after the caregiver's energies are depleted. Dr. Weil strongly suggests for caregivers to put themselves high on the priority list, even at the risk of appearing selfish.

Putting oneself high on the priority list can be especially difficult after having spent a significant period of time being the last one on that list. By now, the person cared for has come to establish expectations that may have been growing and when the caregiver is attempting to rearrange the order on the priority list, resentment from the care-receiver may become apparent. It is extremely difficult to take back what one has already offered in an impulse of sympathy and goodwill. In the ideal case, it would be advisable for the caregiver to know how much time and effort he or she can expand without hurting himself or herself and without building up resentment toward the receiver for "taking it all." In reality, nobody can know better than the care providers how much they can give without impairing their own health and happiness.

Not all caregiving responsibilities are the same in the level of care needed. For those who care for family members enduring chronic and uncontrollable bouts of pain the task can be particularly distressing (Miaskowski, Kragness, Dibble, & Wallhagen, 1997). In addition to emotional distress, caregivers often develop difficulties with their own health over time, such as cardiovascular, neuroendocrine, and immune functioning (Kiecolt-Glaser, Dura, Speicher, Trask, & Glaser, 1991). In situations where a family member acquires severe physical disabilities, such as spinal cord injury (SCI), the pattern of life events in the family system may be disrupted and caregivers face many complicated circumstances.

The chronic stress arising from caring for a spouse with Alzheimer's disease, along with the effects on the psychophysiology and coronary heart disease (CHD) on the caregiver, were the basis for testing a theoretical stress model cross-sectionally and prospectively (Vitaliano et al., 2002). Variables related to the chronic stress in caregiving included vulnerability to anger and hostility; social resources and support; psychological stress (burden, sleep problems); poor health habits; and metabolic syndrome (MS) indicators of blood pressure, obesity, insulin, glucose, and lipids. The participants were 47 older adult men and 105 older adult women (64 not receiving hormone replacement therapy and 41 with HRT).

Results showed that the caregiver men, when compared to noncaregiver men, had a greater prevalence of CHD and poor health habits. In women, no relationship between caregiving and CHD was found, but 15–18 months later "distress-MS" and "MS-CHD" relationships were found in the caregiver women who did not have hormone replacement therapy (HRT). Women who were on HRT did not show "distress-MS" and CHD relationships but exhibited poor health habits.

The metabolic syndrome consists of a group of symptoms that, when present in individuals, markedly increases their chance of developing diabetes, heart disease, and stroke. Feelings of depression, anger, and hostility have been linked to a higher incidence of metabolic syndrome in older men. Compared to nonhostile controls, hostile men who responded to stress in aggressive ways had higher waist/hip ratios, increased body mass index, higher total caloric intakes, higher fasting insulin levels, higher serum triglycerides, and lower high-density lipoproteins—all indicators of metabolic syndrome (Vitaliano et al., 2002).

Similarly in women, anger and depression are associated with higher metabolic syndrome levels. In a longitudinal study of 425 middle-aged women with high levels of depression, anger, and tension at baseline, 7 years later they showed a higher risk for developing metabolic syndrome. Furthermore, metabolic syndrome may cause mood disturbance in a bidirectional manner. For women in this study, having metabolic syndrome at baseline was predictive of higher levels of anxiety and anger 7 years later (Raikkonen, Matthews, & Kuller, 2002).

Parents as Care Providers for Their Chronically Ill Children

For those who are parents of children suffering from a chronic illness, the effects of caregiver stress on their health are no less serious than those of caregiving spouses. Parents who give care to their children with chronic threatening diseases such as cancer show more impairments of the immune system than parents of healthy children (Miller, Cohen, & Ritchey, 2002). In parents who were caregivers to their ill children, the chronic stress resulted in diminished glucocorticoid sensitivity that impaired the immune response and lowered levels of key pro-inflammatory cytokines, such as interleukin-1, interleukin-6, and tumor necrosis factor. In parents affected with this chronic psychological stress, the chances for opportunistic infections were markedly increased.

The health aspects are not the only consideration when addressing the parents' stress in giving care to chronically ill children. The continuous stress takes a significant toll on the quality of the marital relationship. In most families, it is the woman who is in charge of the care for the ill or disabled child while the man is at work, trying to earn enough money to pay for the medical bills. For most men in these families, the work stress is enhanced by the worries about their ability to cope with the financial situation. The after-work hours do not provide for much relaxation either because the wife is waiting for a brief, well-deserved relief from her daily responsibility as the primary caregiver to the child, often without the luxury of taking a deep breath.

Arthur and Debbie's marriage remained childless for several years. They considered the option of adopting a child when Debbie, at 31 years of age, became pregnant. They were overjoyed at the news and set about establishing a college tuition fund for their as yet unborn baby as a celebration. Their son, Rudy, was born with Down syndrome (*trisomy 21*). Children with this condition are mentally retarded and have distinctive facial features and often other physical abnormalities, such as heart defects (Haier et al., 1995). Due to some of the physical abnormalities, the life expectancies of children with Down syndrome are lower than those of normal children, Debbie and Arthur were told by the medical experts. They made the decision that Rudy would be their only child.

Taking care of Rudy was a fulltime job for Debbie. Arthur helped as much as he could after returning home from his job. If Rudy contracted any of the childhood diseases, his parents experienced the additional stress of fearing that their son might not survive the particular disease. But Rudy survived all his illnesses. At 39 years of age, he is still living with his now retired parents. Since his birth, Debbie and Arthur have not taken a single vacation by themselves. Reliable respite care is not easy to find for longer than a day or two. Rudy is enthralled with Disney World and cannot get enough of it. For him, it is part of the real world. His parents take him there as often as they can afford to. They have been told to expect Rudy's memory functions to deteriorate, much as in cases of Alzheimer's disease. That will be another adjustment confronting Arthur and Debbie.

In situations where spouses become caregivers to their partners and grown children or care for their ill or incapacitated parents and other family members, the duration of caregiving may extend from a few years to a decade and termination generally occurs through the death of the impaired person. In contrast, for parents who become the caregivers or custodians of their adult offspring, the duration of care can span a lifetime and in some instances the parents' deaths will terminate the period of care.

Helga and Timothy planned for a family with two children. Two years after giving birth to a beautiful baby girl, Helga was pregnant with a son—their family was complete. Both children were physically healthy but Dean, their little boy, did not respond in normal ways to his environment. He made some grunting noises but his speech functions seemed delayed.

He also did not want to listen to his parents' verbalizations; in fact, he seemed frightened and frustrated by them. Helga was worried when she compared the difference in the development of her two children. Finally, Dean was diagnosed with autism. The prognosis did not leave much room for hope. Dean would always need supervision.

Dean's parents responded in different ways to their son's condition. Timothy focused on his job during the day. The evening hours and weekends were devoted to alcohol intake. Helga changed to part-time employment in order to take care of Dean and to spare her little daughter from being burdened by her brother's condition. Helga reasoned that Lizzie did not deserve anything but a happy childhood and she did her best to protect her daughter from the negative impact of Dean's illness. When it became time to find educational opportunities for Dean, Helga explored available possibilities. She delivered and picked him up daily and worked with him after his school time. Dean was about 11 or 12 years old when residential treatment was suggested. For several years this was a relief for Helga, although she was the one who usually visited Dean in his new environment, sometimes taking her daughter along to maintain the bond between the siblings. Helga returned to fulltime employment.

Over the years different treatment programs were indicated. Helga was the one to research the options, examine them, make decisions, and supervise the treatment. Different housing, different caregivers, different managers—Helga handled all the changes as well as interacting positively with her son and establishing channels of communication with him. Helga's daughter attended college, got married, and moved away to start her own family.

Coping with the difficult adjustments to the needs of an impaired child was not the only challenge in Helga's life. When, as a young woman from Germany she arrived in the United States in 1956, she did not know what to expect. Timothy, the young American man she had met in Europe while on vacation, arranged for her to come to his parents' home in a small Midwestern town. Timothy's parents offered her room and board but emphasized that she would have to obtain work to help with the expenses. They had already found a job for her in a department store nearby. But within a week Helga obtained a better position at a local bank. She had worked for a bank in Germany and was able to transfer some of her knowledge to her new work situation. Like most young people of her generation, Helga had studied English in high school but the American pronunciation was different from what she had been used to. Nevertheless, she prevailed in her efforts to adapt to her new environment.

Timothy's parents, who had exercised poor judgment in some of their financial decisions, seemed eager to see him start his own family; his mother, especially, stressed the importance of marriage. Soon after the wedding Helga became pregnant with their first child. Helga continued to work even after the birth of their second child. She learned some facts about Timothy that she had not known before their wedding. Although a hardworking young man, Timothy had a habit of visiting the local bars in the evening. Several nights a week he was intoxicated upon arrival at home. He was not abusive to Helga but he was no help either when she had to take care of their children. Understandably, her feelings for Timothy deteriorated.

Divorce was not something to be taken lightly in her family of origin. Besides, with her two children she could not return to Germany and she was not about to desert them. Helga continued to work for the bank and received promotions over the years that placed her in a managerial position. With her knowledge of money and investments, she assumed the responsibility for the family's financial planning. Her investments were well placed.

Dean is in his early 40s, living in his parents' home. Timothy and Helga are retired from their jobs. Due to health problems, Timothy has finally reduced his alcohol intake. This means he can be available to supervise Dean at home or go to the gym with him. The marital relationship has evolved to a functional level where both spouses share in the responsibility for their son—not necessarily equally. Although disillusioned about marriage, Helga realizes that it would be even more difficult if she left Timothy and had to take care of Dean all by herself. As long as Dean is alive, he will need to be in a supervised living arrangement and she has been working hard establishing a fund that will enable her daughter to look after Dean when the parents are gone.

Helga's life in the United States may not be what she had dreamed of long ago, but she has used her time well and made her life as meaningful as she could. She now uses her free time to participate in volunteer activities of her interest and enjoys the cultural life the town has to offer. Her friends value her company because of her positive attitude, her lively involvement in community affairs, and her willingness to help.

Helga does not spend time feeling sorry for herself. She enjoys her volunteer activities and interactions with her many friends. Her guidance of Dean has progressed to the point where he can accompany her on some cultural events, such as a concert or a simple show. She takes frequent walks with him and keeps encouraging him to remain active. She is a good model for him when it comes to overcoming obstacles and searching for opportunities to make life meaningful.

Helga's story would have been appropriately placed in the chapter on geographical and cultural relocations. However, a significant part of her life describes events relevant to this chapter. Introducing her here emphasizes the fact that people's life patterns can be interrupted more than once by significant changes, requiring repeated adjustments in the regular flow of their lives.

Stress-Alleviating Public Efforts

Although many states provide programs aimed at personal independence of the disabled person, cutbacks in public funds have significantly limited the vocational rehabilitation services and independent living programs for many disabled individuals (Elliott & Shewchuk, 1998), leaving them no other choice than to depend on family caregiving. Furthermore, most severe physical impairments occur rather suddenly. A subtle developmental course of the illness that would help family members in planning and preparing for the disability does not exist. Instead, lifestyle and role changes arise abruptly at the onset of the disability and usually long-term adaptation is required for disabling conditions that are not typically life threatening or terminal.

To provide interventions to family caregivers, professionals in the mental health field have focused on the notion of wellness for emphasizing physical, psychological, and spiritual health. Wellness does not mean the absence of illness (as defined by health); wellness involves enhanced functioning in all areas of life (Ginter, 1999). Wellness is seen as a proactive lifestyle of individuals who are responsible for choices of self-care, self-sufficiency, and empowerment. When faced with the lifestyle changes presented by a family member's sudden-onset severe physical disability, caregivers often experience an imbalance in one or more of the areas of health. Interventions based on the wellness concept have mainly targeted the provision of respite care and social support. Caregiver support groups and social networks offering assistance have shown some benefits but evidence indicates that this support wears away over time (Quittner, Glueckauf, & Jackson, 1990).

As an alternative, interventions of a social problem-solving approach within an individual counseling context have been considered to help decrease caregiver distress and accentuate wellness in the caregiver. Project FOCUS, a problem-solving training program, was developed specifically for caregivers of family members with spinal cord injury (Kurylo, Elliott, & Shewchuk, 2001). It was thought that effective problem-solving skills are related to increased use of instrumental problem-focused coping in times of stress. Effective problem solvers have a more proactive style of coping and as a result might experience fewer health problems while performing their caregiving activities, regardless of the actual demands of caregiving or the level of physical impairment of the care recipient.

The problem-solving training model for caregivers consists of the following five major components:

1. *Facts/problem definition* involves descriptions of the identified problem and breaking it down into manageable parts. All available facts about the problem should be collected, including relevant information from experts.
2. *Optimism/orientation* is meant to instill in the caregiver the belief of possessing sufficient skills to solve the problem and to motivate initiation and engagement in the problem-solving process. At the same time, regulation of emotional experiences functions to maintain a sense of confidence and pride in the accomplishments achieved so far.
3. *Creativity/generation of alternatives* is a phase of active brainstorming for discovering multiple solutions to the identified problem. Sometimes caregivers may believe that there is only one correct solution but encouragement to explore further may also result in a more complete conceptualization of the problem situation. Being able to develop more options would increase caregivers' optimism and confidence about their abilities.
4. *Understanding/decision making* is the point where all the collected information will be integrated with the purpose of considering which solution to implement. Before actually deciding on a particular solution, potential outcomes are weighed as to their costs and benefits. Each alternative receives a rating relative to its feasibility of achieving the goals and its manageability in coping with obstacles.
5. *Solution/implementation and verification* is the final phase in the problem-solving training process. The particular problem under consideration is being solved and the outcome is reviewed and evaluated as to how well the results matched the expected outcome.

As caregivers evaluate the process and results, this phase becomes a self-monitoring component of the overall process that is crucial to the understanding of the steps that rendered the chosen solution effective or ineffective. This component also provides information about how to implement changes or alternative solutions in future problem situations. Caregivers, having arrived at this phase, often experience a significant increase in self-efficacy and self-confidence.

The phases of this training process model are distributed over the period of a year because it is during the first year of caregiving that family caregivers are faced with several competing demands and problems arising from their multiple roles of having the responsibility for the disabled person as well as their own immediate family, their careers, and various other commitments. In a following the model, the investigators hoped to contribute to caregivers' overall well-being.

Professional Caregivers

Many aging individuals receive some sort of assistance from professional caregivers; it may range from complete care in nursing-home facilities to services from a visiting nurses association to gerontological therapists for guidance in various activities associated with an assisted-living arrangement. Although for professional caregivers the fact that they are not involved in close emotional relationships with their patients provides somewhat of a buffer for the stressors of caregiving activities, the work setting in itself often assigns many competing responsibilities to the individuals. Factors such as high patient-to-caregiver ratio, tight scheduling with lack of time-outs for brief relaxation, excessive continuous direct contacts with patients who may be in pain or in need for assistance with the most basic functions, shift work and long hours leading to chronic fatigue, and maintaining clinical competence in rapidly changing healthcare environments are only a few contributing features to caregivers' fatigue and burnout.

A Life Suspended

Greg remembers not fitting in. As an only child he did not have many socializing opportunities except for school. But school was not a happy place for him. He was intelligent enough to make good grades but did not apply himself consistently. His male classmates regarded Greg as a target for fights. He liked girls but he was too shy to approach them. His parents were always busy; his father worked long hours in the family business. Greg remembers him mostly as being tired and hiding behind the newspaper; he was not approachable. His mother, a peace-loving woman, did the office work for the business.

After graduating from high school Greg worked in his parents' business. It was not something he would have chosen for himself. He was interested in art and received training in commercial art. Writing was another interest. When he was 19 years old he joined the Army to avoid being drafted. It looked like a good decision because he was stationed in Europe for his whole tour of duty. The benefits included the availability of alcohol at low prices in the Class VI store at the base—for many, an opportunity too tempting to pass up. Greg returned to his parents' house after discharge from the Army and helped with the ailing business. He never married and never dated seriously.

Two years after his father had passed away the business closed its doors forever. Greg and his mother were left to themselves. Greg's binge drinking and social withdrawal impeded his job search. They lived on the mother's Social Security and Greg's disability payments. His mother's health deteriorated over the years. Her vision was significantly impaired and later her memory became dysfunctional. Greg assumed the responsibilities of caregiver for his mother. His duties increased with her decreased ability to function. He could not put her in a nursing home because that would result in the loss of his mother's house.

His mother's condition became such that it was dangerous to leave her alone when he had to do the food shopping or attend AA meetings. His drinking had escalated yet he wanted to stop. He looked to AA for help but it seemed that his mother had undergone a personality change. Her behavior became mean and spiteful and Greg tried to escape their unpleasant interactions by withdrawing into drinking. Except for weekly homecare service and nursing help in the last year of her life, Greg had the total responsibility for his mother. He was in a cage, physically and emotionally constrained and isolated. Without a job or money he could not escape. His feelings of anger, resentment, and bitterness led to increased alcohol consumption. There were no friends he could confide in. Attending the structured AA meetings was his only social outlet.

Finally, at the age of 96 years his mother died. Greg was barely able to keep the house with the help of the inheritance from his mother. Relieved of the daily stress of taking care of his mother, Greg has managed to stop drinking. But his outlook for the future is scary and depressing. He is afraid of the freedom he now has. What are his prospects at age 66 without a job and without marketable skills?

The normal changes of life events over time seemed to have passed him by. Except for the years he spent in the Army, he remained in the place and circumstances he was born into, even though he was not happy there. He did not invest himself in any profession and he did not start and raise a family. He did not see grown children leave the home, he did not have a need for job changes or for geographical changes, and he did not experience the search and planning that other people are occupied with when it comes time for retirement. He is suspended in fear and anxiety about how to survive in the present and near future.

Unlike other caregivers who put their lives on hold while they care for a family member, there was nothing Greg had to put on hold. For Greg, the major change was the transition into sobriety, which is a significant achievement. But is it enough to give meaning to the rest of his life? His earlier interest in writing surfaced a few years ago. It is a valuable outlet to express his thoughts and emotions and it may help him in his search for the meaning of his life. Much of his writing reflects his bitterness in the sarcastic tone he uses. Will he find a paying audience for his stories? The likelihood of that to occur is slim. Due to the paralyzing fear of rejection Greg has not submitted his writing to editors and—even worse—he has stopped writing. Similarly, his anxiety keeps him from approaching employers and agencies for jobs that could improve his financial situation.

At this point, Greg's life does not resemble the kind of success story that we would like to see in this chapter. But there are still options for him. Focusing on the wasted times might not be beneficial to acknowledging current opportunities. He might even talk himself out of making use of them. As Greg told his story to be used in this book, it was emphasized that he was in control of the ending. He could still decide whether he wanted to continue in his isolation and remain paralyzed, sitting in a corner of his house until he might be evicted, or, if finally he would rebel against his fear and step out of the corner onto the path of searching for one of the opportunities still available to him, he could write a new beginning to this part of his life story. His deadline for discovering options is as close as the deadline for this book.

CHAPTER **8**

Health-Related Issues Requiring Changes

Chronic illnesses and disabling conditions (CID) can befall anyone. An estimated 54 million Americans suffer from physical, sensory, psychiatric, or cognitive disabilities that interfere with their daily functioning (Bowe, 2000). Individuals with chronic illnesses are impacted by a wide range of stress factors related to their illness. In addition to the functional limitations, prolonged medical treatment with rehabilitation programs and in some cases uncertain prognosis affect not only the individual but also the lives of those living in close proximity, such as family members. For some, financial losses originating from reduced income and increased medical bills present additional concerns, leading to psychological and mental distress.

Adjustment to Long-Term or Chronic Illnesses

About 47% of men and 38% of women are confronted with a diagnosis of cancer during their lifetimes (American Cancer Society, 2000); but mortality rates from cancer are decreasing to the point that certain cancers are currently considered by the American Cancer Society to be chronic rather than acute illnesses. People are living longer now with treatment, but their lives are not necessarily more satisfying in the post-treatment period (Baum & Posluszny, 2001; Kangas, Henry, & Bryant, 2002). Prior to the completion of treatment, cancer patients experience increased anxiety when they prepare to transition from the medical system monitoring their health to assuming self-monitoring responsibility. During this time, fear of recurrence and hope for a permanent cure combine for an emotional roller-coaster experience in the lives of the patients.

Breast cancer can strike women of all ages and when least expected. Some women are in their 50s when confronted with the diagnosis while others have not even reached their 30th birthday. For Libby, a woman in her early 30s, sadness and losses were not new experiences. Illness, deaths, and suicide of family members and friends weighed heavily on her mind. In addition, shortly after giving birth to twin girls, one of them required emergency surgery for congenital heart failure. Her pregnancy with a baby boy ended in miscarriage. But when she was diagnosed with breast cancer, she was not prepared for it. It seemed like a natural law that every recovery from a crisis was to be followed by a new and even greater crisis.

Through the time following the diagnosis, filled with surgeries, chemotherapy, mastectomy, and surgical breast reconstruction, Michael, Libby's husband, became the primary caregiver for the family besides his fulltime job, as described in the chapter on caregiving. While Libby's emotions ranged from anger, depression, self-hate, fear, and anxiety to the dimmest rays of hope, Michael blocked out all his feelings in response to coping with the situation on a daily basis. During this prolonged time of concentrating on the needs of his family, he numbed himself to his own wishes and feelings. Even his memory seemed hazy for this time of excruciating stress; when asked about specific events during this time his mind goes blank.

As Libby's period of physical and emotional recovery was finally under way Michael's resentment and anger flared up. It seemed that the improvement in her condition removed the protective cover of numbness from Michael's being. Internally he rebelled against many of the tasks that still lay ahead. Had he not done enough already? As he expressed his resentment in complaining statements, Libby's feelings of gratitude changed to anger and self-recrimination, which induced guilt feelings in Michael, to be followed by rage and then depression. It was indeed a vicious cycle that their emotions passed through.

Michael's resentment included aspects of self-pity; his needs had been neglected for so long, nobody seemed to care about him. He found solace in the arms of a female coworker, who herself was in an unhappy relationship. But the coworker reconciled with her husband and was no longer available to comfort Michael. He was able to form another fleeting sexual relationship with a female acquaintance who knew about Libby's illness. In order not to disturb Libby's recovery process, Michael thought it best to keep his infidelities a secret.

Libby progressed well in her recovery and began to feel sexually aroused. It had been a long time since their last sexual activity. Michael did not seem interested and he was evasive in his behaviors, pointing out that Libby might need more time as well as expressing a concern about possible pregnancy, which could be a great risk to her health. It was about this time that the female acquaintance met Libby in a store and inquired about Libby's well-being. Her conversation seemed to imply more personal knowledge than Libby would expect from the rather superficial nature of their relationship. Libby's more targeted question resulted in the woman's admission of her sexual involvement with Michael.

After the initial shock wore off, Libby confronted Michael, who hesitatingly admitted his infidelities. He added that he felt entitled to some enjoyment after the long period of worry and concentration on the needs of the family. Libby agreed that indeed he deserved some happier times but she could not understand why he sought his pleasure outside their marriage. Here was another devastating blow to her already fragile condition. How she was supposed to cope with that was her first question to the marriage therapist she contacted. Would Michael's infidelity not have occurred if Libby had not been ill with cancer? As she regained her health, would her marriage to Michael be a loss or were there possibilities for rebuilding their future together? Under what conditions could they go on and reconstruct their family life for their two daughters? Their options included separation, divorce, continuation of the marriage, with allowances for extramarital affairs, or remaining married while demanding absolute fidelity. Each one of the options would carry its own set of mixed emotions with it.

While they were considering these options and the possible losses and gains of each for the family members, they were confronted with another crisis: Both Michael and Libby tested positive for a communicable disease. A new cycle of accusations, defenses, and blaming accompanied by emotions ranging from anger, depression, fear, love, and hate to guilt began. Libby opted for remaining in the marriage; Michael was in favor of separation and divorce. This leaves the possibility that Libby, while adjusting to the consequences of her illness, will also need to cope with the transition to single parenthood.

Process of Adjustment to Chronic Illness

Even without the complications and emotional turmoil involved in Libby's adjustment to her illness, the quality of life of a person with chronic illness is significantly affected by such factors, as body image perceived through the illness can be expected to impact the individual's self-concept. Visible disabilities may illicit prejudicial stereotypical responses from others, leaving the disabled person feeling stigmatized and possibly discriminated against; in turn, this may prompt him or her to withdraw from social encounters (Corrigan, 2000; Falvo, 1999). While in the process of withdrawing, the person may also experience strong fears of being abandoned by those around him and often the withdrawal may be a "protective" act because the withdrawal is seen as preventing the feared abandonment.

Like those who mourn the loss of a loved one, individuals afflicted with a chronic illness may experience similar despair and grieve for the loss of their bodily or mental functioning, independence, and personal authority. They may also respond and adjust to the illness in stages not unlike the grieving process over the death of a loved one. The first reaction is often one of shock, characterized by psychic numbness and followed by anxiety or panic. The defense mechanism of denial becomes mobilized to ward off overwhelming anxiety. During denial, individuals focus attention selectively on their physical and psychological environments. They may indulge in wishful thinking or entertaining unrealistic expectations about recovery.

Anger, hostility, and blame are responses that come into play after denial has outlived its usefulness. Individuals often blame themselves for having neglected signs and symptoms of a developing illness or they may turn the blame toward others, such as medical professionals for unsuccessful treatment efforts.

Finally, as the adjustment process occurs on several levels, there is a cognitive reconciliation of the condition and its impact and permanent nature. This is followed by the individual's internalization or affective acceptance of the self and the condition in terms of a restored self-concept with perhaps modified life values. The modified self-concept and values form the basis for an active planning and pursuit of personal, social, and/or vocational goals (Livnch & Antonak, 2005).

Use of Coping Strategies

Individuals suffering from chronic illness or disability eventually devise a range of coping skills for themselves to overcome some of the distress they are dealing with on a daily basis. Although they may not regain their previous quality of life, there are ways of coping that include a renewed—and sometimes even heightened—zest for life. The case of Jenny, a young woman introduced later in this chapter, is an example of planning and pursuing various new goals in adjustment to and attempts to cope with changes in her lifestyle that resulted from the development of a chronic illness.

Researchers in the area of coping techniques distinguish between different categories of skills (Livnch & Antonak, 2005). Efforts that attempt to deal with stressful events through passive, indirect, or even avoidance-oriented behaviors have been referred to as *disengagement coping strategies*. Wishful thinking and fantasies, denial, blame, and, in some cases, substance abuse are examples of disengagement coping strategies. This type of strategy often leads to increased levels of psychological discomfort and poor adaptation to the condition.

In contrast, *engagement coping strategies* include efforts that defuse stressful situations through active and goal-directed behaviors, such as seeking information, planning, and problem-solving attempts. Individuals applying this type of strategy usually are interested in finding social support. Their strategies in general are associated with higher levels of well-being, acceptance, and successful adaptation. Individuals making use of the engagement types of coping skills are often better able to adapt to the fluctuating course of remitting and exacerbating conditions that are part of chronic illnesses by alternating their strategies accordingly.

A beneficial adjunctive treatment for a medical disease can be found in the application of psychological interventions (Roberts, Kiselica, & Fredrickson, 2002). Therapists working with chronically ill clients are usually experienced in intervention techniques congruent with their theoretical framework. As they introduce particular concepts to their clients, they focus on the usefulness of these concepts within the context of psychosocial adaptation to the client's illness. An effective way of introducing clients to intervention techniques has been to work in a group setting. Individuals often are able to relax when realizing that they are not the only ones experiencing difficulties.

Furthermore, group settings provide an atmosphere of encouragement and good-spirited competition for the exertion of appropriate tasks and activities. Skills of decision making, assertiveness, and stigma management are learned more easily in the presence of others who are beset with equally distressing characteristics due to their illness (Craig, Hancock, Chang, & Dickson, 1998). Information sharing about the availability of advanced medical treatment technology is another valuable aspect of group sessions.

Another benefit of group settings is that it may be the only place where individuals are able to express their greatest fears associated with their illness. Those are the fears that they are not allowing themselves to verbalize to family members because they want to protect them from the potentially terrifying outcomes that occupy their minds.

Jenny and George: Skiing Into Marriage

Jenny and George, the young couple encountered in chapter 2, were forced to make adjustments in their relationship due to Jenny's disabling arthritis. Because Jenny could not ski anymore, her older sister Ellen thought George should be understanding of Jenny's condition and not pursue his interest in skiing any longer. After all, their commitment had been for "in sickness and in health," Ellen pointed out. Jenny, after passing through the different phases of shock, disbelief and denial, and a bout with anger and resentment, disagreed with her sister. It was bad enough that she could no longer engage in her preferred sport, but George should not be deprived of it, too. If George were expected to give up skiing, he would quite likely develop resentment toward Jenny and her illness. Resentment in either one of the spouses would make a damaging impact on their marriage that would be difficult to heal.

Jenny decided that their winter holidays were just as important as before. She would accompany George on the trips but she would not participate in skiing. Instead she would take short walks, read, and catch up with her correspondence with friends and family. At the end of the day, when George returned to the lodge or hotel they would enjoy their time together. Jenny realized that if she asked George not to ski or if she were to begrudge his outings, the harm to their marriage would be far greater than the arthritis damage to her body.

During the times George enjoyed himself on the ski slopes, Jenny had time to think about what she wanted to do for herself. Her life had been so busy before the pain struck. Now she needed to adjust a big part of her life, cutting out vigorous physical activities. Overcoming the shock and anger concerning her condition was only the beginning. What could she put in place of her physical activities to retain a meaningful life? Jenny had decided to focus her overall adaptation to her illness on an engagement rather than a withdrawal or disengagement coping strategy.

During their winter vacation, on a walk through the picturesque village, Jenny had discovered little corners away from the busy path of the tourists. She wished that she had brought a camera along. Fortunately, digital cameras had become popular and were much lighter in weight, so she could carry one along on her walks. "Why not buy one in the village?" Jenny asked herself. She probably would have to pay a higher price here than in New York City, but it would be worth it because she could take advantage now of being where she wanted to take pictures. She could create her own memories of this place and share them with George later.

Jenny was lucky: The store was empty and the clerk was able to devote his time to her, advising her about what type of digital camera would be best for her purposes. Now she regretted that she had not brought her laptop computer along on this trip. But the clerk assured her the camera's memory card would be compatible with her equipment. This is how it started; Jenny soon got deeply involved in her new hobby. Back home in New York, she attended classes and located a photography club. Jenny developed a good eye for unusual scenes and character-filled faces. She talked to the people in the towns and villages George and she visited on their vacations. She collected interesting stories about the people and the histories of the places. Jenny was surprised about her own creative skills as she combined pictures and stories into booklets about the places she and George discovered.

What a thrill it was when George showed her the letter from a travel magazine that wanted to buy one of her stories and expressed an interest in future assignments. George had "borrowed" one of her booklets and submitted it to the editor of the magazine, believing that the quality of Jenny's work would be convincing that her work was of value to the magazine's business.

Jenny had made use of engagement coping strategies by focusing her energies and attention on new goal activities. She achieved renewed meaning in her life by attending to options that were different from the ones she had enjoyed in the past. Other survivors of serious injuries or disabilities may decide to overcome impairments by compensating in the area of their injuries. An example that was recently in the public eye is Heather Mills McCartney (2005), who is a patron of Adopt-A-Minefield and a United Nations Association Goodwill Ambassador. Due to a traffic accident in 1993, she had suffered numerous injuries in addition to having her left leg amputated below the knee. Heather had been invited to participate in the reality TV show "Dancing with the Stars," starting on March 19, 2007. Independent of other publicity information, watching her perform in this competition with an artificial limb makes people marvel at how she could dance, which she stated she always loved to do.

Perhaps Heather's participation in Dancing with the Stars can be understood within the framework of Alfred Adler's "individual psychology" and his concept of *compensation*. Compensation is a process in which individuals attempt to restore equilibrium within the organism. Organic equilibrium may have been disturbed through impairment or inferior functioning of a particular organ or body part and the person compensates for this inferiority by strengthening the particular part or by increased functioning of another organ to make up for the deficiency (Rychlak, 1973). Thus, Heather's outstanding dancing performance in spite of the artificial leg can be viewed as a demonstration of her great efforts to compensate for the loss of her limb.

Progression to a Chronic Condition

For some, illness strikes suddenly as it may happen in an accident; for others there is a warning or a recognition that some disease is progressing perhaps to a chronic condition. When the individual gains awareness of the process and its irreversibility many of the reactions described earlier will be experienced. In addition, there is the agonizing question about how life will be when the disease process has reached its end stage but life is continuing. What quality of life is left for these individuals? How helpless will they become? How dependent will they be on others for the simplest tasks?

Sociologist and writer Susan Krieger, in her book *Things No Longer There* (2005), her memoir of losing her sight, has described the process of anxiety and questioning she experienced after realizing that she was losing her vision due to an eye condition called "birdshot retinochoroidopathy," an inflammation in the back of her eyes. In her own words she explained her experiences:

> When I began to lose my eyesight, the outer world literally became no longer visible to me as it had been before, I soon began to create a counterposing internal vision so that my sense of my own value would remain intact...an interior landscape that is composed of meanings, of sights and sounds, and feelings deeply held. (p. 93)

The author described in extraordinarily colorful detail what she was still able to see as well as what was distorted in her vision as the disease progressed. Her learning to use a white cane and to listen to the smallest sounds and noises around her are reported in a vivid manner. While her vision was in the process of deterioration, she was actively creating memories in the vision of her mind for the time when her eyes could no longer see them.

Jessica, a young woman with physical disabilities, such as chronic back pain and muscular weaknesses stemming from an accident some time ago, told her story about changing her career. For several years Jessica had worked as a teacher but then she decided to branch out and become a counselor. She had been married for almost 20 years and her children were about to leave the home. Due to her physical problems, it took her years of continuous struggle to arrange for the physical accommodations she needed for her coursework and her practicum in counseling.

While working through the program, she realized how her physical problems impeded her but also helped her to learn about herself. Jessica was able to recognize in herself long-standing behavioral patterns of immobilizing herself when she was in pain or facing fear. She was less aware of feeling the underlying anger because it was covered by anxiety. She was embarrassed about looking awkward and foolish when stumbling and even falling down as she tried—unsuccessfully at times—to keep up with others. Although parts of her body were weak, she realized that she was not completely helpless. Other faculties could compensate for some of the physical disabilities.

Her impairments worked both for and against her. Those individuals who was eventually going to help in counseling would recognize that Jessica was able to empathize with them and understand their pain and hardship. But there were also people who might be repulsed by her disabilities. In addition, prospective employers were not easily convinced of her resourcefulness and determination to succeed in her new profession.

Jessica started her work in a spiritually based counseling practice. In her new professional experience she is aware of the occurrence of setbacks and relapses and the importance of reframing them within her abilities in order to keep a healthy perspective. She recognizes and appreciates the opportunities that are available to her. In many ways she has learned to take care of herself in ways similar to those she might suggest to her clients.

During the times that Jessica immobilized herself when facing her own fears in addition to the pain, she operated out of a disengagement coping strategy, but due to her increasing awareness of the debilitating effects of that approach, she shifted to an engagement coping strategy when becoming involved in the lives of others in a meaningful professional way.

For those who are afflicted with a chronic illness and who are cared for by a spouse or family member, there are moments when they experience a fear of being abandoned by the caregiving person. Progress in coping or reaching increased levels of functioning may be accompanied by thoughts about the possibilities of the other person's leaving, whereas remaining incapacitated might ensure the continuing care out of loyalty or a sense of obligation. Available options may be viewed as consisting of progressing in recovery or adjustment and subsequently being abandoned or remaining helpless to assure the love and presence of the caregiver.

Libby, the young woman suffering with breast cancer who was introduced earlier in this chapter, admitted to having fleeting thoughts of being in the position of having to make that choice between remaining dysfunctional or being abandoned. In the case that Michael proceeded with divorce, would she regret the progress she made in recovering from her illness?

Chronic Impairment Aspects of Alcohol and Drug Abuse

In some professional arenas, alcoholism is viewed as a disease. One of the advantages of this notion can be seen in a shift away from a moral or legal perspective to one of medical concern. Furthermore, alcoholism and other addictive diseases have become the focus of scientific investigations as well as the concern of government and employment professionals. The effects of substance abuse (or dependence; for the purpose of this discussion a distinction between the two will not be made) are not limited to the abusing or addicted individual's personal life; they are observed in the workplace as well as in other parts of the communities where impaired behaviors cause accidents and losses.

Whether the abuse of alcohol or recreational drugs is classified as disease, illness, or anything else, it describes a condition that can last over long periods of time and therefore can be viewed as including chronic characteristics, much like other chronic illnesses discussed in this chapter. As with other long-lasting or chronic conditions, substance abuse, as well as the termination of it, is usually accompanied by significant changes in the individual's overall lifestyle.

One of the fundamental changes occurs in the beginning phase of the abuse. The person's thought process turns—perhaps unnoticed at first—onto a different path. As the focus intensifies on the use of alcohol or drugs, different thought patterns develop out of necessity. The individual feels compelled to give explanations (or excuses) to justify some behavioral aspects related to the consumption of chemicals. For instance, occasionally missing an early morning appointment (due to a hangover) will be explained with a malfunctioning alarm clock. Forgetfulness becomes the result of concentrating intently on other things; this, of course, is not a lie because the person's thinking is concentrated on the next "fix." Angry defensiveness may accompany the explanations and pave the way for social isolation.

Explanations are not only constructed for the benefit of others, but also work well for the abusing or addicted person by keeping guilt feelings at bay. The explanations appear so logical most of the time, especially if the person believes that the substance intake served as a coping strategy in finding solutions to a problem or making the problem seem less overwhelming.

As the abuse of or addiction to chemicals intensifies, goals in the person's mind become altered. Long-term professional or personal goals will be replaced by the search for immediate gratification. Psychological dependence on the chemical, which marks the shift in the individual's thought process, starts long before physical dependence becomes a problem. In psychological dependence the alcohol or drug becomes a *priority*; in physical dependence it is a *necessity*. "Dependence means being influenced, controlled, or determined by something; to rely or trust something other than one's self. This is the effect alcohol has on those who develop alcoholism" (Nace, 1987, p. 67).

The purpose of this discussion is not the presentation of knowledge about substance abuse or addiction; neither is it a suggestion for treatment modalities. There are many resources available on these topics. Instead, the focus here is on the changes in lifestyle that individuals affected by this condition are confronted with for significant periods of their lives. In order to simplify the discussion, the word "alcohol" will be used here to include other chemical substances as well.

Matthew, a handsome, competent-appearing businessman, was anxiety ridden when confronted with the requirement of making decisions. These were mostly decisions about his personal life. He was knowledgeable enough to make business decisions without too much trouble. But when it came to major decisions about his personal life he became paralyzed with anxiety. Matthew and Heidi had been married for about 12 years and had several children. There were unresolved issues that Heidi brought into the marriage and Matthew did not understand the origin of these issues. Although extremely attractive, a smoldering anger seemed to darken Heidi's personality. At times, the anger would erupt suddenly, leaving Matthew in a state of anxiety. After a while the anxiety set in even in the absence of Heidi's angry eruptions—just the thought that it might happen at any time was enough for Matthew to be uncomfortable. He seemed to be waiting for "the other shoe to drop."

Heidi's anger distorted her perception in such a way that she found blame for others wherever she looked. When Matthew found out that Heidi had been engaged in an extramarital affair for several years, somehow, while admitting that she was willing to work on improving the marriage, she managed to blame Matthew for her infidelity. This was not the first time that she had been unfaithful. Matthew was shattered by her betrayal. But there was also a decision to make: Should he divorce Heidi or should he forgive her and remain married to her?

What would happen to their children if they divorced? He would miss them if Heidi had custody of them. Matthew had always been afraid of change. He had difficulty adapting to changes because changes often required decisions and decisions involved anxiety. All he ever wanted from life was a loving family.

Every time he contemplated these questions, Matthew felt a wave of anxiety come up in him. He kept thinking, "What if...?" and every "what if" increased the level of anxiety. The main reason for the strong anxiety was his insistence that he make the correct decision. He wanted a guarantee for making the right decision and since that guarantee was not available, he was immobilized. To relieve the strong anxiety feelings, he resorted to alcohol for calming him down—without changing anything. Matthew became a binge drinker when it came to making personal decisions. How long would it take Heidi to figure out the process? The question occurred to Matthew in his therapy session. But how long would it take for him to work through his fear of the anxiety so that he could see himself tackling the task of making reasonably sound, not perfect, decisions and would it be in time to prevent his alcohol binges from developing into alcohol dependence?

When addicted individuals contemplate the cessation of alcohol intake they are confronted by strong fears and insecurities. How can they face the world and its problems without their coping mechanism or their "crutch" and what is left for them after perhaps having eliminated the striving for a future goal or having withdrawn physically or emotionally from previously significant people? The dread of facing any of these possibilities is enough to extinguish lingering thoughts of discontinuing the alcohol intake.

On the other hand, some people, upon starting on the path of sobriety, are rewarded by being flooded with great excitement about life. This excitement for a while overshadows the desire to drink. They may even feel "cured" and look expectantly for the wonders of life to unfold before them. In the euphoria stage of early sobriety there is a tendency to be excited; not drinking or using is a great achievement but it does not change the world around the person. Whatever was dissatisfying at the beginning of the abuse most likely is still there. Few people start drinking or using drugs because they are ecstatically happy. As mentioned earlier, the substance abuse can be seen as the person's distancing attempt from the dissatisfying circumstances—at least spiritually or emotionally. Thus, it is difficult to be "high on life" when life is the same old drag that it was before.

The difference between life as a drag when sober or when intoxicated is that, when sober, the person can do something to change life; when intoxicated, the person tends to take another drink or pop another pill to forget about it. There are no great promises of change in sobriety itself; it does not change the world. The person, however, is better able to modify her or his world when in a clear state of mind.

Maintaining sobriety involves a mental balancing act for the affected person. Amidst this drastic change in daily life, the all-important issue is not to drink. Many spend their days in fear of relapse, a very realistic fear. Recommendations for relapse prevention usually include concentrated maintenance of sobriety through intensive treatment regimens or frequent—almost daily—participation in Alcoholics Anonymous (AA) or similar meetings.

This part amounts to half of the balancing act. The other half is the meaning of life the individual is searching for. For some, sobriety is not enough as the primary source for meaning. After all, it had not been enough before they started drinking. Therefore, it would seem that simultaneously with the concern of maintaining sobriety, the person's chances for succeeding would be greatly enhanced by focusing on stimulating activities with the inherent potential of eliciting a strong interest within the person.

Family members living with an addicted person are affected in significant ways; they share many of the stresses and despair of the recovering individual. Anger, frustration, and emotional upheavals are almost daily occurrences during times of intense alcohol intake. Following the initial relief at the beginning of sobriety, disappointment may set in as the addicted person's intense self-involved focus may shift from how to obtain alcohol and other substances to how to maintain sobriety. Years of focus on oneself do not suddenly give way to other-related interests. Out of necessity and practice, the person's preoccupation is with the self.

The hours in the daily life of the alcoholic person that were previously filled with drinking or spending otherwise in an alcohol-induced haze are there to be filled with meaningful activity to prevent relapse due to boredom. Individuals vary in the behaviors that they demonstrate while in an intoxicated state and they respond differently to abstinence, due to the wide range of attitudes, beliefs, and personality styles they possess. Scientific investigations into the field of substance abuse primarily focus on medical, physiological, pharmacological, and neuropsychological aspects for explanations and treatment modalities. But more than a quarter of a century ago, Gorski and Miller (1982) in their relapse considerations pointed to three different personality styles that often prevent the maintenance of a successful recovery.

Extremely independent people, who believe that they cannot accept help from anyone, have difficulty acknowledging the reality of feeling powerless. The expectations they set for themselves are often impossible to fulfill and the isolation that results from hiding their powerlessness as well as avoiding offers of assistance from others open the door to temptation for relapse.

On the other end of the extreme, highly dependent individuals who believe in their inability to function independently attract others who tend to dominate them. By placing all responsibility on the other person, they will sabotage recovery by not acting in their own best interest and, when they encounter a small disappointment in the relationship with the other, they might resort to drinking again.

Another self-defeating personality style is what the authors called *counterdependence*. This term describes individuals who appear very independent but are actually deeply insecure. The overt behaviors of counterdependent individuals are in direct contradiction to their internal condition. They may evade facing relevant issues by displaying a busy schedule to distract from the void and insecurity deep within them.

Personality regression is another term that has been used in relation to alcoholism and relapse potential (Nace, 1987). This type of regression is a return to earlier modes of psychological functioning. It can be conceptualized as a shift in the level of psychological defenses from a more mature to a less mature level, characteristic of an earlier phase in the individual's development. Examples of immature defenses include impatient, passive–aggressive, or acting-out behaviors. As alcoholic individuals focus on the pleasurable effects of alcohol ingestion, they develop a sense of urgency, a desire for immediate gratification. Delays on the way to the gratification result in increased frustration, prompting some of the immature defenses to take over.

Following a failed early marriage and miscarriage, Helen, an attractive professional woman in her middle 40s, had led a single life for the past 20 years. To all outward appearance, she was a competent and successful professional. However, her brief, unsuccessful marriage and subsequent divorce had not resulted in a true sense of independence. She still yearned for a man to come along and take care of her and her needs. Helen envied her married friends and found reasons to rationalize her withdrawal from them with seeking new attachments to single male and female friends. Her feelings of insecurity were well hidden under the façade of her professional competence. Helen's personality resembled that of a counterdependent individual as described earlier.

Unfortunately, this personality constellation kept her from attracting suitable men. Her seeming independence and overt competence scared away those men who were looking for the more clinging, dependent type of women. And the ones who were initially attracted by her apparent independence became disenchanted when some of her insecurities surfaced. As would be expected, Helen's unsuccessful attempts at attracting a suitable male companion increased her feelings of insecurity and low self-esteem. She was bright, professionally successful, and attractive, so what was wrong with her that she could not find the relationship she craved? Helen looked for answers in the bottles that kept her company during the lonely evenings.

As is often the case with addictions, Helen's alcohol intake did not remain restricted to the evening hours at home. She felt her social interactions were improved by alcohol consumption as her internal fears were numbed by it. Her ability to drive home accident free from parties that involved alcohol intake encouraged her to have a cocktail or some wine at lunch. Over time, errors in her work performance became more frequent. When confronted with the deterioration of her performance, Helen initially responded in a defensive and angry manner. Her supervisor was torn between wishes to support and comfort Helen and the responsibilities of the supervisory position. The supervisor's decision was to strongly recommend treatment for Helen's alcoholism. If she did not follow the recommendation, there would be consequences, which the supervisor outlined for Helen.

Somewhat reluctantly Helen followed the supervisor's recommendations; she knew she could not afford to gamble on the consequences of refusing. Why had previous attempts at sobriety not been successful? Helen was not in favor of rehashing past treatment efforts. But there is a purpose in exploring endeavors at resolving a problem even if they have not been completely successful. Most likely there was a part of the endeavor that precluded success, but the overall approach might have been workable. The consideration of previous attempts will not only prevent repetition of actions that did not work, but will also provide an opportunity for encouragement when focusing on the workable parts of the endeavor. Living in a success-obsessed society, people shy away from failure, treating it like a contagious disease. When focusing exclusively on successful outcomes, opportunities for learning valuable lessons inherent in failures are lost (Maass & Neely, 2000).

In Helen's case, her reluctance stemmed from admitting her problem in front of a group of people. Even if their difficulties were of a similar nature, she did not want to admit that they had anything in common. The stereotypic accounts she had heard regarding people with alcohol problems and the names they were often called made her cringe when she thought of being one of them. At the time, her harsh self-judgment and wish to deny her impairment made it too difficult for her to maintain her sobriety after the initial phases of treatment. When she left the group sessions in a state of depression, alcohol delivered the desired relief.

Exacerbated by her continued drinking, denial became increasingly difficult to maintain and in individual sessions Helen was able to confront her fears and the dislike of herself. What were her options? Continuation with her drinking would most likely result in the loss of her job and an impoverished and socially isolated existence. Abstaining from alcohol intake with continuing her employment and standard of living while exploring paths to supply meaning to her life, even in the absence of a significant romantic partner, was the option Helen chose for the moment.

With her new lifestyle free of alcohol consumption, Helen has noticed that she has more energy as well as more free time in her life. Where previously whole evenings were spent sitting in front of the TV with her favorite alcoholic beverage to keep her company, she now enjoys those evening hours by attending to things that give her pleasure as well as performing maintenance tasks that are necessary for her independent existence. There has even been time for some interesting and meaningful volunteer activities in her community.

Perhaps the most significant change she has observed is that of her interactions with prospective romantic partners. She has become more focused in her observations of their behaviors toward her and others. In the past, she was willing to make excuses for their behaviors, blinding herself about any warning signals regarding the sincerity of their intents and commitments. This neglect on her part was one of the main reasons for the repeated breakups she experienced. Now she is more objective in her observations of their behaviors and commits some of what she perceives as warning signs to her memory. If the pieces of her observations seem to fit into certain patterns of questionable intent on the part of her male partners, she either terminates the relationship or proceeds cautiously.

Interrupted Passage Through Developmental Tasks

Those individuals who started abusing drugs and alcohol in their late adolescent–early adulthood years experience consequences of a different kind and magnitude than those who turned to substance abuse later in their lives. The transition period from late adolescence to early adulthood includes several developmental tasks for individuals to master. It is a time when adolescents' self-concepts become differentiated; they begin to see themselves as somewhat different from those around them. Also, as part of their budding self-confidence, their social and relational skills expand in interactions with family and peers. Important friendships are formed in this period.

As part of adolescents' development, their personality structures undergo changes and deepen as primary traits. Beliefs about the causes of events and circumstances are formed and challenged as part of the social and self-understanding process involving the concept of what has been called "locus of control" (Rotter, 1990). Individuals with an *external* locus of control tend to explain causes of their experiences, such as school failure or alcohol abuse, with reasons outside themselves. On the other hand, individuals with an *internal* locus of control consider personal factors such as ability and effort as determining reasons for outcomes.

There are important links between locus of control and behavioral aspects. Individuals with an internal locus of control are more likely to complete tasks to goal attainment, whereas individuals with an external locus of control would tend to give up or procrastinate (Janssen & Carton, 1999). It has been found that an external locus of control is sometimes linked with certain personality characteristics that include low self-esteem, introversion, and neuroticism (Beautrais, Joyce, & Mulder, 1999).

The early adulthood period is a time when individuals may develop dialectical thought, a type of thought process that involves recognition and acceptance of paradox and uncertainty (Basseches, 1989). Individuals with dialectical thinking expand the ability to deal with the fuzzier issues that are the majority of problems in adulthood. It is the type of thinking that is so useful when contemplating several options and their possible outcomes while adapting to changes in lifestyle circumstances.

Early adulthood is also the time when individuals' *life structures* develop (Levinson, 1990). The concept of life structures includes all the roles an individual occupies throughout life. Different roles function in different relationships and with different tasks and conflicts among them. Entering a new life structure requires a period of adjustment before individuals become competent at meeting the challenges through reassessment and reorganization of the beginning phase of the life structure. The goal is succeeding in the creation of a life structure that permits the individual to manage the demands of the developmental challenges with increased confidence and decreased distress.

As can be understood, the range of developmental tasks individuals are confronted with during late adolescence and early adulthood is immense and the individual tasks are of a complex nature. Mastering the tasks requires the ability to think clearly and critically and, in addition, the awareness of the complexity of the charge. Individuals who have decided to avoid the stresses of this period by withdrawing into the haze of chemicals may pass through this phase without gaining awareness of the requirements and without gaining any of the skills necessary for coping with the challenges of future life structures.

Diana, a graduate student in her late 20s, worked hard to achieve her professional goals. She had spent most of her late adolescence and early 20s drinking alcohol and using drugs along with her peers. Thanks to her high intelligence she was able to obtain her bachelor's degree, although not with the academic distinction one would have expected on the basis of her late childhood IQ scores. Her graduate study program had to be interrupted until after recovery from her addictions. She remained in therapy and worked diligently to make up for lost times. As she was in the stages of collecting data for her Ph.D. dissertation, she attended a professional conference. During the social part toward the end of the conference Diana was greatly relieved to see her therapist. She touched her therapist's elbow and whispered in a faint voice, "Please help me," upon which the therapist turned toward her and realized that Diana was experiencing a panic attack. Diana did not feel competent in the social interaction with other professionals.

Diana's socializing during all those years of her addiction occurred in a state of intoxication that precluded any learning of the skills people employ in regular social interactions. Finding herself in the situation without her previous crutch of alcohol, Diana felt at a total loss as to how to behave and what to say in social conversation with the other professionals she did not know.

Raymond spent an even longer time in his addiction to cocaine and alcohol. Like Diana, he managed to make it through college while partying. Following graduation, he dedicated his life to his addiction to the point of using up his considerable inheritance. He found jobs but could not maintain them for long. They did not pay enough anyway for what he needed. He spent decades before entering a residential treatment program. One of the female patients there caught his interest. She was about to graduate from the program when Raymond was discharged. Both were elated with their new state of being and in the euphoria of early sobriety they decided to get married.

The state of euphoria did not last long. Neither Raymond nor his new wife knew much about life without drugs and alcohol. They began to quarrel, expressing their disappointments, and finally parted, as Raymond realized, to protect and maintain their sobriety. Through some acquaintances of his father, Raymond was able to obtain a position in a major national company. He worked hard at his job and remained in therapy. Slowly he started to take classes toward graduate school; he was now in his 40s. There were several job transfers to different parts of the country, requiring another period of adjustment. Wherever he was transferred, he located another therapist and another university to continue his studies. But his social life had been on hold since the early days of his sobriety.

Raymond was lonely; he would have liked to find a female companion. At his workplace there were many young women who seemed interested in this handsome and intelligent man. But Raymond was too scared to approach any of them. Some colleagues unwittingly introduced him from time to time to a young assistant or secretary. Most of these dates ended in disaster because Raymond was so tense that he did not know how to behave and could not concentrate on conversation. The women found him to be boring. However, social skills could be learned and practiced as part of his therapy sessions.

After several attempts Raymond met a woman he could relate to. She had been divorced years ago. Raymond was in his 50s when they got married. Then the company he worked for went through some reorganization and several employees were offered early retirement as an option. Raymond was ready to move again to another university to pursue a doctoral program in psychology. He was awarded a scholarship, which assured him the money for tuition and a modest amount for living expenses. Early retirement seemed like a good option for him. His wife was willing to move and look for a job in their new environment. At almost 60 years of age, Raymond received his doctoral degree and is ready to start a new career.

Gregg: A New Lease on Life?

Gregg, who was taking care of his mother until her death, is maintaining his sobriety and slowly building a new life. As his story closed in the chapter on caregiving, he had been temporarily submerged in depression. Some of the pro bono counseling helped to revive his sagging spirits. He worked hard at reducing his fear of rejection and took the first steps at finding a job.

Being a delivery person for a florist shop put him in a position to gradually increase his contact with people. Sometimes there was nobody at home and he had to leave the flowers near the entrance to the house. At other times, people would involve him in conversation but he was in control of how long the conversation would last. The ability to leave at any moment with the stated reason that he had to make another delivery put him at ease and gave him partial control of determining the length of contact with customers. The job also brought an element of structure to his life. Not only did he have to show up on time to start his daily delivery load, he had to organize the individual trips along a route that eliminated detours and time delays as much as possible.

Furthermore, he liked flowers and while he was driving to his destinations, his mind could invent stories about the people who ordered the flowers and the people who were to receive them—what was the relationship between them? These thoughts rekindled his interest in writing and since he had already been successful at reducing his fear of rejection somewhat, he submitted two of his short stories to magazines. When the first rejection letter reached his mailbox he was disappointed, of course, but it did not stop him from writing. As he told the members in his writing group, he had a lot to catch up with them, who each had his or her own shares of rejection to swallow.

Gregg recognized the meaning in turning point episodes that people experience at particular times in their lives. The discussion of turning point episodes and personal event memories in the chapter on divorce resonated within him. Two memories surfaced that were influential in Gregg's sense of self-determination. The first one arose in connection with an overly demanding customer in his new job of delivering flowers. Long ago, when he was 6 years old, he stood up to the neighborhood bully. In Gregg's words, it is "a fine glowing memory" and reinforces the idea that he can stand up for himself—a notion that had been forgotten for a long time.

The other event that became a turning point episode for Gregg was the memorial service he had arranged for his mother a few years ago during his struggle of overcoming his long-standing alcohol addiction. His mother was cremated and the socially withdrawn Gregg made all the arrangements for the event. Relatives came from distant parts of the country and he thought this would probably be the last time he would ever see any of them. His anxiety level was high and he expected to fail in his attempts to make it a meaningful frame for his mother's departure. He was confronted by the emotional turmoil that resulted from his mother's death—all the feelings of sadness, guilt, love, anger, and regret. And he had no experience with the death and burial of a person close to him. He did not know much about himself, let alone how to organize such momentous events. He feared rejection from those he had asked to participate.

As Gregg accepted the challenge—even though he was highly anxious—the event proceeded with everybody readily cooperating. He learned that even as a person who did not expect good things to happen to him, going about performing the necessary tasks step by step, he could succeed and, what is even more important, he could find help from those around him.

In the art class he recently joined, Gregg chose as his project painting a portrait of his mother. The class is part of a community project free of charge to the participants. Gregg put this assistance to good use by creating another memorial to his mother, emphasizing the impact of his turning point episode. With his limited funds it was important to obtain the basic materials in order to avail himself of the opportunity for free instruction and critique of his talents. Although he would have preferred to paint in oil, he decided on acrylic because of its lower cost. It was either acrylic or nothing. Because acrylic dries fast, he had to work fast. Many hours were spent in drawing, to become practiced at the shapes and figures in his intended painting, so that he would be able to execute his work within the time span allowed him by the material.

While he labored to frame the painting in time for the graduation of his class, along with the blisters on his hands, he experienced the elation that comes from doing something he never thought he could do. The encouragement offered by the instructor and his fellow students has given Gregg the incentive to participate in the next free painting class when it is offered again. A week later, the members of his writing group were treated to meeting with Gregg's mother, as he showed off his painting to them.

Leaving his long-standing addiction behind, Gregg is busy uncovering and testing new opportunities for constructing a meaningful life for himself. He realizes that there are still developmental tasks he has not conquered yet due to his mental absence during the times these tasks were presented in his life. Some he may still be able to master; others may be lost for the time he has left. He has never been in a position to look for a female companion to share his life. This is a developmental task that may remain unfinished.

CHAPTER 9

Geographical and Cultural Relocations

American history is a history of immigration. Although the United States is not the only place that people immigrate to, its long history of immigration, as well as the sheer number and diversity of origin of its immigrants, makes it a fitting example for exploring the significant impact of geographical and cultural relocating of human beings and their adjustment to the changes.

Brief Historical Observations

Over time, the ethnic composition of the United States has undergone dramatic changes. In the years between 1901 and 1910, the number of admitted immigrants totaled 8,795,386; most of them came from Southern and Eastern Europe (70%). They were principally Catholics and Jews. By 1910, 40% of New York City's population was foreign born and in 1908 *The Melting Pot*, a play by Israel Zangwill, made its appearance.

During the next wave from 1911 to 1920, another 5,735,811 immigrants were admitted and 59% of these came from Southern and Eastern Europe (Menand, 2001). Seemingly as a response to the predominantly Southern and Eastern European immigrant population, the United States had established a quota system to restrict the number of people entering from those regions. In 1914 and the following war years and again in 1921, immigration laws became even more restrictive.

Currently, an unprecedented number of individuals are moving across the world, searching for a better life (Marsella & Ring, 2003). For instance, following the passage of the Immigration Act of 1965, immigrants from Korea arrived with their families in the United States (Hurh, 1998), making

Korean Americans one of the fastest growing Asian American ethnic groups, with more than one million Korean Americans (U.S. Census Bureau, 2000). This community consists mostly of first-generation immigrants with their children who were born in Korea and educated in the United States (Hong & Min, 1999). These immigrants were in search of a better life and a better education for their children.

In the United States, legal immigration refers to relocation of noncitizens who are granted *legal permanent residence* by the U.S. federal government. In 1998, the U.S. Congress lifted the ceiling on the number of work visas that are granted to highly skilled foreigners. They are given the right to remain in the country indefinitely, to be gainfully employed, and to apply for U.S. citizenship through naturalization (Mulder et al., 2001). Not all of them remain in the United States but, according to reports from the U.S. Census Bureau, 10.4% of the U.S. population consists of immigrants (Schmidley, 2001).

The physical proximity of their homeland to the United States has encouraged Mexican people more than other Hispanic groups to enter the United States legally and illegally. Mexicans comprise the largest number of immigrants in the United States and Mexican women make up 64% of the total U.S. Latino population. The second largest Hispanic minority in the United States is made up of people from Puerto Rico. Cuban Americans are rapidly becoming the third largest Hispanic minority in the country (Altarriba & Bauer, 1998).

Political–Philosophical Considerations

In premodern societies, the purpose of life is conceived as the reproduction of practices and customs of the society. Its people are expected to follow their parents' life paths. Thus, the ends of life are determined at the beginning of life—representing a cyclical pattern. Comfort comes from the fact that people know what their life's task is and they also know when it has been completed.

By contrast, in modern societies, the reproduction of customs is not considered to be a main purpose of existence and the ends of life are not thought to be predetermined; instead, they are to be discovered or created. Individuals in modern societies are not necessarily expected to follow their parents' life path; they can plan and construct their own paths. The future is not completely determined by the past in modern societies' thought; changes in unforeseeable directions occur, brought about by the initiative and contributions of individuals within that society. Devotion to preservation and reproduction of the culture of one's group carries with it the risk of obsolescence (Menand, 2001).

Alain LeRoy Locke, the first African American to win a Rhodes scholarship in 1907, stated that modern civilization does not tolerate separateness; modern societies require social assimilation. While people can continue to prepare and consume their ethnic food, overall, it is imperative that they adhere to the dominant standard. In Locke's opinion, the cost of cultural separatism is social subordination. Another modernist, John Dewey, in 1916 warned that it was dangerous for groups to isolate themselves, to attempt to live off their past, and then try to impose themselves upon other elements or to refuse acceptance of the larger culture's offerings and with that to isolate themselves.

In 1924 the term "cultural pluralism," introduced by Horace Kallen in his book *Culture and Democracy in the United States,* first appeared in print. Kallen was born in Silesia, Germany, and came to the United States in 1887 at the age of 5 years. Kallen's notion of pluralism was to keep ethnic groups in their proper places, rather than as a vehicle facilitating social mobility (Menard, 2001).

For some time the presence of large numbers of persons with limited proficiency in English has been a fact of life in the United States. According to the 2000 Census, over 26 million American citizens or residents communicate in Spanish at home and almost seven million persons converse in an Asian or Pacific Island language at home (U.S. Census Bureau, 2000). People with a limited ability to speak, read, write, or understand English are designated to have limited English proficiency, or LEP (U.S. Department of Justice, 2002), and under Title VI of the Civil Rights Act of 1964, they must be provided with assistance when they access Medicaid and other federally funded programs.

As an outgrowth of the Civil Rights Act of 1964, in the late 1960s, the multicultural counseling movement started in the school systems and the mental health field. Its initial goals were to direct attention to and facilitate understanding of the psychological differences among people from various racial–ethnic minority groups within U.S. society (Daniels, D'Andrea, & Arredondo, 2001). These efforts were expected to result in more effective, ethical, and respectful treatment of people from diverse backgrounds. Professionals were trained in multicultural issues to become "multiculturally competent" experts (Holcomb-McCoy & Myers, 1999). The melting pot ideology had changed character; it became more of a stew of individuals retaining their distinct cultural heritage with some flavor from the environment tossed in (Swartz-Kulstad & Martin, 1999).

Describing the changing of the melting pot idea, Linda Chavez (2001), president of the Center for Equal Opportunity in Washington, DC, used the metaphor of the salad bowl where individuals coexist in separate groups, firmly holding on to ancestral identities and affinities. The process of becoming a U.S. citizen has undergone dramatic changes, from dropping or diminishing the English requirement for naturalization to reducing the amount of knowledge of U.S. history and civics required to abandoning portions of the oath of allegiance. According to Chavez, we have been indoctrinated with the cult of multiculturalism for the past three decades and have elevated "diversity" to a civic virtue, without considering that diversity can be good or bad, depending on what we do with it.

Unlike the many new immigrants that arrived in the early part of the twentieth century, many of the high school youth who are immigrants themselves now are confronted with a labor market that does not provide many opportunities except for those who have marketable skills, particularly in the fundamental areas of literacy, numeracy, and problem solving (Marshall & Tucker, 1992). For solving problems in a particular country, the literacy skills would need to be relevant to that country.

To truly help immigrants in their adjustment, Chavez pointed out that our schools should be committed to teaching immigrant children English, which should enable them to fully participate in our society. American history should be taught in depth to all students to enable them to understand the foundations of our democracy. Community organizations have the responsibility to promote civic education for immigrants by setting up classes to aid in their preparation for citizenship. Extreme focus on multiculturalism and diversity entails the risk of turning us back to the corrosive ideology that divides us into factions by emphasizing differences over commonality.

Interestingly, when Altarriba and Bauer discussed the statistical composition of Hispanic minority groups in the United States, they pointed out that within the population of immigrants from Puerto Rico, some desired Puerto Rico's independence from the United States, while others were appreciative of American involvement in Puerto Rico's government. They also stressed the fact that Cuban Americans had attained a high socioeconomic level compared with other Hispanic groups. As rationale for their emphasis of these aspects, they stressed the importance for mental health professionals to be educated about these issues in order to match client–therapist expectations for the effective delivery of mental health care to members of the various Hispanic groups. Of course, it would also be highly desirable for mental health care providers to be proficient in the languages spoken by their immigrant clients.

Educators, researchers, psychologists, and family life educators are faced with an increasing number of culturally diverse clients due to changing demographics, the shrinking of global boundaries, and an increase in the number of immigrants. Ability to understand international clients is considered to be important because the immigrants bring their values, beliefs, and customs with them (Medora, 2005). Even after acculturation into mainstream America, the immigrants transmit their traditions and cultural beliefs from one generation to the next.

Organizations such as the American Counseling Association, the American Psychological Association, and the International Association of Couples and Family Counselors have included into their codes of ethics for their members the requirement of obtaining knowledge for working with ethnically diverse minority U.S. and international clients through coursework regarding cultural differences. Knowledge and understanding about cultural similarities and differences are important for professionals working with clients coming from foreign countries, but, as pointed out by Chavez, there is a fine line between assisting those unfamiliar with the language and customs of their new environment and keeping them dependent upon others and unable to participate freely in American society.

Surely, today's well-meaning recommendations are made in the spirit of easing the immigrants' stress and assisting with the complexities of their lives in an unknown environment, but how far will they go in eventually rendering the immigrant able to function independently in the unfamiliar surroundings? The less people are challenged to achieve knowledge of the unknown, the less they might be inclined to expand the effort—even if it is for their own good. Too much help can be crippling. As individuals are able to transplant their beliefs and cultural background without disturbing or mixing it with those of the outside reality, they can comfortably relax within their group and remain on the periphery of life; they remain marginalized. In the opinion of Woodrow Wilson, America does not consist of groups. Those who consider that they belong to a particular national group in America have not yet become Americans and they may never arrive at that stage (Menand, 2001).

What is more, as they hold on to the bits and pieces of their transplanted cultures, they are not aware that cultures, as responses to the conditions of life, change as the conditions themselves change. In all likelihood, the customs and practices in their original countries are not the same as they were or the same that the immigrants have taken with them and kept holding onto in the new world. If they were to return to their countries of origin, these immigrants might experience shock and disillusionment when confronted by the changes.

Immigrants' Lives in the Nineteenth and Early Twentieth Centuries

Turning the clock back to the nineteenth century when pioneer women from abroad settled with their husbands in northern American states, in 1862 Gro Svendsen, a young woman from Norway, where as a teacher's daughter she had led a sheltered life, accompanied her husband to a frontier settlement in Iowa (Neidle, 1975). She was fond of reading but could indulge in this passion only during the times she was confined to her bed, giving birth to a child. Between childbirths she was deprived of reading; there was too much to do.

At the time that her first child was ready for school attendance, that child was sent to English school accompanied by Mrs. Svendsen, who attended the English school along with her child. What she learned in English school, she taught to other Norwegian settlers in log cabins around the district. She adopted a sense of identification with America and sent all her children to English school and some of them to the Norwegian Sunday school to keep the link to their Norwegian culture alive.

To be congruent with American life, she insisted on giving one of her sons an American name so that he would not have to change it later as a grown-up in the American community. As busy as she was with her farm life and taking care of her large family, she made time available to function as the "secretary of the community" by writing letters on behalf of its members.

Gro Svendsen died at the age of 37 years after the birth of her 10th child. Had she remained in her home country of Norway, her life would have been easier. Perhaps if she had returned to Norway, she might have lived longer. In the process of identification with America, her new home, she was too busy to waste time and energy on grieving over the loss of the lifestyle she left behind. She actively made her life congruent with her new environment. While doing that, she also helped those around her in their attempts to become part of their community.

During the second quarter of the nineteenth century, large numbers of immigrants arrived in Boston. They were quite different from the mostly English, mostly Protestant resident population. Their arrival continued for the remainder of the nineteenth century and well into the twentieth. By 1895, the population in the North End of Boston included 6,800 Irish, 1,200 British, and 800 Portuguese, but also 6,200 Jews, mainly from Russia and Eastern Europe, and 7,700 Italians (Todisco, 1976). As the Irish presence began to dwindle, the Italian community continued to grow and eventually became the dominant ethnic presence in the North End.

By the end of the century, philanthropic efforts assisted the strangers in coping with their alien environment and helped inculcate in them the dominant American culture. Many of the primary agencies in this effort were settlement houses, a phenomenon imported from England, where they had been established to provide educational opportunities to English workingmen. In the United States, the notion of settlement houses was reshaped to serve local goals in Americanizing a diverse population from a variety of ethnic stocks.

One of the women who became a part of this process was a librarian named Edith Guerrier (1870–1958), the daughter of an English immigrant. Edith participated in the efforts to Americanize the individuals arriving in the high tide of immigration from Eastern Europe, but she wanted to give them more than just survival skills. She worked as an aid in the nursery schools supported by philanthropist Pauline Agassiz Shaw and later conducted girls' clubs in several settlement houses and at Shaw's North Bennet Street Industrial School in Boston's North End, where she maintained a reading room and a Boston Public Library book delivery station.

In a comparison of these immigrant women to the general population, it was shown that in 1910 only 3.8% of 18- to 21-year-old women in the United States were in college, a figure that rose to 7.6% in 1920. However, 25% of the settlement house club, called the Saturday Evening Girls, in this sample attended college or professional schools. Of the 48 children of alumnae, 40 attended college (Matson, 1992).

In 1950, 100 comfortably middle-aged, middle-class women, all of them immigrants or children of immigrants and alumnae of the Saturday Evening Girls, gathered in Boston to commemorate the 51st anniversary of the founding of their group. Their guest of honor was Edith Guerrier, the group's founder, who was celebrating her 80th birthday.

The successful assimilation of these women into the middle-class mainstream, from tenement to suburbia, was partly due to the efforts of those who assisted in improving the language, modifying the behavior, and inculcating traditional New England values into the minds of the immigrants and children of immigrants who sought out the settlement houses, night schools, and libraries that offered them a chance at full membership in American society. And assimilation was due to the immigrants' determination to learn a new style of life and make the best of the opportunities that were offered them.

Processes of Assimilation

The immigrants' lives discussed previously can be understood as having undergone the process of assimilation—the process through which an ethnic group loses its distinct cultural and ethnic identity as it becomes absorbed by the larger group (Levinson, 1994). As immigrants conform to and ultimately become part of the dominant cultural group in their new homeland, the process of assimilation proceeds through a series of stages. Cultural assimilation, or acculturation, is the first stage in which immigrant groups change values and norms to conform to the values and norms of the dominant cultural group. Learning and using the language of the dominant group, altering traditional beliefs about the world, becoming citizens of the nation, and, perhaps, changing religious practices to conform to dominant religious practices are parts of this first stage.

When cultural assimilation is followed by structural assimilation, members of the ethnic group begin to interact with institutions and members of the host society. Friendships with people from mainstream society or other ethnic groups develop; use of professional services and civic organizations occurs and increases in frequency. Other types of assimilation, such as identificational assimilation, when one's identity becomes based on membership in the host society, or marital assimilation through intermarriage with members of other groups, proceed. Passage through the various stages provides different sets of opportunities for immigrants.

Another type of assimilation process, known as the "melting pot," suggests that all ethnic groups contribute some parts of their traditional culture, which combine to form a new, distinct culture. In partial assimilations, minority groups adopt several aspects of the dominant culture while at the same time maintaining many of their own customs and beliefs. Some nations resist assimilating groups of culturally or physically different immigrants; on the other hand, there are immigrant ethnic groups that themselves choose to resist assimilation (Levinson, 1994).

Adopting New Gender Roles

Immigration can be an impetus for challenging traditional gender role stereotypes. Women may consider immigration as an opportunity to leave unsatisfying partnerships or improve their gender role status by increasing control over household decisions and developing or strengthening personal autonomy. In some immigrant families, women might seek employment to supplement the family income. Started as a financial necessity, women's working outside the home may eventually change traditional gender roles and power relationships within the family (Gim Chung, 2001; Pyke, 2000). Even if the woman works in a part-time position performing manual labor, she is bound to be exposed to the surrounding culture and language at a higher degree than if she stayed at home. With the increased knowledge and money, her position in the family could become more powerful than it had previously been.

In the 1800s and early 1900s, foreign-born women often were subjected to painful adjustment when they arrived in the United States. A wave of Slavic immigrants coincided with the rise of heavy industry, such as coal mining, steel manufacture, meatpacking, and similar industrial enterprises. Many of these immigrants were illiterate and had been farmers or shepherds in their countries of origin. Accustomed to hard work and outdoor life, these women worked as hard as any of the men.

The story of a strong Croatian woman called Manda Evanich shows how her hard work and her special talents at healing and setting broken bones enabled her to bring her husband and sons to higher levels of responsibility and in time to affluence (Adamic, 1932). Manda shared her countrywomen's strength and willingness to work hard, but, unlike many of them, Manda was not illiterate; she could read and write. At age 19, with a child from a previous marriage, Manda married Mike Evans, her second husband. Mike was the first Croatian to move to Michigan. He worked in the copper mines and intended to return to his native country after saving some money. However, when he contracted an eye disease that doctors were unable to diagnose, he wrote Manda to come as soon as possible with her herbs to help with his eye problem. Mike had been in Michigan for 2 years when Manda arrived at the abandoned log cabin that her husband and a dozen prospective boarders had prepared for her. Mike's eye infection was cured in 2 weeks.

Like many pioneer women at the time, Manda took care of boarders; for $3.00 a month she cooked, cleaned, and did the laundry for them, working more than 16 hours a day. She also nursed their colds, injuries, and wounds. Her husband's daily wage was $1.25. Manda kept her eyes focused on opportunities for improvement. When she heard that other mines paid better wages, she persuaded her husband to move. In the new location, she established another home to which her boarders followed faithfully. In her early 30s, after having been in America for 8 years, she had saved enough money to buy a large house in Calumet and open a saloon.

Twelve of her American-born sons grew to manhood. At the birth of the last, a pair of twins, President Theodore Roosevelt wrote Manda a letter of congratulations. The saloon grew into a thriving establishment, keeping Manda busy with many duties besides serving beer and wine. To help with the many activities, she brought young girls over from Croatia, who stayed and worked with her until they got married. Twice a year she went to Chicago to purchase clothes at wholesale prices for her 12 sons. She also cautiously bought copper stocks, which increased the family's wealth considerably. All her sons grew into successful and respected men; several attended college and law school. At the age of 81 years, now widowed, Manda was living independently, still practicing her healing art.

In Manda's busy days there was no time to grieve for the loss of whatever she had left behind in Croatia. If she had indulged in feeling sorry for anything that was lost to the past, she would have blinded her view to the many opportunities that existed in her new environment. Starting with hard work to supplement her husband's wages, Manda steadily transformed her traditional gender role of wife and mother into a position of personal authority and independence.

In 1731 Lewis and Elizabeth Timothy, a couple born in Holland, immigrated to Philadelphia with their four children. Six years later they moved to Charleston, South Carolina, where they, in partnership with Benjamin Franklin, became publishers of the colony's first permanent newspaper, the *South-Carolina Gazette* (Frost-Knappman, 1994). After her husband's death in 1738, Elizabeth continued to publish the paper under the name of her 14-year-old son Peter. Elizabeth also established a bookshop and her good business sense enabled her to provide well for her children. After Elizabeth's death in 1757, Peter continued to publish the newspaper. According to Benjamin Franklin, Elizabeth was a better business manager than her husband. If Elizabeth and her husband had not immersed themselves in the English language, they could hardly have been so successful in publishing a newspaper and managing a bookstore.

Another newspaperwoman, Anne Catherine Hoof Green, also born in Holland in about 1720, came to America with her parents, who settled in Philadelphia (Frost-Knappman, 1994). Anne married printer Jonas Green, who was employed by Benjamin Franklin. Ten years later, in 1745, Jonas founded the *Maryland Gazette*, one of the colonies' earliest newspapers. Anne must have worked with him in the printing shop because she was able to continue the paper's publication without missing an issue at her husband's death in 1767. She also published other materials, such as almanacs, political tracts, and a book on probating wills and administering estates. Her publishing early accounts of colonial protest against Great Britain furthered the revolutionary cause and made her newspaper the province's main source of news in the period before the American Revolution. She died in 1775.

The preceding stories of two immigrant women for whom English was not their native language tell how they not only mastered the language well enough to publish newspapers, but also took over in the men's positions when their husbands died. They did not select the option to retire permanently into mourning over the loss of their spouses.

A modern story of transformation from traditional female gender role to decision-making head of household was revealed in an interview reported in a professional journal. Claudia Daniels's mother experienced a change in gender role when, with her two young children, she left her husband, a victim of Bolivia's drug culture, in order to build a new life. She was successful working for political party officials in her native country, but in the wake of a transition of power in 1993, Claudia's mother sought political asylum in the United States with 15 year-old Claudia and her younger brother. Arriving in Washington, DC, they had less than $200, and Mrs. Daniels secured work as a housekeeper in a hotel (Kennedy, 2006).

Claudia recalls having a difficult time adjusting to the hardships of her new life. After graduation from high school she enrolled in a local junior college but had to work three different jobs to earn money for tuition and books. Claudia's mother learned English and enrolled in classes to become a medical assistant. Claudia enlisted in the U.S. Navy, which enabled her to pursue a college education in counseling. As a petty officer 2nd class, she has become the only substance abuse counselor for adolescent dependents of U.S. Navy members. Currently a wife and mother of two children, she is still pursuing her education toward a doctorate.

Although an article in *Counseling Today* featured Claudia Daniels, it is really the mother who took decisive action—first when she took her two young children and left her husband and then, as a single mother, became the breadwinner, assuming the traditional role of provider in her native country. When it became necessary to remove her family from her native Bolivia, she sought a safe place in the United States. Her courage and hard work set the example for Claudia to search for opportunities for herself.

Immigration Stress

This section does not address the issues of those who left their countries as refugees. For example, more than 1.5 million Southeast Asian refugees resettled in the United States after the Vietnam War (U.S. Dept. of Health & Human Services, Office of Refugee Settlement, 1990). This group, similar to other refugee populations, is at risk for experiencing serious mental health difficulties, such as post-traumatic stress disorder (PTSD) as result of traumatic war experiences, starvation, dangerous escapes from their homeland, and refugee camp experiences (Chung & Bemak, 2002). These traumatic experiences add significant complications to the stress of immigration and are better discussed in separate writings.

Migration is a highly stressful experience; "it can produce profound psychological distress among the most motivated and well prepared individuals, and even in most receptive circumstances" (Rumbaut, 1991, p. 56). Individuals from different ethnocultural backgrounds often lack the ability to function successfully in their new linguistic environment because the level of proficiency in the host culture's language determines the ease in the socialization process of the individual (Swartz-Kulstad & Martin, 1999). And to the degree that it impedes or enhances the socialization process, it exerts a significant influence on the person's occupational status and, with that, his or her economic class standing (Daniels et al., 2001).

The process of adopting the values and behaviors of a new culture represents another common factor in the consideration of the immigrants' psychological stresses (Flannery, Reise, & Yu, 2001; Hays, 2001). Acculturation proceeds slowly and at different rates for different individuals. Whether consciously or unconsciously, individuals stepping into a second culture are faced with a series of choices about associating with the new culture or holding on to the old, and these choices will be reflected in their behavioral responses. The overall process of acquiring a second culture can be seen as occurring along six paths (Coleman, Casali, & Wampold, 2001): Assimilation, acculturation, and separation are descriptions of linear culture acquisition, while alternation, integration, and fusion present different conceptualizations.

The concept of alternation assumes the possibility of shifting, or alternating, between two cultures; in integration, individuals from different cultures coexist without compromising their original cultural identities. The original culture is maintained while interacting with people from different cultures. The notion of fusion, however, assumes that individuals from different cultures who consistently interact with each other will eventually fuse, creating a new culture that subsumes individuals' original cultures.

Those individuals who give up their culture of origin to achieve competence in a second culture become "assimilated." And those who are able to create a living and working environment in which they can maintain their culture of origin while at the same time interacting with individuals from other cultures become "integrated."

The migration and relocation of nuclear families may be particularly complex for women. In many traditional patriarchal societies women are viewed as the keepers and transmitters of cultural values. Intergenerational conflicts may arise with their children, who often become more readily involved in the new culture, and with older family members, who strongly adhere to the cultural values and gender roles of their native country (Darvishpour, 2002).

A review of five large-scale studies exploring the prevalence of psychological distress among Mexican Americans living in the United States and comparing distress levels among Mexican-born and U.S.-born Mexican Americans revealed higher levels of psychological distress among the U.S.-born Mexican Americans than among those who were born in Mexico (Escobar, Nervi, & Gara, 2000). Newly arrived immigrants from Mexico reportedly were at high risk for depression and suicide (Hovey, 2000).

However, arriving at the conclusion that greater acculturation to the new environment has a direct association to greater mental distress would be a premature speculation as long as there are no definite criteria for what the process of acculturation does or should include. Just spending time in a different environment is not a measure of the degree of acculturation immigrants are actually experiencing. In fact, the data observed in the comparison between Mexican-born and U.S.-born Mexican Americans mentioned earlier could also mean that U.S.-born Mexican Americans experienced greater confusion by being born into a culture different from the one that they were actually living in with their parents, who followed the values and customs of their native country.

Most of the research on acculturation has focused on the experiences of adults, but the children or adolescents of immigrant families experience a different set of distress factors (Sam, 2000). Young people generally face the problems of self-concept, identity conflicts, and generational conflicts with parents typical of adolescence. The relocation aspects of immigration exacerbate these normal developmental conflicts. While attempting to assimilate into American culture, these adolescents are expected to respect and maintain the culture of their countries of origin. The challenge of choosing, juggling, and managing the competing requirements can be extremely stressful, indeed.

The Shifting Self in Young Persons' Negotiations Across Cultures

In order to understand the process of their adjustment and negotiation between various cultural value and belief systems, a group of 13 Korean immigrant youths was recruited from a junior high school in a large metropolitan area in the Northeast and given semistructured interviews (Yeh et al., 2005). The findings indicated that Asian immigrant youth constantly negotiate across different environments, such as school, family, and peer relations. They also seem to shift their identity and value systems according to the norms of these different settings. These identity shifts enable them to fulfill their cultural obligations and to maintain social harmony within and between their two worlds. Identity can thus be conceived of as a fluid and dynamic entity that responds differentially to stimuli and demands emanating from various circumstances.

The notion of the shifting self (Yeh & Hwang, 2000) makes negotiation across cultures possible, as it allows the self to be expressed and understood in multiple ways across various relational and situational aspects. Within interpersonal dynamics the shifting self responds and changes according to various emotional, social, and relationship influences. While functioning within a self-shifting mode, individuals spend time and effort adapting to the continuous shifting, leaving them little time and energy to focus on the losses of things and ideas left behind.

In response to cues in the social environment, individuals may be shifting between interpretive frames that can have roots in different cultures (LaFromboise, Coleman, & Gerton, 1993). Such *frame switching* might occur in response to stimuli that have a psychological connection to one or another culture. Individuals who have internalized two cultures may be guided in their thoughts and feelings by alternating influences from both cultures. These internalized cultures often do not exist in a blended version within the individual. Absorption of a second culture does not necessarily replace the influences of the first one. Concepts of self-shifting and frame switching are not the exclusive domain of young individuals; it just appears easier for them to apply these concepts for their own benefits. However, adults of all ages can make use of them.

As a reference tool in multicultural research, the Dimensions of Personal Identity Model, incorporating three dimensions (A, B, and C) with fixed and fluid or dynamic characteristics of a person's individual identity, has been applied (Arredondo, Rosen, Rice, Perez, & Tovar-Gamero, 2005). Dimension A includes such factors as age, race, culture, ethnicity, gender, language, sexual orientation, and social class, among others. Of these, age, gender, and race are fixed factors, while others, such as language, culture, and sexual orientation, can be considered fluid or changeable. Factors included in the B dimension are educational background, geographical location, work experience, interests, and relationship status, among others.

Contextual and sociopolitical considerations, such as historical moments like wars, slavery, the Depression of 1929–1933, or the Holocaust, are presented in dimension C. These events are not under the control of individuals or small groups but have a direct or indirect impact on the person. The model suggests that dimensions A and C influence the opportunities and experiences that individuals or groups may or may not be able to avail themselves of in the B dimensions.

For instance, persons growing up in war-torn countries (dimension C) may not have been able to attain a solid educational background (dimension B) during their childhood years (dimension A, fixed), but with immigration to another geographical location (dimension B), they could avail themselves of educational or occupational training (dimension B) later in life (dimension A, fixed) and perhaps with the requirement of learning a different language (dimension A, fluid).

Alternating Between Cultures

The condition of shifting between two different cultures is often experienced by individuals who enter another country for professional reasons, as students, or to make more money than they could in the countries of their origin and who plan to eventually return to their native countries. These situations are different from the simultaneous influences of different cultures, which occur with immigrants who are significantly enmeshed with influences from their country of origin, as described in the preceding section.

Under the conditions of the global economy, companies have created branch or daughter companies in countries outside their original sites.

Executives from the main companies are often transferred for varying periods of time to supervise the production in the auxiliary or branch companies. The executive, usually a man, is shielded from immersion into a new culture by his daily work-related contacts, and topics at social events are largely focused on economic rather than personal issues.

For the wife, accompanying the executive husband, the story is somewhat different. She is expected to develop social connections with other executive wives that are beneficial to or supportive of her husband's position. She also knows that this will be a temporary placement while the cultural life at home continues without her. Therefore, it is to her advantage to keep abreast with social, cultural, and political developments in the society she and her husband came from. And there are at least yearly visits to the home country to keep the connection with family and friends or to inspect the condition of the rented-out family residence. Social scientists may consider such situations within the category of transnational migration, as will be discussed later.

Elke, an attractive blond, blue-eyed woman in her early 40s, was in need of a German-speaking therapist upon discharge from the hospital with the diagnoses of depression and alcohol abuse. Alfred, Elke's husband, a vice president of a well-established European company with branch companies around the world, was almost 20 years older than Elke. When they met, Alfred was a widower and Elke's marriage to her first husband had ended in divorce. As a young student, Elke had left the university prematurely, but she had obtained an education suitable for a wife of Alfred's standing.

Officially, their stay in the United States was planned for a period of 3–5 years, with the possibility that Alfred might advance to head of the branch company, staying abroad until the time of his retirement. Elke experienced significant culture shock. She missed the elegance of her European surroundings. Although she had a basic knowledge of the English language, it was not sufficient to discuss topics on a more sophisticated level. She felt inadequate in her conversations at social gatherings. Her self-esteem, which largely depended on approval from outside sources, plummeted. She had learned to drive a car in her native country and had obtained a driver's license in the state she now resided in, but she felt uncomfortable venturing out into unfamiliar territory.

Elke began her therapy with downplaying her alcohol use and reciting a list of complaints: She was bored; there were no interesting activities for her to participate in. Her particular entry arrangements prevented her from seeking employment and, of course, she did not need to work. Initially, people had tried to include her in activities and get-togethers but, out of a mixture of low self-esteem and hypercritical attitude, Elke responded in ways that were interpreted as aloof or even haughty. If she called a taxi for an outing she never knew what kind of automobile would show up. Often it was just a common American car like many people drive, not like in some European countries where taxi drivers used prestigious automobiles for their fares.

After listening for a while, the therapist turned the conversation to what Elke would like to experience during her life in the new environment. Had she thought of options that would make her life more interesting? Although she could not search for a job to hold her interests, she could volunteer for some community agencies. Elke drew herself up; no, volunteer work was not what she had in mind. She did agree, though, that it would be advantageous if she improved her knowledge of the English language.

Her therapy proceeded on several levels: Her depression—partly based in her low self-confidence—and her alcohol abuse needed attention. At the same time, exploration of options, focusing on immediate actions she could take, would supplement the process of dealing with her psychological distress. For application within this chapter, attention will be given primarily to the option exploration part of the therapy process.

What were Elke's options at point A? Although not permitted to work, she could engage herself in volunteer activities. Her initial dislike of volunteer work gave way to a mild interest in the possibility. As her therapist explained, community agencies are usually grateful for the help they receive. Their appreciation of the assistance renders the agencies less critical of restrictions on the part of the volunteer, such as limited knowledge of the language, communicating with an accent, and unfamiliarity with local customs. Elke realized that volunteer activity would be an opportunity to improve her language skills in a nonpunishing situation. It would also enlarge the circle of acquaintances that she could socialize with.

In addition, Elke could participate in community education courses, both to search for an interesting hobby and to upgrade her language competency. Regarding transportation, Elke had the option to ask on the phone for the make and type of automobile the taxi driver used and request another driver with a car that was more to her liking. She could also venture out by herself or with one of her new acquaintances to explore her environment along an increasing radius from her home.

Almost a year had passed since Elke's initial hospitalization. There had been one relapse into alcohol abuse shortly after her start in therapy when her husband was away on a business trip. Through volunteer activities and classes, Elke had become more confident in the use of the English language to the point where she considered attending college. Elke viewed herself at a point B, where her language skills did not constitute a significant limitation anymore and she was in a position to explore new options.

At point B she decided that if Alfred were to remain here for 5 years or even longer, she had at least 3 more years to spend in the United States. She explored local colleges. It looked like a good opportunity to use the time for a big learning experience. Elke applied for admission; excitedly, she called her therapist with the good news of her acceptance. Before the semester began, Alfred received a transfer back to Europe. The company's global reorganization had resulted in the closing of this particular facility in the United States. Elke was devastated. The event she had so hoped for in the beginning now came as a shock. Just as she had begun to feel as if she had conquered a tiny part of the new world, she had to let go of it.

At this particular point, the only viable option for Elke was to return home with her husband. Alfred's position with the company was shaky. Apparently, he had not been able to make a success of the branch operations as had been expected and his employers considered it financially advisable to give up on it.

About 8 months later Elke's therapist received a letter from her. It was a sad letter. Elke's readjustment to her native country had not been easy. While confronted with some of the changes that had occurred there during her absence, her basically negative and passive attitude resurfaced as she focused on her losses. Her family and former friends did not observe any great achievements to celebrate upon Elke's return. In her depression she resorted to self-medication with alcohol again. She was hospitalized for almost 2 months without the benefit of in-depth psychotherapy. At discharge, her prognosis was guarded; it appeared only a matter of time until the next relapse.

Elke's story is one of sadness and disappointment. Although there was a moment of promise, it was short-lived. The combination of her low self-esteem, which needed outside approval to keep her functioning, and her negative attitude regarding changes in a rather passive personality constellation was of long duration and quickly re-established itself upon her return to her home environment. The increased alcohol consumption emphasized her focus on losses and obscured the existence of options from her vision. One brief note informed the therapist that Alfred had been encouraged to take an early retirement and they were moving to another area. The therapist observed the lack of a return address on the envelope; it appeared that Elke did not want to be found.

Transnational Migration

Individuals who routinely cross national and cultural boundaries and maintain ties to their country of origin through ongoing contact with family and friends in their home communities remain intimately connected to their home culture while they are living and working in another country. Their transnational ties may include sending money to family members at home and visiting frequently in their native communities. They may maintain temporary residence in their host countries with the purpose of accumulating sufficient resources for a comfortable life upon permanent return to their home countries. Social scientists have debated whether these transnational migrations lead to a world community or result in cultural variations throughout the world (Levinson, 1994).

The relative ease with which migrants today can communicate with families at home and travel back and forth for visits makes transnational migration more appealing. It may represent a new type of migration pattern as global economic changes might lead to a new world order. In transnational migration, wealth flows from immigrant communities back to the homeland in various ways, as mentioned earlier.

Capital investment in economic institutions in the homeland constitutes another type of economic tie to the homeland. When overseas communities amass significant wealth, such investments are possible (Levinson, 1994). An example was seen in the post-1965 movement of Indian immigrants to the United States. They arrived as professionals, collected significant resources through their work and frugality, and invested resources in the development of new businesses, banks, and industries in India or deposited their money in Indian savings accounts or bonds.

The so-called nonresident Indians (NRIs) may be conflicted in the pull of a satisfactory life in the United States and the loyalty to their home country. Beyond the economic effects, transnational migration impacts the structure and processes of gender relations, child rearing, and family ties in both the homeland and the host country.

Migrant Workers

Migrant workers occupy a somewhat different category under the concept of transnational migration. Around the world, members of one ethnic group have been used by another ethnic group to perform types of labor that held low desirability or was of crucial need for the economic growth of the host ethnic group. In general, nations that do not subscribe to an assimilation ideology permit few of the migrant workers the achievement of their national citizenship (Levinson, 1994).

The European continent has witnessed a drastic shift in the movement of migrants. Prior to 1945, Europe was the scene of emigration; many more people left Europe than moved to Europe. The end of World War II brought the collapse of colonial empires overseas and political realignment of geographical areas, forcing many Europeans to return to their native countries. For instance, French people returned from North Africa, British from India, Dutch from Indonesia, and Germans from Poland and the USSR. These returning migrants were easily absorbed into the populations of their homelands due to the demands of rapid economic reconstruction and expansion. The growing labor demand resulted in bringing in workers from outside Europe. The non-European population in the early 1950s was about 350,000 and increased to about four million by the early 1960s (Levinson, 1994).

By 1973–1974 the immigration of non-European migrant workers was slowed or stopped in most receiving nations. Increase in the numbers of non-Europeans has been mostly due to the arrival of family members from the countries of origin and as a result of children born in Europe. By the 1980s, European and non-European migrants formed separate ethnic communities in France, Germany, and Great Britain. The populations in these communities differ in language, occupation, homeland, religion, and physical appearance from the native population. Each ethnic group exists in isolation, not only from the dominant population but also from other migrant ethnic groups. As a result of high unemployment and recession in Western Europe in the late 1980s, resentment and animosity between the migrant workers and the host societies developed. In times of economic hardships, non-European residents are regarded as outsiders who fit in when their labor was needed but now put a strain on already scarce resources.

The Experiences of Culture Shock

Culture shock is an often encountered and widely accepted ingredient in many immigration scenarios, but there are also those who face a culture shock when they return to their home country, following a sojourn abroad. Individuals who studied abroad for a number of years and then return to their home country with the decision to remain there may experience this phenomenon (Christofi & Thompson, 2007). Roughly half of the students who study abroad decide to return to their home countries. However, 71% of foreign citizens receiving doctoral degrees in the fields of science and engineering from U.S. universities in 1999 were still living in the United States in 2001 (Finn, 2003).

When individuals become immersed in a culture different from the one they grew up in, culture shock can occur. But, after having become acculturated to the new environment, a return to the home country can present a reverse culture shock, which has been defined as the "temporal psychological difficulties returnees experience in the initial stage of the adjustment process at home after having lived abroad for some time" (Uehara, 1983, p. 420).

Variables affecting individuals' readjustment to the home country's culture make up a long list of factors, such as the degree of difference between the two cultures, the individual's length of stay in the new environment, and personal characteristics as well as gender differences. One study demonstrated that Brazilian women experienced more re-entry problems than Brazilian men after having lived in the United States (Gama & Pedersen, 1977), but others found that women experienced greater satisfaction than men upon return to their home culture (Rohrlich & Martin, 1991). Furthermore, the better an individual adapts to the host or temporary culture, the more difficult re-entry into the home culture will be for him or her. The many variables operating around the phenomenon of culture shock make development of explanations that fit the majority of cases difficult.

Investigations with returning Peace Corps volunteers and corporate personnel revealed four coping styles in re-acculturation to home environments (Adler, 1981). Individuals' overall attitude (optimistic or pessimistic) and specific attitude (active or passive) were significant determinants of successful acculturation or re-acculturation. Different combinations of these four dimensions result in the four coping styles of proactive, alienated, resocialized, and rebellious re-enterers. The greatest personal growth is achieved in proactive coping. Proactive people are able to appreciate the condition of being bicultural and use their cross-cultural skills to integrate their foreign and home culture experiences.

A high need for external validation leads the alienated individual to react negatively to the environment and makes adjustment more difficult, as was seen in Elke's case. Individuals operating within the resocialized coping style framework also have a need for external validation and may respond positively to their home environment, but their experience of re-entry appears to be a period of adjustment rather than growth. The rebellious individual, similar to the alienated one, also rejects the home environment, but in an aggressive rather than a passive manner.

Indhira and Ramez, a young married couple and example of transnational migration, left their families of origin behind in India to seek opportunities for financial gain in the United States. Ramez, like many Indian men and women, had a special aptitude for computer work. His engineering degree and computer skills enabled him to obtain a work contract from a well-established American company. With his salary, Ramez believed that in about 5–8 years they would have saved enough money to return to India. Indhira experienced great difficulties in her adjustment to life in the United States. She missed her family and friends in her native country. Although she obtained employment to supplement her husband's income, she was bored and depressed.

While Ramez used opportunities to socialize with his colleagues at work, Indhira made no attempts to become involved with people in their new environment beyond socializing with other couples from India. Weekends were spent visiting with other Indian couples, either in restaurants or their respective homes. They went mostly to places that played Indian music and served Indian food. Indhira did not seem interested in exploring American institutions, such as museums, theatres, seminars, or lectures on any topic that was not related to India. She was unhappy, as she remained focused on what they had temporarily given up to save enough money to return home. To relieve her depressed mood, they spent more and more time with their Indian friends, hardly managing to stay home alone on any weekend.

Their stated goal for coming to the United States was to accumulate, in a relatively short period of time, the financial assets that would later afford them a comfortable life in India. However, the frequent socializing with their Indian friends and acquaintances cost money. And, although they had invested money in buying a house instead of renting, they were not taking advantage of the investment by entertaining themselves at home with reading, watching TV, or listening to music while preparing cost-efficient meals.

As the time passed and their savings remained largely nonexistent, resentment built up in Indhira. It seemed to her that Ramez did not make enough money; they should be able to put money aside while continuing with their current lifestyle. In India, much like in other countries with traditional norms, a woman's chastity along with her abilities as cook and homemaker are highly valued. By the same token, women in these societies value men with ambition and with good financial prospects as well as those holding a favorable social status (Myers, Madathil, & Tingle, 2005). Working outside the home felt like a sacrifice to Indhira, but she thought as long as they did not have children, her work might help accumulate the required financial achievements for returning home.

Indhira reasoned that even the frequent socializing in which they indulged was a far cry from her happy life with her family and all her friends back in India. Here she had to make do with other Indian people that perhaps at home would not have been as desirable to her. Certainly, she did not have as much in common with the people here as she had with her childhood friends. "What was the sense in not being where you wanted to be and not accumulating wealth while sacrificing?" she questioned.

Ramez was torn; eventually he also wanted to return to India, but he was not in as much of a hurry as Indhira. In fact, he would have liked to explore more about life in America, but the overall mood of depression and disappointment in their current living arrangement reduced any ambition he might have had to a passive stance of going to work and participating in Indhira's social plans. It has become apparent to them that, as they will be approaching the end of the 5-year period of living in the United States, their original plans will not materialize. While they are not taking advantage of the current options for betterment of their situation, they eliminate one of the options the transition of their lifestyle was meant to provide for them. Currently, their remaining options are to either return to their native country at the planned time with little more than they came here with or to significantly extend the time period before returning and modifying their current lifestyle.

A Teacher's Legacy

Miss Angelica Meissner (not her real name) knew about immigrants; in fact, she knew them so well she could predict which immigrants would accept the challenges of their new environment and make a successful adjustment, which ones would return to their home countries because they missed the familiar sounds and sights, and which would remain but be disillusioned about their fate. Miss Meissner, a high school teacher, was herself the daughter of immigrants; she understood their true needs.

In the late 1950s to early 1960s some community schools in New Jersey opened their doors to adult learners, offering various courses. Among those were classes for adult learners from different countries who wanted to learn or improve their knowledge of the English language. The courses would run from September through the end of the year and again from January through May. Miss Meissner's course had two class meetings per week scheduled. The first meeting would be devoted to the English language and its grammar, spelling, and sentence structure, while the second class would focus on citizenship, community affairs, relevant laws, and similar topics.

In those days, the typical student population in Miss Meissner's classes would consist of, for example, two young women from Japan, one from South Korea, two from France, two from Germany or Austria, perhaps one from Argentina or another South American country, and two young men from Italy. The only thing they had in common were the few words of English they understood and a desire to learn more. English was the one option for them to communicate with each other and with their teacher. Miss Meissner was strict about homework assignments; every week's English language homework consisted of exercises in vocabulary enrichment, grammar, sentence structure, and the writing of an essay. There were weekly spelling drills, increasing in degree of difficulty with increasing time.

Occasionally, students found it difficult to concentrate so intently on the different language and the content of the history and citizenship topics; they wanted to reminisce about issues familiar to them. One of the German students recalled an experience from her childhood: In the course of the school year a new student had been introduced to the class. Apparently, the girl's father had been given a transfer in his professional life from Austria to Germany. It had been difficult for the new girl to join the class in midsemester. Children are not always on their best behavior toward a newcomer. The situation, however, was exacerbated by the girl herself, who had the habit of prefacing most statements with the words "bei uns in der Ostmark..." (meaning "at home in Austria..."), which placed the content of the statement that followed in competition with something of a similar nature in her home country. The other children in the class did not take kindly to this habit and started to tease her as soon as she raised her hand to answer a question or make a statement. The teacher, of course, reprimanded the students for their teasing behavior, but it did not increase the new girl's popularity. Miss Meissner thought this was a good example of how insisting on comparing everything to past situations not only reduced the speed of becoming familiar with new situations, but also was not beneficial for the social adjustment of the newcomer.

But there was also time for getting to know about each other's cultural backgrounds. Once a month on the class day normally scheduled for citizenship topics, students would take turns preparing and presenting to the class dishes they treasured from their home countries. In addition to providing the various meals, the students would explain the ingredients, the cooking process and—most important—the cultural connection or significance of the prepared food. They would try to serve it the way it was done in the countries of their origin and, if they were in possession of a national costume, they were encouraged to wear it on the occasion of their presentation. At the end of the course, Miss Meissner invited the students to her home, reciprocating the students' hospitality.

To be sure, there was attrition; some students found the lessons too difficult or time consuming, and others might have been bored or embarrassed over attending school at their adult age. Some may have had to drop out due to relocation to other parts of the country. For those who remained and attended both the beginner and the advanced classes, the experience was invaluable. At the graduation exercises at a New Jersey college, one of her students silently thanked Miss Meissner and, when the same student was awarded a doctoral degree several years later, Miss Meissner again was fondly remembered. Sadly, there are no official records available that document Miss Meissner's legacy; the paths of her former students are mostly unknown.

What would be Miss Meissner's most likely response today if she were to pass by a public school with the Spanish word for "entrance" placed next to the English word? Would she approve of it? On the surface, providing

Spanish translations to aid Spanish-speaking immigrants might seem like a welcoming gesture. However, Miss Meissner would probably have frowned if more than a brief welcoming gesture were offered to immigrants. Most likely, she would have seen it as enabling newcomers not to stretch their abilities to forge an independent and meaningful life in their new environment. If people can get along without too much effort, many of them will do so. But in the end they will lose because they continue to feel like strangers in the world they live in.

Not learning the language of the country they live in will relegate them to a life on the periphery; their interests will be focused on the past and the life they knew then. That would not have been Miss Meissner's goal for them. Applying the Dimensions of Personal Identity Model discussed earlier, Miss Meissner's efforts can be understood in influencing immigrants' opportunities for education and occupational training (dimension B) by providing her students with the tools of language and civic knowledge (dimension A), which they could use to advance in social class and improvement of mental well-being (dimension A).

Examples of Famous Immigrants

When considering famous immigrants, the first name that would come to most people's minds now is probably that of California Governor Arnold Schwarzenegger, who was born on July 30, 1947, as the second son of policeman Gustav Schwarzenegger and his wife Aurelia Jadmy Schwarzenegger in the hamlet of Thai bei Graz in Austria. High points in his bodybuilding career are winning the titles of Mr. Universe and Mr. World. He arrived in America in 1968, earned a B.A. degree in business from the University of Wisconsin in 1979, made a name for himself in the movie industry, and became a naturalized U.S. citizen in 1984. Two years later he married Maria Shriver. On November 17, 2003, Schwarzenegger took his oath of office as governor of California. This is the information publicly available on the Internet (http://german.about.com, Flippo, 2007).

How much time did Schwarzenegger spend contemplating the loss of things left behind? We do not know, but it could not have been sufficient to keep him from achieving significant gains. Both his parents and his older brother died while he lived in the United States, where he started his own family. Even without hearing his own statements, we can safely assume that insisting on living primarily according to the customs and practices of his native Austria would not have been an asset in achieving the governorship of a state in America.

Arnold Schwarzenegger is not the only foreign-born governor in American history; Irish-born John Downey served as seventh governor of

California. The state of Nevada had three foreign-born governors; one of them was Reinhold Sadler, who came from Prussia in the 1870s. Illinois, Georgia, Utah, Washington, and Wisconsin are American states with German-born governors in their history. Other U.S. states had governors who were born in Norway, Ireland, Mexico, Scotland, Sweden, England, and Canada. Former secretary of state Henry Kissinger, a German-born American diplomat and national security advisor, played a dominant role in U.S. foreign policy between 1969 and 1977.

To be accepted in public office, these immigrants must have inspired sufficient trust in the people of their states and the United States that any loyalty to their native countries would not interfere with the loyalties they owed the people of the states they served as governors and politicians. They had to be willing to share and accept the values and customs of the country they came to.

Re-entry From Mind-Control Environments

Culture shock of a more complicated nature occurs among those who have left or escaped a mind-control cult, especially if they did not have an opportunity for exit counseling with an experienced professional. Sociologists have warned that people have become vulnerable to persuasion because of today's social isolation, which deprives us of community spirit and communal relationships. In their isolated existence, people become vulnerable to the seduction of cult life because they yearn for the sense of belonging.

The formation of cults is not a new development. Three decades ago the Jones' People's Temple cult in Guyana achieved worldwide attention through the mass suicide of its members (Schroeder, 2002). The Children of God, founded by David Berg, a former Methodist preacher, were forecasting a doomsday scenario because of Americans' obsession with material things. Salvation was possible only through adherence to the doctrine of Moses David, the "Endtime Prophet," but salvation was costly. The members lived in poverty, handing over to the cult any money made on various jobs or other enterprises while Berg himself lived comfortably in affluent surroundings.

The Soka Gakkai cult, claiming a membership of 10 million, was the largest of 180,000 registered sects in twentieth-century Japan and has extended its influence into the twenty-first century in some parts of the world. The Unification Church of the Moonies (formal name: the Holy Spirit Association for the Unification of World Christianity) owns a multibillion-dollar business empire in America. Worldwide, there are several thousands of cults that isolate their members and disciples from the reality of the outside world.

The words "mind control" evoke the term *brainwashing* in most people's minds. Steven Hassan (1990), a former member of the Unification Church ("Moonies"), explained mind control as "a *system* of influences that disrupts an individual's identity (beliefs, behavior, thinking, and emotions) and replaces it with a new identity" (p. 7). The danger in mind control lies in the subtle ways of the process. It works most efficiently within group settings. Those who recruit for cults are usually well-educated people who assess prospective converts according to varying personality types and then package the group to reflect an atmosphere that would be attractive to the prospective convert. Also, it is not unheard of for the wealthy cults to hire public relations firms to create a positive image and to consult marketing experts to design their recruitment campaigns.

During the first few months, newcomers receive exceptional treatment and are made to feel special within the new environment. While the new convert is happy in the fantasy world created for him or her by the group, dependence on the group grows. On a subtle basis, emotional manipulation of the newcomer proceeds. Through observation of other group members' actions and attitudes, individuals change in their own beliefs and attitudes without being aware of it. The power of the contagion of mood in groups brings about the unconscious change in individuals. Cults expertly manipulate feelings of guilt, fear, and shame. In addition, the use of sex and intimacy keeps members dependent on the group (Singer, 2003). Recruitment techniques for the Children of God included sexual persuasion. In Berg's "Hookers for Jesus," attractive female cult members, both married and single, were told to go "flirty fishing" around clubs and bars to seduce men first to bed and then into the cult (Schroeder, 2002).

When joining a cult, individuals break away from the "regular" world and become part of the new social reality that has been constructed by the cult. The regular world becomes an out-group of the unredeemed. To be saved, the new member must obey and act according to the rules of the cult. The convert assumes the social identity of the group and in some cults learns to hate members of the out-group.

For instance, the Children of God were taught that their parents are evil and to hate them; they were not their family anymore. A member's true family was the cult. Similarly, Sun Myung Moon, who never mastered the English language, proclaimed that he and his wife were the heavenly parents of all Moonie followers. He even went so far as to select marriage partners for the members of his flock. Often he united couples that had never met before and who did not even speak the same language (Schroeder, 2002).

Steven Hassan, the youngest of three siblings and the only son, grew up in a conservative Jewish family in Flushing, Queens, New York. His father owned a hardware store and his mother was a junior high school art teacher. In his book, *Combatting Cult Mind Control,* Steven remembers his loving, unconditionally supportive upbringing. He considered himself more a loner than a joiner. His first encounter with the Moonie recruiters occurred at Queens College where he was enrolled for a liberal arts education. After several meetings Steven was convinced that he was invited to join a special community of young, idealistic people. He quit college, turned his bank account over to the cult, and became an active member. For details about the process of recruitment and indoctrination the reader is referred to his book.

More than 2 years had passed when, hospitalized for injuries sustained in an automobile accident, Steven came face to face with his family again. Physically unable to run away, he was confronted by deprogramming experts arranged by his father. Steven went through mental and physical recovery. While he lived with his parents, he returned to normal life and decided to make a public account of his experiences. He returned to college, obtaining an M.Ed. degree in counseling psychology. A licensed mental health counselor and exit counselor, he is the founder of the Freedom of Mind Center, a domestic profit corporation in Massachusetts.

Although Steven left the cult life about three decades ago, his entire life seems to revolve around cults and mind control. As he continues to speak out and write about his experiences in order to help others resist mind control efforts or to free them from being imprisoned mentally, Steven appears to be as much immersed in this topic as he was when we met on a journey to a professional conference in the early 1990s.

Upon leaving the cult, Steven had several options. After his physical injuries had healed, he could have returned to the cult. He could have studied literature and become a writer, as he had contemplated earlier in his life, or he could have remained involved with issues of mind control. His earlier pursuit of writing poetry at the age of 19 years seems to have given way to a lifelong concern and occupation with the forces of mind control. Now in his early 50s, he apparently has made it his life's work. Perhaps one could say that in some way he took the cult with him when he left and made his experiences the basis for his livelihood (Wikipedia, 2007).

Unlike Steven Hassan, who had grown up in the American middle-class culture and who spent a relatively short period of time living the cult life, Camilla was born into a cult atmosphere. Her parents, apparently disenchanted with their middle-class upbringing, had joined the Children of God community at a young age. Also unlike Hassan, who remained in the United States during his involvement with the Unification Church, Camilla's parents were sent to different parts of the world. Although the cult's founder, David Berg, lived in England, he dominated his flock in

Switzerland, Argentina, and other places around the world through letters and pamphlets.

Camilla and her siblings were raised in the cult. As an intelligent and talented girl, learning different languages was easy for Camilla; this, combined with her physical attractiveness, was an asset when it came to recruiting prospective cult members in various countries.

During the late 1970s, police in several countries around the world had been alerted to claims of the cult's child abuse, leading to the cult leaders' instructions in the late 1980s to keep the internal workings secret from the outside world. Escape became increasingly more difficult and risky for cult members if indeed they were able to decide to exit. It is believed that the international headquarters were relocated from Zurich, Switzerland, to India, while Gideon and Rachel Scott, the British-based leaders, left Britain in 1998 for South Africa, where a large part of the remaining membership may have moved (Schroeder, 2002).

Camilla's attempt to leave the cult landed her in an even more restrictive and abusive situation. Finally, she escaped and managed to reach the few remaining members of her family of origin in the United States. There had been no communication and she faced them as the stranger she was. The difference in their backgrounds was difficult to breach; there was no common ground. Nevertheless, the family did what they could to help. It was apparent that she was intellectually gifted and, with financial assistance, Camilla achieved her bachelor's degree with honors in less than the usual time period required. While she excelled in her study subjects, she had difficulty relating to other students on a personal level.

Camilla wanted the emotional closeness of the cult environment. Growing up, she had felt like an important member of a large, closely knit family. She acutely missed the intimacy she had experienced with those around her during her formative years. The focus on her losses resulted in depression and obscured her vision for the future. Her extraordinary intelligence opened the doors of the most prestigious universities for her graduate studies. She entered one of them. Although she graduated, her studies had been impacted to some degree by substance abuse. In her emotional isolation, she avoided the confrontation with accepting and overcoming her chemical dependency by moving to another country. It seems that Camilla traded the wide range of options available to her for the self-made imprisonment of addiction.

Far from being extinguished, "today's cult movements thrive by skillful blending of millenarial paranoia with elements of conventional religious doctrine and ritual. They have thrown up a new breed of cult leaders," Schroeder (2002) cautioned:

[They are] smartly dressed orators with cyberspace know-how, ranging from the intellectually sound to the mentally insane. What they share in common with the "old guard" of cult leaders is the persuasive power to coerce apparently rational people to become thoroughly and, at times, improbably irrational. (p. 125)

Their method is to eliminate in their converts' minds all options except one, the one that carries the undiluted message of the cult.

CHAPTER 10

Career Changes

The first career-related decisions are typically made during adolescence. While such decisions can have lifelong consequences, not only for individuals' vocational future but also for their psychological and physical health and social acceptance, many adolescents are ill equipped to make well-informed career choices this early in their lives. They may want to transfer the decision making to others, such as their parents, in order to avoid taking on the responsibility for the choices and their outcomes.

When choosing an occupation, most individuals are guided by a set of values. Their work participation should satisfy first of all their financial needs but also their achievement needs and perhaps include a certain degree of responsibility and freedom to make work-related decisions. Other values, such as altruism or an outlet for creativity, may be operating in job considerations of other individuals. The primary variables influencing occupational choices, as well as the occupation chosen and the satisfaction with the choices made, are found in the individual's cultural and work values (Brown, 2002). In addition, a person's life role values also have an impact on many aspects of the career-development process. Gender and certain talents and aptitudes are additional characteristics entering into the decision.

A requirement for good occupation choices is to avail oneself of accurate information. Realistic estimates regarding the abilities necessary for successful completion of the tasks that are included in a given occupation will assist the individual in evaluating his or her capacity for the occupation. The information should also include sufficient data for individuals to predict whether or not the particular occupation satisfies important values held by the individuals. Careers and occupations operate within a social context, and information regarding the opportunity structures within one's society will be highly valuable for the overall decision-making process. Thus, attending to social issues and developments will be a worthwhile focus for individuals during this process.

Difficulties in Making Career Decisions

Past explorations about the difficulties connected to making career and educational decisions have focused on the categorization of the types of problems that are the basis for career indecision (Campbell & Cellini, 1981; Osipow & Fitzgerald, 1996; Rounds & Tinsley, 1984; Super, 1953). To address the different types of decision difficulties in detail, a theoretical model was developed to analyze and categorize these problems (Gati, Krausz, & Osipow, 1996). Characterization of the problem types was made on the basis of deviations from the *model of the ideal career decision maker.*

The "ideal career decision maker" was envisioned as a person aware of the need for the decision as well as willing and capable of making the decision "right"—meaning the decision is based on the appropriate process and is compatible with the individual's resources and goals. Deviations from the model of the ideal career decision maker translate into potential difficulties that would influence the person's decision-making process either by preventing the person from making a career decision or by arriving at a less than optimal decision.

In the proposed framework, three major categories of difficulties—"lack of readiness" (due to), "lack of information" (about), and "inconsistent information" (due to)—were divided into 10 more specific difficulty categories. The specific difficulties in the lack of readiness category included problems that would likely arise at or before the beginning of the decision-making process, such as a lack of motivation to engage in the process; a general indecisiveness about decisions in general; and dysfunctional beliefs or irrational expectations, such as believing that there is only one ideal career for the person.

Difficulties that may become apparent during the actual decision-making process would be included in the categories "lack of information" and "inconsistent information," such as lack of information about the particular steps involved in the process, about existence of alternatives, about how to obtain additional data, and about the self. The major category, "inconsistent information," includes problems such as unreliable or incomplete information and internal conflicts, such as contradictory preferences or lack of understanding of the need for compromises. Also included in this category are external conflicts, which can be found in conflicts involving the influence of significant others.

Further research regarding the application of this model would be expected to have implications for career counseling and career-related intervention programs that aim at teaching decision-making skills (Gati & Saka, 2001). Also, a taxonomy of difficulties regarding the process of deciding as developed and described previously can be applied to decision making in other areas of life, such as choosing a life partner, moving to different geographical locations, or preparation for retirement.

Making Wise Vocational Choices

In the early 1900s, Frank Parsons, with the assistance of philanthropist Pauline Agassiz Shaw, proposed the application of the scientific method in order to reach solutions to social problems. Shaw had founded and supported the nursery schools that offered mothers in domestic service a place to leave their children while they went to work (see also discussion in the chapter on relocation). The services were available at girls' clubs in settlement houses and the North Bennet Street Industrial School in Boston's North End in the late 1890s (Matson, 1992) as well as the Vocation Bureau of Boston.

The particular social problem Parsons and Shaw were concerned with at the time was the widespread practice of children leaving school prematurely. Parsons's (1909) tripartite model of the wise choice of a vocation, simply stated, consists of the premises: "Know thyself, know the world-of-work and rationally connect these two groups of knowledge" (Hartung & Blustein, 2002, p. 42). Parsons's work has provided the foundation for much of the literature on career decisions. The vocational guidance movement of the early 1900s, with its theoretical innovation and empirical inquiry, combined with the advances in technology that have occurred since then, still provides guidance for wise vocational decision making for individuals at all stages of the life span.

More recently, proposed models of career decision making fall into two basic types or categories: the rational-choice models and the alternative-to-rational-choice models (Phillips, 1997). The *rational-choice models* have been recognized as the most accurate representation of career decision making. They are valued for the logic, reason, objectivity, and independence they incorporate. In these models, the wise decision maker is compared to an objective scientist who employs a methodical and systematic approach that steadfastly keeps the ultimate goal of maximizing personal gain in focus. While rational models emphasize the individual—the person as decision maker—alternative models underscore the circumstances within which decision making occurs. The context and environment surrounding the decision-making process are viewed as meaningful and important elements.

Instead of regarding the two decision-making types as opposites along a continuum of the process, suggestions for integrating both approaches would provide a framework for attending to both—the individual as the agent in the process and the circumstances and environment as the meaningful context that exerts influence on the whole process (Hartung & Blustein, 2002). The combination of the two approaches facilitates the focus on individual differences in decision making within the particular person, while at the same time exploring the influences of social and economic opportunities available or accessible to the individual.

In response to the needs of high school students regarding vocational choices, researchers at Boston College have been involved in the formulation of the School-to-Career program within the Boston Public Schools. The program addresses students' problems, such as their uncertainty about career choices and lack of internalized skills in exploring and decision making, as well as other psychosocial issues, intrapersonal difficulties, family problems, and lack of financial resources (Hartung & Blustein, 2002).

The Tools for Tomorrow (TFT) intervention approach, developed by the School-to-Career Office, is organized around four themes: (1) self-knowledge (Who am I?), (2) identification of resources and barriers, (3) connecting school and work, and (4) building personal strengths. Most of these themes would be appropriate to keep active in people's minds throughout the life span.

New Discoveries and Dead-End Jobs

Generations ago one job or one career would last for a person's lifetime. An apprenticeship in one's youth laid the foundation for one's livelihood. But now new advances in science and technology can render whole lines of occupations obsolete. Therefore, while a chosen career may appear to have as long a life as the individual who is involved in it, it would be wise to keep abreast with new developments in the labor market. Many occupations have either reduced their need for workers or even eliminated them through the development and use of computers. By the same token, whole new careers became available through and with the application of computers. A whole new brand of *information technology* has developed—along with other branches within the networks of computer science and technology.

On the other hand, when a new career field opens up, many more people may flock to it than can be accommodated in the field. The computer industry serves as an example for this situation, too. Colleges were flooded, and they trained and turned out armies of computer-literate professionals. There were many who found it difficult to keep up with the continuing developments in the computer industry and became obsolete within a short time in their new career paths. In other instances, there were just too many professionals entering the computer labor market.

Eric, a bright young man, envisioned a stimulating and lucrative career in computer engineering. It seemed tailor-made for him, engaging his creative abilities in combination with his sense for detail. Fresh out of college he was hired by Digital Equipment Corporation. It was an exciting time for Eric to be involved vocationally at the leading edge of a new industry. He especially enjoyed his activities in DEC's worldwide training programs with the travel and the challenging and stimulating aspects of teaching and training.

In the early 1980s Eric met the woman he wanted to start a family with. Tammy was a high school teacher with an interesting teaching load that included teaching English, art, and physical education classes. In short succession they became parents of two sons and a daughter. Life was good until sales at Digital Equipment Corporation faltered, and in the early 1990s the company announced some layoffs. Eric was able to see the handwriting on the wall and considered his options. With his background he would have been able to find another job in the computer industry—but for how long? Perhaps the situation at DEC was a sign of the times; besides, it seemed that, while the industry might be slowing down somewhat, colleges and universities turned out more and more graduates in the computer field.

Another consideration was the financial need for his growing family. He wanted to collect his paychecks for as long as possible, but at the same time take action to prepare himself for the uncertainty of his situation. Tammy and Eric brainstormed and researched several occupational possibilities until they concentrated on teaching. Of course, there would be no comparison between the salary of a high school teacher and what Eric currently earned. On the other hand, it seemed that there would be no dearth of children needing an education. There were also the summer months that could provide time for additional income-producing activities.

With his knowledge of computers, he would be an asset to any school, especially if he were able to pass on that knowledge to his pupils. Many computer professionals lack the patience and skills to teach others what they know. Eric's training work for DEC had been a good experience. Mathematics and computer science and application seemed the natural combination for Eric to base his teaching activities on. He also had an interest in history so that looked like a possibility for rounding out his high school teaching career.

Tammy had been thinking about some type of learning activities for children during the summer. She discussed it with Eric. With their combined teaching experiences, they could in due time open something like a summer day camp for students who wanted either extra help or to start on more advanced topics. With their own three children, the need for meaningful activities during the months of summer vacation was a concern that they could expand into a business. Another option for Eric was to phase into consulting work on his own, in addition to teaching.

As Eric, in discussions with Tammy, came to decide on the teaching option, he set out taking classes in the evenings and on weekends toward his teaching certifications. It would take time but he felt that, with every step in his preparation, while still holding his employment with DEC, he was getting closer to the solution of what to do when or if his layoff came. In his opinion, the time for preparation in a new direction would be a better investment than using the time for exploring and applying for other jobs in his field. The time when he received his layoff notice coincided with the need for making daytime available for his student teaching involvement.

The Digital Equipment Corporation went through several changes, being acquired by Compac in 1998 and later merging with Hewlett-Packard in 2002. Such changes are usually accompanied by organizational restructuring and possibly downsizing of the workforce. Eric had no guarantee that his job would not be affected by these changes when he explored his options and chose the one he thought would serve him best.

The Threat of Downsizing—Am I Next?

Jason, a man born in 1930, thought he had made a solid investment in his future when he obtained his B.S. degree in chemical engineering from the University of Minnesota. He worked for several big companies, among them McDonald Aircraft in California, and felt good about his professional choice. He had been married for only 2 weeks when he was drafted into the armed services for the Korean War, but he was fortunate enough to be stationed within the United States. Jason and his wife became the parents of three sons and one daughter. Life seemed stable; but then in the middle to late 1960s, the chemical industry experienced a slowdown and many chemical engineers were faced with unemployment. Jason was one of them.

With a family to support, what were his options? Had the degree that seemed like a promise of financial security if he was just willing to work worn out its utility? Jason could not afford to focus his energies on the loss of his career; he decided to get into computer programming. He learned different computer languages, such as Fortran IV and Cobol, and worked for several companies, most recently for the local government in the city in which he lives. Although Jason is now receiving Social Security benefits, he still works part-time and helps one of his sons with his new computer business.

His chemical engineering career was not the only aspect of his life that did not survive the changing times; his marriage ended in divorce. About 25 years later Jason married the mother of four children. They had been living together in her house for several years prior to their marriage. They wanted to make sure that they were compatible. Their relationship stood the test of time and cohabitation progressed to marriage. The children and grandchildren from both their prior marriages are getting along very well. Jason is proud of his artist wife and enjoys accompanying her on meetings across the country.

When asked if he would have stayed with his first career if that had been possible, Jason replied that if he had not been laid off from his chemical engineering job, he would have stayed with it because he liked it. However, he has been enjoying his second career even more—a fact he would never have known. He also admitted that the option he exercised at the critical transition time in his life left him in a far better situation financially than if he had stayed in his previous profession. Professionally, he enjoys the greater independence that the computer field affords him. All in all, a good change occurred in his life when he explored his options and chose the one he thought would suit him best.

Douglas, though almost 15 years older than Jason, had similar experiences. He received his B.S. degree in chemical engineering from the University of California at Berkeley. Before he could actually start on a career in this field, he was drafted into the Armed Forces in early 1941. Finally, after returning from overseas at the end of World War II, he was hired in late 1945 as a chemical engineer by Union Carbide Corporation to work in San Francisco. He thought he had the best job in the world. He got married and he and his wife settled down in the Bay area with their two children. Several years later he was able to build his dream house, designed by a student of a well-known architect. Life seemed good; Douglas had dreams of owning a vineyard but this would have to be far in the future if he ever made enough money to afford it.

His family did not have much time to settle in their wonderful new home because Douglas was transferred to the Midwest. It was a tough decision to leave his native California and his beautiful house, but the responsibilities of a family mandated job security. Life in the Midwest was quite different, with harsh winters and different lifestyles. The family adapted more or less well to the dramatic changes. Douglas and his wife enrolled on a part-time basis at the local university. They had just barely completed their master's degrees in counseling psychology, a field quite different from chemistry or engineering, before it was time for another transfer with the company—this time to the East Coast.

By now Douglas had experienced some doubts about his future with the company. It did not appear that he was on an upward path. His responsibilities were still many and varied, but they did not indicate great opportunities for advancement. Still, his salary was needed for the children's college fund, as the older one was just about ready to apply to different educational institutions. Around his 55th birthday Douglas was given the feared news: early retirement—the battery in the standard gold watch he had received earlier for his 25 years of service with the company just gave up its life—with six monthly paychecks and a tiny pension. As in Jason's case, the marriage did not survive the changes.

Considering his options, Douglas knew that the chemical industry was not the place to look for further employment. He searched for another university to continue with the studies he had begun when living in the Midwest. Because he wanted to be available to his children, a move back to California, his home state, was not a feasible option. After several years of study, an internship, and writing his dissertation, Douglas received his Ph.D. degree and embarked upon a new career as a clinical psychologist. At the time that he decided to take that option, he had to make considerable investments in time, effort, and money—the very things he did not have much of. Some people might think that all this just to be able to work for a few more years would not be worth the investment. But the option of sitting back and waiting to die was not to his liking. Somewhere along the journey, Douglas found a new companion to share the rest of his life with. In his second career Douglas can still work part-time, while the Union Carbide Corporation has long ceased to exist.

There are similarities in the stories of Jason and Douglas beyond the obvious likeness of their first career choice. They were aware of some concerns about the stability of their professions but they tried to ignore or explain them away in the hope that they might be overreacting and worrying when it was not necessary. In that respect, neither one took a proactive stance, although Douglas had started to involve himself in studies within a different discipline. When they were faced with the fact that their jobs had been eliminated, they immediately explored their options and acted decisively without spending time and effort to bemoan the loss of what they thought they had had.

Both Jason and Douglas made wise decisions upon confrontation with the termination of their careers as they knew them. Both did well in their future endeavors. If they had discussed their earlier concerns about the stability of their professional situation with a therapist, most likely they would have been encouraged to explore the situation more deeply, rather than distract themselves from realistically interpreting the signs, and to prepare themselves ahead of time.

Searching for Career Happiness—An Adventure

Some time ago Joseph Campbell (1988) explained the notion of *career happiness* as an adventure for one to explore what one's career might be and what one's nature or personality might be. Studying the mythologies of the world, Campbell recognized a special kind of life journey: one that discloses profound purpose and meaning and that permits an opening or blossoming of one's potential. The fulfillment of the individual's potential does not represent the endpoint of the journey, however; it continues throughout the course of life. It is a lifelong journey of self-exploration and consequential self-expression, which demands the individual's investment of energy and consciousness into those activities that create an emotional satisfaction. The guiding light for this journey does not come from external expectations, such as other people or society's requirements, but rather from a resonance from within the individual.

Although much research on job satisfaction has been involved with external work factors (Nichols, 1990), some theorists have pointed out that work satisfaction depends on individuals' ability to recognize and pursue their interests. This was the underlying assumption for the development of the Strong Interest Inventory (Campbell & Hansen, 1981). But beyond the urges and promises of immediate interests, individuals should be encouraged to continually recognize and reevaluate their beliefs and assumptions about themselves and their perceived abilities to facilitate the search for fulfilling career choices (Krumboltz, 1994).

Based on these considerations, how do individuals who appear happy with their work and who seem to others to be deeply satisfied with their work life explain their contentment? A study intended to answer this question involved eight male and female Caucasian participants who self-identified as happy in their work (Henderson, 2000). Personal interviews with open-ended queries were designed to elicit information about the participants' work and the challenges and aspects they enjoyed and disliked. Personal strengths, their attitudes toward risk, their strategies for coping with obstacles, and the development of their careers as well as their outlook for the future were explored.

The results of these interviews indicated that seven out of the eight participants followed a meandering career path. They tried out one or more jobs in one direction but then refocused toward a different and better path. They seemed to conceive of the final path as one that they ended up in by accident rather than design. They all remained with work that held their interest and what they could succeed in. Although the work environments differed widely, there were common characteristics, such as a relative freedom to perform the work, intellectual challenge, a positive work atmosphere, and opportunities for tangible meaning.

The investigator was aware that the small sample size and lack of ethnic variability constituted limitations of the study when considering a general application of the results. Furthermore, whether the participants' positive work experiences were the cause or the result of their overall sense of happiness was not explored. Perhaps the most important aspect of this study is the fact that most of the participants did not embark on one career path early in their lives and make it their life's work. They allowed themselves the freedom to change directions when it appeared to be in their best interest.

This finding should serve to remove some of the stress young people experience when they think they have to decide what will be the best career for them for the rest of their lives. Many of the current advances in science and technology render some job skills obsolete in relatively short time spans. To demand correct decisions that impact a large part of one's life at the beginning of it seems to parallel facing the request for a commitment without being informed about the variables and conditions inherent in the commitment.

When the Excitement of One Career Does Not Last a Lifetime

After 22 years working in the banking insurance business, Wes and his wife Claire were ready for a change. They decided to invest in an interest Wes had been aware of for most of his life: art (Cohen, 2007). In 1998, when the couple was in their mid-40s, a lifetime of being practical was going to be changed to taking risks by opening an art gallery and framing shop. Wes stated that he felt he was getting stale in his career in the insurance industry. It took about a year for the transition from start to an early success.

Wes and Claire had spent time and effort in their background research for the new adventure long before he left the insurance business. Talking to other gallery owners and attending trade shows were valuable learning experiences and brought them in contact with people who eventually became their suppliers. They also worked out a special niche for themselves by taking in artworks that people in their state would have to travel to major cities to enjoy. And, most important, they specialized in artists who were not represented in any other show in their home state.

Although Wes and Claire had done a lot of work in preparation for their new adventure, they admitted that they should have planned more down to the details, beyond the big strategy. Wes appreciates the challenges he now faces because it convinces him that he will not have to look back later, feeling sad that he let opportunities for happiness pass by. The process of planning and replanning and finally acting on the plans can be full of excitement that one does not get to experience staying in the same mold.

"What made you decide to take up art when you were in your late 40s?" the interviewer asked a female artist who is now approaching age 80. She responded, "When you're young, people tell you just to be yourself. But you don't know who you are yet. It takes a while" (Berry, 2007, p. 16). The former teacher was 52 years old when she graduated from art school.

Gender Differences in Career Decision Making

Research concerned with career decision-making points to significant differences between men and women engaged in the process. For women, external barriers include gender stereotypes, lack of appropriate role models, and discrimination, while internal barriers are thought to be a tendency to avoid mathematics, low levels of self-esteem, and low success expectations (Ancis & Phillips, 1996). The external messages from parents, teachers, and religious doctrine emphasize the importance of girls' family pursuits and deferring to the career priorities of their husbands or male partners (Betz, 1994).

Some young women may perceive the career decision-making situation as one of having to choose between a successful career or marriage and motherhood. When motherhood is the stronger goal, women may adopt a career option with flexibility that allows the major direction of time and energy toward raising a family and permits job activities to be structured around the main goal. The stories of Nancy and Linda in the chapter on marriage are examples of this approach to career decision making.

However, decisions like those take on a different significance in situations where marriage ends in divorce. While some judges and lawyers recommend that women's career sacrifices for the benefit of the family should be considered when determining appropriate compensation, divorce mediators and some lawyers have argued that if a wife chose a low-paid profession for the purpose of devoting time to the children of the marriage while her husband was engaged in a time-consuming and lucrative career, the wife had the full responsibility for her career choice and need not be considered for extra compensation (Bohmer & Ray, 1996). In other words, a woman deciding on a career that will enable her to also function fully as a nurturing parent may later, if the marriage ends in divorce, be penalized for not having chosen a more lucrative career.

Although some women recognize and act on the importance of their own concerns, many others are discouraged by social and family pressures from doing so, and their existence in an atmosphere of self-sacrifice is

often associated with depression (Seligman, 1994). It should not be surprising to find depression associated with situations where individuals
spend long hours on a daily basis in activities that they do not enjoy and
that they have not chosen for themselves, but rather to comply with the
wishes or demands of others. These would be examples of career decisions
made within the alternative-to-rational models, as discussed earlier in the
section "Making Wise Vocational Choices" (Phillips, 1997).

In a vocational guidance-related therapeutic context, goal exploration
for young women would seem especially pertinent in regard to the priority
of their goals. If the wish and need for motherhood determine the career
choice, women need to be aware of possibly limiting their occupational
options as well as initiating consequences they may later come to resent.
Therapists, rather than to assume that motherhood naturally is the goal of
priority for women, need to provide special guidance in helping their female
clients explore all options and alternatives with great care and deliberation.

Information from university counseling centers indicated that a large
proportion of women requesting help with career decision making—significantly more than men—admit struggling with problems of depression
in addition to their career problems (Lucas, 1993). A study at the counseling center of a large mid-Atlantic university evaluated information from
18 female students seeking assistance in deciding on a career and who also
reported feeling depressed or unhappy. The modal age of the participants
was 19 years (Lucas, Skokowski, & Ancis, 2000).

Most of the women described their career decision-making process in
the context of their relationships with parents and significant others. The
primary external theme centered on issues pertaining to family conditions,
such as parental expectations, criticism, and parents' authoritarianism.
Some of the young women who presented family issues also reported
relationship problems with significant others. Still others admitted to
having difficulties with boyfriends only.

When it was time to think about her future, Nadine, the daughter of an
authoritarian father and a passive, placating mother, expressed her wishes to
become a lawyer. Her parents, however, strongly opposed her wishes. They
determined that Nadine was to become a schoolteacher and they refused
to spend a penny on tuition toward a law degree. Nadine, used to conform-
ing to her parents' demands, attended a local teachers' college. Once she
obtained her teaching certificate, she found a position teaching first and
second grades in an elementary school. For the first time in her memory,
her father openly approved and her mother appeared silently supportive of
her. Her parents expected her to live at home until she got married. In fact,
her mother countered Nadine's attempts to move into her own apartment
with the statement that it would reflect poorly on Nadine's moral character

if she lived by herself in the town where her parents resided. After complying with her parents' wishes for so long Nadine became disappointed in herself. Her self-esteem was at a low point when she met Burt, whose charming behavior camouflaged his underlying mental rigidity—at least, in Nadine's eyes. She did not recognize the similarities between Burt and her father until they were married. Very much like her father, her husband did not tolerate any opinions that were at variance from his own and the marriage deteriorated to the point of divorce.

Nadine, who had quit her job when Burt's work took them to another town, now was forced to return to teaching in order to support herself. She had kept her credentials current but she felt hopeless; it seemed to her that she was doomed to spend the rest of her life in a profession she had never wanted to choose for herself. Her parents pointed out how fortunate she was to have some kind of career to fall back on after she had failed in her marriage. Her father added that as long as people continued to reproduce there was always a need for teachers. To Nadine, this statement sounded like the final closing on what she had once wanted for herself. Her divorce papers were the official documents of her poor judgment skills.

Although Nadine was able to separate from her domineering husband, she could not shake the influences from her authoritarian father. He had created a lasting legacy in her mind; important life situations were reduced to one option—the one he dictated. Perhaps if her mother had expressed a different view instead of silently complying with her husband, Nadine would have been better equipped to examine the reasonableness of her own opinions. As it was, Nadine capitulated under the onslaught of her father's rules.

Women's Vulnerability to Distraction From the Career Path

According to some scholars, at the birth of the first child, women's paths divide into two different groups: those who remain in the workforce and those who are homemakers, although there may be some crossovers at different times during the women's childrearing years (Klerman & Leibowitz, 1999). During the early 1990s, about one third of the women who were employed during their first pregnancy terminated their jobs or were laid off around the time of the birth of the child; 86% of them left their jobs voluntarily (Smith, Downs, & O'Connell, 2001).

But data from the Survey of Income and Program Participation indicated that of the women who had left their jobs during pregnancy, 58% re-entered the labor market within 12 months of the birth of their first child (Smith et al., 2001). In addition, information from analysis of the job histories of retired women showed that 11% of them had careers that progressed on an intermittent basis (Han & Moen, 1999; Williams & Han, 2003).

To examine women's employment trajectories across the period of early parenthood, Hynes and Clarkberg (2005) used data from the National Longitudinal Survey of Youth 1979 and found implications for as many as six typical employment trajectories around the birth of a child. A substantial group of women tended to leave employment around the time of childbirth and there are also groups who remain employed on a stable basis and those who stay out of the labor force. When employment patterns of women across two births were examined, even less continuity in employment was found. There was a wide variation in the individual women's paths through their first and second birth periods.

Another complicating factor in women's career paths is the actual timing of childbearing on the women's wages (Taniguchi, 1999). Early childbearers are particularly vulnerable to experience a higher wage penalty because their career interruptions occur during the critical period of career building. Those women who delay childbearing face a less aversive impact. The women's level of education is thought to reduce the magnitude of the wage penalty they are confronted with. But even when controlling for women's "human capital"—education, work experience, and job characteristics that appear to be related to pay status—mothers' earnings are lower than those of their childless counterparts (Anderson, Binder, & Krause, 2002; Budig & England, 2001). The negative association between wages and motherhood has been called the *motherhood penalty*. Studies with cohorts of young women drawn from the National Longitudinal Survey of Young Women and the National Longitudinal Survey of Youth have shown the wage penalty associated with motherhood has not diminished over time and that each additional child is linked to negative effects on the women's wages (Avellar & Smock, 2003).

As was described in the Lucas et al. study (2000), some women experience difficulty with following their career path due to their involvement with a romantic partner. Doreen and Dennis started dating in college. He was a year ahead of her, majoring in history and political science, while Doreen's major was sociology. Dennis had definite plans about his future; he was planning on attending law school and possibly later entering politics. To help with tuition money, Doreen had a part-time job as a kind of assistant to an assistant administrator. She realized that her options in sociology were limited unless she could go on to graduate school, but that seemed far off for the moment.

Dennis graduated with honors and was accepted at law school when Doreen had about three semesters to go before graduating. At this time the assistant administrator Doreen worked for was promoted to a higher position in another town and Doreen was offered to succeed her. She would, however, have to work fulltime. Dennis was impressed that her superiors thought so highly of Doreen's work and encouraged her to accept the position. "But what about my college attendance?" Doreen asked. Dennis had the solution: They could get married and Doreen could finish her studies in evening classes while Dennis was busy with law school and apprenticing in some law firms. The thought of getting married was exciting to Doreen. She accepted the fulltime position and was able to finish the current semester as planned. Some of her final grades came down from the A's she was used to, but it was a compromise well worth it with the money she made in her new job.

Doreen could have taken classes during summer school, but with the wedding and search for living quarters for Dennis and herself she was too busy to think about school. Instead, she registered for the fall semester, planning to attend two evening classes. Married life was different from what she had expected. She actually saw her new husband less than during the time they were dating. He was grateful for her help as she typed his notes from the lectures for him and she enjoyed the responsibilities of her job. Her studying time was greatly reduced. At the end of the fall semester she was able to pass one of the classes; for the other class she requested an "incomplete" with the hope of completing the work during the short semester break.

At the beginning of the new semester her hopes had not materialized. Study for the new classes in addition to the work necessary for removal of the "incomplete" became too stressful. She was confronted with the decision to either quit her job or drop out of college. Dennis suggested that leaving college at this point was the better option. Through her job she had been able to obtain medical insurance for both of them and that benefit was too valuable to give up. It would be easier for Doreen to return to school after he had graduated from law school and entered employment that would provide for their future medical insurance. It seemed to be the logical solution to Doreen's difficulty of pursuing her career in sociology. Did Doreen view this decision as a sacrifice on her part? The answer is not known. However, her options for a career in sociology are still available if she believes that vocational decision making and pursuit are appropriate for individuals at all stages of the life span.

On the other hand, the issue of medical insurance benefits can turn out to be a double-edged sword for some women, as Rita's life story demonstrated. Rita had earned a bachelor's degree in social work and intended to work toward her master's degree and possibly her doctorate when she and Tim got married. Soon thereafter Tim lost his job at the printing company he worked for. Instead of going to graduate school, Rita decided to accept a job offer to work for an insurance company. It was a fulltime job with excellent benefits. Tim settled into another job and they decided to start a family.

From time to time Rita thought about graduate school, but now seemed a good time to have children. After the birth of her second daughter Rita quit her job. She wanted to be with her daughters on a fulltime basis until they were in school. When her youngest daughter was in second grade, Rita returned to work on a part-time schedule for the same insurance company. Perhaps after the girl transferred to high school she could return to school herself for her master's degree, Rita thought. Tim disclosed that his job was less secure than he had expected. There was talk about layoffs and, in addition, Tim had become disenchanted about being an employee. He thought he could do better starting his own business. At first, he wanted to get started on a business in the evening hours while still employed.

It seemed like a sound strategy when he talked about it. As an afterthought he added that now that the girls were getting closer to high school age, it might be a good idea if Rita worked fulltime again, just to make sure they were financially safe, in case he lost his job before his own business was established. Again, it sounded reasonable. The insurance company was happy to have Rita work fulltime; she was a valued employee. Her full medical insurance benefits for the family were back in place by the time Tim was let go from his job.

True, there was a reduction in the family's overall income, but thanks to their careful planning, they did not have to worry about the astronomical costs of medical care without insurance. Now Tim had the incentive and all the time he needed to build up his business—but what about Rita's master's degree? It would have to wait.

As discussed earlier, the stories of Nadine, Doreen, and Rita are reflective of the alternative-to-rational model of vocational decision making. In Nadine's case, the demands of her father obviously were external influences that eliminated a rational approach to choosing a career. For Doreen and Rita, it seemed that their initial vocational decisions were subjected to detours and delays due to external circumstances based in family dynamics.

Although in general the consideration of various career options can occur at almost any time in an individual's life, for women changes in lifestyle may be accompanied by a reduction in career options. In Rita's case, when she changed her lifestyle from that of a single young woman to wife, her option of attending graduate school diminished at the time when Tim lost his job. In her transformation from wife to mother, she again put graduate school on hold while her daughters were young. Finally, when her daughters were almost ready for high school, Rita's fulltime job with medical insurance benefits was needed for the family's safety while Tim pursued his own business.

Similarly, Doreen's transformation from single to married status brought with it the requirement for fulltime employment, thus reducing her options to continue her studies and obtain even her bachelor's degree, let alone graduate study. After Dennis had completed law school, would her time come to return to college or would another lifestyle change—that to mother—put her career considerations on hold indefinitely? Both Doreen and Rita might be at risk for encountering unfavorable legal definitions in the significance of the responsibility for their career decision making should their marriages end in divorce, as discussed earlier.

Neither Rita nor Doreen had sought professional help when she had to make decisions regarding the continuation of educational endeavors or the interruption of plans to accommodate for other changes in her life, such as marriage and motherhood. They had not seriously considered the difficulties in the attainment of their goals that might arise from such delays. Within a therapeutic framework there would have been opportunity to evaluate whether the sacrifices of the moment might prove to be serious obstacles in their vocational futures.

Another critical issue for employed women is that of health insurance for the family, which can be obtained through their employment. As in Rita's case, husbands may pursue their goals of establishing their own business and cannot afford to provide health insurance for their families. Leaving a job that provides health insurance to follow their own career dreams would seem to most mothers to jeopardize the lives of their children. Again, these are issues that can be explored in therapy in order to assist women in making the very best decisions for their own lives.

Accommodating the "new mommy track," some companies allow their female (and some male) professionals flexible work schedules that allow them to combine career and parenthood (Palmer, 2007). The new generation of American mothers, who are rejecting the "soccer mom" stereotype of the 1990s and the older "superwoman" image of the 1990s, are ready to negotiate flexible schedules at work. They also demand more participation of their husbands in household and child-raising responsibilities. The Full Circle program instituted at Price Waterhouse Cooper even allows certain female professionals to temporarily stop working while they are busy taking care of their children. Continuing contact is managed through networking and training events. When the mothers are ready to return to their jobs, they may not have sacrificed their position along the career track.

A word of caution is in order though: These practices are far from being the norm and even participation in the Full Circle program is highly selective. If options like those in the Full Circle program are available, they are mostly there to accommodate professional women, who represent a particular value to the company. Women working in low-skilled jobs will have greater difficulty when negotiating for flexible work schedules. Another option taken by women is that of starting their own business from home while also being in a position of supervising their children.

When considering career choices and training, in addition to knowing one's interests and talents, being aware of the options of motherhood along with the various possibilities of holding a job or working independently would follow Parsons's tripartite model of the wise choice of a vocation—know thyself—includes knowledge of one's talents and interests and awareness of one's personality or working style, such as preferring working in connection with others or independently, as well as the wish for motherhood. Knowledge of the world of work requires an ongoing process of observation, and the rational connection of the two groups of knowledge calls for continuing flexibility on part of the individual. These are the requirements for today's women's wise choices among the options.

When Careers and Personal Lives Do Not Match

As observed in the case histories and outlined in the preceding discussion, women's careers often do not follow original plans because of demands placed on them as a result of significant lifestyle changes from single to married life and again to motherhood. In addition, depending on the number and spacing of children, the period of motherhood can stretch from one to several decades and may include intermittent periods of less intense mothering demands. In any event, during this time the order of priority becomes reversed for most women. At the beginning of young adulthood there may be a stronger concentration on career issues, perhaps similar to their male counterparts. However, when family concerns become an issue, contrary to males in our society, women feel obliged to place their career aspirations below their family responsibilities along the list of priorities. Some women, as shown in the case histories in the chapter on marriage, calculate these factors when they decide upon a career, while others might not be convinced that this type of planning is useful.

Irene had always wanted to be a nurse. Her parents agreed that Irene seemed well suited for that profession. She was the youngest of their three pretty daughters and the one who was always willing to take care of anybody who needed it. Irene was a good student and although there was much competition for acceptance into the school of nursing at the local university, Irene easily gained admission and graduated with honors.

After several years of working at local hospitals, Irene was offered a position as research assistant/nurse supervisor in a prestigious hospital in New York. The opportunity was too good to pass up. Irene loved the challenges of her new position. She thought she had found the career of her life. Then she met Wolfgang, the dashing young airline pilot from Germany who was in the United States for a training mission. Following a whirlwind romance and wedding Irene started married life in Germany. Before Irene could consider options for her own career she realized that she was pregnant. In due course, Wolfgang and Irene became the parents of two daughters. Wolfgang's career as pilot required frequent absences from home with an unreliable schedule. Under those circumstances it was essential that Irene assume the responsibilities of a fulltime parent. Also, there was Wolfgang's mother, who looked to Irene for help.

This marriage was not what Irene had dreamed of as a young girl. She was tied to the house while her husband flew to different corners of the world accompanied by a crew of admiring female flight attendants. The frequent overnight stays in different cities provided opportunities for extramarital affairs. During his times at home he was tired and needed rest. Their sex life deteriorated and Irene felt old beyond her years. When her daughters were spending more time in school, Irene thought about looking for a job, but it was not easy to find work in her profession because she did not have the necessary certification for Germany. Besides, unemployment was on the rise. As a registered nurse, she could have found employment on a U.S. Armed Forces base but there was no such installation within commuting range from her home.

Wolfgang's affairs had not been without consequences: his current romantic involvement resulted in the woman's pregnancy, which she had apparently not disclosed while in the early stages of her pregnancy. Now tests revealed that she would have a baby boy. It was too late for an abortion; besides, Wolfgang liked the idea of having a son. After weeks of arguments, trial separation, reconciliation, and more arguments, Wolfgang and Irene agreed on a divorce. She would return to America with their two daughters. Wolfgang was willing to let the girls move with Irene but he wanted his pregnant girlfriend to move into the home that he had occupied with Irene. His reasoning was that the young woman needed all the help he could give her in her stressful situation until they could get married.

Irene agreed; her main goal was to return home to the States with her daughters. She knew her family would be there to help her. They filed for divorce. Irene packed up her belongings to make room for Wolfgang's future wife. Apparently, Irene was not familiar with the German divorce laws. She was informed that after filing in court there was a waiting period of 12 months where she and the children could not leave the country.

Wolfgang's vision was focused on the future; he could not spend much money on a family that was going to be a part of the past.

Until they were able to leave the country, Irene and her daughters were taken in by Wolfgang's parents. It was a traumatic time. The girls did not want to leave Germany. They could not understand why their father was willing to abandon them. It must be Irene's fault. They rebelled against her and tried unsuccessfully to convince their grandparents to let them live with them. They again blamed Irene for their grandparents' rejection. Money was scarce. While she was waiting for the divorce to be finalized, Irene finally obtained work cleaning people's houses.

Irene's original career choice was an excellent one. She enjoyed her profession and would have continued in it, had her personal life not brought her to a different country and into circumstances where it was difficult to maintain her professional standing. Upon her return to her country of origin, after an absence of 13 years, she may have had to study to update her credentials but she would again be living in an environment where her professional qualifications were accepted and highly respected.

However, considering the impact of the stress that their transition to America would have on Irene's daughters, it would be beneficial to enroll the family into therapy. Just being in a more advantageous environment may not be sufficient to prevent major difficulties in the girls' adjustment to their new community, schools, grandparents, language differences, and, not least of all, Irene's parental authority. As the girls already blamed her for the emotional upheaval of losing their father and his parents along with the home and culture they were born into, additional problems could be expected to develop during the period of adjustment to this new lifestyle.

For many people making an early career decision, the three major categories of difficulties—"lack of readiness" (due to), "lack of information" (about), and "inconsistent information"—as discussed earlier in this chapter, are obstacles to making a wise decision. For some professions, it is difficult to obtain accurate information that is detailed enough for deciding whether it is something one wants to spend a major part of one's life in. This is especially true for those occupations that are of rather recent development, and experts who are knowledgeable in the field are not easy to access for the needed information.

The field of communication technology and what was soon to be called information technology was in its infancy when Amber faced her career decision-making time. Entering a brand new field seemed like a sound decision and it was interesting, too. She enjoyed her studies in college. It was not difficult to get a job after graduation but, as promising as some of the jobs sounded, Amber spent a lot of time at the computer, answering customer questions from different parts of the world or transferring them to other workers, depending on the category of inquiries. For some of the requests, Amber had to do some research before she could provide the answers.

Although most of her working hours were spent in communication with people, she never saw any of them. But in due course, Amber got married, had a couple of children, and moved to another state with her new family. She worked part-time to supplement her husband's income—again, mostly on computers. When she and her husband divorced after several years of marriage, Amber considered herself lucky that her employer offered to extend her part-time work into a fulltime position. At the time her children had started college, Amber moved back to her home state.

She was now thoroughly disenchanted with her career. Her jobs had been more like a data-entry and retrieval type work than creative endeavors in the communication or information technology field. She missed personal interactions with people and sitting all day in front of the computer had made her sluggish. At the local YMCA she started on a strict physical exercise regimen and after some time started to work as personal trainer with a few people. Her main earnings, however, came from jobs as a waitress. She knew she could not continue with this work indefinitely.

What should her next career be? At this time in her life she had more knowledge about herself than when she faced the career decision in her late adolescence. She knew that she wanted the people contact and she knew she did not want to sit in the same spot all day. At the age of 56 years she decided to become a beautician. She had to continue her work as waitress because she needed the money for her living expenses and the tuition it cost for her new training. Amber likes what she is doing; her fingers, though, do not seem to move as adroitly and quickly as those of the younger students, but she is good at the work. She is about 2 months away from graduating as beautician but may have to interrupt her training to work fulltime for a while as she is running out of financial resources. As she stated, she is in a survival mode and although there will be breaks along the path, the end is in sight.

Amber will be at least 57 years old before starting a job as a beautician. Although she is in excellent physical condition now, for how long will she be able to work at such a physically demanding job? Aside from what Social Security benefits she will receive, she has no retirement funds at her disposal. She will have less than two decades to work and save money for her old age. Remembering the premises of Frank Parsons's tripartite model of the wise vocational choice of connecting the two aspects of knowledge—knowing oneself and knowing the world of work—discussed earlier, Amber's knowledge of herself has grown insofar that she knows what she does not like. However, as she grows older, how realistic is it to embark on a physically demanding career at this point in her life? Her current degree of physical fitness does not give a hint of future impairments, except for the slowness in her fingers, which is probably age related and may not improve much, even with continued practice.

As far as knowing the world of work is concerned, again, how realistic is Amber's outlook? Admittedly, she looks much younger than her actual age, but disclosing her age to an employer when Amber is in her 60s might not enhance her chances for employment. Having no significant financial resources of her own, she cannot seriously consider opening her own beauty salon in the near future. It is almost as though Amber made an age-inappropriate reversal in her career choices by choosing a sedentary occupation in her youth and a physically stressful work experience in her advancing years.

"Job shadowing" is a practice used for young people to become familiar with the details of the various occupations they are interested in. Spending time in an apprenticeship-like situation, following an experienced worker and observing the daily activities and decisions that are part of a certain job performance, provides an almost "hands-on" experience that can be extremely valuable in the career decision-making process of a young adult. Amber was at that point about 40 years ago and if that option had been available to her, she might have been in a better position to obtain accurate information regarding the decision she was about to make.

Occupational and Marital Aspects in Dual-Earner Couples

The question of the likelihood of associations between husbands' and wives' experiences at work and their attitudes about marriage and their behaviors within the marriage was the basis for a study involving 167 dual-earner couples with at least two children. The couples had been married for 18.6 years on average and each spouse worked at least 20 hours per week in his or her job. Couples with spouses who had been married and divorced prior to the current marriage were not included in the study (Klute, Crouter, Sayer, & McHale, 2002). The investigators' particular interest was focused on how work experiences may shape individuals' values, which may, in turn, affect their attitudes and behaviors related to marriage.

On the basis that women are generally employed in different types of jobs than men, it was expected that these work experiences with their differential opportunities for self-direction would influence the type of marital relationship they valued and preferred. The investigators examined the obtained information within the framework of two conceptual models about the link between spouses' employment and egalitarianism in marriage: the function of values as mediators of occupational self-direction in relationship to attitudes regarding marital roles and in relationship to the division of feminine sex-typed household tasks.

The hypotheses that experiences of self-direction at work would be associated with greater endorsement of self-direction-related values and that individuals who value self-direction more would prefer and adopt more egalitarian arrangements in their marriages were both supported by the data. Spouses who endorsed values of self-direction held less traditional attitudes toward marital roles and more equal division of household tasks than spouses who adhered to values of conformity. The investigators explained that the obtained evidence for the mediating effect of values on the relationship between occupational self-direction and attitudes about marital roles suggests that work experiences may function as a socializing force shaping individuals' values.

In general, a confirmation of the link between greater endorsement of self-directed values and more egalitarian attitudes and behaviors in marriage would not seem surprising; however, assigning work experiences a socializing function that carries over into marital life would point to the need of additional research. An equally likely expectation could be stated that individuals who adhere to values of self-direction would endorse egalitarian attitudes and would also gravitate to employment that allows for the opportunity to express this preference.

Analyzing the relationship between labor force participation and risk of spousal violence against women on the basis of information obtained from 8,641 women, Macmillan and Gartner (1999) found that the effect of one spouse's employment is conditioned by the employment status of the other spouse. Women's participation in the labor force may lower the risks of spousal abuse when the male partners are also employed. However, when husbands are not employed the women's participation in the workforce substantially increases the risks of spousal violence against them.

As stated in the beginning of this chapter, career-related decisions are generally considered during adolescence and early adulthood, a period of insufficient information for most people in modern times. Instead of one career, people's thinking could switch to the concept of a series of careers with individual periods of occupations that may not even follow the same general path. Particularly for women with the complicating factors described before, there may be opportunities for different careers before and after childrearing. Modifying the thinking from one career to several careers would eliminate the pressure of having to make the correct decision in the face of insufficient knowledge and could add the excitement of meeting new challenges and options for untried adventures to the general concept of working for a living.

CHAPTER 11

Retirement
A Diverse Menu of Options

Most recent retirees in the United States are married, and the timing of retirement for working spouses occurs in relation to one another. However, in couples' voluntary retirement, the process of arriving at the decision and the perception of the spousal influence on the decision are interactions characteristic of the relationship dynamics and the marital quality of the particular couple. In previous times, retirement meant a transition for both spouses. If the working husband retired, his wife's lifestyle was usually affected in major ways. Where prior to his retirement, her days might have been her own to spend as she decided as long as the evening meal was prepared and ready to serve, with his retirement she may have had to adapt to her husband's company during the day as well as in the evening.

If they had planned to move to a warmer climate to spend their days at sunny beaches, both of them would move together. Studies from more than two decades ago showed that age was an important predictor of retirement for both men and women (George, Fillenbaum, & Palmore, 1984) and married women, when compared with divorced or never married women, tended to retire at an earlier age (O'Rand & Henretta, 1982).

Currently, however, for many couples retirement of one does not necessarily coincide with retirement of the other, especially in those unions where it is the husband's second marriage. The current wife's age might not be as close to retirement as his is. She may continue in her employment for several years after he has made the transition to retirement. Similar situations may arise in first marriages where the wife started employment after the couple's children had reached a certain age. To be eligible for certain retirement benefits, her years of employment may stretch after the termination of his work history.

The intertwining of spouses' retirement timing was the focus of a study involving married retirees of Florida's state employee retirement system (Szinovacz, 1989). The findings seemed to confirm the preceding statements, revealing gender differences in retirement behavior based on the spouse's retirement. Women were more likely to retire later than their husbands; 42% of the women retired more than 1 year after their husbands retired, compared with 25% who retired before. Forty-nine percent of the men retired earlier than their wives. One can think of retirement as a life course or lifestyle transition as the combination or integration of two work trajectories over time.

The Gendered Nature of Spousal Influence on Retirement

If over the life span of the marriage one or the other spouse has assumed the position of greater power, it can be expected that when considering retirement options, the spouse who holds the greater power will be the one with the greater influence. Predictions can be made based on previous decision-making processes and outcomes.

Information from 151 retired men and their wives and from 77 retired women and their husbands was collected to explore whether or not husbands and wives agree about their spouses' influence on the decision to retire (Smith & Moen, 1998). Another question asked by the investigators was whether retired husbands and their wives differ from retired wives and their husbands in the factors related to spousal influence on the retirement decision. The data collection consisted of face-to-face interviews, which included a structured battery of questions and extensive life history reviews.

Analyzing the information regarding individual perceptions of the spouses' influence on retirement decisions, it was found that husbands' and wives' perceptions of the wife's influence on the husband's retirement decision differed considerably. Retired husbands perceived their wives as having more influence on their retirement decision than the wives themselves reported. Additionally, it was observed that a couple's gender role ideology and several retirement transition variables were related to husbands' and wives' perceptions of their spouses' influence. Husbands holding traditional gender beliefs but married to women with a modern gender role ideology stated that their decision was due to retirement incentives. Those husbands who discussed the retirement issue with their wives stated poor relations with a boss or supervisor as reason for retirement.

The retired wives' perceptions of their husbands' influence on their retirement decision also seemed higher than the husbands' own perception of their influence, but the difference between them was not as pronounced as in the case of the retired husbands. In those instances where the wife retired because of her husband's retirement, they both agreed that the husband was influential. In this group, wives embracing modern ideas about gender roles were more likely to see their husbands as influential, independent of the husbands' gender role ideology. In those situations where both spouses held modern gender role beliefs, wives gave the most credit to their husbands.

Looking at couples' joint perceptions of spousal influence, it was found that in couples where the husband's retirement was the focus, 43% agreed that the wife had influence at least equal to or more than that of the husband. Planning and preparing for the transition to retirement mattered; if the husband discussed retirement aspects with his wife, both spouses agreed that the wife was influential. In the group of retired wives and their husbands, more than two in five (45%) couples agreed that the husband had influenced the wife's decision to retire.

The investigators pointed to the gendered nature of spousal influence on the process of transition to retirement. Both spouses perceive a man's retirement as a family event, whereas a woman's retirement is seen as an isolated occurrence, except when it is closely followed by her husband's retirement. "The effects of the husband's retirement reverberate through-out the family. A wife's life transition to retirement seems to fall into the tagalong category" (Smith & Moen, 1998, p. 743).

The End of the Line or a New Beginning?

Anne and Louis planned to have a smooth transition from work to retire-ment. There would be the end of their working careers and a transition period of intensifying their already established hobby activities. Both held government jobs and looked forward to their retirement and pensions. They had developed an interest in arts and crafts and selling their products at state and community fairs as well as at craft shows around the country. They made an investment in a comfortable, efficient camper that they could use for their travels on the arts and crafts show circuit. It was big enough to sleep in when appropriate and to hold the items they had produced in their workshop at home.

Anne had been a high school art teacher before changing to her govern-ment job and it was natural for her to remain involved in arts and crafts production in her spare time. Stimulated by Anne's achievements, Louis discovered in himself a talent for woodcarving. The range of their talents grew as they immersed themselves in what seemed to be hobbies—until one day when on their vacation they visited an outdoor arts and crafts show. They looked around at the products offered and realized that their own efforts would fit in quite well. To learn more about it, they talked to several of the vendors and exchanged addresses to keep in touch and inform each other of fairs and crafts shows in their communities.

That was the last vacation Anne and Louis took just as a vacation. From then on they devoted their free time to research the opportunities that might open up for them in participating in this aspect of life. They learned all about the paperwork, permits, and licenses as well as tax regulations and they made the necessary applications. For the first few tours they used a rented camper. They were cautious and wanted to make sure that they were able to objectively assess their chances in this new business before investing a significant amount in the transportation mode.

Their experiences were gratifying because visitors to the fairs liked their products, which, in turn, stimulated their productivity after returning home. Another rewarding aspect of their involvement in traveling from fair to fair was the atmosphere of camaraderie they experienced with the other vendors. It was a whole new world for Anne and Louis. They used all the vacation time from their jobs to become part of the life into which they wanted to immerse themselves more intensely during the years of their retirement.

Not everybody can become involved in preferred retirement activities while still remaining actively employed for a livelihood. But as people near the age of retirement, many of them are healthy and alert and want the next decades of their lives to be as interesting and meaningful as the earlier ones. For them, planning for their activities during their retirement years is logical and it can be exciting to think about the various possibilities available to them. Obtaining sound information about the appropriateness of a particular path is an important first step in the planning process and can be engaged in some time prior to the actual time of retirement. In effect, exploring the aspects of a retirement career can be similar to the vocational explorations individuals have pursued in their young-adult years.

A shift of emphasis may differentiate earlier career searches from those in retirement. Where in early vocational explorations financial considerations may have been a prominent concern for young people starting careers and planning for a family, in the retirement years the focus might shift to occupations that are rewarding to the individual in other than financial aspects. Perhaps a long-held thought of engagement in creative activities beckons as a goal or another vocation that had seemed interesting but inappropriate for earlier life circumstances could be realized now. To help with the exploration and decision-making process, there are now opportunities for people to try out what it would be like to run a certain business or start a new career. "Vocation Vacations" can provide these opportunities.

Whether the wish is to operate a bed and breakfast or become a sword-maker, a sports announcer, or a brewmaster, people can use the vacations from their regular job to apprentice in the field they are interested in for their retirement years. "Vocation Vacations" is a developing company that enables interested customers to try out their new jobs or vocations in a hands-on experience (Villano, 2007). The company reportedly provides immersions in more than 110 careers that people might have dreamed about over the years. The brief intensive exposure to a given occupation can either add aspects of reality to the dream or lay it to rest and make space for the search for other options.

Retirement and Marital Relationships

When thinking about retirement, most people focus on the professional aspects of it. Will it be a transition from a hectic work schedule to a life of leisure, reaping the rewards of decades of hard work? But this stage of life can bring with the shift in occupation and activities a change in the marital relationships of the retiring spouse. The majority of retiring people are married. Therefore, a significant impact on the quality of retirement for married couples can be expected to come from the quality of their marriage. Most of the buffers that existed during the different phases of the marriage are gone. The daily trips to the workplace have ended; the children are grown and have moved out of the house. For many, this is the time when the two spouses face one another across the breakfast table, wondering about the stranger on the other side.

The increased exposure to one another gives rise to opportunities for emphasis on disagreements that previously did not seem to matter as much. Some spouses may even decide to terminate the marriage along with the employment.

Marital Relationships and Quality of Retirement

Factors considered to have long-term impact upon the quality of marriages and family life were investigated in a study involving 190 dual-earner couples with adolescent children (Crouter, Bumpus, Hedad, & McHale, 2001). The variables chosen for this study were men's long working hours and role overload. In the study, role overload was assessed using the Role Overload Scale (ROS; Reilly, 1982). On this instrument, respondents expressed their feelings of being overwhelmed by multiple commitments and not having sufficient time for themselves.

As would be predicted, high levels of role overload resulted in less positive marital relationships. Difficulties in the father–adolescent–child relationships were traced back to a combination of long working hours and role overload. Perhaps more surprising was the finding that the men's long working hours reduced the time spent with their wives but seemed to be of little consequence to the partners' subjective evaluations of their marital relationships.

The implications from this study would point to role overload, a factor that produces a higher level of frustration and therefore a higher level of stress on men than long working hours by themselves, leading to significant marital discord. Role overload presents a situation where the individual is required to alternate between patterns of cognition in addition to demands for decisions. The resulting experiences of stress and frustration can be anticipated to give rise to complaints and arguments. Research focusing on physiological factors has shown that men's heart rate and tonic skin conductance were elevated after reading vignettes about conflicts with an intimate partner (Moore & Stuart, 2004). The anticipation of conflict with a significant partner, which can be expected to occur as part of role overload, thus increases the felt frustration.

On the other hand, spending less time together seemed less detrimental to the marital relationship at this time in their lives, especially in dual-earner couples where both partners are equally busy with external commitments. The real effects of the degree of marital estrangement developing at this period in their lives will most likely be disclosed at a later time, such as in retirement.

How the two spouses experienced the marriage will set the tone for their relationship during retirement. Both "his" marriage and "her" marriage combine into "their" retirement life. In their study of midlife marriages Huyck and Gutmann (2006) identified several patterns of marital politics that reflected the ways spouses dealt with potential or actual conflict regarding the allocation of attention, time, and energy within the marital dyad.

Among the sample of 131 wives, the patterns of marital politics included patriarchal, conceding to the husband; passive management of covert anger; ambivalent overt assertiveness; unambivalent overt assertiveness; and matriarchal nurturance. In the wives' perception of their marital relationships, a significant connection to the ages of their children still living in the parental home was noted. With reduced responsibilities for children at home, women's tendency to assert themselves in the marriage was increased. Overall, the wives' marital politics style showed a strong relationship to the husbands' ratings of marital satisfaction. High marital satisfaction for both spouses was found in relationships either where wives described the husband as the family leader (patriarchal) or where they viewed themselves as in charge (matriarchal). The lowest ratings for marital satisfaction in both spouses were observed in marriages where wives were unambivalently assertive.

For the sample of 107 husbands, the following patterns of marital politics were observed: patriarchal; patriarchal but under pressure; crisis; egalitarian; separate peace; conceding dominance generally; conceding dominance because of his ill health; conceding to a domineering wife; and post-transitional union (minimizing differentiating roles, interests, or activities). Husbands who reported the lowest marital satisfaction described themselves as giving in to a domineering wife or as distancing themselves from the troubled relationship by establishing a separate peace.

Men who had turned the marital power over to their wives due to their own poor health reported relatively high satisfaction. Men who saw themselves in a nonconflictual union, men who resisted the pressure to change, and men who viewed their marriage as a differentiated but egalitarian relationship all expressed relatively high marital satisfaction. Overall, the husbands' marital satisfaction seemed to depend on the lack of conflict with the spouse, regardless of the husband's dominant, detached, or submissive marital politics pattern.

While the time of middle adulthood often is characterized by marital stability and increased satisfaction because of reduction in conflicts over child rearing and due to an increased sense of control (Lachman & Weaver, 1998), preretirement is a stage where people take stock of what they have achieved compared to what they had wanted to accomplish. For men, the pride derived from having been a good provider for their families may be mixed with conflict if the "good provider" considerations took precedence over the rewards that would have come from the fulfillment of more meaningful career aspirations that involved a certain degree of risk (Carr, 2005).

The emotional struggle between what one wanted to do and what one thought one ought to do at the time of decision might have lingered silently within the man's memory. When retirement is considered to be a point of no return, the sadness over doing one's duty instead of choosing what one wanted may turn into resentment and anger. Similarly, wives may have given up promising careers for the purpose of raising a family and providing support to the husband. The memory of lost opportunities can evoke bitterness and anger.

The Rose-Colored Glasses of Global Sentiment

The concept of *sentiment override,* as proposed by Weiss (1980), can be seen as a global dimension of affection or disaffection for one's partner and one's marriage, which influences the individual's perception of the partner's objective response during interactions. Spouses with positive sentiment override tend to interpret their partners' messages in positive terms regardless of the message's objective quality. Spouses with a negative sentiment override, on the other hand, tend to interpret their partners' communications in a negative manner, independently of the objective quality of the message.

Considering global sentiments or sentiment override as a type of *marriage bond*, Hawkins, Carrère, and Gottman (2002) investigated their effects on spouses' perceptions of their partners' specific feelings. Realizing that different negative emotions and behaviors can take on different levels of toxicity in terms of relationship outcomes, the investigators believed that it would be important to examine their impact on the perceptual filtering of specific types of marital communication. It was hypothesized that sentiment override would influence both positive and low-intensity negative affects but not high-intensity negative affects. High-intensity negative affect has been observed to be predictive of marital instability and would show little influence from the marital bond.

It was found that sentiment override functions as a perceptual filter through which wives evaluate their husbands' behaviors. Those wives who scored low on the marriage bond measures rated their husbands' behaviors as expressing low-intensity negative affect as negative emotion. In comparison, wives who had high scores on the marriage bond measures rated their husbands' low-intensity negative affect behaviors as neutral in emotional content. As had been predicted, neither husbands nor wives were influenced by sentiment override when rating their spouses' behaviors that reflected high-intensity negative affect.

It is interesting to note that the significant findings regarding global sentiments appeared to be gender specific. In contrast to the findings related to wives, sentiment override did not seem to influence husbands' ratings of their wives' expression of positive affect, low-intensity negative affect, or even high-intensity negative affect. According to the researchers, in wives at least, the marital bond—through the operation of positive sentiment override—may protect couples at times when disagreements evolve. However, the absence of a similar impact of global sentiments on the husbands would indicate that husbands are not aware of the effect and its protective functioning. The lack of awareness might prevent them from seriously considering the importance of the marital bond when opportunities for its development present themselves.

The Correlation of Equity and Relationship Distress Level

According to early studies, lack of equity in intimate relationships seems to be correlated with distress levels in relationships. Those who experienced personal inequity felt high levels of distress, whereas individuals who experienced equity in their relationships reported the lowest level of distress. When inequity strains the relationship, individuals experience distress accompanied by lower satisfaction and commitment to the relationship (Sabatelli & Cecil-Pigo, 1985; Sprecher, 1988).

How is equity or the lack thereof represented and experienced in relationships? Some may measure equity by the amount of money partners are able to control or spend; others see it as the role they play in decision-making events, and still others perceive the level of equity through a division of labor that the partners perform within the relationship.

One area commonly investigated regarding perceived relationship equity is the allocation of household tasks. Research about the division of household labor during the 1990s has shown that men's contributions to the performance of household tasks has increased; however, women still are responsible for twice as much of the routine housework as men are (Coltrane, 2000). Consequently, for women, inequality in the division of household labor is related to marital dissatisfaction and depression.

Equity and Gender Role Ideology

However, the impact of inequality in household labor division is influenced by *the mediating hypothesis of perceived fairness* and further complicated by *the moderating hypothesis of gender role ideology*, which shapes the individual's perception of fairness. Thus, gender role ideology can influence the connections of division of labor, perceived fairness, and marital satisfaction in various ways. In general, couples that endorse traditional gender role orientation will accept less equal participation between men and women in household tasks, whereas the perception of unfairness affects the perceived marital quality more strongly for egalitarian wives than for traditional wives (Kluwer, Heesink, & Van de Vliert, 1997).

The concept of equity in heterosexual relationships is confounded with concepts of gender role identity and gender role rigidity, as mentioned earlier. Partners adhering to a traditional view of marriage would be expected to apply different criteria to the factor of equity than those that subscribe to more egalitarian-based relationships. In addition, while it may seem logical to consider the notion of gender ideology on the basis of two categories, such as traditional and egalitarian, individual couples may not neatly and permanently fall into one or the other of these categories.

Some researchers conceive of gender ideology as falling along a continuum (Lavee & Katz, 2002) or occupying a third category—that of transitional gender ideology (Greenstein, 1996). Thus, while definitely exerting influence on marital satisfaction or dissatisfaction, gender ideology is not a variable that can be measured and assumed to remain stable over time, even though changes seem to occur at a slow pace.

The women's movement may have succeeded in women's increased awareness of opportunities for deeper personal satisfaction within marriage, but role rigidity still remains as much a problem as it was generations ago (Tuch, 2000). Current social structural conditions still support male privileges. In a self-esteem poll, Anderson and Hayes (1996) found that 78% of women respondents agreed that their partners do not share child-rearing responsibilities equally.

Communication

All through the issues presented in this book, communication is the vehicle for expressing what we want and declaring what we do not want to experience. Communication is the way to make ourselves understood and to learn about the intentions and wishes of those around us. Unfortunately, communication can also provide opportunities for misunderstandings.

Men and women have different styles of communicating, as pointed out by sociolinguist Deborah Tannen (1990) in her book, *You Just Don't Understand: Women and Men in Conversation*. Women in their communications often expect or are looking for a response that expresses understanding and support, whereas men address the problem described in the communication and try to offer solutions. Women then are disappointed at not receiving what they were looking for and perceive the man's response as one of superiority because he tells her what to do. Men, on the other hand, do not understand why their offer of a solution to the perceived problem does not receive the appreciation it deserves. This is only one aspect of many that affect relationships.

Equally important in the area of partner communication are concerns that in modern considerations of the reason–emotion dichotomy, characterizations of masculine aspects of behaviors—as based on reason and logic—and feminine behavior—as rooted in emotion—stemming from the nineteenth century seem to have been rejuvenated. Current reasoning explains that while men may lack emotional expressions, it does not mean that men do not experience them. Rather, it is interpreted to mean that men are capable of controlling their strong emotions for the sake of preserving an atmosphere of logic and reason. By comparison, women's expression of emotion becomes just ineffective emotionality (Shields, 2005).

According to this characterization, there are different, gender-linked styles of emotion experienced by both men and women—but in unequal proportions. Strong emotions, such as anger or rage, are part of manliness, whereas openly displayed feminine emotions, such as nurturing behavior and expressions of intimacy, fall under the label of emotionality and could be called *extravagant expressiveness*. But *manly emotion*, the other emotional style, can best be described as a "subtle expression of intense emotion under control" (Shields, 2005, p. 9).

As the two styles are considered to communicate different aspects of emotion, the extravagant expressiveness of women seems to focus on the interpersonal relationship in which the emotional encounter takes place, but the manly emotion constitutes a statement about the individual's relationship to his emotion. Linking manly emotion to rationality and self-control, our culture places less value on the feminine standards of expressiveness and the manly emotional standard exerts greater influence on the way male–female interactions occur and on the consequences of such interactions (Maass, 2006).

The literature on marital development emphasizes the importance of the nature of spousal communication in predicting marital satisfaction and divorce (Gottman, Coan, Carrere, & Swanson, 1998). Particularly, the way spouses interact in marital conflict resolution appears to be a significant predictor of marital satisfaction and stability (Karney & Bradbury, 1995).

It is also important to remember that communication does not consist of the spoken word only; facial expressions, body language and, most important, what is not expressed verbally—what is left unsaid—are parts of communication. In fact, when there is lack of congruence between someone's words and actions, many consider the actions as the more important part of the communication. In other words, if the live-in boyfriend promises that both partners will share everything equally but "forgets" to clean the bathroom when it is his turn, his communication may well amount to "I don't clean bathrooms. That is your job."

Investment in Relationships: Costs and Rewards

Explorations of the impact of rewards received through a relationship and costs of investing in relationships on satisfaction and commitment of partners have indicated that satisfaction is associated with rewards but commitment is associated with both investment and rewards (Sacher & Fine, 1996; Simpson, 1987). Rewards and costs form a fluctuating system that influences the quality of relationships in different ways. To produce satisfaction, the individual may compare the receipt of rewards from the relationship with expected or hypothesized rewards from other relationships with other partners. It could be viewed as a comparison between different partners one would encounter in different relationships. In the case of commitment, individuals compare the rewards coming from the partner with the expenditures made by the individuals themselves. "Do I get a fair share for my investment?" is the comparison in commitment.

Considering the fact that married couples may have several decades together in the retirement phase of their lives, exploring and modifying their marital relationship in the decades prior to retirement can be a significant part of the overall preparation process for retirement. Once in the situation, the balance sheet of the past has left its impression on the partners and is not subject to change. Furthermore, the old established patterns of marital interaction that might have perhaps resulted in an unbalanced commitment account are more difficult to change.

Kevin and Lisa's Commitment Balance Sheet

Kevin appeared to be a born leader when Lisa first met him. He fit the traditional image of men as being in control of their emotions and having a solution for any problem. As long as she was with Kevin, Lisa did not have to worry—he had the answer to everything (low cost). She considered herself lucky (reward) when Kevin proposed marriage. Kevin's behavior included aspects of benevolent sexism, which initially can be so seductive—as described in another chapter. At first, Lisa sought Kevin's advice on most decisions (low cost) and he was glad to give it.

Over time Lisa learned that there were unpleasant consequences if she did not follow Kevin's advice. He was offended when she did not apply his recommendations. His modes of response took one of two paths: He would complain and accuse Lisa of playing games with him and his sincere wish to help or he would be withdrawn and silent for several days. Lisa could not decide which of the two ways she disliked most (cost). By then Lisa had given birth to two daughters and did not feel she was in a position to assert herself. Often after the birth of the first child, the woman's bargaining power is significantly decreased when she requests that the husband take on an equal share of the household tasks (Crittenden, 2001) and each subsequent child reduces her bargaining power further.

Lisa's circle of friends gradually shrank over time (cost). Kevin had succeeded in letting them know that their phone calls and visits were not desirable and Lisa had few opportunities to leave the house for more than a shopping trip. Kevin became increasingly more demanding (rewards) about her household performance as well as her willingness to have sex. He felt entitled to sexual activities according to his wishes, although Lisa's desire for sex had diminished significantly. The lack of arousal on her part made intercourse painful for her (cost). But she was in no position to refuse. Without a job or financial resources, she had to comply for the sake of her children.

What would be the predictions for Lisa and Kevin's relationship as they pass into retirement age? Lisa's role transition to wife and fulltime mother gave her the opportunity to devote herself to her daughters and develop strong bonds with them (rewards, costs, rewards = satisfaction + commitment). The girls' attachment to their mother, in combination with Kevin's authoritarian parenting style, might eventually leave Kevin emotionally isolated from the family (zero rewards, costs). The increased marital stability that often develops during middle adulthood after the children have left the home probably cannot be expected to occur in a marriage like theirs (Maass, 2006). Upon experiencing the "empty nest" syndrome, Lisa might become depressed (zero rewards). On the other hand, she may find a job (rewards) and ways to leave the marriage. Middle-aged women at times show more resilience than younger women when it comes to managing transitions such as divorce, according to research findings (Marks & Lamberg, 1998).

The balance sheet for Kevin and Lisa does not look promising for a pleasant retirement situation; Lisa's side especially seems low on rewards, which does not lead to significant satisfaction and additionally is not available for sufficient balancing costs in order to establish strong commitment in the marriage. For Kevin, although the rewards seem to be reduced over time and his level of satisfaction may not be at an optimum, his costs appear low enough not to overwhelm the rewards and his commitment would be stronger than Lisa's. Of course, the relationship bookkeeping system is not as simple as described. Rewards and costs do not appear in well-defined units of measurement; instead, they are filtered through individuals' perceptions of them.

If Kevin and Lisa remain married, they would enter the retirement phase of their life as two partners who have little compassion for each other. Should they divorce, Kevin may marry again and start another family, which, in turn, would most likely postpone his retirement because of financial obligations to the new family. If indeed he remarries, Kevin might find out again that domineering and controlling behaviors work for a short time to keep those around him in his power. In the end, however, they will distance themselves from his influence—leaving him emotionally isolated at the time of a major transition in his life.

Spouses like Kevin and Lisa may decide to terminate the marriage along with the employment. For others, the time period between the children's leaving the home and the actual retirement from work can be a period of transition for their marital relationship. Instead of continuing with the distance that might have developed during the years when the spouses were busy with raising the children and focusing on careers, they can use this time to get to know each other again and to deepen and stabilize their relationship. It could become a time of discovering and rediscovering the delightful characteristics of the person who long ago shared the transition from single life to married and family life. It can be an exciting journey bringing these characteristics to the surface again.

If their lives did not focus much on pleasuring each other during the busy time of raising children and developing careers, preparation for retirement would present the couple with another opportunity to establish a degree of intimacy that previously may not have existed between them. Taking the time and making the effort for exploration of each other's wishes and desires and taking pleasure in fulfilling them would seem like a sound investment in life during the couple's remaining years. Donald and Cornelia, whose story ends this chapter, decided on such a preparation for their retirement.

Emotional Disorders Over the Life Span

The experience of childhood or adolescent anxiety is often a predictor for later anxiety symptomatology and, in addition, it may also be associated with the development of a mood disorder, such as unipolar depression. Anxiety and depression symptomatologies affect the lives of individuals in various ways. But the afflicted persons are not the only ones suffering; their partners in intimate relationships are also being exposed to the negative emotions, and with that the quality of their relationship is impacted negatively.

Self-centeredness of anxiety was at the bottom of what had brought Paul and Monica to the brink of separation, as was described in the chapter on divorce. After Monica and Paul had been married for 28 years, their children had graduated from college and were busy forging their own careers. Marital therapy was Monica's idea. She had felt neglected during most of their marriage. Paul could not be described as the ideal lover; in fact, they had not engaged in sexual intercourse for years. Monica, an extremely attractive, lively woman with a fulltime job, explained that Paul had no sexual desire. In addition, Monica reported, Paul was not emotionally available to her and did not support her with their children or with his mother. Monica had been taking the brunt of their complaining and rude behaviors for years. In situations where the children misbehaved and were disrespectful toward their mother, Paul did not step in to let them know that their behavior was unacceptable.

A similar situation had developed with Paul's mother. She criticized Monica, who tried to show her the respect a mother-in-law deserved in Monica's eyes. Again, Paul was of no help. He had never got along with his mother and tried to stay quietly in the background. Paul hated confrontations and suffered from anxiety and depression, for which he was prescribed medication. He was able to function adequately in his business, perhaps because being his own boss eliminated some of the anxiety he would have experienced had he worked for someone else. In his personal life, however, he refrained from asserting himself to avoid feeling the anxiety that accompanied confrontations with his mother, his children, and Monica. Monica felt that Paul had abandoned her and his outward behavior confirmed her suspicion.

When Paul talked about himself, he admitted that he was afraid of criticism; his mother had supplied it all his life. He had been afraid of not saying or doing the right thing. His older brother had committed suicide and Paul felt defenseless at home. The strong anxiety, co-occurring with depression, clouded his thinking in emotionally charged situations. His sexual desire had long been extinguished by the fear of not pleasing Monica, but he was also too anxious to verbalize his fears and ask her for her opinion about his sexual performance. It was easier not to say or do anything.

Monica, who had poured her energies into her job, the only place where she was rewarded for what she did, faced competition from younger coworkers and did not feel as secure in her job anymore as she had in the past. She could not imagine life with Paul, whom she still loved, when they were alone without jobs to go to or work to distract them. She felt that for all the years she had spent emotionally isolated, she wanted to pull Paul into the intimate relationship they did not develop in the past. Paul voiced agreement with Monica's suggestion. However, on a daily basis, will he be able and willing to overcome his fears and anxiety and become emotionally available to Monica instead of remaining in his self-centered emotional paralysis? Does he realize that tomorrow's life starts today?

The "Tripartite Model" of Emotional Disorders

A study of adolescents with a primary diagnosis of anxiety disorder revealed that about two thirds of them later in life also developed a diagnosis of depressive disorder (Orvaschel, Lewinsohn, & Seeley, 1995). The rates for comorbidity between emotional disorders in adulthood are high, but not surprising when considering the variety of similar factors in their development and their shared latent structure (Allen, Ehrenreich, & Barkow, 2005). The latent structure of anxiety and depression has been explained on the basis of the "tripartite model" of emotional disorders (Clark & Watson, 1991).

The first factor in this model, negative affect (NA), is a common factor for both anxiety and depression. The second factor, positive affect (PA), differentiates depression from anxiety. Depression results in a reduction of positive affect and increase in negative affect. Anxiety may be characterized by negative affect alone, but positive affect reflects the degree of zest a person feels for life and is demonstrated by the person's active and enthusiastic engagement in pleasurable activities. Physiological arousal (PH), the third factor, is independent of the other two and seems to represent the phenomena of panic states (Barlow, 2002). Interestingly, the application of this model indicates that mood disorders show greater overlap with certain anxiety disorders, such as generalized anxiety disorder (GAD), than with others.

The tripartite model has been applied within research in the child and adolescent as well as the adult literature, which would indicate that the same pattern of changes in negative affect and positive affect observed in adults characterize the symptom constellations of anxiety and depression in children and youth. Based on the shared etiologic pathways, structural commonalities, and responses to similar psychological and pharmacological interventions across anxiety and mood disorders, the development of a coherent treatment approach, a unified protocol (UP), appeared promising (Ehrenreich, Buzzella, & Barlow, 2007). The main elements of this approach consist of introducing the client to general psychoeducation about the nature of emotions and their relationship to behavior, which is followed by explanation of the three components: (1) modification of antecedent cognitive reappraisals, (2) prevention of emotional avoidance, and (3) alteration of emotionally driven behaviors to include new, adaptive responses to emotions.

It is not the aim here to present this treatment approach in all its theoretical and practical elements, but it is applicable to the case of Paul and Monica. Paul's old evaluations of interactions with his mother and confrontations in general would be examined as to their realistic degree of danger or discomfort along with his exaggerated perceptions of the level of his helplessness, leading to new, reality-based appraisals. Instead of his previous response of withdrawing, which was based on his experience of anxiety, Paul would be able to handle the situation appropriately. For instance, he would be able to remind his children of the respectful treatment that they owed their mother and that there would be consequences if they did not treat her with respect.

Similarly, he would assert his choice of a wife to his mother, demonstrating his close connection to Monica. No doubt Monica would richly reward Paul's modified behaviors, and the experience of success instead of the expected helplessness would eventually lead to Paul's change in attitude about life itself. His transition into retirement with Monica could be marked by a zest for life that he had not experienced previously. This brief outline of the possible changes would be enhanced through the use of psychotherapy—in addition to the pharmacological treatment Paul is currently receiving.

The Concept of Sociosexuality

A person's willingness to engage in sexual activity with a variety of partners not restricted to romantic relationships has been referred to as sociosexuality (Simpson & Gangestad, 1991). Persons who adhere to an "unrestricted" sociosexual orientation do not need romantic relationships for engaging in sexual activities. In contrast, individuals with a restricted sociosexual orientation prefer sharing an emotional bond with partners prior to engaging in sex.

Sociosexuality seems to be linked with different characteristics in men and women. For instance, some researchers found sociosexuality in men to be associated with attitudes related to sexism and traditional masculinity (Walker, Tokar, & Fischer, 2000). Additionally, unrestricted sociosexual men reported personality characteristics similar to those of narcissistic individuals and psychopaths; they were unlikely to feel guilt and lacked the capacity for close relationships. Unrestricted sociosexual women, on the other hand, described themselves as fun-loving, self-absorbed, and somewhat shallow (Reise & Wright, 1996).

To investigate correlations between sociosexuality and behaviors, motives, and attitudes, Yost and Zurbriggen (2006) collected self-report measures from a community sample of 88 men and 80 women between the ages of 21 and 45. Overall, men reported being more unrestricted than women in their sociosexual orientation, as men seemed to be more willing than women to participate in sexual activities without an emotional connection. Both unrestricted men and women admitted having engaged in sexual intercourse at a younger age than did the more restricted individuals.

Regarding the construct of sexual conservatism (a rejection of casual-sex attitudes), the investigators observed gender differences. For women, sociosexuality was negatively correlated with sexual conservatism, but not so for men. Women who viewed themselves as unrestricted sexually apparently did not believe that women should be held to a different, more restricted sexual standard than men, while men who considered themselves as sexually unrestricted may have still endorsed greater sexual restriction for women. Thus, while claiming a sociosexual attitude for themselves but not for women, men may in fact live up to a traditionally masculine gender role. The investigators explained that, for men, sociosexuality may be a concept relevant to the self, but sexual conservatism is primarily applied to women. For women, on the other hand, both sexual conservatism and sociosexuality are personally relevant constructs.

The Costs of "Inconsequential" Involvements

Cornelia and Donald were happily married for several years. After the birth of their two children a change developed gradually. Donald's work entailed some travel, which provided opportunities for infidelity. He liked being married to Cornelia but the little sexual encounters were tempting and seemingly inconsequential—in Donald's mind. Cornelia did not agree when she found about them. Donald promised behavior change, Cornelia forgave, and life continued.

Some time later Cornelia found out that Donald had not kept his promise. This time she did not forgive; in fact, she considered leaving him. But disrupting the family would be traumatic for the children. She decided to remain married to Donald but there would not be any physical intimacy between them. Her trust in him was shaken, along with her confidence in herself. "What did I do wrong or not enough of that Donald felt the need to pursue sexual encounters outside our marriage?" she asked herself. In those days, from the many suggestions in women's magazines on how to keep one's husband sexually stimulated and entertained, one could easily get the impression that it was the wife's task to curtail her husband's roving by fulfilling his every fantasy before he could act on it out in the world (in other words, by sexually satiating him).

Cornelia poured her energies into motherhood and community activities. Almost 20 years passed; the children had left the family home and the time for retirement appeared on the horizon. How were Cornelia and Donald going to approach this stage in their life?

Donald could not imagine the rest of his life without Cornelia, but what would their relationship be like if they spent all their time together? He promised behavior change again; without the regular travel, his opportunities for outside involvement would be eliminated, he argued. Cornelia did not believe his promises. She had built up resentment; for years she had led a sexless life and yet she was a sensuous and sexual being. Cornelia strongly believed in the family values her parents had taught her; the notion of sociosexuality was not relevant to her life. But she felt cheated out of experiencing the joys of sexual intimacy that she expected to find in marriage. Donald and Cornelia sought the help of the therapist they had seen years ago.

The Triangle of Living Model

Luciano L'Abate (2005) from Georgia State University, as part of his work on a theory of personality socialization and psychopathology in intimate and nonintimate relationships, proposed the model of the "triangle of living." According to this model, personality can be viewed relationally through competencies in the three components or modalities of the triangle: (1) being or presence, (2) doing, and (3) having. The components function as modalities of exchange within relationships. The content of the exchanges falls into different resource classes, such as status or importance, love or intimacy, services, information, goods or possessions, and money.

The modality of "being" or "presence" combines the resources of importance and intimacy and is therefore relevant to intimate relationships, as presence is understood as an emotional availability to oneself and significant others. Presence is something to be shared; it is different from performance and production. It is to be negotiated if it is to function in healthy ways. Being includes the ability to allocate importance to self (status) and to others (spouses, friends, etc.) and the capacity to be intimate—sharing joy, pleasure, pain, and fears of being hurt.

The combination of the resource information and services forms the modality of performance or doing. Doing is the important modality within educational and teaching institutions, the media, welfare agencies, and professional settings. Examples of extreme doing can be seen in "Type A" personalities and obsessive–compulsive personalities. In these examples, the inability to set limits to one's work schedule is a handicap that severely limits the individual's ability to be close and committed to prolonged relationships.

The modality of production or having includes the combination of the resources possessions and money. Having is relevant to banks and savings institutions, to agriculture and industry. Tycoons whose major aim in life is the accumulation of wealth and goods are examples of extremes in having. It has been shown with empirical data that individuals who organize their lives primarily around materialistic pursuits do so at the expense of the other two modalities: being and doing (Kasser, 2002).

All three modalities are found to varying degrees in most people. It is the inordinate stress on any one of these modalities at the expense of the others that characterizes an unhealthy condition. The type of resource that is exchanged classifies the circumstances or settings. For instance, the resource information is available in schools or libraries; services are found in transit settings; industries and retail stores offer goods and possessions; money is located in banks and other financial institutions; and intimacy is found in the home, where all resources are exchanged.

The distinction between modalities of exchange in this model can be likened to influential distinctions made by other investigators between communal and agentic relationships (Bakan, 1968), where presence or being is related to community and power, while doing or having are related to agency. Often these constructs are linked to differential socialization for men and women. Thus, agency may be defined as a focus on self and forming separations, which is often equated with a masculine orientation. Communion may mean to reflect a focus on others and developing connections, which are regarded as feminine characteristics. The occurrence of one in the absence of the other may result in negative health aspects. Communion may be linked to social support, whereas agency seems related to control (Helgeson, 1994).

The Meanings of Power

Performance (doing) and production (having) combined define the construct of power in this model. But there are different definitions and different aspects of power. Being powerful could be conceived of as having the ability to transform resources into influence within a given system. This conception includes three general aspects of power. The *bases* of power (possession of resources) are transformed into *manifestations* (the expression of the resources) of power through the *processes* (how the resources are shared) of power. Power can be shared and delegated reciprocally in democratic relationships or it can be kept autocratically by dominant individuals.

Sex: Performance or Intimacy?

Applying the distinction of power (performance and production) and presence (importance and intimacy) to the area of sex and sexuality, L'Abate and Hewitt (1988) explained sexual dysfunctions on the basis of inability to be present emotionally to self and to one's partner. One-night stands and short-lived sexual encounters are expressions of sex as performance, representing the physical act of intercourse at the cost of emotional presence. Sex as production can be seen in the frequency of sex as well as the use of "tools" for achieving sexual pleasure (pornography, prostitutes, vibrators, etc.). Stressing performance or production with little or no presence results in deviations and disturbances that impact the further development of sexuality in individuals and their partners (Andersen, Cyranowski, & Aarestad, 2000).

According to L'Abate's model, competence is demonstrated by what an individual *is, does,* and *has* in different circumstances. The two sets of abilities and the resource classes delineate various skills. According to the different circumstances and task requirements, presence needs to be balanced with power. In sex and sexuality, being together and connecting emotionally is more important than "doing" it—the performance or production of it (Abramson & Pinkerton, 2002).

Application of the Triangle of Living Model

L'Abate's model has utility in the case of Donald and Cornelia, introduced earlier. The personality constellations of Donald and Cornelia incorporated all three of the modalities, but Cornelia's personality reflects an emphasis on being or presence, while Donald shows a noticeable focus on doing and particularly on production or having. His high level of energy results in the production of many things in his work and his home. He possesses many skills and is resourceful in solving practical problems and producing articles that please others and gain him the gratitude of others. Performance and production may combine here to the existence of power, as pointed out by L'Abate. There are many tangible representations of his efforts. He wants to be thought of and remembered as a nice, helpful person.

At times, his strong problem-solving activities can create difficulties between him and Cornelia. She may have started to work on a project but Donald, in his usual helpful way, jumped in and finished it for her. Certainly, he meant well, but Cornelia experienced irritation and anger: "Why didn't he allow me to finish it by myself? Don't I have a right to be proud of my skills, too?" she asked. To her, Donald's taking over her project seemed like an intrusion or invasion of her space, or even as belittling her abilities. She saw it as a form of competition that she was not allowed to enter. Her overt response, however, was to withdraw quietly from the project and avoid starting another one.

Competition is closely related to the construct of power. Studies have shown that objective indicators of financial adequacy or inadequacy were significantly associated with the likelihood of domestic violence, indicating that women's earnings relative to their husbands' income may increase women's vulnerability to violence from their partners (Fox, Benson, DeMaris, & Van Wyk, 2002). Of course, Donald was without question the one with the higher earning power and engaging in physical violence would not have been something he would resort to in his relationship with Cornelia or any other woman. Nevertheless, his taking over Cornelia's projects could be interpreted as a type of competition and asserting his power.

Communication has been another area leading to difficulty and isolation. Cornelia, as can be seen from the earlier example, did not express her anger and disappointment in a verbally appropriate manner. In Donald's family of origin, verbalizations were used to communicate about things that needed to be done, in order for life to function adequately. Verbal expressions were used mainly in communications about actions, not feelings.

Donald sees himself as optimistic, looking on the bright side of life. He prefers not to think about unpleasant things. Although seemingly socially extroverted, he does not share much about himself, just as he keeps his strong sense of competitiveness hidden under a pleasing façade. Cornelia finds him emotionally unavailable in their relationship. In her opinion, the moments of an intimate connection between the two are brief. Donald becomes impatient and attempts to escape to his activities. He does not offer explanations unless they are demanded of him and then only sparingly and reluctantly.

Donald's past lack of emotional presence during lovemaking can be seen to confirm L'Abate and Hewitt's (1988) explanations about sexual actions regarding one-night stands and short-lived sexual encounters as expressions of sex as performance and is also congruent with the earlier discussion of sociosexuality. In the past, Donald seemed to engage in the physical act of intercourse at the cost of emotional presence.

The years of activity and raising children covered up or camouflaged many of these internal aspects. With the reduction of this type of buffer, what will the transition to retirement be like? Normally, during retirement, people give up most of their professional pursuits and scale down their style of living, trading their living quarters for smaller places that are easier to maintain. A general scaling down would afford Donald fewer opportunities for the activities that he is so used to for his escape as well as his sense of competition.

At the threshold to retirement, what are Cornelia's options? She can continue her life in a sexless marriage to Donald, she can leave the marriage and find a male partner with whom she can share her stored-up desires instead of going to her grave without expressing her own sensuality, or she can—as long as he avoids extramarital sex—re-enter into a sexual relationship with Donald. The first two options are probably the easier ones; the third option is complicated by a mixture of conflicting emotions. If Cornelia was willing to enter into an intimate relationship with Donald, would that not mean that she has forgiven him and is actually rewarding his past actions?

Sidestepping the notion of forgiving and forgetting for the moment, how could the third option work out in Cornelia's (and also Donald's) best interest? Any resentment over his betrayal could be confronted with the wish to experience and express her sexuality. Shedding the role of the betrayed wife along with any responsibility for Donald's infidelity, she could concentrate on a sexual relationship that is satisfying to her. In other words, she can assume the freedom of acting on how she feels and asking for what she wants sexually. Only if she engages in sex for her own enjoyment can she bypass negative feelings such as anger and resentment or the wish for revenge.

If Cornelia chooses the third option, she would also decide to allow Donald time to change. Now would be the time to prepare for his lifestyle in retirement by exploring and deepening the "being or presence" part of his personality. Another question remains: Assuming that Donald will enlarge his being part, how much will he be willing to share of himself? Will he recognize the difference between "giving" and "sharing" in his concentration on giving with the underlying thought of gaining something, such as the gratefulness or admiration of others? Sharing is not producing something to give it away; sharing is opening and giving of oneself, one's feeling, thinking, and wishing as well as one's fears and anxieties.

Learning to share will not be an easy transition for Donald. After a lifetime of being encased in his own sphere, he will need to learn step by step to have the confidence in himself and in Cornelia to open the doors and invite her in. Most of his past communications about himself have been in responding or reacting rather than in offering in a proactive style. He will need frequent reminders in his thought processes and he will need to incorporate Cornelia in his thought processes—not only at particular times but as a continuous and essential part of his thinking.

Cornelia, on the other hand, has begun to communicate her likes and dislikes calmly but clearly to Donald, leaving no doubt as to what she wants to experience in her life with him. As she confirms her privileges to act and feel according to her wishes, she continues to share parts of herself with Donald.

Wedding anniversaries are highlights on the path of shared life experiences. Some couples celebrate the occasion in the circle of their family and close friends; others may want to mark the significance of the day by repeating their wedding vows and renewing their commitments. On the occasion of their wedding anniversary—the last one prior to retirement— Donald and Cornelia requested the option to start the day with a session in their therapist's office to discuss and outline the path for their changing relationship. They wanted to define some steps as road signs along their future path so that they could recognize them as landmarks to confirm that they are on the right path. In the event that they had unwittingly embarked upon a detour, they wanted to make sure to recognize the signals.

CHAPTER **12**
Conclusions

A life course perspective reflects differences in the structure of individuals' lifestyles and changes in the configuration of their needs, desires, abilities, goals, and resources. As historical events and phases of social change give rise to incentives for forging innovative pathways, traditional lifestyle scripts may loosen or disintegrate, leaving individuals in situations of uncertainty. The traditional markers of transition into adult status as established in previous generations do not reflect accurately the realities of the present. Finishing school, leaving home, finding appropriate employment, getting married, and raising a family—markers of adulthood that operated in a more or less orderly process in the past—do not occur anymore in roughly the same order in everybody's life.

For many, the education–work–retirement lockstep is out of step; education may follow work experience and in some instances even retirement. Family constellations erupt and re-form into different patterns. For some, they may be more or less loosely held together in the absence of legal commitments and boundaries. As people live longer, health and illness situations impact individuals in different ways than they did in the past. Giving and receiving care may occur for more years than ever before and impact individuals' lives and the lives of their families in unexpected ways. Geographical relocation as part of immigration and economic globalization has been increasing in numbers over the twentieth century, breaking up communities and resulting in the formation of new communities with different mixtures of people.

This book has examined a broad spectrum of circumstances that carried with them significant changes in people's lifestyles. Some of the changes may have been expected; others came as surprises to the individuals involved. Responses to changes also come in a wide variety, according to individual differences inherent in the people involved. Some resist changes by ignoring their existence and holding on to their old ways; others might view changes cautiously and more or less reluctantly adapt to them, and still others may open their minds and arms in embracing incentives for creating new options.

Although the individual chapters of the book focus on one or two specific areas of circumstances, that does not mean that people only face circumstances of changes in one particular area of their lives. From the stories of many of the participants it can be seen that they have had to cope with transformations from one lifestyle to another time and again for various reasons and in various areas of their lives. Several of the individuals whose stories appeared in this book could appropriately be featured in more than one of the chapters because they experienced changes in their lifestyles in more than one area of their lives.

There is Larry, who had just moved his family to a different town upon changing his job, when his wife suddenly and tragically died, requiring additional lifestyle decisions. Jenny was stricken with a severe case of arthritis just after having transitioned from single to married life with a partner as devoted to skiing as she had been. Several lifestyle changes were in store for Karen when she married a man addicted to drugs. For financial reasons, soon after the wedding she and her husband had to move in with his mother. Almost simultaneously she was hit by the news of her husband's incarceration and her own pregnancy. As a temporarily single parent she had to make life-changing decisions about her own and her daughter's life.

As the widowed mother of three children, Nora had a difficult path in assuming the authority over her children, increasing her work hours, and, finally, moving to another state. There are those who suspend significant parts of their own lives to care for ill or incapacitated family members—such as Arthur and Debbie who devoted their lives to the care of their son, born with Down syndrome, or Nancy, the mother of a special-needs child, who was left with all the decisions regarding her son's educational development while her husband withdrew from the family. Helga, the mother of a child diagnosed with autism, had already made a major change in her life when she immigrated to the United States. And there are those who were caregivers for ailing parents or spouses like Marian, Sally, Christian, Patrick, and Michael.

Other lifestyle changes were encountered by individuals who relocated to different countries or different cultures and those who made significant changes in their professional careers either out of necessity, as Eric, Jason, and Douglas did, or because of their personal desire, as happened in the case of Wes and Claire. For many, retirement is a period to look forward to for relaxation, while others face different challenges that have perhaps unexpectedly developed out of their past life histories.

Retirement is not only a time of change in one's activities, such as transitioning from scheduled daily work activities to the freedom of performing activities of one's choice and at one's impulse or personal planning. Retirement also presents the likelihood for changes in one's intimate relationships. Spouses have the opportunity to interact more frequently and more directly with one another than they did before, when children and work schedules provided buffers for some of the more critical encounters between husband and wife. As the case of Donald and Cornelia demonstrates, adjustments that go beyond just the additional time available to spouses may be required.

For many, the changes have challenged their ability to adapt and draw on talents or strengths they did not know were available to them. Others, like Curt, were limited by their individual resistance to opening their minds for the inclusion of different attitudes or beliefs. Most individuals face significant changes that require decisions and coping activities several times during their lifetime. The case of Christian is a relevant example. After marrying at a young age, he was drafted into the Armed Forces, became a father, and moved many times with his young family to accommodate for the changes in his work career. Planning carefully for retirement, he had not been prepared for his wife's illness. After taking care of her needs during this time he had to adjust to widowhood. Always open to new experiences and to meeting new people, he found another person with whom to share his life and devotion. Terminal illness interfered again and after taking care of the second woman in his life, he was forced to forge yet another life for himself, while all the time coping with and adjusting to the physical impairments of his own condition.

Christian, saddened by the loss of his beloved Pat, the love that came late into his life, does not feel sorry for himself. He is too busy for that; life has to be lived in ways different from before but not less involved. He will find meaning for his life wherever he turns. As with many of the other individuals, Christian's story would have been appropriate for inclusion into several chapters of this book. He has experienced the changes that come with marriage and raising a family, in his work life, and geographical relocations; he has been primary caregiver to significant life partners and has adapted to the challenges of widowhood while also adjusting to the demands of his own chronic physical ailment.

The life stories of Helga and Christian illustrate the main points expressed in this book: Over their lifetimes, people will be presented with various alterations in the styles of their living; while each alteration brings an end to some familiar aspects of life, it also can introduce new opportunities, new vistas, new adventures. Whether individuals respond to changes by focusing sadly on the losses of those familiar aspects or they look excitedly and with hope on the opportunities and possible adventures lies within their individual personal control. Just because one has responded for most of one's lifetime in a particular way does not mean one has to continue with this approach, especially if it is not in the individual's best interest. As change is part of life, it presents options to those who want to avail themselves of them.

A cognitive–behavioral therapy approach includes several elements that constitute systematic phases in the overall therapy process (Maass & Neely, 2000). Following the presentation of the problem or conflict the client wants to resolve, a brief period is spent in identifying efforts that have not been successful. Clients may have attempted a solution before seeking therapy. If the strategies did not prove successful, that may have been due to some small parts of the overall attempt. Instead of rejecting the whole approach, those parts that seemed to work could be useful again in another attempt. Explorations of previous attempts not only avoid repeating those steps that did not succeed, but also offer opportunities for encouragement.

In the phase of introducing the idea of choices, different approaches will be outlined with estimation of the possible or probable consequences for each approach. Once a particular approach has been selected, action occurs along the chosen path, using skills such as mental imagery, behavior rehearsal, reality checks, and similar techniques. Techniques for proceeding along a chosen path are behaviorally based, but the emotions accompanying actions are closely related to clients' underlying values and beliefs. Incongruity between behaviors and values could lead to emotional dissonance and may jeopardize the achievement of goals, a possibility therapists will be aware of.

As clients work through a given conflict situation, there comes a time to evaluate the gains or losses encountered in the process so far. Reevaluation is an opportunity for detecting necessary shifts in the process or for emphasizing the importance of small successes as building blocks for future greater achievements. Finally, the phase of generalizing learning onto other life situations proceeds with a double impact. The repeated applications of newly acquired thinking and acting skills result in the strengthening of their effectiveness. In addition, through repeated applications the new skills pervade increasingly more life areas and eventually the person's overall quality of life will improve.

The therapy process as outlined here lends itself very well to working on the resolution of different conflicts and in achieving healthy adaptations to the various lifestyle changes described in this book.

References

Abma, J. C., Chandra, A., Mosher, W. D., Peterson, L. S., & Piccinino, L. J. (1997). *Fertility, family planning, and women's health: New data from the 1995 National Survey of Family Growth.* (Vital and Health Statistics, Series 23, No. 19). Hyattsville, MD: National Center for Health Statistics.

Abramson, P. R., & Pinkerton, S. D. (2002). *With pleasure: Thoughts on human sexuality.* New York: Oxford University Press.

Adamic, L. (1932). *Laughing in the jungle.* New York: Harper & Bros.

Adler, N. J. (1981). Re-entry: Managing cross-cultural transition. *Group & Organization Studies, 6,* 341–356.

Allen, L. B., Ehrenreich, J. T., & Barlow, D. H. (2005). A unified treatment for emotional disorders: Applications with adults and adolescents. *Japanese Journal of Behavior Therapy, 31,* 3–31.

Altarriba, J., & Bauer, L. M. (1998). Counseling the Hispanic client: Cuban Americans, Mexican Americans, and Puerto Ricans. *Journal of Counseling & Development, 76,* 389–395.

Amato, P. R. (1991). The "child of divorce" as a person prototype: Bias in the recall of information about children in divorced families. *Journal of Marriage and the Family, 53,* 59–69.

Amato, P. R. (1996). Explaining the intergenerational transmission of divorce. *Journal of Marriage and the Family, 58,* 628–640.

Amato, P. R. (2002). Good enough marriages: Parental discord, divorce, and children's well-being. *Virginia Journal of Social Policy & the Law, 9,* 71–94.

Amato, P. R., & Booth, A. (1997). *A generation at risk: Growing up in an area of family upheaval.* Cambridge, MA: Harvard University Press.

Amato, P. R., & DeBoer, D. D. (2001). The transmission of marital instability across generations: Relationship skills or commitment to marriage? *Journal of Marriage and Family, 63,* 1038–1051.

Amato, P. R., & Hohmann-Marriott, B. (2007). A comparison of high- and low-distress marriages that end in divorce. *Journal of Marriage and Family, 69,* 621–638.

Amato, P., Johnson, D., Booth, A., & Rogers, S. (2003). Continuity and change in marital quality between 1980 and 2000. *Journal of Marriage and the Family, 65,* 1–22.

American Cancer Society. (2002). *Cancer facts and figures.* Atlanta, GA: Author.

Ancis, J. R., & Phillips, S. D, (1996). Academic gender bias and women's behavioral agency self-efficacy. *Journal of Counseling & Development, 75,* 131–137.

Andersen, B. L., Cyranowski, J. M., & Aarestad, S. (2000). Beyond artificial, sex-linked distinctions to conceptualize female sexuality. Comment on Baumeister (2000). *Psychological Bulletin, 126,* 380–384.

Anderson, D., Binder, M., & Krause, K. (2002). The motherhood wage penalty: Which mothers pay it and why? *The American Economic Review, 92,* 354–358.

Anderson, D. Y., & Hayes, C. L. (1996). *Gender, identity, and self-esteem: A new look at adult development.* New York: Springer Publishing Company, Inc.

Aneshensel, C. S., Pearlin, L. I., Mullan, J. T., Zarit, S. H., & Whitlatch, C. J. (1995). *Profiles in caregiving: The unexpected career.* San Diego: Academic Press.

Arredondo, P., Rosen, D. C., Rice, T., Perez, P., & Tovar-Gamero, Z. G. (2005). Multi-cultural counseling: A 10-year content analysis of the *Journal of Counseling & Development. Journal of Counseling & Development, 83,* 155–161.

Artis, J. E. (2007). Maternal cohabitation and child well-being among kindergarten children. *Journal of Marriage and Family, 69,* 222–236.

Aseltine, R. H., Jr., & Kessler, R. C. (1993). Marital disruption and depression in a community sample. *Journal of Health and Social Behavior, 34,* 237–251.

Avellar, S., & Smock, P. J. (2003). Has the price of motherhood declined over time? A cross-cohort comparison of the motherhood wage penalty. *Journal of Marriage and Family, 65,* 597–607.

Avison, W. R. (1999). Family structure and processes. In A. V. Horwitz & T. L. Scheid (Eds.), *A handbook for the study of mental health: Social contexts, theories, and systems* (pp. 228–240). New York: Cambridge University Press.

Axinn, W. G., & Barber, J. S. (1997). Living arrangements and family formation attitudes in early adulthood. *Journal of Marriage and the Family, 59,* 595–611.

Axinn, W. G., & Thornton, A. (1992). The relationship between cohabitation and divorce: Selectivity or causal influence? *Demography, 29,* 357–374.

Axinn, W. G., & Thornton, A. (1993). Mothers, children, and cohabitation: The intergenerational effects of attitudes and behavior. *American Sociological Revue, 58,* 233–245.

Bakan, D. (1968). *Disease, pain and sacrifice: Toward a psychology of suffering.* Boston: Beacon Press.

Ball, F. L. J., Cowan, P., & Cowan, C. P. (1995). Who's got the power? Gender differences in partner's perception of influence during marital problem-solving discussions. *Family Process, 34,* 303–321.

Bandura, A. (1997). *Self-efficacy: The exercise of control.* New York: Freeman.

Barlow, D. H. (2002). *Anxiety and its disorders: The nature and treatment of anxiety and panic* (2nd ed.). New York: Guilford.

Bart, M. (1999). Rising numbers of single fathers reflect changing attitudes in society. *Counseling Today, 41,* 14–16.

Basseches, M. (1989). Dialectical thinking as an organized whole: Comments on Irwin and Kramer. In L. M. Commons, J. D. Sinnott, F. A. Richards, & C. Armon (Eds.), *Adult development: Vol. 1, Comparisons and applications of developmental models* (pp. 161–178). New York: Praeger.

Batalova, J. A., & Cohen, P. N. (2002). Premarital cohabitation and housework: Couples in cross-national perspective. *Journal of Marriage and Family, 64,* 743–755.

Baum, A., & Posluszny, D. M. (2001). Traumatic stress as a target for intervention with cancer patients. In A. Baum & B. L. Anderson (Eds.), *Psychosocial interventions for cancer* (pp. 143–174). Washington, DC: American Psychological Association.

Baumeister, R. F., Bratlavsky, E., Finkenauer, C., & Vohs, K. D. (2001). Bad is stronger than good. *Review of General Psychology, 5,* 323–370.

Beautrais, A., Joyce, P., & Mulder, R. (1999). Personality traits and cognitive styles as risk factors for serious suicide attempts among young people. *Suicide & Life-Threatening Behavior, 29,* 37–47.

Bennett, N. G., Blanc, A. K., & Bloom, D. E. (1988). Commitment and the modern union: Assessing the link between premarital cohabitation and subsequent marital stability. *American Sociological Review, 53,* 127–138.

Bentler, P. M., & Newcomb, M. D. (1978). Longitudinal study of marital success and failure. *Journal of Consulting and Clinical Psychology, 46,* 1053–1070.

Berry, S. L. (2007). Conversation, Q&A, Lois Main Templeton, artist. *Indianapolis Star/Indy Sunday* (April 15, 2007, pp. 16–17).

Betz, N. E. (1994). Basic issues and concepts in career counseling for women. In W. B. Walsh & S. H. Osipow (Eds.), *Career counseling for women* (pp. 1–14). Hillsdale, NJ: Erlbaum.

Bianchi, S., & Casper, L. M. (2000). American families. *Population Bulletin, 55*(4). Washington, DC: Population Reference Bureau.

Bird, C. E. (1997). Gender differences in the social and economic burdens of parenting and psychological distress. *Journal of Marriage and the Family, 59,* 809–823.

Blackwell, D., & Lichter, D. (2000). Mate selection among married and cohabiting couples. *Journal of Family Issues, 21,* 275–302.

Blanton, P. W., & Vandergriff-Avery, M. (2001). Marital therapy and marital power: Constructing narratives of sharing relational and positional power. *Contemporary Family Therapy: An International Journal, 23,* 295–308.

Blood, R., Jr., & Wolfe, D. (1960). *Husbands and wives: The dynamics of marital life.* New York: Free Press.

Bloom, B. L., White, S. W., & Asher, S. J. (1979). Marital disruption as a stressful life event. In C. Levinger & O. C. Moles (Eds.), *Divorce and separation: Context, causes, and consequences* (pp. 184–200). New York: Basic Books.

Blumstein, P., & Schwartz, P. (1983). *American couples.* New York: William Morrow.

Bohmer, C., & Ray, M. L. (1996). Notions of equity and fairness in the context of divorce: The role of mediation. *Mediation Quarterly, 14,* 37–52.

Bolger, N., DeLongis, A., Kessler, R. C., & Wethington, E. (1989). The contagion of stress across multiple roles. *Journal of Marriage and the Family, 51,* 175–183.

Booth, A., & Amato, P. (1991). Divorce and psychological stress. *Journal of Health and Social Behavior, 32,* 396–407.

Booth, A., & Amato, P. (1994). Parental gender role nontraditionalism and offspring outcomes. *Journal of Marriage and Family, 56*, 865–877.

Booth, A., Amato, P. R., & Johnson, D. R. (1998). *Marital instability over the life course: Methodology report for fifth wave.* Lincoln: University of Nebraska Bureau of Sociological Research.

Booth, A., Amato, P. R., Johnson, D., & Edwards, J. N. (1993) *Marital instability over the life course: Methodology report for fourth wave.* Lincoln: University of Nebraska Department of Sociology.

Booth, A., & Crouter, A. C. (2002). *Just living together: Implications of cohabitation for children, families, and social policy.* Mahwah, NJ: Lawrence Erlbaum.

Bowe, F. (2000). *Physical, sensory, and health disabilities: An introduction.* Upper Saddle River, NJ: Merrill.

Brines, J., & Joyner, K. (1999). The ties that bind: Principles of cohesion in cohabitation and marriage. *American Sociological Review, 64*, 333–355.

Bronfenbrenner, U. (1995). Developmental ecology through space and time: A future perspective. In P. Moen, G. H. Elder, Jr., & K. Luscher (Eds.), *Examining lives in context* (pp. 619–647). Washington, DC: American Psychological Association.

Brown, D. (2002). The role of work and cultural values in occupational choice, satisfaction, and success: A theoretical statement. *Journal of Counseling & Development, 80*, 48–56.

Brown, G. W., Andrews, B., Harris, T., Adler, Z., & Bridge, L. (1986). Social support, self-esteem and depression. *Psychological Medicine, 16*, 813–831.

Brown, S. (2003). Relationship quality dynamics of cohabiting unions. *Journal of Family Issues, 24*, 583–601.

Brown, S. L. (2000a). Fertility following marital dissolution: The role of cohabitation. *Journal of Family Issues, 21*, 501–524.

Brown, S. L. (2000b). Union transitions among cohabitors: The significance of relationship assessments and expectations. *Journal of Marriage and the Family, 62*, 833–846.

Brown, S. L. (2004). Family structure and child well-being: The significance of parental cohabitation. *Journal of Marriage and Family, 66*, 351–367.

Brownridge, D. A., & Hall, S (2002). Understanding male partner violence against cohabiting and married women: An empirical investigation with a synthesized model. *Journal of Family Violence, 17*, 341–361.

Budig, M. J., & England, P. (2001). The wage penalty for motherhood. *American Sociological Review, 66*, 204–225.

Bumpass, L. L. (1990). What's happening to the family? Interactions between demographic and institutional change. *Demography, 27*, 483–498.

Bumpass, L., & Lu, H. H. (2000). Trends in cohabitation and implications for children's family contexts in the United States. *Population Studies, 54*, 29–41.

Bumpass, L. L., Martin, T. C., & Sweet, J. A. (1991). The impact of family background and early marital factors on marital disruption. *Journal of Family Issues, 12*, 22–42.

Bumpass, L. L., & Sweet, J. A. (1989). National estimates of cohabitation. *Demography, 26*, 615–625.

Bumpass, L. L., Sweet, J. A., & Cherlin, A. (1991). The role of cohabitation in declining rates of marriage. *Journal of Marriage and the Family, 53*, 913–927.

Burgess, E., & Cottrell, L. (1939). *Predicting success or failure in marriage.* New York: Prentice-Hall.

Buss, D. M. (1994). *The evolution of desire: Strategies of human mating.* New York: Basic.

Byrne, G., & Raphael, B. (1999). Depressive symptoms and depressive episodes in recently widowed older men. *International Psychogeriatrics, 11,* 67–74.

Byrne, G., Raphael, B., & Arnold, E. (1999). Alcohol consumption and psychological distress in recently widowed older men. *Australian & New Zealand Journal of Psychiatry, 33,* 740–747.

Calhoun, L. G., Cann, A., Tedeschi, R. G., & McMillan, J. (2000). A correlational test of the relationship between posttraumatic growth, religion, and cognitive processing. *Journal of Traumatic Stress, 13,* 521–527.

Call, V., Sprecher, S., & Schwartz, P. (1995). The incidence and frequency of marital sex in a national sample. *Journal of Marriage and the Family, 57,* 639–652.

Campbell, D. P., & Hansen, J. C. (1981). *Manual for the Strong–Campbell Interest Inventory* (3rd ed.). Stanford, CA: Stanford University Press.

Campbell, J. (1988). *The power of myth.* New York: Doubleday.

Campbell, R. E., & Cellini, J. V. (1981). A diagnostic taxonomy of adult career problems. *Journal of Vocational Behavior, 19,* 175–190.

Carr, D. (2004a). Gender, preloss marital dependence, and older adults' adjustment to widowhood. *Journal of Marriage and Family, 66,* 220–235.

Carr, D. (2004b). The desire to date and remarry among older widows and widowers. *Journal of Marriage and Family, 66,* 1051–1068.

Carr, D. (2005). The psychological consequences of midlife men's social comparisons with their young adult sons. *Journal of Marriage and Family, 67,* 240–250.

Carr, D., House, J. S., Kessler, R. C., Nesse, R., Sonnega, J., & Wortman, C. B. (2000). Marital quality and psychological adjustment to widowhood among older adults: A longitudinal analysis. *Journal of Gerontology: Social Sciences, 55,* S197–S207.

Casper, L. M., & Bianchi, S. M. (2002). *Continuity and change in the American family.* Thousand Oaks, CA: Sage.

Chase-Landsdale, P. L., & Hetherington, E. M. (1990). The impact of divorce on life-span development: Short and long term effects. In P. B. Baltes, D. L. Featherman, & R. M. Lerner (Eds.), *Life-span development and behavior* (Vol. 10, pp. 107–151). Hillsdale, NJ: Erlbaum.

Chavez, L. (2001). The melting pot still trumps the salad bowl. *Indianapolis Star/ Sunday Star,* 9/30/01 Focus, D2.

Chen, J., Bierhals, A., Prigerson, H., Kasl, S., Mazure, C., & Jacobs, S. (1999). Gender differences in the effects of bereavement-related psychological distress in health outcomes. *Psychological Medicine, 29,* 367–380.

Cherlin, A. J. (2004). The deinstitutionalization of American marriage. *Journal of Marriage and Family, 66,* 848–861.

Christensen, A. (1990). Gender and social structure in the demand/withdrawal pattern of marital conflict. *Journal of Personality and Social Psychology, 59,* 73–81.

Christensen, A., & Heavey, C. L. (1993). Gender differences in marital conflict: The demands/withdraw interaction pattern. In S. Oskamp & M. Costanzo (Eds.), *Gender issues in contemporary society* (Vol. 6, pp. 113–141). Newbury Park, CA: Sage.

Christian, J. L., O'Leary, D. K., & Vivian, D. (1994). Depressive symptomatology in mutually discordant women and men: The role of individual and relationship variables. *Journal of Family Psychology, 8,* 32–42.

Christofi, V., & Thompson, C. L. (2007). You cannot go home again: A phenomenological investigation of returning to the sojourn country after studying abroad. *Journal of Counseling & Development, 85,* 53–63.

Chung, R. C-Y., & Bemak, F. (2002). Revisiting the California Southeast Asian mental health needs assessment data: An examination of refugee ethnic and gender differences. *Journal of Counseling & Development, 80,* 111–119.

Clark, L. A., & Watson, D. (1991). Tripartite model of anxiety and depression: Psychometric evidence and taxonomic implications. *Journal of Abnormal Psychology, 100,* 316–336.

Clarke, S. C. (1995). *Advance report of final divorce statistics, 1998 and 1990* (Monthly Vital Statistics Report. Vol. 43, No. 9, Supplement). Hyattsville, MD: National Center for Health Statistics.

Clarkwest, A. (2007). Spousal dissimilarity, race, and marital dissolution. *Journal of Marriage and Family, 69,* 639–653.

Clay, R. A. (2003). Researchers replace midlife myths with facts. *Monitor on Psychology, 34,* 38–39.

Clements, M. L., Stanley, S. M., & Markman, H. J. (2004). Before they said "I do": Discriminating among marital outcomes over 13 years. *Journal of Marriage and Family, 66,* 613–626.

Cobb, N., Larson, J., & Watson, W. (2003). Development of the attitudes about romance and mate selection scale. *Family Relations, 52,* 222–231.

Cohan, C. L., & Kleinbaum, S. (2002). Toward a greater understanding of the cohabitation effect: Premarital cohabitation and marital communication. *Journal of Marriage and Family, 64,* 180–192.

Cohen, B. E. (2007). "Art & Soul" man: A life-long love of art channels into new career. *The Indianapolis Star/Indy Sunday* (April 8, 2007, p. 27).

Cohen, G. (2000). *The creative age: Awakening human potential in the second half of life.* New York: Avon Books.

Coleman, H. L. K., Casali, S. B., & Wampold, B. E. (2001). Adolescent strategies for coping with cultural diversity. *Journal of Counseling & Development, 79,* 356–364.

Collins, T., & Collins, B. G. (2005). *Crisis and trauma: Developmental ecological intervention.* Boston: Houghton Mifflin.

Coltrane, S. (1996). *Family man: Fatherhood, housework, and gender equity.* New York: Oxford University Press.

Coltrane, S. (2000). Research on household labor: Modeling and measuring the social embeddedness of routine family work. *Journal of Marriage and the Family, 62,* 1208–1233.

Conger, R. D., Elder, G. H., Lorenz, F. O., Conger K. J., Simons, R. L., Whitbeck, L. B., et al. (1990). Linking economic hardship to marital quality and instability. *Journal of Marriage and the Family, 52,* 643–656.

Conger, R. D., Patterson, G. R., & Ge, X. (1995). It takes two to replicate: A mediational model for the impact of parents' stress on adolescent adjustment. *Child Development, 66,* 80–97.

Connidis, I. A., & McMullin, J. A. (2000). Sociological ambivalence and family ties: A critical perspective. *Journal of Marriage and Family, 64,* 558–567.

Cooksey, E. C., & Fondell, M. F. (1996). Spending time with his kids: Effects of family structure on fathers' and children's lives. *Journal of Marriage and the Family, 58*, 693–707.

Coombs, R. H. (1991). Marital status and personal well-being: A literature review. *Family Relations, 40*, 97–102.

Corrigan, P. W. (2000). Mental health stigma as social attribution: Implications for research methods and attitude change. *Clinical Psychology: Science and Practice, 7*, 48–67.

Cott, N. F. (2000). *Public vows: A history of marriage and the nation.* Cambridge, MA: Harvard University Press.

Cowan, C. P., & Cowan, P. A. (1992). *When partners become parents: The big life change for couples.* New York: Basic Books.

Cowart, M. E. (1996). Long-term care policy and the American family. *Journal of Aging and Social Policy, 7*, 169–184.

Cox, M., & Paley, B. (1997). Families as systems. *Annual Review of Psychology, 48*, 243–267.

Cox, M. J., Paley, B., Burchinal, M., & Payne, C. C. (1999). Marital perceptions and interactions across the transition to parenthood. *Journal of Marriage and the Family, 61*, 611–625.

Craig, A., Hancock, K., Chang, E., & Dickson, H. (1998). The effectiveness of group psychological intervention in enhancing perceptions of control following spinal cord injury. *Australian and New Zealand Journal of Psychiatry, 32*, 112–118.

Crawford, D. W., Houts, R. M., Huston, T. L., & George, L. J. (2002). Compatibility, leisure, and satisfaction in marital relationships. *Journal of Marriage and Family, 64*, 433–449.

Crittenden, A. (2001). *The price of motherhood.* New York: Henry Holt and Company.

Crosnoe, R., & Elder, G. H., Jr. (2002) Life course transitions, the generational stake, and grandparent-grandchildren relationships. *Journal of Marriage and Family, 64*, 1089–1096.

Crouter, A. C., Bumpus, M. E., Head, M. R., & McHale, S. M. (2001). Implications of overwork and overload for the quality of men's family relationships. *Journal of Marriage and Family, 63*, 404–416.

Csikszentmihalyi, M. (1990). *Flow: The psychology of optimal experience.* New York: Harper & Row.

Daniels, J., D'Andrea, M., & Arredondo, P. (2001). Multicultural counseling and clients' economic class backgrounds. Dignity, development & diversity (column). *Counseling Today, 43*, 24, 26.

Daniluk, J. C. (1997). Gender and infertility. In S. R. Leiblum (Ed.), *Infertility: Psychological issues and counseling strategies* (pp. 103–125). New York: Wiley.

Daniluk, J. C., & Tench, E. (2007). Long-term adjustment of infertile couples following unsuccessful medical intervention. *Journal of Counseling & Development, 85*, 89–100.

Darvishpour, M. (2002). Immigrant women challenge the role of men: How the changing power relationship within Iranian families in Sweden intensifies family conflicts after immigration. *Journal of Comparative Family Studies, 33*, 270–296.

Davies, L., Avison, W. R., & McAlpine, D. (1997). Significant life experiences and depression among single and married mothers. *Journal of Marriage and the Family, 59,* 294–308.

de Jong Gierveld, J. (2004). Remarriage, unmarried cohabitation, living apart together: Partner relationships following bereavement or divorce. *Journal of Marriage and Family, 66,* 236–243.

Dekovic, M., & Meeus, W. (1997). Peer relations in adolescence: Effects of parenting and adolescents' self-concept. *Journal of Adolescence, 20,* 163–176.

DeMaris, A. (2000). Till discord do us part: The role of physical and verbal conflict in union disruption. *Journal of Marriage and the Family, 62,* 683–692.

DeMaris, A. (2001). The influence of intimate violence on transitions out of cohabitation. *Journal of Marriage and Family, 63,* 233–246.

DeMaris, A., & Greif, G. L. (1992). The relationship between family structure and parent–child relationship problems in single father households. *Journal of Divorce & Remarriage, 18,* 55–77.

DeMaris, A., & Rao, K. V. (1992). Premarital cohabitation and subsequent marital stability in the United States: A reassessment. *Journal of Marriage and the Family, 54,* 178–190.

Demo, D. H., & Cox, M. J. (2000). Families with young children: A review of research in the 1990s. *Journal of Marriage and the Family, 62,* 876–895.

Denes-Raj, V., & Epstein, S. (1994). Conflict between intuitive and rational processing: When people behave against their better judgment. *Journal of Personality and Social Psychology, 66,* 819–829.

de Ridder, D. (2000). Gender, stress and coping: Do women handle stressful situations differently from men? In L. Sherr & J. S. St. Lawrence (Eds.), *Women, health and the mind* (pp. 115–135). Chichester, England: Wiley.

Deveraux, L. L., & Hammerman, A. J. (1998). *Infertility and identity: New strategies for treatment.* San Francisco: Jossey-Bass.

Didion, J. (2005). *The year of magical thinking.* New York: Alfred A. Knopf.

Domar, A. D. (1997). Stress and infertility in women. In S. R. Leiblum (Ed.), *Infertility: Psychological issues and counseling strategies* (pp. 67–82). New York: Wiley.

Dukakis, O. (2007). Heartfelt decisions. *AARP Bulletin* (May 2007). Opinion/In the Know, p. 35.

Dunifon, R., & Kowaleski-Jones, L. (2007). The influence of grandparents in single-mother families. *Journal of Marriage and Family, 69,* 465–481.

Dwyer, J., & Coward, R. T. (1991). A multivariate comparison of the involvement of adult sons versus daughters in the care of impaired parents. *Journal of Gerontology: Social Sciences, 46,* S259–269.

Ehrenreich, J. T., Buzzella, B. A., & Barlow, D. H. (2007). General principles for the treatment of emotional disorders across the life span. In S. G. Hofmann & J. Weinberger (Eds.), *The art and science of psychotherapy* (pp. 191–209). New York: Routledge, Taylor & Francis Group.

Elder, G. H., Jr. (1998). Life course and human development. In W. Damon (Ed.), *Handbook of child psychology* (pp. 939–991). New York: Wiley.

Elliott, T., & Shewchuk, R. (1998). Recognizing the family caregiver: Integral and formal members of the rehabilitation process. *Journal of Vocational Rehabilitation, 10,* 123–132.

England, P., & Farkas, G. (1986). *Households, employment, and gender: A social, economic and demographic view.* New York: Aldine.

Erikson, E. H. (1963). *Childhood and society* (2nd ed.). New York: Norton.

Escobar, J. I., Nervi, C. H., & Gara, M. A. (2000). Immigration and mental health: Mexican Americans in the United States. *Harvard Review of Psychiatry, 8*(2), 64–72.

Ewart, C. K., Taylor, C. B., Kraemer, H. C., & Agras, W. S. (1991). High blood pressure and marital discord: Not being nasty matters more than being nice. *Health Psychology, 10,* 155–163.

Falvo, D. (1999). *Medical and psychosocial aspects of chronic illness and disability* (2nd ed.). Gaiterhsburg, MD: Aspen.

Fields, J., & Casper, L. (2001). *America's families and living arrangements: March 2000.* Washington, DC: U.S. Census Bureau.

Finn, M. G. (2003). Stay rates of foreign doctorate recipients from U.S. universities, 2001. Retrieved October 9, 2006, from http://www.abtassoc.com/reports/stayrate03.pdf.

Flannery, W. P., Reise, S. P., & Yu, J. (2001). An empirical comparison of acculturation models. *Personality & Social Psychology Bulletin, 27,* 1035–1045.

Flippo, H. Schwarzenegger not the first. http://german.about.com/cs/culture/a/foreignguvs.htm, retrieved 2/25/02.

Foster, M. E., Jones, D., & Hoffman, S. D. (1998). The economic impact of nonmarital childbearing: How are older, single mothers faring? *Journal of Marriage and the Family, 60,* 163–174.

Fowers, B. J. (1994). Perceived control, illness, status, stress, and adjustment to cardiac illness. *Journal of Psychology, 128,* 567–576.

Fox, G. L., Benson, M. L., DeMaris, A. A., & Van Wyk, J. (2002). Economic distress and intimate violence: Testing family stress and resources theories. *Journal of Marriage and Family, 64,* 793–807.

Fredrickson, B. L. (2000). Cultivating positive emotions to optimize health and well-being. *Prevention and Treatment, 3.* Retrieved January 20, 2001, from the World Wide Web: http://www.journals.apa.org/prevention/volume3/pre0030001a.html.

Fredrickson, B. L. (2001). The role of positive emotions in positive psychology: The broaden-and-build theory of positive emotions. *American Psychologist, 56,* 218–226.

Frick, P., Christian, R., & Wooton, J. (1999). Age trends in association between parenting practices and conduct problems. *Behavior Modification, 23,* 106–128.

Frost-Knappman, E. (1994). *The ABC-CLIO companion to women's progress in America.* Santa Barbara, CA: ABC-CLIO, Inc.

Futris, T. G., & Pasley, K. (1997, November). *The father role identity: Conceptualizing and assessing within-role variation.* Paper presented at the Preconference Theory Construction and Research Methodology Workshop, annual meeting of the National Council on Family Relations. Crystal City, VA.

Gallagher, S. K., & Gerstel, N. (2001). Connections and constraints: The effects of children on caregiving. *Journal of Marriage and Family, 63,* 265–275.

Gama, E. M. P., & Pedersen, P. (1977). Readjustment problems of Brazilian returnees from graduate studies in the United States. *International Journal of Intercultural Relations, 1,* 46–58.

Ganong, L., & Coleman, M. (1989) Preparing for remarriage: Anticipating the issues, seeking solutions. *Family Relations, 38,* 28–33.

Garcia, L. T., & Markey, C. (2007). Matching in sexual experience for married, cohabiting, and dating couples. *Journal of Sex Research, 44,* 250–255.

Gardner, H. (1993). *Creative minds.* New York: Basic Books.

Gati, I., Krausz, M., & Osipow, S. H. (1996). A taxonomy of difficulties in career decision making. *Journal of Counseling Psychology, 43,* 510–526.

Gati, I., & Saka, N. (2001). High school students' career-related decision-making difficulties. *Journal of Counseling & Development, 79,* 331–340.

George, L. K., Fillenbaum, G. G., & Palmore, E. (1984). Sex differences in the antecedents and consequences of retirement. *Journal of Gerontology, 39,* 364–371.

Gibson, D. M., & Myers, J. E. (2000). Gender and infertility: A relational approach to counseling women. *Journal of Counseling & Development, 78,* 400–410.

Gilbert, D. T., Pinel, E. C., Wilson, T. D., Blumberg, S. J., & Wheatley, T. P. (1998). Immune neglect: A source of durability bias in affective forecasting. *Journal of Personality and Social Psychology, 75,* 617–638.

Gim Chung, R. H. (2001). Gender, ethnicity, and acculturation in intergenerational conflict of Asian American college students. *Cultural Diversity and Ethnic Minority Psychology, 7,* 376–386.

Ginter, E. J. (1999). David K. Brooks' contribution to the developmentally based life-skills approach. *Journal of Mental Health Counseling, 21,* 191–202.

Gordon, H. S., & Rosenthal, G. E. (1995). Impact of marital status on outcomes in hospitalized patients. *Archives of Internal Medicine, 155,* 2465–2471.

Gorski, T. T., & Miller, M. (1982). *Counseling for relapse prevention.* Independence, MO: Herald House-Independence Press.

Gottman, J. (1994). *Why marriages succeed or fail.* New York: Simon & Schuster.

Gottman, J. M., Coan, J., Carrère, S., & Swanson, C. (1998). Predicting marital happiness and stability from newlywed interactions. *Journal of Marriage and the Family, 60,* 5–22.

Gottman, J. M., & Levenson, R. W. (2000). The timing of divorce: Predicting when a couple will divorce over a 14-year period. *Journal of Marriage and the Family, 62,* 737–745.

Graefe, D. R., & Lichter, D. T. (1999). Life course transitions of American children: Parental cohabitation, marriage, and single motherhood. *Demography, 36,* 205–217.

Greenstein, T. N. (1996). Gender ideology and perceptions of the fairness of the division of household labor: Effects on marital quality. *Social Forces, 74,* 1029–1042.

Greif, G. L. (1995). Single fathers with custody following separation and divorce. *Marriage & Family Review, 20,* 213–231.

Gupta, S., Smock, P. J., & Manning, W. D. (2004). Moving out: Transition to non-residence among resident fathers in the United States, 1968–1997. *Journal of Marriage and Family, 66,* 627–638.

Hager, D. L. (1992). Chaos and growth. *Psychotherapy, 29,* 378–384.

Haier, R. J., Chueh, D., Touchette, P., Lott, I., Buchsbaum, M. S., McMillan D., et al. (1995). Brain size and cerebral glucose metabolic rate in nonspecific mental retardation and Down syndrome. *Intelligence, 20,* 191–210.

Hall, D. R., & Zhao, J. Z. (1995). Cohabitation and divorce in Canada: Testing the selectivity hypothesis. *Journal of Marriage and the Family, 57,* 421–427.

Hall, L. D., Walker, A. J., & Acock, A. C. (1995). Gender and family work in one-parent households. *Journal of Marriage and the Family, 57,* 685–692.

Han, S. K., & Moen, P. (1999). Work and family over time: A life course approach. *Annals of the American Academy of Political and Social Science, 562,* 98–110.

Hartung, P. J., & Blustein, D. L. (2002). Reason, intuition, and social justice: Elaborating on Parsons's career decision-making model. *Journal of Counseling & Development, 80,* 41–47.

Hassan, S. (1990). *Combatting cult mind control.* Rochester, VT: Park Street Press.

Hawkins, M. W., Carrère, S., & Gottman, J. M. (2002). Marital sentiment override: Does it influence couples' perceptions? *Journal of Marriage and Family, 64,* 193–201.

Hays, P. A. (2001). *Addressing cultural complexities in practice: A framework for clinicians and counselors.* Washington, DC: American Psychological Association.

Heath, T. D., & Orthner, D. K. (1999). Stress and adaptation among male and female single parents. *Journal of Family Issues, 20,* 557–587.

Heavey, C. L., Christensen, A., & Malamuth, N. M. (1995). The longitudinal impact of demand and withdrawal during marital conflict. *Journal of Consulting and Clinical Psychology, 63,* 797–801.

Heavey, C. L., Layne, C., & Christensen, A. (1993). Gender and conflict structure in marital interaction: A replication and extension. *Journal of Consulting and Clinical Psychology, 61,* 16–27.

Heckert, D. A., Nowak, T. C., & Snyder, K. A. (1998). The impact of husbands' and wives' relative earnings on marital disruption. *Journal of Marriage and the Family, 60,* 690–703.

Heidemann, B., Suhomlinova, O., & O'Rand, A. M. (1998). Economic independence, economic status, and empty nest in middle marital disruption. *Journal of Marriage and the Family, 60,* 219–231.

Heider, F. (1958). *The psychology of interpersonal relations.* New York: Wiley.

Heimdal, K. R., & Houseknecht, S. K. (2003). Cohabiting and married couples' income organization: Approaches in Sweden and the United States. *Journal of Marriage and Family, 65,* 525–538.

Helgeson, V. S. (1994). Relation of agency and communion to well-being: Evidence and potential explanations. *Psychological Bulletin, 116,* 412–428.

Helms-Erikson, H. (2001). Marital quality ten years after the transition to parenthood: Implications of the timing of parenthood and the division of housework. *Journal of Marriage and Family, 63,* 1099–1110.

Helson, H. (1964). *Adaptation-level theory: An experimental and systematic approach to behavior.* New York: Harper.

Henderson, S. J. (2000). "Follow your bliss": A process for career happiness. *Journal of Counseling & Development, 78,* 305–315.

Heuveline, P., & Timberlake, J. M. (2004). The role of cohabitation in family formation: The United States in comparative perspective. *Journal of Marriage and Family, 66,* 1214–1230.

Heyn, D. (1997). *Marriage shock: The transformation of women into wives.* New York: Villard Books, a division of Random House, Inc.

Holcomb-McCoy, C. C., & Myers, J. E. (1999). Multicultural competence and counselor training: A national survey. *Journal of Counseling & Development, 77,* 294–302.

Holstein, M. (1997). Ethics and public policy: A normative defense of age-based entitlements. In R. B. Hudson (Ed.), *The future of age-based public policy* (pp. 25–35). Baltimore: Johns Hopkins University.

Hong, J., & Min, P. G. (1999). Ethnic attachment among second generation Korean adolescents. *Amerasia Journal, 25,* 165 178.

Horowitz, A. V., Raskin White, H., & Howell-White, S. (1996). The use of multiple outcomes in stress research: A case study of gender differences in response to marital dissolution. *Journal of Health and Social behavior, 37,* 278–291.

Hooyman, N., & Gonyea, J. (1995). *Feminist perspective on family care.* Thousand Oaks, CA: Sage.

Hovey, J. D. (2000). Acculturative stress, depression, and suicidal ideation in Mexican immigrants. *Cultural Diversity and Ethnic Minority Psychology, 6,* 134–151.

Hurh, W. M. (1998). *The Korean Americans.* Westport, CT: Greenwood Press.

Huston, T. L., Caughlin, J. P., Houts, R. M., Smith, S. E., & George, L. J. (2001). The connubial crucible: Newlywed years as predictors of marital delight, distress, and divorce. *Journal of Personality and Social Psychology, 80,* 237–252.

Huston, T. L., & Houts, R. M. (1998). The psychological infrastructure of courtship and marriage: The role of personality and compatibility in romantic relationships. In T. N. Bradbury (Ed.), *The developmental course of marital dysfunction* (pp. 114–151). New York: Cambridge University Press.

Huston, T., McHale, S., & Crouter, A. (1986). When the honeymoon's over: Changes in the marriage relationship over the first year. In R. Gilmour & S. Duck (Eds.), *The emerging field of personal relationships* (pp. 109–132). Hillsdale, NJ: Lawrence Erlbaum Associates.

Huyck, M. H., & Gutmann, D. L. (2006). Men and their wives: Why are some married men vulnerable at midlife? In V. H. Bedford & B. F. Turner (Eds.) *Men in relationships: A new look from a life course perspective* (pp. 27–50). New York: Springer Publishing Company.

Hynes, K., & Clarkberg, M. (2005). Women's employment patterns during early parenthood: A group-based trajectory analysis. *Journal of Marriage and Family, 67,* 222–239.

Ingersoll-Dayton, B., Neal, M. B., Ha, J.-H., & Hammer, L. B. (2003). Redressing inequity in parent care among siblings. *Journal of Marriage and Family, 65,* 201–212.

Ingersoll-Dayton, B., Starrels, M. E., & Dowler, D. (1996). Caregiving for parents and parents-in-law: Is gender important? *The Gerontologist, 36,* 483–491.

Jacquet, S. E., & Surra, C. A. (2001). Parental divorce and premarital couples: Commitment and other relationship characteristics. *Journal of Marriage and Family, 63,* 627–638.

James, R. K., & Gilliland, B. E. (2005). *Crisis intervention strategies* (5th ed.). Pacific Grove, CA: Brooks/Cole.

Janssen, T., & Carton, J. (1999). The effects of locus of control and task difficulty on procrastination. *Journal of Genetic Psychology, 160,* 436–442.

Jepsen, L. K., & Jepsen, C. A. (2002). An empirical analysis of the matching patterns of same-sex and opposite-sex couples. *Demography, 39,* 435–453.

Johnson, D. R., & Wu, J. (2002). An empirical test of crisis, social selection, and role explanations of the relationship between marital disruption and psychological distress: A pooled time-series analysis of four-wave panel data. *Journal of Marriage and Family, 64,* 211–224.

Johnson, M. P. (1995). Patriarchal terrorism and common couple violence: Two forms of violence against women. *Journal of Marriage and the Family, 57,* 283–294.

Joseph, S., & Linley, P. A. (2005). Positive adjustment to threatening events: An organismic valuing theory of growth through adversity. *Review of General Psychology, 9,* 262–280.

Kallir, J. (2001). Grandma Moses in the 21st century. *Women in the Arts, 19,* 6–11, 30.

Kalmijn, M. (2001). Joint and separated lifestyles in couple relationships. *Journal of Marriage and Family, 63,* 639–654.

Kangas, M., Henry, J. L., & Bryant, R. A. (2002). Posttraumatic stress disorder following cancer: A conceptual and empirical review. *Clinical Psychology Review, 22,* 499–524.

Karney, B. R., & Bradbury, T. N. (1995). The longitudinal course of marital quality and stability: A review of theory, method, and research. *Psychological Bulletin, 118,* 3–34.

Kasser, T. (2002). *The high price of materialism.* Cambridge, MA: MIT Press.

Katz, J., & Beach, S. R. (1997). Self-verification and depressive symptoms in marriage and courtship: A multiple pathway model. *Journal of Marriage and the Family, 59,* 903–914.

Kelly, G. A. (1963). *A theory of personality: The psychology of personal constructs.* New York: W. W. Norton & Company, Inc. (Original work published 1955)

Kelly, G. A. (1991). *The psychology of personal constructs, Vol. 1: A theory of personality.* London: Routledge. (Original work published 1955).

Kennedy, A. (2006). An American success story. *Counseling Today, 49,* 16.

Kenney, C. (2004). Cohabiting couple, filing jointly? Resource pooling and U.S. poverty policies. *Family Relations, 53,* 237–247.

Kiecolt-Glaser, J. K., Dura, J. R., Speicher, C. E., Trask, O. J., & Glaser, R. (1991). Longitudinal changes in immunity and health. *Psychosomatic Medicine, 53,* 345–362.

Kiecolt-Glaser, J. K., & Newton, T. (2001). Marriage and health: His and hers. *Psychological Bulletin, 127,* 472–503.

Kiecolt-Glaser, J. K., Newton, T., Cacioppo, J. T., MacCallum, R. C., Glaser, R., & Malarkey, W. B. (1996). Marital conflict and endocrine function: Are men really more physiologically affected than women? *Journal of Consulting and Clinical Psychology, 64,* 324–332.

Killian, T., & Ganong, L. H. (2002). Ideology, context, and obligations to assist older persons. *Journal of Marriage and Family, 64,* 1080–1088.

Kim, K. H., & McKenry, P. C. (2002). The relationship between marriage and psychological well-being. *Family Issues, 23,* 885–911.

King, V., & Elder, G. H. Jr. (1995). American children view their grandparents: Linked lives across three rural generations. *Journal of Marriage and the Family, 57,* 165–178.

King, V., & Scott, M. E. (2005). A comparison of cohabiting relationships among older and younger adults. *National Council on Family Relations Report, 50*(3), Family Focus On … (September), F11, F13.

Klerman, J., & Leibowitz, A. (1999). Job continuity among new mothers. *Demography, 36,* 145–155.

Klute, M. M., Crouter, A. C., Sayer, A. G., & McHale, S. M. (2002). Occupational self-direction, values, and egalitarian relationships: A study of dual-earner couples. *Journal of Marriage and Family, 64,* 139–151.

Kluwer, E. S., Heesink, J. A. M., & Van de Vliert, E. (1997). The marital dynamics of conflict over the division of labor. *Journal of Marriage and the Family, 59,* 635–653.

Knott, J. E., & Wild, E. (1986). Anticipatory grief and reinvestment. In T. A. Rando (Ed.), *Loss and anticipatory grief* (pp. 55–60). Lexington, MA: Lexington Books.

Kogan, L. (1999). Ninety-nine and a half won't do: The art of Nellie Mae Rowe. *Women in the Arts, 17,* 6–7.

Krieger, S. (2005). *Things no longer there: A memoir of losing sight and finding vision.* Madison, WI: Terrace Books, a division of The University of Wisconsin Press.

Krokoff, L. J. (1991). Communication orientation as a moderator between strong negative affect and marital satisfaction. *Behavioral Assessment, 13,* 51–65.

Krokoff, L. J. (1992). Hidden agendas in marriage: Affective and longitudinal dimensions. *Communication Research, 17,* 483–499.

Krumboltz, J. D. (1994). The Career Beliefs Inventory. *Journal of Counseling & Development, 72,* 424–428.

Kulik, L. (1999). Marital power relations, resources and gender role ideology: A multivariate model for assessing effects. *Journal of Comparative Family Studies, 30,* 189–206.

Kurdek, L. A. (1991). Marital stability and changes in marital quality in newly wed couples: A test of the contextual model. *Journal of Social and Personal Relationships, 8,* 27–48.

Kurdek, L. A. (1999). The nature and predictors of the trajectory of change in marital quality for husbands and wives over the first 10 years of marriage. *Developmental Psychology, 35,* 1283–1296.

Kurdek, L. A. (2002). Predicting the timing of separation and marital satisfaction: An eight-year prospective longitudinal study. *Journal of Marriage and Family, 64,* 163–179.

Kurdek, L. A. (2005). Gender and marital satisfaction early in marriage: A growth curve approach. *Journal of Marriage and Family, 67,* 68–84.

Kurylo, M. F., Elliott, T. R., & Shewchuk, R. M. (2001). FOCUS on the family caregiver: A problem-solving training intervention. *Journal of Counseling & Development, 79,* 275–281.

L'Abate, L. (2005). *Personality in intimate relationships: Socialization and psychopathology.* New York: Springer Science + Business Media, LLC.

L'Abate, L., & Hewitt, D. (1988). Toward a classification of sex and sexual behavior. *Journal of Sex and Marital Therapy, 14,* 29–39.

Lachman, M., & Weaver, S. (1998). Sociodemographic variations in the sense of control by domain: Findings of the MacArthur studies of midlife. *Psychology & Aging, 13,* 553–562.

LaFromboise, T., Coleman, H. L., & Gerton, J. (1993). Psychological impact of biculturalism: Evidence and theory. *Psychological Bulletin, 114,* 395–412.

Lamb, K. A., Lee, G. R., & DeMaris, A. (2003). Union formation and depression: Selection and relationship effects. *Journal of Marriage and Family, 65,* 953–962.

Lamborn, S. D., Mounts, N. S., Steinberg, L., & Dornbusch, S. M. (1991). Patterns of competence and adjustment among adolescents from authoritative, authoritarian, indulgent, and neglected families. *Child Development, 62,* 1049–1065.

Lampard, R., & Peggs, K. (1999). Repartnering: The relevance of parenthood and gender to cohabitation and remarriage among the formerly married. *British Journal of Solciology, 50,* 443–465.

Lancaster, J. (1994). Human sexuality, life histories, and evolutionary ecology. In A. Rossi (Ed.), *Sexuality across the life course* (pp. 39–62). Chicago: The University of Chicago Press.

Larson, R. W., & Almeida, D. M. (1999). Emotional transmission in the daily lives of families: A new paradigm for studying family process. *Journal of Marriage and the Family, 61,* 5–20.

Laumann, E. O., Gagnon, J. H., Michael, R. T., & Michaels, S. (1994). *The social organization of sexuality: Sexual practices in the United States.* Chicago: University of Chicago Press.

Lavee, Y., & Katz, R. (2002). Division of labor, perceived fairness, and marital quality: The effect of gender ideology. *Journal of Marriage and Family, 64,* 27–39.

Lee, G. (1977). Age at marriage and marital satisfaction: A multivariate analysis with implications for marital stability. *Journal of Marriage and the Family, 39,* 493–504.

Lee, G. R., DeMaris, A., Bavin, S., & Sullivan, R. (2001). Gender differences in the depressive effect of widowhood in later life. *Journal of Gerontology: Social Sciences, 56,* S56–S61.

Lee, G. R., Dwyer, J. W., & Coward, R. T. (1993). Gender differences in parent care: Demographic factors and same-gender preferences. *Journals of Gerontology: Social Sciences, 48,* S9–16.

Leonard, J. (2006). Introduction. In Didion, J. *We tell ourselves stories in order to live* (pp. ix–xxiii). New York: Everyman's Library, Alfred A. Knopf.

Leonard, K. E., & Roberts, L. J. (1998). Marital aggression, quality, and stability in the first year of marriage: Findings from the Buffalo Newlywed Study. In T. N. Bradbury (Ed.), *The developmental course of marital dysfunction* (pp. 44–73). New York: Cambridge University Press.

Leonard, K. E., & Senshak, M. (1996). Prospective prediction of husband marital aggression within newlywed couples. *Journal of Abnormal Psychology, 105,* 369–380.

Levenson, R. W., & Gottman, J. M. (1985). Physiological and affective predictors of change in relationship satisfaction. *Journal of Personality and Social Psychology, 49,* 85–94.

Levinson, D. (1994). *Ethnic relations: A cross-cultural encyclopedia.* Santa Barbara, CA: ABC-CLIO, Inc.

Levinson, D. J. (1990). A theory of life structure development in adulthood. In C. N. Alexander & E. J. Langer (Eds.), *Higher stages of human development* (pp. 35–54). New York: Oxford University Press.

Lewin, E. (2004). Does marriage have a future? *Journal of Marriage and Family, 66,* 1000–1006.

Lichter, D. T., Batson, C. D., & Brown, J. B. (2004). Welfare reform and marriage promotion: The marital expectations and desires of single and cohabiting mothers. *Social Service Review, 78,* 2–25.

Lindsay, J. W. (Warren) (1995). *Teenage couples coping with reality: Dealing with money, in-laws, babies and other details of daily life.* Buena Park, CA: Morning Glory Press.

Litvak, E. (1980). Research patterns in the health of the elderly. In E. Borgatta & N. McCluskey (Eds.), *Aging and society: Current research and policy perspectives* (pp. 79–130). Beverly Hills, CA: Sage.

Liu, C. (2000). A theory of marital sexual life. *Journal of Marriage and the Family, 62,* 363–374.

Livnch, H., & Antonak, R. F. (2005). Psychosocial adaptation to chronic illness and disability: A primer for counselors. *Journal of Counseling & Development, 83,* 12–20.

Locke, H. J., & Wallace, K. M. (1959). Short marital adjustment and prediction tests: Their reliability and validity. *Marriage and Family Living, 21,* 251–255.

Lovallo, W. R. (1997). *Stress & health: Biological and psychological interactions.* Thousand Oaks, CA: Sage.

Loving, T. J., Heffner, K. L., Kiecolt-Glaser, J. K., Glaser, R., & Malarkey, W. B. (2004). Stress hormone changes and marital conflict: Spouses' relative power makes a difference. *Journal of Marriage and Family, 66,* 595–612.

Lown, J., & Dolan, E. (1988). Financial challenges in remarriage. *Lifestyles: Family and Economic Issues, 9,* 73–88.

Lown, J., McFadden, J., & Crossman, S. (1989). Family life education for remarriage focus on financial management. *Family Relations, 38,* 40–45.

Lucas, M. S. (1993). A validation of types of career indecision at a counseling center. *Journal of Counseling Psychology, 40,* 440–446.

Lucas, M. S., Skokowski, C. T., & Ancis, J. R. (2000). Contextual themes in career decision making of female clients who indicate depression. *Journal of Counseling & Development, 78,* 316–325.

Maass, V. S. (2002/2006). *Women's group therapy: Creative challenges and options.* New York: Springer Publishing.

Maass, V. S. (2006). Images of masculinity as predictors of men's romantic and sexual relationships. In V. H. Bedford & B. F. Turner (Eds.), *Men in relationships: A new look from a life course perspective,* (pp. 51–78). New York: Springer Publishing Company.

Maass, V. S. (2007). *Facing the complexities of women's sexual desire.* New York: Springer Science + Business Media, LLC.

Maass, V. S., & Neely, M. A. (2000). *Counseling single parents: A cognitive-behavioral approach.* New York: Springer Publishing Company.

Mackey, R. A., & O'Brien, B. A. (1995). *Lasting marriages: Men and women growing together.* Westport, CT: Praeger.

Macklin, E. D. (1983). Nonmarital heterosexual cohabitation: An overview. In E. D. Macklin & R. H. Rubin (Eds.), *Contemporary families and alternative lifestyles: Handbook on theory and research.* (pp. 49–74). Newbury Park, CA: Sage.

Macmillan, R., & Gartner, R. (1999). When she brings home the bacon: Labor-force participation and the risk of spousal violence against women. *Journal of Marriage and the Family, 61,* 947–958.

Maddux, J. E. (1991). Personal efficacy. In V. Derlega, B. Winstead, & W. Jones (Eds.), *Personality* (pp. 231–262). Chicago: Nelson–Hall.

Manning, W. (2001). Childbearing in cohabiting unions: Racial and ethnic differences. *Family Planning Perspectives, 33,* 217–223.

Manning, W. D. (1995). Cohabitation, marriage, and entry into motherhood. *Journal of Marriage and the Family, 57,* 191–200.

Manning, W. D. (2002). The implications of cohabitation for children's well-being. In A. Booth & A. C. Crouter (Eds.), *Just living together: Implications of cohabitation for children, families, and social policy* (pp. 121–152). Mahwah, NJ: Erlbaum.

Manning, W. D. (2004). Children and the stability of cohabiting couples. *Journal of Marriage and Family, 66,* 674–689.

Manning, W. D., & Landale, N. S. (1996). Racial and ethnic differences in the role of cohabitation in premarital childbearing. *Journal of Marriage and Family, 58,* 63–77.

Manning, W. D., Longmore, M. A., & Giordano, P. C. (2007). The changing institution of marriage: Adolescents' expectations to cohabit and to marry. *Journal of Marriage and Family, 69,* 559–575.

Manning, W. D., & Smock, P. J. (2002). First comes cohabitation and then comes marriage? *Journal of Family Issues, 23,* 1065–1087.

Markman, H. J., Stanley, S. M., & Blumberg, S. L. (2001). *Fighting for your marriage: New and revised.* San Francisco: Jossey-Bass.

Marks, N., & Lamberg, J. (1998). Marital status continuity and change among young and midlife adults. *Journal of Family Issues, 19,* 652–686.

Marks, N. F., Lambert, J. D., & Choi, H. (2002). Transition to caregiving, gender, and psychological well-being: A prospective U.S. national study. *Journal of Marriage and Family, 64,* 657–667.

Marsella, A. J., & Ring, E. (2003). Human migration and immigration: An overview. In L. L. Adler & U. P. Gielen (Eds.), *Migration: Immigration and emigration in international perspective* (pp. 3–22). Westport, CT: Praeger.

Marshall, R., & Tucker, M. (1992). *Thinking for a living: Education and the wealth of nations.* New York: Basic Books.

Marsiglio, W., Day, R., & Lamb, M. E. (2000). Exploring fatherhood diversity: Implications for conceptualizing father involvement. *Marriage and Family Review, 29,* 269–293.

Mastekaasa, A. (1992). Marriage and psychological well-being: Some evidence on selection into marriage. *Journal of Marriage and the Family, 54,* 901–911.

Mastekaasa, A. (1994). The subjective well-being of the previously married: The importance of unmarried cohabitation and time since widowhood or divorce. *Social Forces, 73,* 665–692.

Masten, A. S. (2001). Ordinary magic: Resilience processes in development. *American Psychologist, 56,* 227–238.

Masters, W., Johnson, V., & Kolodny, R. (1992). *Human sexuality.* New York: Harper Collins.

Matousek, M. (2007). Writing to live. *AARP The Magazine. 50,* No. 2C, Dropping By, 25–26.

Matson, M. (Ed.). (1992) *An independent woman: The autobiography of Edith Guerrier.* Amherst, MA: The University of Massachusetts Press.

Matthews, L. S., Wickrama, K. A. S., & Conger, R. D. (1996). Predicting marital instability from spouse and observer reports of marital interaction. *Journal of Marriage and the Family, 58,* 641–655.

McAdams, D. P. (2001). The psychology of life stories. *Review of General Psychology, 5,* 100–122.

McCarthy, B., & MacCarthy, E. (2003). *Rekindling desire: A step-by-step program to help low-sex and no-sex marriages.* New York: Brunner–Routledge.

McCartney, H. M. (2005). *About Heather,* short biography. http://www.heathermills.org/about.php, retrieved 4/7/07.

McClun, L., & Merrell, K. (1998). Relationship of perceived parenting styles, locus of control orientations, and self-concept among junior high age students. *Psychology in the Schools, 35,* 381–390.

McGinnis, S. L. (2003). Cohabiting, dating, and perceived costs of marriage: A model of marriage entry. *Journal of Marriage and Family, 65,* 105–116.

Medora, N. P. (2005). International families in cross-cultural perspective: A family strengths approach. *Marriage & Family Review, 38,* 47–64.

Menaghan, E. G., & Lieberman, M. A. (1986). Changes in depression following divorce: A panel study. *Journal of Marriage and the Family, 48,* 319–328.

Menand, L. (2001). *The metaphysical club (a story of ideas in America).* New York: Farrar, Straus and Giroux.

Merrill, G. (1997). *Caring for elderly parents.* Westport, CT: Auburn House.

Meyer, D. R., & Cancian, M. (1998). Economic well-being following an exit from aid to families with dependent children. *Journal of Marriage and the Family, 60,* 479–492.

Meyerowitz, B. E., Heinrich. R. L., & Schag, C. C. (1983). A competency-based approach to coping with cancer. In T. Burish & L. Bradley (Eds.), *Coping with chronic illness: Research and applications* (pp. 137–158). New York: Academic Press.

Miaskowski, C., Kragness, L., Dibble, S., & Wallhagen, M. (1997). Differences in mood states, health status, and caregiver strain between family caregivers of oncology outpatients with and without cancer-related pain. *Journal of Pain and Symptom Management, 13,* 138–147.

Miller, G. E., Cohen, S., & Ritchey, A. K. (2002). Chronic psychological stress and the regulation of pro-inflammatory cytokines: A glutocorticoid-resistance model. *Health Psychology, 21,* 6.

Mitchell, T. (2007). Far from home? *USA Weekend,* February 2–4,2007. Special Health Report, pp. 6–8.

Moen, P. (1996). Gender, age, and the life course. In R. H. Binstock & L. K. George (Eds.), *Handbook of aging and the social sciences* (4th ed., pp. 171–187). San Diego, CA: Academic Press.

Moore, T. M., & Stuart, G. L. (2004). Effects of masculine gender role stress on men's cognitive, affective, physiological, and aggressive responses to intimate conflict situations. *Psychology of Men and Masculinity, 5,* 132–142.

Mulder, T. J., Hollmann, F. W., Lollock, L. R., Cassidy, R. C., Constanzo, J. M., & Baker, J. D. (2001). *U.S. Census Bureau measurement of net international migration to the United States: 1990-2000.* Retrieved January 3, 2004, from http://www.census.gov/population/www/documentation/twps0051.html.

Murray, S. L., Holmes, J. G., & Griffin, D. W. (1996). The self-fulfilling nature of positive illusions in romantic relationships: Love is not blind, but prescient. *Journal of Personality and Social Psychology, 71,* 1155–1180.

Musick, K. (2002). Planned and unplanned childbearing among unmarried women. *Journal of Marriage and Family, 64,* 915–929.

Myer, R. A. (2001). *Assessment for crisis intervention: A triage assessment model.* Belmont, CA: Brooks/Cole.

Myer, R. A., & Moore, H. B. (2006). Crisis in context theory: An ecological model. *Journal of Counseling & Development, 84,* 139–147.

Myers, J. E., Madathil, J., & Tingle, L. R. (2005). Marriage satisfaction and wellness in India and the United States: A preliminary comparison of arranged marriages and marriages of choice. *Journal of Counseling & Development, 83,* 183–190.

Nace, E. P. (1987). *The treatment of alcoholism.* New York: Brunner/Mazel Publishers.

National Alliance for Caregiving (April 2004). Caregiving in the U.S. Key findings: 2004. *National Alliance for Caregiving and AARP.* www.caregivingorg/data/04keyfindings.pdf.

National Center for Health Statistics (2004). *Births, marriages, divorces, and deaths.* Retrieved May 17, 2004, from htpp://www.cdc.govnchs/data/nvsr/nvsr52/nvsr52_20.pdf.

Neff, L. A., & Karney, B. R. (2007). Stress crossover in newlywed marriage: A longitudinal and dyadic perspective. *Journal of Marriage and Family, 69,* 594–607.

Neidle, C. S. (1975). *America's immigrant women.* New York: Hippocrene Books, Inc.

Neugarten, B. L. (1979). Time, age, and the life cycle. *American Journal of Psychiatry, 136,* 887–894.

Nichols, C. W., Jr. (1990). An analysis of the sources of dissatisfaction at work (doctoral dissertation, Stanford University, 1990). *Dissertation Abstracts International, 51-11B,* 1–267.

Nickerson, R. S. (1998). Confirmation bias: A ubiquitous phenomenon in many guises. *Review of General Psychology, 2,* 175–230.

Nock, S. L. (1995a). Commitment and dependency in marriage. *Journal of Marriage and the Family, 57,* 503–514.

Nock, S. L. (1995b). A comparison of marriages and cohabiting relationships. *Journal of Family Issues, 16,* 53–76.

Nock, S. L. (2001). When married spouses are equal. *Social Policy and the Law, 9,* 48–70.

Nomaguchi, K. M., & Milkie, M. A. (2003). Costs and rewards of children: The effects of becoming a parent on adults' lives. *Journal of Marriage and Family, 65,* 356–374.

Norton, A. J. (1983). Family life cycle: 1980. *Journal of Marriage and the Family, 45,* 267–275.

O'Leary, K. D., & Smith, D. A. (1991). Marital interactions. *Annual Review of Psychology, 42,* 191–212.

Ono, H. (1998). Husbands' and wives' resources and marital dissolution. *Journal of Marriage and the Family, 60,* 674–689.

O'Rand, A. M., & Henretta, J. C. (1982). Delayed career entry, industrial pension structure, and early retirement in a cohort of unmarried women. *American Sociological Review, 42,* 365–373.

Orvaschel, H., Lewinsohn, P. M., & Seeley, J. R. (1995). Continuity of psycho-pathology in a community sample of adolescents. *Journal of the American Academy of Child and Adolescent Psychiatry, 34,* 1525–1525.

Osipow, S. H., & Fitzgerald, L. F. (1996). *Theories of career development* (4th ed.). Boston: Allyn & Bacon.

Overskeid, G. (2000). The slave of the passions: Experiencing problems and selecting solutions. *Review of General Psychology, 4,* 284–309.

Palmer, K. (2007, September 3). The new mommy track. *U.S. News & World Report, 143,* 7, 40–45.

Parkes, C. M., & Weiss, R. S. (1983). *Recovery from bereavement.* New York: Basic Books.

Parsons, F. (1909). *Choosing a vocation.* Boston: Houghton–Mifflin.

Pasch, L. A., & Bradbury, T. N. (1998). Social support, conflict, and the development of marital dysfunction. *Journal of Consulting and Clinical Psychology, 66,* 219–230.

Pasch L. A., Dunkel-Schetter, C., & Christensen, A. (2002). Differences between husbands' and wives' approach to infertility affect marital communication and adjustment. *Fertility and Sterility, 77,* 1241–1247.

Pearlin, L. I. (1999). Stress and mental health: A conceptual overview. In A. V. Horwitz & T. L. Scheid (Eds.), *A handbook for the study of mental health: Social contexts, theories, and systems* (pp. 161–175). New York: Cambridge University Press.

Pederson, L. M., & Valanis, B. G. (1988). The effects of breast cancer on the family: A review of the literature. *Journal of Psychosocial Oncology, 6,* 95–118.

Peek, M. K., Coward, R. T., Peek, C. W., & Lee, G. R. (1998). Are expectations for care related to the receipt of care? An analysis of parent care among disabled elders. *Journal of Gerontology: Social Sciences, 53B,* S127–136.

Peters-Davis, N. D., Moss, M. S., & Pruchno, R. A. (1999). Children-in-law in caregiving families. *The Gerontologist, 39,* 66–75.

Phillips, S. D. (1997). Toward an expanded definition of adaptive decision-making. *The Career Development Quarterly, 45,* 275–287.

Piercy, K. W. (1998). Theorizing about family caregiving: The role of responsibility. *Journal of Marriage and Family, 60,* 109–118.

Pillemer, D. B. (1998). *Momentous events, vivid memories.* Cambridge, MA: Harvard University Press.

Pillemer, D. B. (2001). Momentous events and the life story. *Review of General Psychology, 5,* 123–134.

Porter, L. S., & Stone, A. S. (1995). Are there really differences in coping? A reconsideration of previous data and results from a daily study. *Journal of Social and Clinical Psychology, 14,* 184–202.

Posner, R. (1992). *Sex and reason.* Cambridge, MA: Harvard University Press.

Proulx, C. M., Helms, H. M., & Buehler, C. (2007). Marital quality and personal well-being: A meta-analysis. *Journal of Marriage and Family, 69,* 576–593.

Pyke, K. (2000). "The normal American family" as an interpretive structure of family life among grown children of Korean and Vietnamese immigrants. *Journal of Marriage and the Family, 62,* 240–255.

Quittner, A. L., Glueckauf, R. L., & Jackson, D. (1990). Chronic parenting stress: Moderating versus mediating effects of social support. *Journal of Personality and Social Psychology, 59,* 1266–1278.

Rabin, B. S. (1999). *Stress, immune function, and health: The connection.* New York: Wiley-Liss & Sons.

Raikkonen, K., Matthews, K. A., & Kuller, L. H. (2002). The relationship between psychological risk attributes and the metabolic syndrome in healthy women: Antecedent or consequence? *Metabolism, 51,* 1573–1577.

Rait, D., & Lederberg, M. (1989). The family of the cancer patient. In J. C. Holland & J. H. Rowland (Eds.), *Handbook of Psychooncology* (pp. 585–597). New York: Oxford University Press.

Raley, K. (2001). Increasing fertility in cohabiting unions: Evidence for the second demographic transition in the United States? *Demography, 38,* 59–66.

Raley, R. K., & Wildsmith, E. (2004). Cohabitation and children's family instability. *Journal of Marriage and the Family, 66,* 210–219.

Rando, T. A. (1986). Understanding and facilitating anticipatory grief in the loved ones of the dying. In T. A. Rando (Ed.), *Loss and anticipatory grief* (pp. 97–130). Lexington, MA: Lexington Books.

Raschke, H. (1987). Divorce. In M. Sussman & S. Steinmetz (Eds.), *Handbook of marriage and the family* (pp. 597–624). New York: Plenum.

Raush, H. L., Barry, W. A., Hertel, R. K., & Swain, M. A. (1974). *Communication, conflict, and marriage.* San Francisco: Jossey–Bass.

Reilly. M. D. (1982). Working wives and convenience consumption. *Journal of Consumer Research, 8,* 407–418.

Reise, S. P., & Wright, T. M. (1996). Brief report: Personality traits, cluster in personality disorders, and sociosexuality. *Journal of Research in Personality, 30,* 128–136.

Reiss, D., & Oliveri, M. F. (1983). The family's construction of social reality and its ties to its kin network: An exploration of causal direction. *Journal of Marriage and the Family, 45,* 81–91.

Rindfuss, R. R., & VandenHeuvel, A. (1990). Cohabitation: A precursor to marriage or an alternative to being single? *Population and Development Review, 16,* 703–726.

Risman, B. J., & Johnson-Summerford, D. (1998). Doing it fairly: A study of post-gender marriages. *Journal of Marriage and the Family, 60,* 23–40.

Roberts, L. J. (2000). Fire and ice in marital communication: Hostile and distancing behaviors as predictors of marital distress. *Journal of Marriage and the Family, 62,* 693–707.

Roberts, S. A., Kiselica, M. S., & Fredrickson, S. A. (2002). Quality of life of persons with medical illnesses: Counseling's holistic contribution. *Journal of Counseling & Development, 80,* 422–432.

Robinson, J., Moen, P., & Dempster-McClain, D. (1995). Women's caregiving: Changing profiles and pathways. *Journals of Gerontology: Social Sciences, 50B,* S362–373.

Rogers, S. J. (2004). Dollars, dependency, and divorce: Four perspectives on the role of wives' income. *Journal of Marriage and Family, 66,* 59–74.

Rogge, R. D., & Bradbury, T. N. (1999). Till violence does us part: The differing roles of communication and aggression in predicting adverse marital outcomes. *Journal of Consulting and Clinical Psychology, 67,* 340–351.

Rohrlich, B. F., & Martin, J. N. (1991). Host country and reentry adjustment of student sojourners. *International Journal of Intercultural Relations, 15,* 163–182.

Rosen-Grandon, J. R., Myers, J. E., & Hattie, J. A. (2004). The relationship between marital characteristics, marital interaction processes, and marital satisfaction. *Journal of Counseling & Development, 82,* 58–68.

Ross, C. E. (1995). Reconceptualizing marital status as a continuum of social attachment. *Journal of Marriage and the Family, 57,* 129–140.

Ross, C. E., & Van Willigen, M. (1996). Gender, parenthood, and anger. *Journal of Marriage and the Family, 58,* 572–584.

Rossi, A. S., & Rossi, P. H. (1990). *Of human bonding: Parent–child relations across the life course.* New York: Aldine.

Rotter, J. (1990). Internal versus external control of reinforcement: A case history of a variable. *American Psychologist, 45,* 489–493.

Rounds, J. B., & Tinsley, H. E. A. (1984). Diagnosis and treatment of vocational problems. In S. D. Brown & R. W. Lent (Eds.), *Handbook of counseling psychology* (pp. 137–177). New York: Wiley.

Ruggles, S. (1997). The rise of divorce and separation in the United States, 1880–1990. *Demography, 34,* 455–466.

Rumbaut, R. G. (1991). The agony of exile: A study of the migration and adaptation of Indochinese refugee adults and children. In F. L. Ahearn & J. L. Athey (Eds.), *Refugee children: Theory, research, and services* (pp. 53–91). Baltimore: Johns Hopkins University Press.

Rusbult, C. E., Arriaga, X. B., & Agnew, C. R. (2001). Interdependence in close relationships. In G. J. O. Fletcher & M. S. Clark (Eds.), *Blackwell handbook of social psychology: Interpersonal processes* (pp. 359–387). Malden, MA: Blackwell.

Rusbult, C. E., Johnson, D. J., & Morrow, G. D. (1986). Impact of couple patterns of problem solving on distress and nondistress in dating relationships. *Journal of Personality and Social Psychology, 50,* 744–753.

Rusbult, C. E., & Martz, J. M. (1995). Remaining in an abusive relationship: An investment model analysis of nonvoluntary dependence. *Personality and Social Psychology Bulletin, 21,* 558–571.

Rychlak, J. F. (1973). *Introduction to personality and psychotherapy: A theory-construction approach.* Boston: Houghton Mifflin Company.

Sabatelli, R. M., & Cecil-Pigo, E. F. (1985). Relational interdependence and commitment in marriage. *Journal of Marriage and the Family, 47,* 931–937.

Sacher, J. A., & Fine, M. A. (1996). Predicting relationship status and satisfaction after six months among dating couples. *Journal of Marriage and the Family, 58,* 21–32.

Sam, D. L. (2000). Psychological adaptation of adolescents with immigrant backgrounds. *Journal of Social Psychology, 140,* 5–25.

Sanders, M. R., Halford, W. K., & Behrens, B. C. (1999). Parental divorce and premarital couple communication. *Journal of Family Psychology, 13,* 60–74.

Sandfort, J. R., & Hill, M. S. (1996). Assisting young, unmarried mothers to become self-sufficient: The effects of different types of early economic support. *Journal of Marriage and the Family, 58,* 311–326.

Sassler, S. (2004). The process of entering into cohabiting unions. *Journal of Marriage and Family, 66,* 491–505.

Sassler, S., & McNally, J. (2003). Cohabiting couples' economic circumstances and union transition: A reexamination using multiple imputation techniques. *Social Science Research, 32,* 553–578.

Schmidley, A. D. (2001). *Profile of the foreign born population in the United States: 2000* U.S. Census Bureau, Current Population Reports, Series P23-206). Retrieved January 3, 2004, from http://www.census.gov/prod/2002pubs/p23-206.pdf.

Schneider, D., & Schneider, C. J. (1993). *The ABC-CLIO companion to women in the workplace.* Santa Barbara, CA: ABC-CLIO.

Schneider, J. (2003). Living together. *U.S. News & World Report*, March 24.

Schoen, R., & Weinick, R. M. (1993). Partner choice in marriages and cohabitation. *Journal of Marriage and the Family, 55,* 408–414.

Schroeder, J. (2002). *Cults: Prophecies, practices & personalities.* Dubai: Carlton.

Schuchter, S. R. (1986). *Dimensions of grief: Adjusting to the death of a spouse.* San Francisco: Jossey–Bass.

Scovell, J. (1998). *Oona: Living in the shadows: A biography of Oona O'Neill Chaplin.* New York: Warner Books, Inc.

Seaburn, D. B. (1990). The ties that bind: Loyalty and widowhood. *The Psychotherapy Patient, 6,* 139–146.

Seccombe, K., James, D., & Battle Walters, K. (1998). "They think you ain't much of nothing": The social construction of the welfare mother. *Journal of Marriage and the Family, 60,* 849–865.

Sedikides, C., Campbell, W. K., Reeder, G. D., & Eliot, A. J. (1997). The self-serving bias in relational context. *Journal of Personality and Social Psychology, 74,* 378–386.

Seff, M. A. (1995). Cohabitation and the law. *Marriage and Family Review, 21,* 141–168.

Seligman, L. (1994) *Developmental career counseling and assessment* (2nd ed.). Thousand Oaks, CA: Sage.

Seligman, M. E. P. (1999). Seligman on positive psychology: A session at the National Press Club. *The General Psychologist, 34,* 37–45.

Seltzer, J. A. (2000). Families formed outside of marriage. *Journal of Marriage and the Family, 62,* 1247–1268.

Seltzer, M. M., & Li, L. W. (2000). The dynamics of caregiving: Transitions during a three-year prospective study. *The Gerontologist, 40,* 165–178.

Shanas, E. (1979). The family as a social support system in old age. *The Gerontologist, 19,* 169–174.

Shapiro, A., & Lambert, J. D. (1999). Longitudinal effects of divorce on the quality of the father–child relationship and on fathers' psychological well-being. *Journal of Marriage and the Family, 61,* 397–408.

Shields, S. A. (2005). The politics of emotion in everyday life: "Appropriate" emotion and claims on identity. *Review of General Psychology, 9,* 3–15.

Shuey, K., & Hardy, M. A. (2003). Assistance to aging parents and parents-in-law: Does lineage affect family allocation decisions? *Journal of Marriage and Family, 54,* 418–431.

Simmons, T., & O'Connell, M. (2003). Married-couple and unmarried partner households: 2000. *Census Special Report* CENSR-5. Washington, DC: U.S. Census Bureau.

Simons, R. L., Beaman, J., Conger, R. D., & Chao, W. (1992). Gender differences in the intergenerational transmission of parenting beliefs. *Journal of Marriage and the Family, 54,* 823–836.

Simons, R. L., Beaman, J., Conger, R. D., & Chao, W. (1993). Childhood experience, conceptions of parenting, and attitudes of spouse as determinants of parental behavior. *Journal of Marriage and the Family, 55,* 91–106.

Simons, R. L., & Johnson, C. (1996). Mother's parenting. In R. L. Simons (Ed.), *Understanding differences between divorced and intact families: Stress, interaction, and child outcome* (pp. 81–93). Thousand Oaks, CA: Sage.

Simpson, J. A. (1987). The dissolution of romantic relationships: Factors involved in relationship stability and emotional distress. *Journal of Personality and Social Psychology, 53,* 683–692.

Simpson, J. A., & Gangestad, S. W. (1991). Individual differences in sociosexuality: Evidence for convergent and discriminant validity. *Journal of Personality and Social Psychology, 60,* 870–883.

Singer, M. T. (2003). *Cults in our midst* (Rev. ed.). San Francisco, CA: Jossey-Bass.

Skaldeman, P. (2006). Converging or diverging views of self and other: Judgment of relationship quality in married and divorced couples. *Journal of Divorce & Remarriage, 44,* 145–160.

Skinner, K. B., Bahr, S. J., Crane, D. R., & Call, V. A. (2002). Cohabitation, marriage, and remarriage: A comparison of relationship quality over time. *Journal of Family Issues, 23,* 74–90.

Smith, D. B., & Moen, P. (1998). Spousal influence on retirement: His, her, and their perceptions. *Journal of Marriage and the Family, 60,* 734–744.

Smith, K., Downs, B., & O'Connell, M. (2001). *Maternity leave and employment patterns: 1961–1995* (Current Population Reports, P70-79). Washington, DC: U.S. Census Bureau.

Smock, P. J. (2000). Cohabitation in the United States: An appraisal of research themes, findings, and implications. *Annual Review of Sociology, 26,* 1–20.

Sniezek, J. A., & Buckley, T. (1993). Becoming more or less uncertain. In N. J. Castellan, Jr. (Ed.), *Individual and group decision-making* (pp. 87–108). Hillsdale, NJ: Erlbaum.

South, S., & Lloyd, K. M. (1995). Spousal alternatives and masrital dissolution. *American Sociological Review, 60,* 21–35.

Spitze, G., Logan, J. R., Joseph, G., & Lee, E. (1994). Middle generation roles and the well-being of men and women. *Journals of Gerontology: Social Sciences, 49,* S107–116.

Sprecher, S. (1988). Investment model, equity, and social support determinants of relationship commitment. *Social Psychology Quarterly, 51,* 318–328.

Stack, S., & Wasserman, I. (1993). Marital status, alcohol consumption, and suicide: An analysis of national data. *Journal of Marriage and the Family, 55,* 1018–1024.

Stafford, L., & Canary, D. J. (1991). Maintenance strategies and romantic relationship type, gender, and relational characteristics. *Journal of Social and Personal Relationships, 8,* 217–242.

Stambor, Z. (2006). Caring for caregivers. *Monitor on Psychology, 37,* 46–47.

Statistics Canada. (2002, December 2). Divorce. *The Daily,* pp. 9–11.

Stein, C. H., Wemmerus, V. A., Ward, M., Gaines, M. E., Freeburg, A. L., & Jewell, T. C. (1998). Because they're my parents: An intergenerational study of felt obligation and parental caregiving. *Journal of Marriage and Family, 60,* 611–622.

Steinberg, L., Darling, N. E., Fletcher, A. C., Brown, B. B., & Dornbusch, S. M. (1995). Authoritative parenting and adolescent adjustment: An ecological journey. In P. Moen, G. H. Elder, Jr., & K. Lüscher (Eds.), *Examining lives in context: Perspectives on the ecology of human development* (pp. 423–466). Washington, DC: American Psychological Association.

Steinberg, L., Lamborn, S. D., Darling, N., Mounts, N. S., & Dornbusch, S. M. (1994). Over-time changes in adjustment and competence among adolescents from authoritative, authoritarian, indulgent, and neglectful families. *Child Development, 65,* 754–770.

Stoller, E. P. (1990). Males as helpers: The role of sons, relatives and friends. *The Gerontologist, 30,* 228–235.

Stoller, E. P., Forster, L. E., & Duniho, T. S. (1992). Systems of parent care within sibling networks. *Research on Aging, 14,* 28–49.

Stroebe, M., Stroebe, W., & Schut, H. (2001). Gender differences in adjustment to bereavement: An empirical and theoretical review. *Review of General Psychology, 5,* 62–83.

Super, D. E. (1953). A theory of vocational development. *American Psychologist, 8,* 185–190.

Surra, C. A., & Gray, C. R. (2000). A typology of the processes of commitment to marriage: Why do partners commit to problematic relationships? In L. J. Waite (Ed.), *The ties that bind: Perspectives on marriage and cohabitation* (pp. 253–280). New York: Aldine de Gruyter.

Swann, W. B., Jr. (1983). Self-verification: Bringing social reality into harmony with the self. In J. Suls & A. G. Greenwald (Eds.), *Social psychology perspectives* (Vol. 2, pp. 33–66). Hillsdale, NJ: Erlbaum.

Swartz-Kulstad, J. L., & Martin, Jr., W. E. (1999). Impact of culture and context on psychosocial adaptation: The cultural and contextual guide process. *Journal of Counseling & Development, 77,* 281–293.

Swensen, C. H., & Fuller, S. R. (1992). Expression of love, marriage problems, commitment, and anticipatory grief in the marriages of cancer patients. *Journal of Marriage and the Family, 54,* 191–196.

Swensen, C. H., & Trahaug, G. (1985). Commitment and the long-term marriage relationship. *Journal of Marriage and the Family, 47,* 939–945.

Szinovacz, M. (1989). Decision making on retirement timing. In D. Brinberg & J. Jaccard (Eds.), *Dyadic decision making* (pp. 293–303). New York: Springer Verlag.

Tanfer, K. (1987). Patterns of premarital cohabitation among never-married women in the United States. *Journal of Marriage and the Family, 49,* 483–497.

Taniguchi, H. (1999). The timing of childbearing and women's wages. *Journal of Marriage and the Family, 61,* 1008–1019.

Tannen, D. (1990). *You just don't understand: Women and men in conversation.* New York: William Morrow.

Teachman, J. D. (2003). Premarital sex, premarital cohabitation, and the risk of subsequent marital dissolution among women. *Journal of Marriage and Family, 65,* 444–455.

Teachman, J. D., & Polonko, K. A. (1990). Cohabitation and marital stability in the United States. *Social Forces, 69,* 207–220.

Tedeschi, R. G., & Calhoun, L. G. (1995). *Trauma and transformation: Growing in the aftermath of suffering.* Thousand Oaks, CA: Sage.

Tedeschi, R. G., & Calhoun, L. G. (2004). Posttraumatic growth: Conceptual foundations and empirical evidence. *Psychological Inquiry, 15,* 1–18.

Thornton, A., Axinn, W. G., & Hill, D. H. (1992). Reciprocal effects of religiosity, cohabitation, and marriage. *American Journal of Sociology, 98,* 628–651.

Thornton, A., & Young-DeMarco, L. (2001). Four decades of trends in attitudes toward family issues in the United States: The 1960s through the 1990s. *Journal of Marriage and Family, 63,* 1009–1037.

Timmer, S. G., & Veroff, J. (2000). Family ties and the discontinuity of divorce in Black and White newlywed couples. *Journal of Marriage and the Family, 62,* 349–361.

Todisco, P. J. *Boston's first neighborhood: The North End.* Boston: Boston Public Library, 1976.

Treas, J., & Giesen, D. (2000). Sexual infidelity among married and cohabiting Americans. *Journal of Marriage and Family, 62,* 48–60.

Trentham, S., & Larwood, L. (2001). Power and gender influences on responsibility attributions: The case of disagreements in relationships. *Journal of Social Psychology, 141,* 730–751.

Tuch, R. (2000). *The single woman–married man syndrome.* Northvale, NJ: Jason Aronson Inc.

Udry, R., Deven, F., & Coleman, S. (1982). A cross-national comparison of the relative influence of male and female age on the frequency of marital intercourse. *Journal of Biosocial Science, 14,* 1–6.

Uehara, A. (1983). The nature of American student re-entry adjustment and perceptions of the sojourner experience. *International Journal of Intercultural Relations, 10,* 415–438.

Umberson, D., & Gove, W. (1989). Parenthood and psychological well-being: Theory, measurement, and stage in the family life course. *Journal of Family Issues, 10,* 440–462.

U.S. Bureau of the Census (1997). *Statistical abstract of the United States.* Washington, DC: U.S. Government Printing Office.

U.S. Census Bureau (2000a). Profile of general demographic characteristics for the United States: 2000 [table]. Retrieved April 8, 2002, from http://www.census.gov/Press-Release/www/2001/tables/dp_us_2000PDF.

U.S. Census Bureau (2000). *Statistical abstract of the United States,* 120th ed. (Table 58) Washington, DC: Government Printing Office. www.census.gov/stat_abstract.

U.S. Census Bureau (2005). America's families and living arrangements, 2005. Retrieved February 14, 2005, from http://www.census.gov/population/www/socdemo/hh-fam/cps2003html.

U.S. Department of Health and Human Services, Office of Refugee Resettlement (1990). *Refugee resettlement program.* Washington, DC: Author.

U.S. Department of Justice (2002, July 8). *A Message to Recipients from Ralph F. Boyd, Jr., Assistant Attorney for Civil Rights, United States Department of Justice.* July 8, 2002. Washington, DC: Office of the Assistant Attorney General, Civil Rights Division. (Available at http://www.usdoj.gov/crt/cor/Pubs/BoydLEPArt.htm)

Ventura, S. J., Martin, J. A., Curtin, S. C., Menacker, F., & Hamilton, B. E. (2001). *Births: Final data for 1999, National Vital Statistics Reports* (Vol. 49, No. 1). Hyattsville, MD: National Center for Health Statistics.

Villano, M. (2007). NRTA live & learn—Try on a new career. http://www.aarp.org/about_aarp/nrt/livelearn/try_on_a_new_career.html, retrieved 3/27/07.

Vitaliano, P. P., Scanlan, J. M., Zhang, J., Savage, M. V., Hirsch, I. B., & Siegler, I. C. (2002). A path model of chronic stress, the metabolic syndrome, and coronary heart disease. *Journal of Psychosomatic Medicine, 64,* 418–435.

Waite, L. (1995). Does marriage matter? *Demography, 32,* 483–507.

Waite L. J., & Joyner, K. (2001). Emotional and physical satisfaction with sex in married, cohabiting, and dating sexual unions: Do men and women differ? In E. O. Laumann & R. T. Michael (Eds.) *Sex, love, and health in America* (pp. 239–269). Chicago: University of Chicago Press.

Walker, D. F., Tokar, D. M., & Fischer, A. R. (2000). What are eight popular masculinity-related instruments measuring? Underlying dimensions and their relations to sociosexuality. *Psychology of Men and Masculinity, 1,* 98–108.

Walker, W. R., Skowronski, J. J., & Thompson, C. P. (2003). Life is pleasant—and memory helps to keep it that way! *Review of General Psychology, 7,* 203–210.

Waller, M. R., & McLanahan, S. S. (2005). "His" and "her" marriage expectations: Determinants and consequences. *Journal of Marriage and Family, 67,* 53–67.

Wang, H., & Amato, P. R. (2000). Predictors of divorce adjustment: Stressors, resources, and definitions. *Journal of Marriage and the Family, 62,* 655–668.

Watson, D., Klohnen, E. C., Casillas, A., Simms, E., & Haig, J. (2004). Match makers and deal breakers: Analyses of assortative mating in newlywed couples. *Journal of Personality, 72,* 1029–1068.

Watzlawick, P. (1983). *The situation is hopeless, but not serious.* New York: W. W. Norton and Company, Inc.

Weil, A. (2007). Taking care of the caregiver. *USA Weekend,* May 4–6, 2007. Health, p. 22.

Weiner, I. (1995). *Judgments of responsibility.* San Francisco, CA: Jossey–Bass.

Weiss, R. L. (1980). Strategic behavioral marital therapy: Toward a model for assessment and intervention. In J. P. Vincent (Ed.), *Advances in family intervention, assessment and theory* (Vol. 1, pp. 229–271). Greenwich, CT: JAI Press.

Weiss, R. L., & Heyman, R. E. (1990). Observation of marital interaction. In F. D. Fincham & T. N. Bradbury (Eds.), *The psychology of marriage* (pp. 150–171). New York: Guilford.

Weiss, R. L., & Summers, K. (1983). The Marital Interaction Coding System-III. In E. E. Filsinger (Ed.), *A sourcebook of marriage and family assessment* (pp. 85–115). Beverly Hills, CA: Sage.

Welcome to Las Vegas: Weddings (always and forever). (November 7–20, 2006). *What's on: The Las Vegas Guide, 52,* #24, 35.

Wheaton, B. (1999). The nature of stressors. In A. V. Horwitz & T. L. Scheid (Eds.), *A handbook for the study of mental health: Social contexts, theories, and systems* (pp. 176–197). New York: Cambridge University Press.

Whitehead, B. D. (1996). *The divorce culture.* New York: Alfred Knopf.

Wikipedia, the free encyclopedia. http://en.wikipedia.org/wiki/Steven_Hassan. Retrieved 4/22/07.

Williams, S., & Han, S. K. (2003). Forked roads: Career pathways of men and women in dual-earner families. In P. Moen (Ed.), *It's about time* (pp. 80–97). Ithaca, NY: Cornell University Press.

Wineberg, H., & McCarthy, J. (1998). Living arrangements after divorce: Cohabitation versus remarriage. *Journal of Divorce and Remarriage, 29,* 131–146.

Wu, Z., & Schimmele, C. M. (2005). Repartnering after first union disruption. *Journal of Marriage and Family, 67,* 27–36.

Yalom, I. D. (1980). *Existential psychotherapy.* New York: Basic Books.

Yee, J. L., & Schulz, R. (2000). Gender differences in psychiatric morbidity among family caregivers: A review and analysis. *The Gerontologist, 40,* 147–164.

Yeh, C. J., & Hwang, M. Y. (2000). Interdependence in ethnic identity and self: Implication for theory and practice. *Journal of Counseling & Development, 78,* 420–429.

Yeh, C. J., Ma, P-W., Madan-Bahel, A., Hunter, C. D., Jung, S., Kim, A. B., Akitaya, K., & Sasaki, K. (2005). The cultural negotiations of Korean immigrant youth. *Journal of Counseling & Development, 83,* 172–182.

Yost, M. R., & Zurbriggen, E. L. (2006). Gender differences in the enactment of sociosexuality: An examination of implicit social motives, sexual fantasies, coercive sexual attitudes, and aggressive sexual behavior. *The Journal of Sex Research, 43,* 163–173.

Author Index

A

Aarestad, S., 270
Abma, J. C., 126
Abramson, P. R., 270
Acock, A. C., 132
Adamic, L., 205
Adler, N. J., 216
Adler, Z., 135
Agnew, C. R., 41
Agras, W. S., 41
Allen, L. B., 265
Almeida, D. M., 20
Altarriba, J., 198
Amato, P. R., 19, 24, 25, 51, 65, 71, 80, 81, 83, 91, 92, 127
American Cancer Society, 177
Ancis, J. R., 237, 238
Andersen, B. L., 270
Anderson, D., 240
Anderson, D. Y., 260
Andrews, B., 135
Aneshensel, C. S., 161
Antonak, R. F., 180
Arnold, E., 120
Arredondo, P., 199, 210
Arriaga, X. B., 41
Artis, J. E., 65
Aseltine, R. H., Jr., 80
Asher, S. J., 91
Avellar, S., 240
Avison, W. R., 80, 90, 135
Axinn, W. G., 51, 54, 71

B

Bahr, S. J., 55
Bakan, D., 269
Ball, F. L. J., 82
Bandura, A., 16
Barber, J. S., 54, 71
Barlow, D. H., 265, 266
Barry, W. A., 76
Bart, M., 129
Batalova, J. A., 63
Batson, C. D., 65
Battle Walters, K., 137
Bauer, L. M., 198
Baum, A., 177
Baumeister, R. F., 4
Bavin, S., 102
Beach, S. R., 15
Beaman, J., 137, 140
Beautrais, A., 192
Behrens, B., 25
Bemak, F., 207
Bennett, N. G., 70
Benson, M. L., 271
Bentler, P. M., 22, 39
Berry, S. L., 237
Betz, N. E., 237
Bianchi, S. M., 46, 54
Binder, M., 240
Bird, C. E., 30
Blackwell, D., 52
Blanc, A. K., 70
Blanton, P. W., 41

Subject Index